PROS & CONS

PROS & CONS
A DEBATER'S HANDBOOK

SEVENTEENTH EDITION BY
Michael D. Jacobson

ROUTLEDGE & KEGAN PAUL
London

First edition by J. B. Askew
published in 1896

Seventee··'h edition published in 1987 by
Routledg· & Kegan Paul Ltd
11 New Fetter Lane, London EC4P 4EE

Set in Linotron Sabon
by Input Typesetting Ltd, London
and printed in the British Isles
by the Guernsey Press Co Ltd
Guernsey, Channel Islands

British Library Cataloguing in Publication Data

Jacobson, Michael D.
  Pros & Cons: a debater's handbook.—
  17th ed.
  1. Social policy
  I. Title
  300   HN17.5

  ISBN 0–7102–1044–2

CONTENTS

PREFACE TO THE SEVENTEENTH EDITION ix

ADVERTISING, PUBLIC CONTROL AND
TAXATION OF 1
ANARCHISM 6
ANIMALS, RIGHTS OF
(and the Animal Liberation Front) 7
ARCHITECTURE, MODERN: Has It Lost Its Way? 11
ARMAMENTS, LIMITATION OF
CONVENTIONAL 14
AWARDS FOR ARTISTIC ACHIEVEMENT:
Too Much of a Good Thing? 15
BIRTH CONTROL: VOLUNTARY OR
COMPULSORY? 17
BIRTH RATE, HIGH 20
BISHOPS: Should They Be Excluded
from the House of Lords? 22
BLOOD SPORTS: Should They Be Abolished? 23
BRITISH COMMONWEALTH:
Is It a Reality? Can It Survive? 28
BROADCASTING, PUBLIC CONTROL OF 31
CABINET GOVERNMENT 34
CALENDAR REFORM 35
CAPITAL PUNISHMENT, RESTORATION OF 37
CENSORSHIP 39
CHANNEL TUNNEL:
Should the Project Be Scrapped? 40
CHRISTENDOM, REUNION OF 44
CHURCHES: Should They Take Part in Politics? 45
CIVIL DISOBEDIENCE 46
CLASSICS (LATIN AND GREEK) IN EDUCATION 48
CLOSED SHOP: Should It Be Banned? 49
COALITION GOVERNMENT 51
CO-EDUCATION 53
COMMERCIAL RADIO: Should It Be Abolished? 56
COMMON CURRENCY 57
COMPREHENSIVE SCHOOLS 59

CONTENTS

CONTRACEPTION FOR GIRLS UNDER 16   61
CO-OPERATION: Compared with Capitalism   62
CO-OPERATION: Compared with Socialism   63
CO-PARTNERSHIP IN INDUSTRY   64
CORPORAL PUNISHMENT: Should It Be Retained?   66
DEGENERACY OF MODERN CIVILISATION   67
DELEGATION v. REPRESENTATION   70
DIRECT ACTION (The Use of Industrial Strikes to
   Affect Political Issues)   71
DIRECTION OF LABOUR   72
DISESTABLISHMENT OF THE CHURCH OF
   ENGLAND   74
DIVORCE   77
DIVORCE, EASIER: Has It Gone Too Far?   79
EIGHTEEN-YEAR-OLD MPs   81
EUTHANASIA: Should It Be Legalised?   82
EXAMINATIONS: Should They Be Abolished?   84
FASCISM: Should It Be Outlawed in Britain?   86
FREEDOM OF INFORMATION ACT   87
FULL EMPLOYMENT   90
GAMBLING, MORALITY OF   91
HOMOSEXUALS, SOCIAL RECOGNITION OF:
   Has It Gone Too Far?   93
IMMIGRATION: Should The Present Restrictions
   Be Lifted?   95
INDETERMINATE SENTENCES FOR
   PROFESSIONAL CRIMINALS   98
INDUSTRIAL EXPANSION   99
INDUSTRIAL PSYCHOLOGY, APPLIED   102
INTELLIGENCE TESTS   103
INTERNATIONAL AUXILIARY LANGUAGES   105
INTERNATIONALISM   106
IRELAND: Should Ulster Join Eire?   108
JURY SYSTEM: A Serious Need for Reform?   110
LAND, NATIONALISATION OF   113
LIQUOR LAWS: Should They Be Relaxed?   115
LORDS, REFORM OF THE HOUSE OF   117
LOTTERIES   119
MARRIAGE AS AN INSTITUTION:
   Is It an Outmoded Concept?   121

MILITARY TRAINING, COMPULSORY:
Should It Be Restored?   123
MINORITIES, RIGHTS OF   125
MOTOR TRAFFIC: Should It Be Restricted?   126
MULTI-NATIONAL FIRMS   129
NEWSPAPERS: Should They Be Reformed?   133
NUCLEAR WEAPONS:
  Should They Be Banned Completely?   135
OLYMPIC GAMES: Back to Square One?   137
PACIFICISM   139
PARLIAMENT, REFORM OF: Devolution   141
PARTY GOVERNMENT   142
PAYMENT BY RESULTS IN INDUSTRY   144
POLLUTION OF THE ENVIRONMENT:
  Are Tougher Laws Needed?   144
PREMATURE BURIAL:
  Are the Safeguards Inadequate?   150
PRESERVATION OF BEAUTY SPOTS AND SITES
  OF SPECIAL SCIENTIFIC INTEREST:
  Are the Laws Inadequate?   152
PRISON REFORM   157
PRIVATE MEDICINE   160
PRIVATISATION   162
PROFIT-SHARING   166
PROHIBITION   167
PROPORTIONAL REPRESENTATION   168
PSYCHO-ANALYSIS   171
PUBLIC OPINION POLLS   173
PUBLIC SCHOOLS   175
PUBLIC TRANSPORT, FREE   177
RATING REFORM   178
RECALL OF REPRESENTATIVES   181
THE REFERENDUM, MORE USE OF   182
REGISTRATION, NATIONAL, IN PEACE-TIME   186
RELIGIOUS TEACHING IN SCHOOLS   187
SCHOOL-LEAVING AGE:
  Should It Be Lowered Again?   188
SCHOOL SPORT, COMPULSORY   190
SCIENCE: Is It a Menace To Civilisation?   191
SCIENTIFIC MANAGEMENT   192

───────────── CONTENTS ─────────────

SECOND BALLOTS   193
SINGLE-CHAMBER GOVERNMENT   194
SOCIAL SERVICES CONSCRIPTION (FOR BOTH
  SEXES)   197
SOCIALISM AND COMMUNISM   198
SOFT DRUGS, LEGALISATION OF   207
SPACE EXPLORATION: International Only?   209
SPECULATION, SUPPRESSION OF COMMERCIAL   211
SPELLING REFORM   212
SPIRITUALISM   213
STATE MEDICAL SERVICE   217
STATE-REGISTERED BROTHELS   219
STERILISATION OF THE UNFIT   221
SUNDAY ENTERTAINMENT; SUNDAY
  SHOPPING   223
SURROGATE MOTHERS   225
TAXATION, DIRECT, ABOLITION OF   227
TAXATION OF SINGLE PEOPLE   229
TERMINATION OF PREGNANCIES, LEGALISED   230
TERRORISM   231
THEATRES: Are They In Need of Reform?   233
TIED (PUBLIC) HOUSES, ABOLITION OF   235
TRADE UNIONS:
  Do Their Powers Need Further Restriction?   237
UNEMPLOYMENT, STATE REMEDY FOR   240
UNITED NATIONS ORGANISATION   241
UNITED STATES OF EUROPE   244
UNIVERSITY REFORM   246
VACCINATION   248
VEGETARIANISM   250
VIVISECTION AND EXPERIMENTS ON ANIMALS   253
VOTING, COMPULSORY   258
WAR: Is It Desirable?   259
WAR: Is It Inevitable?   261
WOMEN, MARRIED, MORE JOBS FOR   262
WOMEN'S RIGHTS MOVEMENTS:
  Are They Too Aggressive?   265
WRITTEN CONSTITUTION   272

INDEX   275

PREFACE TO THE SEVENTEENTH EDITION

The object of *Pros & Cons* is to give debaters a useful guide to
for-and-against arguments on a wide range of controversial
issues. It not only provides up-to-date material on the standard
subjects long familiar to debating societies but also covers many
newly urgent topics – to the extent, it is hoped, that anyone
reading right through the book would emerge with a fair idea
of the contemporary climate of society and most of the principal
political, social, industrial, educational and moral questions of
the day.

All the opposing arguments, numbered successively, appear
in adjacent columns, so that (as far as possible) each Pro corresponds with the relevant Con. For the sake of convenience, the
debating subjects are arranged in alphabetical order, even
though this may sometimes result in a separation of subjects
which logically ought to go together. Attention is always drawn,
however, to any themes related to each other, through cross-
references both in the text and in the Index. The opinions and
factual details in the debates could not possibly be comprehensive but are intended, rather, as guidelines which the debater
could develop or which might suggest other points worth
exploration.

This is the seventeenth edition of *Pros & Cons*, which was
first published in 1896 and has since been revised at regular
intervals, often so substantially that later versions bear only
minimal resemblance to their predecessors. In the preface to the
sixteenth edition, published in 1977, I expressed doubt whether
the pace of change since the previous one, which appeared in
1965, had ever before required such a large volume of modifica-

tions and entirely new matter. That view must now be applied equally to the present book. Since 1977, at least 15 debating subjects have disappeared entirely. Anglo-French political imperatives have decisively reversed the debate on whether the Channel Tunnel project should be restored; whether nudism should be permitted in allotted public places has been rendered uncontroversial by franker modern moralities; sharp commercial realities have made a nonsense of such questions as whether Britain could retain any truly amateur sports. Even among titles which have been repeated, very few have escaped radical alteration to their texts.

It is a sad commentary on trends in British life, all too frequently taking their cue from Parliament itself, that it has become so much more common for issues to be 'politicised' – for reasoned argument to give way, on one side or the other, to the confrontational. But one consolation, at least, is the nature of those topics which, as a reflection of changing public perceptions about their relative importance, are not merely virtually new in detail but also, often, well over double their previous lengths. To cite just a few examples: the rights of animals, blood sports, the British Commonwealth, public control of broadcasting, the jury system, pollution of the environment and the preservation of beauty spots and sites of special scientific interest.

Among official bodies to which the reviser gratefully acknowledges help with information and debating points are the British Field Sports Society, the Countryside Commission, the League Against Cruel Sports and the Nature Conservancy Council. The many individuals to whom his thanks are due for their suggestions and advice include, in particular, PDB, IB, Harry Coen, GJJ, Judith Judd, ML, G. L. Leigh, D. A. Orton, Andrew Samuels and the Timpsons.

M.D.J.

PROS & CONS

ADVERTISING, PUBLIC CONTROL AND TAXATION OF

Pro: (1) The case for public control is demonstrated above all by the general lack of trust in advertising now evident. Only new legislation, and the creation of a State-backed controlling body with 'teeth' to impose penalties on offenders, will ease the present widespread public suspicion of advertising – notably as regards its cost, waste of manpower and material, and the belief that too many advertisements, if not actually dishonest, are downright misleading. The fact that the Advertising Standards Authority launched a national campaign, inviting members of the public to send in complaints if they saw a Press, poster, cinema or direct mail advertisement which they believed to have broken the Code, was a clear recognition of the likelihood that such contraventions are still to be found.

(2) The expense of advertising adds greatly to overall production costs and thus to the prices of goods or services when they reach the public. Too much money is spent on advertising, in relation to the scale of any benefits it may bring in making products known or giving people information they genuinely wish or need to acquire.

Con: (1) Advertising is perhaps the most closely regulated form of communication in the UK. There are more than 80 statutes which affect what people may do or say in advertisements. Print advertising is governed by the British Code of Advertising Practice, administered by the Advertising Standards Authority. Television and radio 'commercials' come under the auspices of the Independent Broadcasting Authority. The control of print advertisements is described as voluntary and means that the industry is responsible for ensuring that no advertisements break the Code – so there is considerable moral pressure on everyone to conform to it. If an advertisement is published which breaks the Code, the ASA takes immediate steps to have the ad withdrawn or corrected and to make it known publicly that the Code has been breached. The system has the support of consumer organisations and is one of the most efficient and effective ways of controlling advertisements and protecting the consumer from misleading advertising.

(2) Businessmen are always seeking the lowest costs they can find. For

1

(3) Much of the huge sum devoted to advertising each year is unnecessary and could be used more fruitfully to bring down prices. There is particular public resentment at the mass advertising for rival brands of products such as petrol or detergents – which, most people suspect, are so similar in character as to be virtually indistinguishable except in their packaging. Another wasteful practice is the 'prestige' advertising placed by big companies whose names are so familiar that, in reality, people no longer need even occasional reminders of them. In some cases, too, the products advertised are so specialised that it seems pointless to tell the general public about them in this way. The only material return from such advertisements, one may deduce, is that the companies concerned can claim the cost against tax. In effect, therefore, the practice denies revenue to the Exchequer.

(4) The advertising industry employs an undue number of people, a large proportion of whom could be put to better and more constructive use in other fields.

(5) Advertising is, by its very nature, a subterfuge – the head of a leading British advertising agency once described himself as being 'in the myth-making business'. Although blatant lying in advertisements has become much less common, not only because of the Code but because it is counter-productive once detected, advertisers still believe nevertheless that it is legitimate to mislead people, without actually telling them lies. And people *are* misled, through being persuaded to buy products which may well be good of their kind but which they don't really need. This almost amoral attitude among advertisers should, clearly, be subjected to much

example, they decide to buy their own lorries, for delivering their goods, only if they believe this is cheaper and more efficient than using the railways or other means of public transport. Equally, they would not spend a penny on advertising unless they felt it did an essential job in helping to increase the sale of their products – nor would they spend a penny more than they deemed necessary for the purpose.

(3) Under the principle of 'economies of scale', advertising may actually lead to lower prices: the better a product becomes known and the bigger its sales volume, the more chance there is of bringing down its unit cost. Petrol companies gain much of their custom because motorists come to recognise that garages selling a particular brand usually have a higher standard of service than others – the implicit object of the advertising; detergent manufacturers insist that their products *do* differ, whatever some people may imagine. In relation to the size of their businesses, anyway, their spending on advertising is quite small. Indeed, the total level of advertising expenditure in Britain annually represents under 1.5 per cent of the Gross National Product. Even in the USA, the world's most advertising-conscious nation, it is still under 2 per cent of the GNP.

(4) The industry does not make a large use of labour. In 1985, the total number of people employed in all the advertising agencies in Britain (including secretaries and accountants, etc.) was only about 14,000.

(5) Visiting a factory, one may see chemists or scientists producing some new, anonymous liquid, developed to fulfil a particular function or meet a specific need. They have created it, but that's where their job ends. They have no idea how to sell it; except, perhaps,

more rigorous restriction and control, through new legislation.

(6) The Press depends for its very survival on its income from advertisements. Most British newspapers have to rely on advertising for about 50 per cent of their revenues. Those papers which fail to attract sufficient advertisements face the prospect either of closing down or, perhaps, of continuing to exist only through the financial buttressing of another, healthier newspaper in the same 'stable'. (For example, the *Guardian* would probably not have survived some years ago without its support from the highly profitable *Manchester Evening News*.) This is a lamentable state of affairs, and it opens the door to all sorts of pressures from advertisers. In the past, it was quite common for newspapers to be threatened with the withdrawal of advertising if they published stories the advertiser didn't like. While such threats are now almost unheard of (except, perhaps, on some small local papers), and journalists would in any case strongly resist that kind of blackmail, there are other, subtler pressures which are even more harmful. The bigger a newspaper's circulation, the more it can charge for its advertising space. Popular papers therefore have a compulsion to get a bigger audience – as, indeed, do commercial TV and radio companies – and they try to acquire it, all too often, by lowering their editorial standards: hence their resort to pin-ups, sex stories and other superficialities which, they believe, appeal to mass tastes. This pernicious struggle to gain more readers, in order to get more advertising, at higher rates, would be unnecessary if each paper had a fair share of all the advertising available. The only way to achieve that would be to channel the

for a long technical name, they don't even know what to call it. That is where an advertising agency comes in, by creating a personality for the product. It is a perfectly valid task – no matter whether the liquid concerned happens to be, say, a new stain-remover, lawn-mower lubricant or even some new, life-saving medicine. Advertisers create symbols, sell ideas and associations, and thereby bring awareness of a product to people who will be glad to make use of it. The advertising industry knows better than anyone the importance of public trust in advertisements, because lack of it means a loss of advertising effectiveness which can cost clients millions; apart from their social responsibility, therefore, it is in advertisers' own best commercial interests that advertising should be both as trustworthy and as trusted as possible. They remain convinced that the industry itself can achieve this more surely than could any form of governmental control.

(6) Far from decrying the importance of advertising to newspapers, we should recognise it as being one of the ways we get a free Press. It is an essential pillar not only for a newspaper's solvency but for its very independence. Without advertisements, the full economic price per copy that newspapers had to charge their readers would be so high, compared with the present levels, that their circulations would be extremely limited. Advertising, therefore, performs a useful social function, in addition to its own purpose, since it enables a much larger number and wider variety of newspapers to reach the public than would be possible without it. No form of State control has yet been devised which would improve matters, in this field, without

3

advertising through a central, officially-established body, responsible for ensuring its equitable allocation. Such a measure would not merely save a number of worthwhile publications from extinction but help to raise editorial standards in others. Proposals of this nature, in fact, have already been discussed in Parliament.

(7) Some publications do already survive healthily without advertisements. The French humorous weekly *Le Canard Enchaîné* is a case in point. Soviet newspapers, too, had no advertising for years and still contain very little. Accordingly, querying the basic assumption that advertising is essential to the Press in Western countries, one parallel suggestion mooted in Britain is that newspapers' financial security (and thus their existence) should be assured instead by means of a Government subsidy. This would have no 'strings' attached, as regards editorial control, and would presumably be along the lines of the system for the BBC, which receives its money via the State but in principle remains autonomous, free to decide its policies and attitudes without Government interference.

(8) The Press is only one of many aspects of advertising marked by abuses which require remedying by stricter public control. Among examples: the defacement of the countryside by huge billboards along the trunk roads; and the apparently unrestricted rash of neon signs, flashing lights and other such illuminated advertisements in the towns, which are usually ugly and may even be positively dangerous when they obscure or clash with road and traffic signs. Deceptive packaging, phoney price reductions and 'gifts', and the excessive use of children in TV

interfering unwarrantably with other aspects of a newspaper's work. Various Government Departments are themselves among the biggest individual advertisers; like any private advertiser, they buy space in publications which are the most 'cost effective' (i.e. which provide the largest audience for a given sum of money), irrespective of whether or not they approve of the policies of the publication concerned. If a governmental body were given responsibility for allocating all advertising, it might well be more likely to threaten a reduction in the share-out to newspapers of which it disapproved. It is public opinion, not the influence of advertisers, which newspapers consider when deciding their attitudes to given issues. In 1956, two leading British national papers showed very heavy circulation losses, within a month, when they opposed Britain's participation in the Suez invasion. That was solely the pressure of public opinion – and it proves that Government control would be both unnecessary and irrelevant.

(7) The examples given opposite are special cases. Russian newspapers did not have advertising originally because the Soviet economy at the time put little or no emphasis on consumer goods; but their level of advertising in recent years has been increasing steadily (even though they still tend to talk of 'realisation of a schedule' rather than 'selling'). A Government subsidy, however well-meaning, would have several drawbacks; not the least is that, ultimately, the responsibility for handing out the money would rest with a small committee set up for the purpose – and that committee, even if it did not mean to, would be bound to exercise an influence on editorial content,

4

commercials to persuade mothers to buy foods or other products they don't really need, are further menaces to the housewife in particular. Perhaps the most dangerous development in recent years is subliminal advertising, whereby the 'message' is implanted in people's minds without them being consciously aware of it.

(9) There are two product areas in which it is now widely accepted that firmer control of advertising has become increasingly necessary: cigarettes and tobacco products, and alcohol. In an age when the medical profession is adamant that smoking can aggravate the risks of developing cancer and other grave maladies, it is inexcusable that various forms of publicity for it are still countenanced. The partial restrictions on its advertising, as with the futile warnings about dangers to health which the Government demands must be shown on posters and packaging, do not go far enough. There are good grounds for a total ban on cigarette and other tobacco advertisements (and that includes 'back-door' advertising by means of cigarette companies sponsoring big sporting events and the like). After all, nobody suggests that advertisements for such drugs as cannabis should be permitted. Similar considerations apply to alcohol publicity. Apart from alcoholism as such – far more widespread than is generally realised – alcohol abuse and illnesses associated with it are probably responsible for a greater loss of manhours, in industry and commerce, than any other single factor. Clearly, advertising which encourages people to drink more should likewise be banned. It is disgraceful that the main reason successive Governments have failed to do so, in both cases, is their desire not to reduce the huge tax

because newspapers would depend so heavily on its largesse.

(8) The advertising industry itself has instituted a whole series of 'watchdog' bodies, at different levels, to ensure that the consumer is not misled by what an advertiser says or by any promises he makes about his products. Not a single TV commercial can be transmitted in Britain until several such bodies have scrutinised it at each stage – from the original script up to the final film. In Britain, the authorities already impose considerable restrictions on the nature, number, size and siting of street advertisements; these controls have avoided the hideous jumble of roadside advertising seen in the USA and, indeed, have greatly improved the situation even in this country, compared with that between the wars. In packaging and all other aspects affecting household shopping, new measures of consumer protection are being introduced all the time, and advertisers automatically conform to them. Subliminal advertising has never been used by the advertising business and is, in any case, banned by the IBA Code.

(9) Critics of tobacco and alcohol advertising fail to make a crucial distinction. In both cases, it has the particular aim of drawing attention to individual brands, which, while obviously hoping to improve their sales over those of their competitors, is *not* the same as setting out to increase consumption in general. The view that advertising does not stimulate an overall rise in the number of people smoking is borne out by extensive research projects, which have failed to find any evidence showing a correlation between the level of media advertising, as such, and the total volume of cigarette and tobacco sales. Similarly, alcohol advertisements are

revenues which tobacco and alcohol bring in.

(10) The case for specific taxation on advertising makes sense on several different grounds. It would reinforce the effectiveness and authority of the reforms proposed above. In these days of high taxation, it is an appropriate and fully justifiable new source of Government revenue. It would reduce the volume of unnecessary or dubious advertisements and thereby serve the cause of worth-while advertising. A Press baron who had a leading part in founding one of the regional independent television companies in Britain once described commercial TV as 'a licence to print money'. If the profits of those who hold the commercial television franchises were not so excessive, they would have less temptation to put on so many programmes appealing to the lowest common denominator.

directed towards selling specific products and never encourage people to drink larger quantities than they do already. (Indeed, generic publicity by such bodies as the Wine Development Board always stresses the importance of drinking only in moderation.) Alcohol abuse is associated with many socio-cultural, genetic and psychological factors. There is no research evidence to indicate that advertising is one of those factors.

(10) Apart from the fact that companies are already hit by Corporation Tax and other forms of taxation, a direct tax on their advertising would have one serious outcome: it would increase marketing costs and thus, inevitably, result in higher prices to the consumer. The suggestion that taxing advertisements would reduce the amount of commercially unnecessary advertising does not hold water; contrary to popular myth, companies do not advertise for fun. Proposals for the taxation of advertising were first made as long ago as 1947, but were rejected by the Labour Government at that time because the measures were seen to be both unfair and impracticable. No new proposals have yet been devised which overcome those objections.

ANARCHISM

(Anarchism, as a political philosophy, opposes any form of established government or imposed authority and is summed up by the belief that 'every man should be his own government, his own law, his own church'. Holding that each community should run its affairs by voluntary, co-operative means, it shares Communism's ultimate goal of a classless society but differs from Communism in that it rejects control by the State or by any other organised authorities such as political parties or trade unions.)

Pro: (1) Universal suffrage and representative institutions do not

Con: (1) Government is necessary to prevent a minority of fanatical, self-

prevent governments from being as hostile to liberty as aristocracies or monarchies were in the past. Only the abolition of governments and of all compulsory associations can secure the right of liberty, because people who make it their profession to control others will always be tyrannical in practice, however well-meaning they may be in principle.

(2) Voluntary association has always accomplished much more than is commonly recognised. It is a generally accepted right that one can refuse to work with, or for, those who have failed to act honourably or conscientiously. Men are social beings and behave socially, except when prevented by anti-social institutions.

(3) There can be no real liberty as long as a constant check is imposed from external sources on the actions of the individual.

(4) Anarchism won large-scale support in Spain, particularly in the 60 years up to the outbreak of the civil war in 1936; far from being just a theory, it proved extremely efficient and had many achievements to its credit.

(5) If adopted, anarchism would not mean disorder. The mere fact that it has not been tried out recently is not a valid argument against it.

seeking or unprincipled people from exploiting the common man. If as many abuses as possible are prevented, it is better to risk the occasional diminishing of liberty, through governmental control, than to run the greater risks from private tyranny. Most people do not want the trouble of managing their own communal affairs. Some degree of uniform behaviour and of controls over the individual, within generally accepted limits, is necessary for the development of social life and civilisation.

(2) Boycotts, strikes and refusal to co-operate are just as much instruments of coercion as fines and imprisonment. Most of the important so-called voluntary associations, in this context, rest either on some government's coercive resources of equally coercive conditions.

(3) 'Liberty' is equivocal. Liberty to do good is desirable, not liberty to do evil – but which is which often depends on the individual's point of view.

(4) While the Spanish Anarchists taught peasants to read and worked to form self-governing groups of workers in industry and agriculture, they resorted to widespread murder and violence to try to achieve their political aims. No end can justify such means.

(5) Institutions are a necessity for any form of social life. Without them, there would be chaos.

ANIMALS, RIGHTS OF
(and the Animal Liberation Front)

Pro: (1) Most forward-thinking countries recognise that animals do have rights – in particular, those according

Con: (1) The treatment of animals must be related to the needs of mankind. We should be kind to

them the 'restricted freedom' to live a natural life, in harmony with the human community's fundamental requirements. Some people have difficulty in deciding what animal rights mean: are they analogous with human rights or of a quite different order? One immediate answer is that rights are conferred on other creatures by human beings who recognise that they do have obligations (to themselves as well as to others). An unborn child, obviously, is totally unaware of its 'rights', or of what use these may be to it; but the obligations we acknowledge towards that child *are* of use to it – and, thus, can be regarded as the child's rights. This philosophy applies precisely to animal rights as well.

(2) The rights of animals have long been recognised by thinkers (e.g. Jeremy Bentham) and emphasised by several religions (e.g. Buddhism).

(3) It is absurd to make a distinction between domestic and other animals whereby the former are given appreciably more legal protection from the infliction of pain and from the excesses of hunting and other blood sports. The failure to recognise that other animals are equally entitled to such rights tends to result in greater cruelties, under the pretexts of the needs of scientific research, man's food requirements, and so on.

(4) It is nonsense to assert, as some people do, that rights are tenable only if they are reciprocal. Otherwise, what claims could infants or the mentally sick have on our protection? All research workers have a sense of obligation not to cause unnecessary suffering – an obligation which does, effectively, confer 'rights' on animals. But what awareness of any theoretical obligations they might have could we reasonably expect of animals, in

animals for the sake of our own self-respect and because of material considerations (e.g. conservation), not because they themselves have any specific rights. The most that is feasible is, for example, the task of preventing cruelty which the RSPCA has set itself – a limited goal which is largely achievable. But to try to bestow amorphous, undefined 'rights' on animals is an unlimited goal incapable of achievement. Any such attempt would entail, for example, man's total conversion to vegetarianism, since the first right we would have to accord would be the right to life. This would, in fact, be self-defeating, because the outcome would be that, with the end of any need for animal husbandry, there would be fewer animals . . .

(2) These theories relate to mysticism, vegetarianism, and the like, which have little or no bearing on the issue for the majority of people who do not subscribe to such specialist views.

(3) We protect domestic animals because they are personally valuable to us, either emotionally or materially, and not because they have any special claims beyond those of other animals. At the same time, only extremists would deny that human law fails to protect animals used in controlled scientific research. While it is true that there is still room for improvement in this field, giving animals such 'rights' is merely common sense, since the benefits from this research – to animals themselves as well as to man – have been beyond measure.

(4) It is specious to suggest that people critical of the entirely nebulous concept of animal 'rights' would claim, as part of their argument, that these would have to be a two-way traffic. To do so would be tantamount

return? Their rights are implicit – it is up to *us* to recognise them.

(5) The feeling of community among all sentient creatures is clearly desirable – and mutually beneficial.

(6) Cases of animal abuse investigated by the RSPCA in 1985 were at their highest level for more than 150 years. The complaints investigated, covering everything from neglect to malnutrition and sadistic treatment, totalled 64,678 – compared with 47,362 the previous year. Similarly, the number of court convictions for animal cruelty reached a post-war record: 2,112, against 1,889 in 1984. Frustration at the laggardly official reaction in dealing with this horrific trend led a number of young activists – notably those of the Animal Liberation Front – to embark on overtly militant tactics in support of animal rights. As examples: captive mink and laboratory animals have been set free from their cages; death threats have been issued (though not implemented); the home of a leading scientist has been set on fire; and it was claimed that pieces of chicken and Mars bars on supermarket shelves had been injected with poison. Whether or not this last was a hoax – warning was given before anyone was actually poisoned – it served to show what *could* so easily have been perpetrated. Other than the militants, no reasonable person could condone any of these exploits; the use of such violence is deplorable, no matter how just the cause may be deemed. But, however wrong-headed the tactics, at least they have put the spotlight on the whole subject of animal rights and have made members of the public more aware of the issue today than ever they were before.

(7) The book *Animal Liberation* by the Australian-born philosophy

to sheer anthropomorphism – a characteristic far more typical of the Pros than the Cons, on this issue! It has been said that rights are a human invention, derived from the system of laws for the regulation of human societies, and that other species have no part in them. The same laws have laid down duties – indeed, rights and duties are effectively inseparable. But what duties, as such, could be formally ascribed to animals? To what or to whom would they be owed? Certainly not to humans . . . Solidarity between members of the same species is natural and necessary. It is not so between members of different species.

(5) This feeling would be one-sided and, in practice, would often entail putting man's interests second to those of animals.

(6) The main reason for the sharp rise in complaints investigated is not an increase in cruelty, compared with the past, but a much greater public awareness and concern. This stems from the efforts of many respected animal welfare workers and organisations over the years. Thanks to their long, patient work, the message had begun to get through: more and more people *cared* about short-comings in the way we look after animals, which had already started to bring about improved legislation on the issue. The heightened awareness is also evident through the questions being raised about such matters as: the need for dolphins and killer whales in marine parks to have larger pools; calls for a ban on the import of pâté de foie gras (alleged to involve cruelty through the force-feeding of geese); querying of the methods used in the slaughter of animals, for religious reasons, by Orthodox Jews and Muslims. All these, be it stressed, relate to our own responsibility towards animals and are

lecturer Peter Singer, published in 1975, has become the 'bible' of ALF activists (in much the same way as *The Female Eunuch*, by his fellow-Australian Germaine Greer, helped to establish the Women's Lib movement in Britain). Briefly, Singer argues that the moral case for treating all humans as equal does not involve accepting that all humans are equal in all ways, but rather, simply, that they deserve equal consideration; and there is no logical or moral reason for failing to extend this 'consideration' to animals. It is an argument that seems irrefutable.

quite distinct from according them any notional 'rights'. But now, through the excesses of the Animal Liberation Front militants, even some of the most reasonable reforms have been jeopardised. The ALF's hoaxes and threats are not merely despicable in themselves but, worse, are counter-productive – deterring people who were in process of being won over and stirring up potential opposition, often where none existed before, to the whole question of improving animal protection. Scotland Yard, which has had to set up a special squad to combat them, estimates that the Front's activities cause damage costing more than £6 million a year. There are even good grounds to suspect that some of the militants are not genuinely interested in animals but have seized on the ALF as a means of furthering their own, more sinister political aims. Some ALF exploits have been utterly heedless, to put it mildly. Many of the caged animals they have released, for instance, were thereby doomed to a much crueller fate, since they were unfitted to look after themselves in the wild. Both in this respect and in the overall loss of public goodwill, the real victims of the militants' activities are the very animals they claim to defend.

(7) All the criticisms we have made of the ALF activists are underlined by one simple fact: Peter Singer is now howled down by some of his erstwhile followers, who condemn his attempt to promote the aims of animal liber-ation by using all available democratic means – giving lectures, writing letters, lobbying political parties, etc – and who attack his campaigning methods as 'too soft'.

(See also BLOOD SPORTS; VIVISECTION)

ARCHITECTURE, MODERN:
Has It Lost Its Way?

Pro: (1) For the purposes of this debate, it may be assumed that 'modern architecture' is the form represented by disciples and followers of such high priests of modernity as Mies van der Rohe, Le Corbusier and Gropius. In one sense, of course, almost every generation – or anyway, almost every half-century or so – produces its own 'modern' architecture, whose supporters can usually be relied on to decry the creations of their immediate predecessors. But rarely, if ever, can an architectural fashion have become more disliked, even hated, than that which reached its peak in the 1950s and '60s, and on into the '70s: the uncompromising glass towers and featureless concrete blocks which have come to symbolise the period initiated by the re-building of Britain's cities after the last world war. The trend is not over. Too many buildings of this nature are still going up.

(2) Architects responsible for such designs spoke solemnly about 'functionalism' – with never a mention of pride or identity. Their work became separated from true style and, instead, invaded politics and posed as social engineering. The buildings were so anonymous that the few outstanding exceptions – e.g. the once-controversial Sydney Opera House – became landmarks almost overnight, instantly recognisable world-wide.

(3) In building their impersonal tower-block housing estates, theatre complexes and other developments that were all supposed to be for the public good, modernist architects spoke of transforming post-war London (for instance) into 'clusters of

Con: (1) As with any other art form, opinions about architecture are always bound to be highly subjective – 'one man's meat is another man's poison' . . . But the crux of what is generally understood by 'modern architecture' can be summed up by these words from Mies van der Rohe: 'The decisive achievements in all fields are impersonal and their authors are for the most part unknown. They are part of the trend of our time towards anonymity.' This is not at all cold and unfeeling, as some people interpret it. What it pointed towards was the reticence which characterised most big architectural clients in the post-war era (a natural reaction after the lack of personal privacy so many individuals had suffered throughout the war years). Hence the wide demand for designs of reserve and restraint, for buildings which hid their actual functions behind bland understatement. In short, like it or not, the architecture was an accurate reflection of the age.

(2) Many criticisms of modern architecture stem partly from lack of knowledge about it and partly from the fact that it was never given as much chance in Britain as in some other countries. Years of planning controls and other official restrictions in this country led to an all-round lowering of aspirations. As a result, the principles of functionalism, technology, spareness of line and absence of ornament, as imbibed from the modernist masters, have never really come to full fruition here. Even so, many of the so-called exceptions often fit much more closely to such principles than the layman may realise. Let

villages turned on end' – with their slab-like office blocks described as 'cities in the sky' and high-rise lift shafts as 'vertical pavements'. It was not many years before the buildings themselves proved to be as flawed as the supposed social engineering concept. (Inside one new glass tower at Sheffield University, for instance, the 'greenhouse effect' brought about an internal temperature of 97 deg F. – on a February day when it was snowing outside! And because of the wind vortex formed at the base of the tower, there were 16 days a year, on average, when the staff couldn't open the front door against it and had to enter the building round the back . . .) What many of the architects responsible for such flaws had apparently failed to realise was that their own high priests had long since abandoned many of these concepts. Le Corbusier, though initially attracted to the idea of glass towers, carried out some small-scale experiments and discovered the problems of solar overheating, which he duly warned against in some of his papers. Similarly, while he remained the arch-exponent of high-rise, he also came to see that there were more efficient ways of organising space. In like vein, the Quickborner team, inventors of the open-plan office floor, holding 80 to 100 people, now say that staff should be partitioned into groups of not more than 10 – and the American architect Philip Johnson, a prime disciple of Mies van der Rohe, also dispensed with large open floors and went back to more or less conventional spaces in his famed AT&T skyscraper in New York (one of *the* great new buildings, anywhere). So it would seem that many of Britain's supposedly modernist architects are now, in fact, simply out of date!

(4) The Prince of Wales used a

it not be forgotten, for instance, that Sydney Opera House originally aroused fierce hostility and ridicule from a majority of the general public – and that it, too, is very much a product of modern architecture.

(3) The probable watershed for modern architecture in this country was reached in 1985 when the then Environment Secretary finally rejected a superbly thought-out scheme, centred on a 290ft tower designed by Mies van der Rohe, for Mansion House Square – immediately opposite the Lord Mayor of London's official residence. This ended a battle between developers and conservationists which had raged for some 20 years. Prevailing opinion in the City of London, originally in favour of the scheme, had swung over in support of conserving the 180,000 sq. ft. of Victorian office space on the site – nine listed buildings which are not in very good condition and, in truth, are of no particular distinction, either architecturally or historically. In exchange for this victory for the conservationists, London lost £100 million-worth of private sector construction, an ultra-modern bank building, an enclosed shopping centre and a public square flanked by works of unquestioned architectural genius. The would-be developer could have made a handsome profit by simply refurbishing the listed buildings, plus some small-scale in-filling, but remained faithful to his dream of giving London a building by the greatest and most influential architect of the 20th century. The underlying point here is that, compared with the cheap post-war office boxes which deservedly aroused public hostility, this kind of architecture is in an utterly different league. So is a good deal more which merits far more discrimination in its

phrase which has now become folk-lore when, in a speech to the Royal Institute of British Architects in 1984, he criticised the design then chosen for an extension to the National Gallery in London's Trafalgar Square, describing it as 'like a monstrous carbuncle on the face of a much loved and elegant friend'. Since then, in his evident opposition to the uglinesses perpetrated by the moderns, the Prince has consistently espoused the cause of 'community architecture', in which the architect collaborates on-site with the people who will live or work in the new building – in effect, using his professional skills to give them what *they* want, not imposing his own solutions. Prince Charles also sees this as offering hope of a regeneration of Britain's decaying inner city areas (especially as another feature of community architecture is that the architect should, wherever possible, use local people's energy and labour, thus providing jobs as well as urban renewal). In launching an appeal in November 1986, to raise funds for the purpose, the Prince asked: 'Can't we raise the spirit by restoring a sense of harmony, by re-establishing human scale in street patterns and heights of buildings, by redesigning those huge areas euphemistically known as "public open space" between tower blocks which lie derelict, festering and anonymous?' More and more people have come to believe that this is the direction in which architects should be heading. In their view, modern archi-tecture, as previously understood, has lost its way – and here, now, is the *real* modern architecture.

appraisal than the blanket dismissal customarily accorded by ill-informed critics. To give just two more exam-ples in or near London: the TV-am headquarters in Camden Town could hardly be more modern, yet fits into its Victorian canal-side surroundings without giving the least offence; and the new dormered and hipped-roof town hall at Hillingdon, Middlesex, attracts visits from architects all over the world.

(4) It is thought that there are now about 1,000 architects practising community architecture in Britain. It is *known* that they do not all agree with each other ... However, few would dispute that many of community architecture's aspirations are admirable. At the same time, there are one or two aspects on which a word of caution needs to be sounded. While it is an estimable idea that people who are going to use a building should be consulted about its design, and that their wishes should be taken into account as fully as possible, such consultation – particularly for public housing projects – can merely formalise the desires of present resi-dents, whose occupancy may be rela-tively transitory; it takes no account of what the needs and wishes of future tenants might be. Again, while it's a nice idea to create jobs and cut building costs by using the (usually unskilled) labour of the local people, might it not also increase the risk of shoddy construction? Finally, one hidden hazard is that the community architect's personal prejudices may work *against* the people he professes to serve. By going through a charade of canvassing tenants' views, architec-tural fads can be and *are being* foisted upon them. Such is the opposition to concrete and glass, for example, that pitched roofs and brick walls (say)

may be proffered as the 'right' solution – whereas, plainly, there will be occasions when they *won't* be. Whatever criticisms may be made of modern architecture, its unilateral imposition on doubting clients is not one of them.

ARMAMENTS, LIMITATION OF CONVENTIONAL

Pro: (1) Swollen armaments encourage militant nationalism, and often misplaced pride, in the countries which maintain them. At the same time, they create distrust and fear among other nations, leading them to increase their armaments in turn. In this mad race, each nation's defensive measures become interpreted by its neighbours as preparations for aggression.

(2) Experience has shown that schedules of disarmament are possible. Even with nuclear weapons, the Soviet Union and the USA have made some progress towards agreement to reduce their stockpiles. The limitation of conventional armaments, with a corresponding reduction in the size of armies, would lessen the danger of local wars – which always risk becoming bigger conflicts.

(3) The Geneva disarmament conference has served a useful purpose in forcing its participants to lay their cards on the table and in fostering an atmosphere of greater frankness. Its imperfections are admitted but, though ignored by some powers, it is generally recognised as a forum which it is essential to maintain.

(4) The burden of armaments is heavy in all countries and crushing in some. If it could be removed, trade

Con: (1) Armaments are not a cause but a symptom of the causes which bring about war. Whatever governments may say for public consumption, their intelligence services can distinguish perfectly well between countries which are taking defensive precautions and those which are prepared to use war as a specific policy.

(2) It is exceptionally difficult to bring about any effective limitation of conventional forces and armaments because qualitative reckonings are more important than quantitative. This has been the big problem for NATO and the Warsaw Pact powers, in their negotiations for mutual and balanced force reductions. In any case, America and the Soviet Union have given priority – quite rightly – to the much graver threat of nuclear arms.

(3) Without the participation of two of the world's nuclear powers, China and France, the Geneva disarmament conference is worthless. It has become a mere ritual and continues only because, politically, none of the major UN powers dares to take the responsibility of admitting the fact.

(4) One lesson war has taught all countries is that, unless armaments are kept up-to-date and in sufficient stock,

would have a chance to improve, taxation would be lessened and all countries would become more prosperous.

(5) Large armies and navies involve the existence of a large class of professional military men, who are naturally prone to warlike ambitions.

(6) Disarmament on a large scale would secure at any rate a considerable delay before war was resorted to, and the time taken to raise a nation to the pitch of warlike efficiency would give the forces of peace a better chance of prevailing.

(Some) Disarmament by one country (without waiting for agreement from others) would be a courageous step which would prove that country's good faith and help to break down the atmosphere of distrust.

a war can easily go in favour of the aggressor in the early days and be prolonged, if not lost altogether.

(5) In the most powerful countries especially, the professional soldier is essentially peaceable. Trained for war, he wants to prevent it from happening. The fomenters of modern war are the civilians.

(6) It is impossible to disarm any modern country, because armament is co-extensive with the country's organised knowledge and resources. Unilateral disarmament is a Utopian idea. It would merely be regarded as a sign of weakness by other countries.

(Some) What protagonists of unilateral disarmament tend to forget is that, in terms of *realpolitik*, only a lead from the two super-powers, the USA and the Soviet Union, could bring about anything effective. Without their participation, disarmament by any other country would be virtually irrelevant.

(See also NUCLEAR WEAPONS: SHOULD THEY BE BANNED COMPLETELY?)

AWARDS FOR ARTISTIC ACHIEVEMENT:
Too Much of a Good Thing?

Pro: (1) Such has been the growth in the number of prize competitions and awards in the artistic field – whether for music, painting or literature – that their validity has largely become debased. So many big commercial companies have jumped on the bandwagon, in search of easy publicity for their names or wares (notably tobacco groups now debarred from many other forms of advertising, as well as brewery groups in search of a bit of

Con: (1) In times gone by, creative artists in every field were largely dependent for their livelihoods on the patronage of enlightened wealthy individuals. Many big industrial and business companies have recognised that, with the virtual disappearance of private patrons, it is up to them to take on this responsibility (or its present-day equivalent). While they naturally hope to gain kudos for their companies by sponsoring awards of

respectability), that any worthwhile aims behind such awards have tended to become obscured or forgotten.

(2) In the musical field, the worst aspects of excessive prize competition are seen in such ventures as the BBC's Young Musician of the Year scheme, which puts too much emphasis on the mere business of 'winning', with all its attendant commercial rewards, at the expense of the steady, gradual development essential to young performers with genuine promise and of the crucial need to shield such gifted players from premature exposure.

(3) In the fine arts – painting, sculpture, print-making – a plethora of prize trophies exists for young students at the principal art colleges, and there are also a fair number of award distinctions open to artists who have established themselves. But the very people who need help most – the young artists who have left college and are struggling to make ends meet until they can start earning a living from their work – are almost entirely ignored by the firms sponsoring schemes of this nature.

(4) The decline in the merit of artistic awards is probably seen at its most acute in the literary field. Even the most famed distinction of all, the Nobel Prize for Literature, has become subject to increasing criticism and controversy, with accusations that the committee responsible has tended to make its decisions on political rather than literary grounds. It can certainly be held that, in the decade after Saul Bellow received the award in 1976, all but one of the ensuing winners (William Golding) were relatively unknown to the general public and could not be identified by anything more than a quite restricted circle outside their own countries. It is equally true that, further demon-

this nature, they have accepted that they are now almost the only sources – other than the Government – with enough financial resources to spare for the purpose. Repeated appeals from successive Arts Ministers for industry to devote more money to such sponsorships are clear evidence that, in the official view, the trend has *not* gone too far.

(2) Events such as the international Tchaikovsky piano competition held every four years in Moscow, as well as the Leeds piano competition in Britain, have acquired unquestioned status as virtually guaranteeing a career of world-wide distinction to the winners (and quite probably to a fair number of the other finalists as well). Winners of the Young Musician competition are always given most careful advice afterwards, both towards furtherance of their musical development and in avoiding undue attempts to exploit them commercially (e.g. not to accept too many of the concert engagements offered as a result of their success).

(3) Would-be sponsors are well aware of this particular gap, but so far it has proved impossible to structure an award scheme which would be sufficiently equitable or comprehensive, without being fiendishly expensive. Money apart, the mere mechanics of trying to reach all (or as many as feasible) of the young artists concerned would be unbelievably complex. At the same time, many of these artists do now have far more exhibition opportunities than was formerly the case.

(4) The criteria for these awards are frequently misunderstood (in particular, by literary critics themselves). The Nobel Prize has served to draw attention to the work of a good number of writers which was

strating the eccentricity of the prize committees, English-speaking writers passed over for the award in the past have included such literary giants as James Joyce, Thomas Hardy, Conrad, Henry James, D. H. Lawrence, Virginia Woolf and W. H. Auden. At a more blatantly commercial level, the list of various prizes available, as shown in a publishers' directory, runs to many pages in length. The best known of these, perhaps, are the annual Booker McConnell Prize for Fiction and the Whitbread prizes. Nothing could have revealed the underlying question-marks more plainly than the manner in which the money on offer for the latter was nearly doubled, suddenly, in an effort to steal Booker's limelight. On the other hand, the Booker Prize itself has produced so many apparently odd choices as winner, in recent years, that at one time many people were seriously querying whether it could continue to survive such idiosyncracy for very much longer. As a serious attempt to discover the way present-day fiction is going, or to uncover the most promising new work, it had ceased to have any genuine relevance, in their view.

previously unfamiliar to a wide international audience but well deserved to be much better known. (Among examples in the decade since Saul Bellow were I. B. Singer and the Czechoslovak dissident poet Jaroslav Seifert.) With the Booker, a former chairman of the judging panel once explained that, as he and his colleagues saw it, their task was not to tell the public what it ought to be reading but to select books that people were likely to *want* to read. Indeed, apart from the prize money, the main benefit from the award is in vastly increasing the sales of the winning work: one recent, pretty controversial winner sold more than 40,000 hardback copies within only a month, against the total of 3–4,000 copies that could normally have been expected; an earlier winner, less disputed, sold 177,000 in hardback and 300,000 in paperback. In addition, the success also sparked off further interest in other books by the authors concerned. And this, surely, is the crux of the matter, whether for literature, fine art or music: if prize competitions lead to much wider public interest in the arts, what greater justification for such awards could there be?

BIRTH CONTROL: VOLUNTARY OR COMPULSORY?

Pro: (1) Left to the operations of nature, men, like plants and animals, tend to outrun the supplies available to satisfy their wants. Fierce competition and destruction of the weaker is the usual way of meeting the difficulty, but this is a wasteful method and not

Con: (1) The imposition of world-wide birth control programmes, as a means of easing pressure on natural resources, would put the cart before the horse (quite apart from any moral objections). The danger of food shortages, apart from special causes, has

in accord with man's increasing mastery over nature. For centuries, man has been learning and practising the control of nature's productivity in the plant and animal worlds, yet the application of such principles to man himself is still hardly out of the elementary stages. By the turn of the century, it is estimated, the world's population will reach 6,130 million – an increase of 50 per cent in only 23 years (according to previous UN figures). But the Earth's natural resources are finite and such huge population growth will make shortages of food and raw materials inevitable. It is urgently necessary that birth control education and facilities should become universal. The only arguable point is whether these should be voluntary or compulsory.

(2) The wider provision of reliable medical advice on birth control has not been followed by the upsurge of immorality that the prophets of gloom predicted. There is now a strong movement in favour of allowing birth control even in the Roman Catholic Church, many of whose adherents already practise it.

(3) In more and more countries, abortion is now legal (under specified conditions, the most common being those cases when birth would be dangerous to the mother's health). Many of these operations could have been avoided by the wise use of birth control. There is no evidence, in general, that birth control does any harm to those who practise it or to their potential fertility. In fact, the contrary has been proved by the population increases in the advanced countries since the last world war. The law still controls methods which might be harmful if wrongly applied. For instance, the Pill can be obtained only on medical prescription to ensure

arisen in the past from large-scale devastation due to war, from inadequate knowledge locally, and also partially from the artificial restrictions resulting from financial difficulties and manipulations. But any shortages could be overcome – or avoided – by proper international co-operation (as already seen in part through the UN Food and Agricultural Organisation). Science and technology have made such progress that an increase in supplies at least proportionate to population could be effected without difficulty – and the latest statistics indicate that this is, in fact, already in process of being achieved.

(2) To check the birth rate artificially is immoral. It is rankly disobedient to the teaching of the Roman Catholic Church and, indeed, of many other religions. The motive of limitation is nearly always selfish, fundamentally.

(3) From the huge demand for abortions, since their legalisation, it is obvious that only a relatively small proportion of them are really necessary, on strictly medical grounds. Birth control has been used too often to avoid imagined risks for purely selfish reasons. Furthermore, there are indications that the continued practice of birth control actually reduces fertility. Even the Pill, supposedly 'safe', has made some women permanently infertile – and has been blamed for occasional deaths by thrombosis. When birth control is used to prevent child-bearing altogether, women are denying themselves the exercise of their natural functions. It is well established medically that, in most cases, child-bearing has a beneficial effect on a woman's mental and physical health.

(4) The desire for small families often springs from less worthy motives

women get the type most suitable for them (as regards oestrogen, etc.).

(4) Birth control is used mainly to limit, and not to avoid, child-bearing. In Western countries, the rise in the standard of living of the poorer classes has coincided with a decrease in the size of their families, and they no longer regard their children from a largely economic point of view. It is only in some developing nations, such as India, that peasant parents still regard having a large number of children as an insurance – a means of adding to the family's earning power and of safeguarding the parents' keep in their old age. But massive family planning campaigns are gradually succeeding in cutting the annual birth rate in such countries, even so.

(5) With attitudes towards women's position in society now becoming more enlightened, their freedom to practise birth control is among those rights which are already widely accepted as fundamental. Many women are no longer content to spend the most active years of their adult lives solely in bearing and rearing children; they wish to play their full part in the life of the community, which requires more time than traditional family ties would usually allow them; such women should have the practical means of deciding for themselves on the extent of family responsibilities they are willing to accept.

(6) The spread of birth control education and facilities, with official encouragement, has not only helped to eradicate dubious, hole-in-the-corner sources which existed formerly but has made people franker and more honest in their approach to the whole subject of sex. Except, perhaps, for the greater Press publicity it receives, sexual immorality is no greater today

than regard for the welfare of the children. Many selfish people decide against having children merely because they don't want to cut back on expensive enjoyments, such as foreign holidays. These people frequently offer proof that the retention of material amenities, at that price, may well be outweighed by the loss of spiritual values. In the poorest countries, the prime need is not family planning but the achievement of higher economic standards – and that's where concerted international action should mostly be directed. The Chinese, with more inhabitants than any other nation, insist that this presents no problems because, whatever the growth in the population, the country's economic growth has been at an even higher rate.

(5) To suggest that birth control gives women more freedom to widen their horizons, socially or intellectually, just isn't true. Only a relative minority of women show any real interest in the life and welfare of the community at large. Of those who do take an active role, very few manage to combine their public and private responsibilities without difficulty (or without some loss on one side or the other). For the average mother of a small family, with no other interests, extra spare time is rarely of any particular benefit. Some, feeling lonely, may enter industry – for the sake of the companionship as much as for the extra cash – but this will often be to the detriment of what remains of family life.

(6) The almost unrestricted availability of birth control appliances (even the Pill, from complaisant doctors) is encouraging immorality in the young and already leading many of them to reject the concepts of a society founded on the family and

than in past ages when birth control was unknown.

monogamic marriage – essential cornerstones of Western civilisation.

(See also the next article; MARRIAGE AS AN INSTITUTION; TERMINATION OF PREGNANCIES)

BIRTH RATE, HIGH

Pro: (1) A country's prosperity is bound up with the size of its working population. It cannot be developed, nor its economy carried on adequately, with too small a population. That is why some of the oldest and largest Commonwealth countries, such as Australia and Canada, were only partly developed until relatively recently, when intensified campaigns to encourage immigration gradually alleviated their shortage of manpower.

(2) Earlier alarm was accentuated by forecasts of a world population of 7,500 million by the year 2000 (and possibly reaching 10,000 million 30 years later). With more accurate data, such estimates have since been successively revised downwards. A similar change of thinking applies to modern methods of production and scientific improvements in agriculture, which make it possible to support larger populations than our ancestors ever imagined. The balance of probability is that, by the end of this century, food production will have grown faster than population. Britain's population has increased fourfold in the last century; the average standard of living of her people, particularly the poorer classes, has risen beyond measure in that time.

(3) Populations cannot be reduced harmoniously at all levels, unless by emigration on an enormous scale. A low birth rate really means a gradual decrease in the number of young

Con: (1) Most nations should be striving for lower, not higher birth rates. It's true that such countries as Australia and Canada still have many resources which they are only just beginning to exploit, as well as wide open spaces able to take huge populations. But with the world's total population expected to reach 6.13 billion by the turn of the century (an increase of two billion since the mid-1970s!), it is anything but certain that our resources will be sufficient by then, which could well mean increasing shortages of food supplies and raw materials, greater health hazards, fewer job opportunities, lower educational and living standards.

(2) The wealthier nations, which consume a much higher proportion of the world's resources than anyone else, have long benefited unfairly from the poor but heavily populated countries' huge pool of cheap labour. For our common survival, a more equitable situation is essential. Britain herself, despite her huge rise in agricultural production since 1939, is still quite unable to feed her own population. Economically and environmentally, she would probably be most viable and self-sufficient with a population one-quarter its present size.

(3) The expectation of life has risen by more than 20 years in the last century or two, and we can already see the first signs of people habitually

people and a corresponding increase in the old. For instance, it has been estimated that, by the end of the century, Britain will probably have as many people over 65 as under 15, while the number of people aged over 75 will increase by ten per cent in the next twenty years. That will mean a decrease in the manpower available for industry – as already seen in West Germany, where, with insufficient men of her own, the post-war 'economic miracle' could not have been achieved without bringing in millions of 'guest workers' from other, poorer countries.

(4) A falling birth rate is one sign of an increasing sense of insecurity among the people. The world-wide wars and economic depressions of the last seventy years are responsible for this; although a temporary increase in the birth rate is a common wartime phenomenon, such rates are not normally reached again in times of peace. (Between the 1950s and mid-1970s, Britain's birth rate was declining by up to 7 per cent annually; since then, the country's population has become more or less static.)

(5) The vast majority of families in Britain today have two children at the most – in 1982, the national average was 1.75 – and the proportion of single-child families has naturally continued to show a steady increase. Such children are usually at a disadvantage in life compared with children from large families, who have undergone the salutary discipline of having to consider other people's needs and feelings. The incidence of infantile mortality has been very much reduced by modern science, and financial hardships to the parents of large families are alleviated by the State, through child benefit payments.

(6) A large population is necessary

working fewer days a week and retiring at an earlier age (having learned to put their extra leisure time to worthwhile use). Modern technical advances make possible a vastly increased production at the cost of much less human effort; here again, therefore, the long-term trend is not towards a bigger labour force but towards a smaller, more highly trained one.

(4) Who can blame young couples if, in face of the nuclear threat, pollution and other adverse conditions in the world today, they decide to restrict their families to only one or two children at the most (or even to have none at all)? In fact, a lower birth rate may well be a positive, not a negative development. For Britain, one of the world's most densely populated industrial countries, halting her population growth would be beneficial rather than harmful.

(5) A high birth rate is always accompanied by a high death rate and, despite medical advances, by an increased level of invalidism in mothers. In present circumstances, few parents can support a large family properly. Overcrowding is one of the chief factors contributing to child mortality and inferior health. Quality is more necessary than quantity. The theory that children in large families are better balanced socially, and more self-reliant, simply does not stand up to closer examination.

(6) Numbers are not necessarily decisive in war; victory is more likely to depend on a sufficiency of weapons and a high level of industrial production generally. But even if numbers were decisive, who could possibly condone the idea of appraising life from the military standpoint alone?

(7) It is impossible to organise

21

from a military point of view. No country can reckon to defend itself successfully if it has a stationary or falling population. In war, numbers are always a decisive factor.

(7) If the morale of society were good and purely artificial hindrances to family life were removed, much recent social legislation would have been unnecessary and parents would be willing and able to cope with the tasks of raising more children than they intend to have at present. The housing shortage will not be a permanent problem, and progressive local authorities are already making provision, in their housing schemes, for the accommodation of larger families.

society satisfactorily if the proportion of children is unduly large. For instance, many of the improvements envisaged in the crucial 1944 Education Act, setting Britain's entire post-war educational pattern, later proved largely unworkable because of the fluctuations in the child population and the tremendous amount of money and labour required.

(See also the preceding article)

BISHOPS:
Should They Be Excluded from the House of Lords?

Pro: (1) Bishops have quite enough to do in looking after their dioceses. They are rarely fitted by circumstances or temperament to be legislators and, as a body, have an unfortunate history in this capacity.

(2) When the bishops were temporal powers, their presence in the House of Lords was necessary and natural. Today, their original status and duties have gone; the country holds many faiths and no faith. Their presence occasions resentment among those who are not members of the Established Church. It is a further infringement of the democratic principle that members of a legislature should be elected.

(3) Religion should have no place in politics. It appears to give no sure guidance in the problems before

Con: (1) Being independent of party, the bishops do very useful work as guardians of the interests of religion and the Church. They can take a statesmanlike view of public policy. As the clergy are not allowed to sit in the Commons, the bishops are all the more needed in the Lords.

(2) Long before the creation of life rather than hereditary peerages became the general practice, bishops were among the few Lords who sat by virtue of merit and not by accident of birth. The bishops' continued presence, therefore, is sound political science.

(3) Their exclusion would mean a further divorce between religion and politics. Most English people are religious, and the Church of England is still the State Church and the one

22

Government. Now that the Church has a much larger measure of self-government than it used to have, the bishops' defence of its interests in the Lords is no longer necessary.

(4) (Some) However commendable the idea of 'widening the spread' may be in theory, it is clearly significant that no great enthusiasm for it was shown by any of the other leaders suggested for the honour. Another MP, opposing the proposal, said the Lords was not a representative chamber and the bishops were not there as representatives; he doubtless didn't intend to, but he could hardly have made a better case for their total removal from the Lords!

which best represents the national feeling.

(4) (Some) One Conservative MP proposed in the Commons, early in 1986, that nearly half the 26 Anglican bishops in the Lords should be replaced by the UK leaders of other faiths — in particular, the Roman Catholic archbishops and bishops, the Chief Rabbi and his deputy, and the heads of the Free Churches. This would, he suggested, achieve a 'more balanced view' and help to 'reduce tension and a sense of alienation'. Clearly, though, it still reflected a view that senior clerics had a valuable role to play in the Upper House.

(See also CHURCHES, SHOULD THEY TAKE PART IN POLITICS?;
DISESTABLISHMENT OF THE CHURCH OF ENGLAND; LORDS, REFORM
OF THE HOUSE OF)

BLOOD SPORTS:
Should They Be Abolished?

Pro: (1) Blood sports involve the infliction of suffering and death in the name of human entertainment. To perpetrate this for such a trivial purpose is immoral. There can be no justification for treating other animals as though they existed only to serve man's ends. Besides the great cruelty inherent in blood sports and their fostering of a too ready acquiescence in the causing of pain, they are in any case a most inefficient method of exterminating noxious animals.

(2) In the hunting of deer, foxes and hares, the chase is deliberately prolonged through the use of slow-running, high-stamina hounds, to enable mounted hunt followers to enjoy a long gallop. If the purpose of

Con: (1) Blood sports, otherwise known as field sports, are defined as any activity which involves the pursuit of wild animals and which also engenders enjoyment, interest or recreation for human beings. As all mammals, birds and fish are 'animals', the activities covered in Britain by this definition include most forms of hunting with dogs or hounds, all forms of angling, and all shooting except target and clay pigeon.

(2) Field sports all exist on the same moral base. Those who engage in them believe that their enjoyment is legitimate so long as it does not involve unnecessary suffering. All the animals taken in field sports are either pests or edible, or both, and would

23

the hunt were a quick kill, fast dogs such as lurchers would be used. Among many other examples of a deliberate extension of suffering, it is common for a Hunt Servant to be employed to block up fox earths and badger setts the night before a meeting, to ensure that the quarry has no choice but to run until exhausted. Again, it is also common for fox hunting to continue not merely through the fox's mating season but even until after the cubs are born. This, obviously, can lead to cubs being orphaned and starving to death.

(3) Fox hunts build artificial earths to ensure a readily available supply of foxes, making a nonsense of their claims to be carrying out 'pest control'. The high level of sustained fox persecution has no effects on the animal's overall population. This is because the fox, being a predator/scavenger which has never had a serious natural enemy, controls its own population level through the year-long availability of food in a defended territory. It is also an acknowledged fact that, in areas of high fox persecution and mortality, vixens have larger litters than those in areas where they are virtually undisturbed. Thus, killing foxes is pointless in terms of population control. As for claims about the depredations allegedly wreaked by foxes, modern scientific studies prove that foxes are, in fact, insignificant predators of lambs and poultry. In the Highlands of Scotland, for instance, up to 24 per cent of lambs die from exposure, disease or malnutrition, or are stillborn, whereas only around one per cent are taken by foxes.

(4) The hunting of deer with hounds is alien to the principle of 'natural selection', in that strong, fit deer are selected for the hunt, to

still be killed even if field sports did not exist. What matters, therefore, is whether the alternatives which would replace hunting, shooting and angling are more humane. In the view of regular participants in field sports, they are not. These participants say that they ask no special favours but merely wish to enjoy the same freedom of conscience as their fellow-citizens. They point out that it is, for instance, quite unnecessary for anyone to eat meat; the existence of many thousands of healthy vegetarians proves this (see Vegetarianism). Accordingly, it is both logical and obvious that, if meat is not eaten from necessity, it must be eaten for pleasure – from which it follows that those who eat meat must support the killing of animals for this reason. If such people suggest that fishing or hunting is immoral, they can hardly be surprised that others may consider them to be hypocrites.

(3) The argument that the fox is not a pest and does not need control is totally fallacious. Figures produced by the League Against Cruel Sports show that thirty per cent of farmers suffered damage from foxes in a single year, in spite of the fox being already heavily controlled. According to statistical data produced by one fox expert, Dr David McDonald, of Oxford University, 80 to 90 per cent of farmers consider the fox to be a pest which requires control. In such circumstances, to suggest that the fox can be left to control its own numbers is simply ridiculous. Contrary to the claims opposite, fox controls – including hunting – do have an effect on the fox population. Foxes breed only once a year, and any fox killed after the end of the breeding season cannot be replaced until the following spring. No one has asserted that foxes

ensure a long chase. In earlier times, natural predators, such as wolves, would have predated on the old, sick and weak, not on the fit and strong animals of breeding-standard. While periodic culling is essential to ensure that over-population does not imperil their survival in the wild, deer can be killed humanely – using high-powered rifles in the hands of experts – instead of chasing them to a standstill with hounds. The vast majority of deer killed for control purposes in the UK are, in fact, shot by rifles. Moreover, hounds frequently trespass on land where they are not welcome, sometimes stampeding cattle or killing sheep and lambs, as well as many domestic cats. Stag hunt riders and supporters following the hunt on motor-cycles also cause damage to valuable moorland – notably, for example, on Exmoor and on the Quantock Hills in Somerset.

(5) There can be no possible defence for the unspeakable cruelties committed in the alleged 'sport' of hare coursing, with the quarry often literally torn to pieces by rival greyhounds. This apart, there is another, broader issue on the conservationist front. Hare numbers are declining in Britain, due to intensive mono-culture farming methods. A species under such pressure ought to be officially protected.

(6) The shooting of pheasants involves the artificial production of this (non-British) species of bird in huge numbers, purely for the purpose of killing them for 'sport'. In carrying out their job of protecting the birds, gamekeepers snare, trap or shoot vast numbers of British native species of predators and have been responsible for the deaths of countless thousands of now-rare birds of prey. The snares and traps used by gamekeepers have

can or even should be eradicated from whole sections of rural England – only the opponents of hunting claim this to be the aim of fox control. What such bodies as the British Field Sports Society do seek is a reduction in fox density, with a consequent reduction in damage – and this, they insist, is precisely what is being regularly achieved. They also make the point that a ban on fox-hunting with hounds could be justified only if it could be shown that the fox itself would be better off as a result. But the plain facts are that fox control continues in all of the many places where hunting already does not exist and that the methods which replace hunting – gassing, snaring, poisoning, shooting – are recognised as facing the fox with a greater risk of real physical suffering than does hunting. Unlike all the alternatives, moreover, fox hunting is the only system which allows the fox any close season during which to rear its cubs in peace. In addition, hunting with hounds approximates more closely than any other technique to a biological control. Healthy, strong foxes tend to escape; weak, sick, injured and old foxes tend to be caught. This is as Nature intended. In no sense are foxhounds slow, as claimed in (2) opposite. They can outpace a thoroughbred horse across country and can run at least as fast as a fox. During a hunt, they frequently go much slower than this, not because they are slow but because they have to follow the delicate, twisting and fast-fading scent left by their quarry. They could not be replaced by greyhounds or lurchers, because these dogs lack the toughness to face the dense cover where foxes are found, do not have the exceptional noses which enable foxhounds to follow a fox when it is not in sight, nor the power to

caused injury or death to large numbers of non-target animals, such as badgers, otters and domestic pets and livestock. Gamekeepers protect grouse in a similar way. The cumulative effect of their depredations on raptors (wild predatory birds) has been to lead many of these to become extinct or to be added to the endangered species list. Another very harmful aspect is that shooting results in 3,000 tons of lead being discharged into the environment every year – a particular threat near lakes and other waterways. Many swans and other waterfowl have died from the effect of accidentally ingesting shotgun pellets.

(7) Claims are sometimes made that fish caught by skilled anglers feel little or no pain – but what clear evidence has ever been produced to prove this? Apart from the very real possibility of cruelty (however unintentioned), it is undeniable that great harm is caused to wild life by anglers carelessly abandoning lead weights or pieces of nylon fishing line. The swan population, alone, is believed to suffer several hundred losses from these causes every year. Responsible angling organisations have tried for some years to make anglers bear such dangers in mind – urging them continually to gather up any left-over bits of line and to use harmless new alternatives introduced in place of the conventional lead weights. But the response from lazy anglers has been so inadequate that, by the autumn of 1986, the Government was led to announce that it would have to ban lead weights by law.

(8) Public opinion polls conducted by reputable polling companies, such as NOP and Gallup, all indicate that a vast majority of the British public, both urban and rural, is opposed to hunting wild animals with hounds. In

guarantee the instantaneous kill achieved by the foxhound.

(4) Stag hunting with hounds is limited to England's West Country and enjoys enormous support from the farming community in that area. It is now universally recognised that the survival of the wild red deer is inextricably linked with the survival of stag hunting. Deer are both valuable meat-producing animals and a serious pest to agriculture and forestry. In spite of this, they are almost universally preserved by the farming community, simply because of its traditional love of stag hunting. If such hunting were abolished, the deer's survival would be put to the gravest risk. Hunted deer are not killed by the hounds or touched by them in any way. At the end of a hunt, deer go to water and stand at bay, where they are shot at point-blank range with a firearm specially suited for the job. The particular circumstances of deer hunting permit the hunt's marksman to approach so close that the loss of a wounded deer is literally unheard of.

(5) Hares are an important game animal and an actual or potential pest to agriculture, horticulture and forestry. Their numbers are limited in some areas by climate, altitude or certain types of farming regime; but they occur in considerable numbers in areas suited to them. There is absolutely no truth in the claim that the hare is a threatened species. Control is necessary in many areas – and in most, harvesting the annual surplus of hares for food is both legitimate and an acceptable conservation practice. Hares may be shot, hunted with scent hounds or coursed with greyhounds. The idea that they are torn to pieces, in hare coursing, is completely fallacious; on the contrary, using greyhounds or lurchers to catch them

26

striking contrast to this majority, hunting is very much a minority activity, with fewer than 16,000 subscribers to fox hunts, fewer than 1,000 subscribers to stag hunts and fewer than 350 to hare-coursing clubs. (Figures published by the Standing Conference on Countryside Sports in 1983.)

(9) The abolition of hunting need not affect employment, because it is a simple matter to convert a pack of hounds to 'drag-hounds'. These follow an artificially laid trail and the riders gallop along behind in the same way as on a fox hunt. The trail can be laid to avoid crops, livestock, roads and railway lines, thus avoiding the damage, anger and conflict which often occur when hunts are pursuing a quarry which is running for its life. Hunting and shooting do not have significant value in the conservation of habitat. Since the Second World War, 60 per cent of Britain's heathlands have been destroyed, as have 40 per cent of our ancient woodlands and 125,000 miles of hedgerows; every year, many thousands more acres of moorland and wetland are lost. This destruction of habitat has contributed to 80 species of birds, 60 species of plants and 40 species of animals being added to the endangered species list. Accordingly, despite Britain having more packs of hounds than any other country in the world, as well as nearly a million shotguns in private hands, these blood sports have contributed virtually nothing to the preservation of habitat. In 1911, Parliament made the 'infliction of unnecessary suffering' on to domestic and captive animals a criminal offence. There is no logical reason why the law should not regard the inflicting of unnecessary suffering on to wild animals as equally criminal.

is a traditional method of 'filling the pot' in many country areas.

(6) Game shooting, like all other field sports, is closely controlled by statute law and by self-imposed codes of conduct which go much further than normal legal requirements. Where winged game is concerned, there is, of course, no alternative to shooting. If you want to eat a partridge or a pheasant, the only way of taking it is with a gun – and in this sense, shooting is almost beyond attack.

(7) Angling is probably best defended by comparing the fate of a fish caught by an angler with that of one destined for a fish-and-chip shop. The angler's fish, after a fight of no great duration, is either killed instantly or gently returned to the water; the fish caught for commercial sale lies choking to death for hours, crushed in a welter of blood and scales in the hold of a ship.

(8) Opponents of field sports make much of opinion polls which purport to show that a majority of the population disapproves of hunting. But disapproval is vastly different from an explicit desire to end people's freedom to take part in hunting, if they wish. In any case, it is known that at least 90 per cent of those polled have no first-hand knowledge of what hunting is. Much better tests of informed opinion were provided by two polls little mentioned by the 'antis'. The first was a referendum held in the Hertfordshire village of Redbourne on whether the local hunt should be banned. It was a poll in which an effort was required to vote, staged in a locality where most of the inhabitants had at least seen hounds – and the motion was soundly defeated, with only 13 per cent voting for a ban. The second poll was conducted by the

27

National Society for the Abolition of Cruel Sports into the attitude of veterinary surgeons to hunting. More than 90 per cent of the vets who responded were pro-hunting. Such a result from an informed and caring profession is worth all the crude opinion polls put together.

(9) Banning field sports is not a trivial matter. In the UK, more than four million people fish, well over a million shoot, and around one million take a friendly interest in hunting. It is beyond dispute that field sports contribute positively towards employment, recreation, rural access and the conservation of the landscape and the wildlife it supports. To put all this at risk to please a prejudiced clique, and with no clear evidence of beneficial results for the quarry species, would be plain madness.

(See also ANIMALS, RIGHTS OF; VIVISECTION)

BRITISH COMMONWEALTH:
Is It a Reality? Can It Survive?

Pro: (1) Today, the Commonwealth comprises most of the nations which were formerly part of the British Empire. It is the only multi-racial, multi-ethnic, multi-religious group of freely associating independent states in the world. Its continued existence, despite such wide variations, not only bears out the wisdom of achieving independence by consent – the principle originally applied by Britain, for these countries – but also shows that the Commonwealth still has a highly useful function.

(2) The mother country's help was made readily available to all the old Empire's former Asian and African

Con: (1) The British Empire was assembled from a haphazard series of conquests and otherwise had no discernible pattern, either strategic or economic. On the contrary, its defence eventually became a strategic liability. When pressures after the last world war speeded up the process of independence (much against many Britons' will, if truth be told), Britain's dominant economic ties with the new Commonwealth nations were still mutually beneficial; but this has since largely changed. Today, the Commonwealth is bound together by the force of inertia alone and, in the course of time, is bound to disintegrate.

colonies, after independence, and was just as readily accepted by each of them, in coping with the problems of building their own new nation. This is only one of many factors explaining why, despite occasional strains on the surface, fundamentally friendly relations continue between them to this day.

(3) The old-established Dominions, settled largely by people of British stock, are firmly linked to Britain by emotional as well as economic ties. Hence their support in times of war. South Africa left the Commonwealth for special reasons – was, in effect, expelled because of its hated racial policies – and in any case had less of an emotional tie since more than half its white population is not of British but of Boer (Dutch) descent.

(4) Britain bequeathed her system of parliamentary democracy both to the older Dominions and to the new Commonwealth nations, many of whose future leaders were educated in the mother country and came to have great respect for many British institutions.

(5) Like the United Nations, the 49-member Commonwealth is a loose association of sovereign states. But one way it differs from the UN is, precisely, that it has an accepted titular head, the Queen, to whom all its members look with affection and respect. Except for the Queen's unique role – taking account of those member-nations which have remained monarchies, she is in effect 17 Queens in one – the fact that the Commonwealth has a pretty loose structure works extremely well. None of its members, with their varying needs and ways of life, would wish to be bound in detail by inflexible decisions. In practice, however wide their individual differences, the vast majority

(2) While the new nations accepted British help, they made it very plain that they did not feel in any way bound by British policies. Some of them now lean more towards links with countries which have never been in the Commonwealth.

(3) Among the former Dominions, Canada has had no vital economic dependence on Britain for a very long while, and Australia has not only turned more towards the USA in recent years but has also built up its political and economic links within the whole Far East sphere – a process given added impetus after Britain joined the EEC. South Africa felt able to dispense entirely with any supposed benefits brought by Commonwealth membership – and, in fact, suffered no economic ill-effects as a result of its withdrawal.

(4) The Dominion Parliaments were profoundly modified and several are now closer to the American model. Experience among many of the African member-nations, in particular, indicates that they have found the traditions of parliamentary democracy may not be best suited to them – as witness the number which have since established one-party governments (or which aim to).

(5) The monarchical tie has much less meaning now that so many of the Commonwealth nations have become republics. Even in her role as individual sovereign, the Queen is often obliged to say quite contradictory things – as between the policies of one member-country and another – when giving the Speech from the Throne (announcing governmental legislative plans) in different countries' Parliaments. There might be some point in a Commonwealth Federation, if this were compatible with Britain's membership of the EEC. As now

of the Commonwealth peoples share fundamental beliefs in democracy, racial equality and tolerance – beliefs which many other nations might do well to adopt.

(6) One traumatic episode which amply proved the viability of the Commonwealth was British entry into the EEC in 1973. The other Commonwealth members backed the decision, recognising the realities of Britain's best future interests. At the same time, the entry terms finally negotiated took due account of Britain's continued relationships with her Commonwealth partners.

(7) The underlying strength of the Commonwealth was also borne out by its survival from the latest and by far the biggest strain on the bond: the British Government's reluctance to impose large-scale economic sanctions against South Africa, despite the report by the Commonwealth Eminent Persons Group (in June 1986) warning that only such 'concerted action' by the Commonwealth and the whole international community could avert what it described as 'the terrible fate' now awaiting all South Africa's communities. In July 1986, this British unwillingness led many member-nations to withdraw from the Commonwealth Games in Edinburgh; and genuine fears were expressed that, at the ensuing Commonwealth summit meeting in London, the entire organisation might collapse. There could hardly be more convincing proof of its viability that, notwithstanding the deep difference of view, the Commonwealth did *not* disintegrate, after all.

constituted, though, the Commonwealth is an anachronism.

(6) Despite the lip service paid to consulting the Commonwealth, Britain's decision to 'go into Europe' was taken unilaterally. The older members were strong enough to begin establishing alternative trading links (if they hadn't done so already). The newer, still developing member-countries could only hope to derive benefit from the Common Market via their association with Britain. Either way, though, none of the other partners was given any real choice in the matter.

(7) The sanctions row in the summer of 1986 could hardly have provided clearer proof of the underlying fragility of the Commonwealth. Some sort of agreement was reached, temporarily, for Britain to remain the 'odd man out' on the issue. On this occasion, despite many very angry criticisms of the British standpoint, matters were not allowed to reach the stage of an irretrievable head-on confrontation. But for how much longer? It has to be said bluntly, too, that some of the most vociferous critics could stand accused of hypocrisy, in the light of their own racial and political records. In general, be it noted that (for instance): Kenya, Malawi, Sierra Leone and Zambia are one-party states; Ghana and Nigeria are military regimes; in the latter case, the Nigerians have had six military coups since independence and are not expected to return to civilian rule until 1990, at the earliest; Zimbabwe's ruling party has been widely accused of atrocities against followers of its main rival political party (who are also from a rival tribe) in Matabeleland; it was Uganda, Kenya and Tanzania which threw out their own Asian populations in the 1970s, ostensibly in furtherance of their drives for

'Africanisation'. Should Britain accept attempts by states like these to impose on her, in the name of 'Commonwealth unity', policies which the British Government deems as contrary to the national interest or running counter to its own judgment? It would not be altogether surprising if a time came when moves to end the Commonwealth charade were initiated not by the other partners but by Britain herself.

BROADCASTING, PUBLIC CONTROL OF

Pro: (1) As a method of conveying both education and political propaganda, broadcasting – by which is meant sound radio as well as television – is probably the most potent there is. Its influence is so pervasive that the service cannot be left with safety to private concerns; some form of public control (and, indeed, of management) is essential. The BBC, which is established by Government charter and gets its finance from licence fees, provides its public service autonomously and is – in theory, anyway – free of Government intervention. While it is far from perfect (with such a huge daily output, there are bound to be occasional hiccups), many other countries still regard it as the best possible model.

(2) Commercial television has lowered programme standards. Public control, as exercised in Britain by the BBC, enables all tastes to be catered for, to some extent, whereas a commercialised service tends to pander to the lowest common denominator (to boost the size of its audience and thus increase its advertising

Con: (1) Because of its power to shape or even manufacture opinion, broadcasting ought not to be subject to governmental control, much less to public management. One consequence of such control must always be the danger of programmes being biased in favour of the prevailing Government's viewpoint, with minority bodies and views given little or no hearing and live controversial subjects often suppressed from discussion. One notable example of these drawbacks was provided by TV and radio in France under the rigid state control imposed by General de Gaulle (and maintained by most of his successors). The BBC may claim to have avoided all this, but the potential precariousness of its position became all too evident under the Conservative Government in the mid-1980s, through Ministerial attempts to stop certain programmes being transmitted (e.g. the 'Real Lives' controversy). Moves to get the (Government-appointed) Board of Governors to take a more direct hand in such matters were also interpreted as

revenues). No privately owned broadcasting company would have initiated Radio 3, for example. The BBC has accomplished much in raising the general level of public taste, particularly in music and drama, and in stimulating a thirst for knowledge. Its schools broadcasts are recognised world-wide as the best of their kind anywhere. Television, particularly, is in need of public control. The low standard of the majority of programmes in the USA shows the depths of taste to which television can descend when left in private hands. Above all, freedom of speech is more likely to be preserved by an impartial authority than by purely commercial companies which have a vested interest in keeping 'on side' with the advertisers who ultimately pay for their programmes . . . 'He who pays the piper calls the tune.'

(3) Technical advances in immediate or near-prospect include world-wide communications satellites, the institution of pan-European TV transmissions through ECS-1 (European Communication Satellite-1), the growth of cable television, and, ultimately, the advent of a new type of television, DBS (Direct Broadcasting by Satellite), in which programmes will be beamed directly into viewers' homes. All these changes indicate a need for a greater measure of international control, as well as public control at home, rather than allowing the air to be thrown open to unrestricted competition. Partly to consider the impact of these innovations, and partly to study the best ways of financing the BBC, the latest big inquiry into public broadcasting in Britain was that of the committee under Professor Alan Peacock, which delivered its report in July 1986. Although its main proposals included

containing a surreptitious threat of greater official control.

(2) Public control is, in effect, a form of dictatorship by people who, as in the BBC, are virtually inaccessible to the public. In the BBC, a 'civil service' attitude prevailed which resulted all too often in lack of enterprise. It was only under the stimulus of competition from the livelier independent TV companies that the BBC brightened its own offerings. There have even been justifiable complaints that it was sometimes guilty of lowering standards, in an effort to compete for audience ratings. Nowadays, in any case, it is quite untrue that the BBC has an 'edge' in programme quality. Many ITV programmes – in fields ranging from music and drama to current affairs and sport – have set equally high if not higher standards. The independent Channel 4 explicitly caters for minority interests. As for the open discussion of controversial subjects, freedom of speech certainly fares no worse on commercial TV and radio than under the BBC.

(3) The alternative to public or quasi-public control and management is not unrestricted competition but regulated competition under private management. This already exists in Britain, where the private companies in both commercial TV and commercial radio are still subject to the regulations of their own centralised authority – and where advertising sponsors have no control whatever over the actual programmes, as they do in the USA. The Peacock committee recognised that the needs of the consumer – the viewer and the listener – must be paramount. Accordingly, given the wide choice of channels that will soon be open to us, it proposed that broadcasting should be financed by a kind

a recommendation that the BBC should have the option to sell Radios 1 and 2, as well as local radio, into private hands, it is significant that the idea of financing the BBC by allowing it to take advertising – as the Government had wished – was *not* espoused. The report suggested that, with the incursion of advertising, the quality of programmes would be likely to suffer and that in any case there would not be enough advertising revenue to go round. It also proposed that the licence fee should be index-linked, to take account of the inflation rate; that the BBC should take over collection of the fee from the Post Office; and that, by the end of the century, the fee should be abolished in favour of a system of payment per programme watched – the idea being that TV sets would be adapted so that people watching BBC, cable or satellite programmes could insert credit cards into them on a 'pay as you view' basis. Overall, in short, despite the changes recommended by the Peacock committee to make the BBC better fitted to meet the 21st century, what it did *not* recommend was the abolition of public service broadcasting, as such. The committee said explicitly, indeed, that it wanted to see BBC Radio 3 and 4 preserve their present character.

of 'mixed economy' system: a combination of paying directly for programmes and of subsidising, from the public purse, programmes which are of national interest. (Professor Peacock himself has drawn a parallel with reading: we pay for the individual book, magazines and newspapers we want to buy, but at the same time everyone approves of public libraries being financed out of taxes and the rates.) On another aspect of this 'mixed economy', the committee also recognised the imperatives of market forces and proposed that the franchises for commercial television companies should be put out to competitive tender. It would expect the Independent Broadcasting Authority (which regulates the commercial companies) to lay down minimum standards that bidders must meet. The IBA would be required to publish a detailed statement of its reasons if it awarded a franchise to any company other than the highest bidder; but it would be entitled to allot the contract to a company offering a lower price if, for example, it decided that this bidder was giving more value for money in terms of a public service. In addition, again accepting the claims of economic reality over exclusively public control, the committee suggested that night hours on both ITV and BBC television which are not usually occupied at present – as a general rule, 1 a.m. to 6 a.m. – should be sold for broadcasting purposes. None of the Peacock report's recommendations is likely to be implemented much before 1990, if then. It has to be said frankly that Parliament's immediate reaction to them was anything but favourable, with the Conservative Government disappointed about not getting its way over financing the BBC through advertising and with the Labour Opposition rejecting nearly every proposal. However, even if the report remains pigeon-holed, its conclusion that there is no case for increased public control has undoubtedly confirmed the pattern for the future of broadcasting in this country.

(See also COMMERCIAL RADIO: SHOULD IT BE ABOLISHED?)

CABINET GOVERNMENT

Pro: (1) Under Cabinet Government, the more important Ministers are supreme in their respective departments and at the same time benefit from their colleagues' advice and support.

(2) By giving each Government department a political chief of wide outlook and experience, the prejudices of permanent civil service officials in that department are counter-balanced.

(3) The House of Commons does not exercise direct authority over Government departments, but it does have ultimate control over the system, through the power of dismissing Ministers.

(4) The Cabinet connects the executive with the legislative branch of government and protects the departments from hasty and disastrous interference by Parliament.

(5) A complexity of affairs can be managed only by a small and united group; hence the success of our system. The business of the Cabinet is to formulate a general policy as the outcome of calm discussion. The temperamental differences among its members are sufficient to prevent its becoming a rigid machine. That the system works well is also proved by the fact that there is no need for notes

Con: (1) The joint responsibility implicit in Cabinet Government often compels Ministers to give a colleague indiscriminate support and to compromise over the interests of their own departments.

(2) Permanent officials inevitably dominate the inexperienced and harassed Minister. In the eyes of senior civil servants, a 'good' Minister is one who always follows their advice.

(3) Cabinet Government has reduced the House of Commons to impotence. In practice, the House does not dismiss either Ministries or Ministers. Because of the Cabinet system, an attack on one department has the often-unwanted effect of being taken as an attack on the whole Government.

(4) It subordinates administration to the political vagaries of a few men, who are both inexpert and primarily concerned with the fortunes of their party. Departments should have permanent heads directly responsible to Parliament.

(5) Once established, a Cabinet, provided it remains unanimous, has all the power and the characteristics of an oligarchy. This can lead to an even more intensive form of abuse –

to be taken at the end of the Cabinet's discussions – virtually all its decisions are by consensus (the 'feeling of the meeting').

as exposed by the Westland helicopter controversy, early in 1986, when one of the principal allegations voiced was that crucial decisions were being taken by small, inner groups of Ministers and not by the Cabinet as a whole.

(See also COALITION GOVERNMENT; PARTY GOVERNMENT; WRITTEN CONSTITUTION)

CALENDAR REFORM

Pro: (1) Our present calendar, devised by Pope Gregory XIII in 1582, is both inconvenient and illogical. It was a correction of the Julian Calendar drawn up by Julius Caesar in 46 BC, which reckoned the length of a year as 365¼ days, whereas it is actually 365.2422 days. But its irregular and arbitrary division of the year into months of uneven length could easily be improved upon. Various associations exist with the object of bringing about such reform, and it would not be difficult to arrange for international action. The matter was under consideration by the League of Nations as long ago as the 1930s, and about 200 different proposals were investigated.

(2) There are definite advantages in such a tidying up, and several excellent schemes have been put forward. The simplest was one suggested by a Yugoslav who would abolish weeks and months altogether, and distinguish the date only by number. Thus one might make an appointment for 11 a.m. on the 159th. Leap Year, according to this plan, would merely stop at the 366th day instead of the 365th.

(3) In spite of British conservatism, some such scheme is bound to come sooner or later. The principal

Con: (1) The Gregorian Calendar has been used satisfactorily for nearly four centuries. The only people who wish to change it are a handful of cranks, who would find themselves in a very small minority if any of their schemes were taken seriously. The whole civilised world would be thrown out of gear by such a change and would gain in compensation nothing but a rearrangement or re-shuffling of names and days. The calendar might look a little better to people who set logical tidiness before practical convenience, but there would be no real advantage whatever.

(2) Such a scheme would be of little value unless universally adopted. Great Britain, of all countries, is least likely to agree to it. We waited 170 years before accepting the Gregorian Calendar and began to use it long after the rest of Europe had fallen into line.

(3) Similar schemes have been put forward before and have met with no lasting success, since they gave no fundamental advantage. The French Revolution Calendar, introduced in 1793, had twelve equal months of thirty days, each subdivided into ten-day weeks, or decades. The year was completed by five national holidays. The months were named according to their traditional weather – Brumaire,

improvement needed is a perpetual calendar that remains unchanged year after year. There are two main schools of thought – the equal months school, and the equal quarters school. British reformers largely incline to the latter, and Americans, exemplified by the International Fixed Calendar Association, to the former.

(4) It is generally agreed nowadays that a perpetual calendar would have great advantages in business and accounting. Such a one is the international fixed calendar, advocated mainly by the International Fixed Calendar League. This calendar has thirteen months, each of twenty-eight days, and a New Year's day which comes between 28 December, the last day of one year, and 1 January, the beginning of the next. The thirteenth month, named Sol, comes between June and July, and in Leap Year an extra day is inserted between June and Sol, which would be a general holiday. The advantage of this scheme, which has won an increasing measure of support, is that the same date always falls on the same day of the week.

(5) There are already business concerns which have successfully worked the thirteenth-month system, e.g., Kodak. Many companies in France pay monthly salaries on the basis of a thirteenth month, added to payments at the beginning of December (and thus a welcome bonus before Christmas).

(6) There is a clear public demand for a fixed Easter, which makes itself heard every year as that holiday comes round. According to the British scheme (usually known as the Desborough plan), not only would the date of Easter be fixed but other important social fixtures, such as August Bank Holiday and school and university terms, could also be standardised.

Frimaire, Nivôse, Pluviôse and so forth. This calendar was abandoned in 1806. Russia in 1929 abolished Saturday and Sunday in favour of a five-day week, but the final result has been merely an arrangement comparable to our own. During the Fascist regime, Italy introduced a system which counted years from the beginning of the regime instead of the birth of Christ, but the change had no effect on everyday life in the country.

(4) Because of deep-seated superstition, the number 13 is widely unpopular. An unofficial committee on calendar reform has already considered this scheme and has described the 13-month year as 'definitely repugnant to British feeling'. Moreover, it has several disadvantages for business purposes. The number 13 is difficult to divide by and impossible to divide into. Neither the quarters nor the half-year would contain a whole number of months; a quarter would consist of three and a quarter months. Thirteen monthly balancings, stock-takings, and payments would increase trouble and complicate business.

(5) The exception does not prove the rule. If there were any genuinely widespread desire for calendar reform, we should hear the issue discussed much more than we normally do.

(6) There is still a considerable body of opinion, especially religious opinion, opposed to a fixed Easter. And those religious bodies which approve a fixed Easter would show great divergence of views about how and when it should be fixed. If school and university terms were permanently stabilised, the hard-won public acceptance of the need for the staggering of holidays would inevitably be jeopardised.

CAPITAL PUNISHMENT, RESTORATION OF

Pro: (1) Experience since its abolition has proved that capital punishment is a stern, though regrettable, necessity. Without it, our lives and property have become less secure and crimes of violence have increased. In the present unsettled state of the world, its restoration is becoming more, not less, necessary. The police say that, now criminals do not have to fear hanging, the numbers who carry guns when committing robberies or other crimes have risen enormously.

(2) Capital punishment should be used to rid society of its enemies, instead of keeping them for the remainder of their lives as a perpetual charge upon the public purse. Some of the countries which had virtually ceased to carry out capital punishment, e.g. France, have since found it necessary to draw back from its complete legal abolition.

(3) The reformation and re-education of some types of criminal may be possible, and it is recognised that a high proportion of those convicted of unlawful killing are 'one-off' cases, not normally involved in serious crime; but a hardened murderer is beyond hope of reform. Are we to allow such men, ready to kill without compunction not once but several times, to live and return to society as a source of danger to their fellows on the expiry of their sentences (for even a life sentence may, in practice, sometimes amount to little more than 10–12 years)?

(4) If there is the slightest doubt in the minds of the jury, a verdict of guilty is not returned. Despite public concern over the possibility of

Con: (1) The death penalty is an anachronism in the modern penal code. It is a relic of an age when all punishments were savage and vindictive, and will be regarded by our successors with the same horror with which we now look upon the hanging of little children for theft. Up to the early part of the nineteenth century, the death penalty could be, and was, inflicted for more than 200 different offences. Hanging is now recognised to be a revolting and cruel punishment. Its abolition was a major step towards our claim to be more civilised.

(2) Capital punishment is not an effective deterrent. In fact, the statistics of crime in all countries prove that violent punishment does not tend to bring about a decrease in violent crime. In spite of the death penalty, the average number of murders in Britain each year remained almost stationary for half a century – and the annual total (London had 204 murders in 1980 and 187 in 1985) has continued to be virtually static, as well, since capital punishment was abolished.

(3) Out of about thirty countries that have abolished the death penalty, not one has reported any increase in murders, and several have reported decreases. A penal code based on the idea of education and reformation of the offender is far more likely to reduce the amount of crime. In the USA, neither the recent few years without executions nor the resumed implementation of the death penalty in several states has had any appreciable effect, one way or the other, on

mistakes, only one wrongful conviction and execution (that of Timothy Evans) is known out of the many thousands of murder cases in Britain since the last world war.

(5) Discrimination between degrees of homicide, and the possibility of returning a verdict of manslaughter, gives juries plenty of opportunity for clemency. Insane murderers are never executed. It might be argued that the majority of murderers are insane – temporarily, anyway – and that there is a case for revising the present somewhat restricted legal definition of insanity. But the prospect of facing the supreme penalty, not just a long jail sentence, is the only way to deal with the clearly threatening rise in the proportion of hardened killers and those who murder in the course of other crimes. A life sentence is in some ways even more cruel than a death sentence, and there have been some convicted murderers who would actually have preferred the latter.

(6) That many people habitually signed petitions seeking clemency for convicted murderers was often merely the result of mass suggestion or hysteria – due, it may be, to newspaper 'hype'. It proved nothing.

(7) The State has a duty to its people to act harshly, if need be, to help preserve the good order of society.

the country's already horrific murder rate (New York alone had 1,392 murders in 1985). It is the tide of violent crimes that has continued to increase, not the number of murders, as such.

(4) The death sentence is irrevocable. A mistake once made cannot be put right. Even a single mistake, among no matter how many thousands of cases, is one too many for a civilised society to chance.

(5) Murderers did sometimes escape all legal punishment because the jury refused to convict, but this has become less likely now there is no death penalty. In many cases, death sentences were passed as an empty and cruel formality, when there was no intention of carrying them out. Very few of the murders committed really are premeditated. Up to 80 per cent are committed by people who are found to be insane – and no threatened penalty is likely to deter a lunatic – while in the great majority of those cases in which the murderer is held to be sane, the crime is committed under the temporary stress of violent passion or anger. That such people had to be condemned for premeditated murder, under the previous law, was a travesty of justice.

(6) That thousands were always eager to sign petitions for reprieve, even in cases where murder was definitely proved, shows how deep is the feeling that infliction of the death penalty is against the conscience of civilised man.

(7) Whether by the State or by an individual, the plain fact remains that the destruction of human life is a crime.

CENSORSHIP

Pro: (1) The purpose of enlightened censorship is to protect the public, and especially to prevent young people from being exposed to films, plays or books which centre on violence, pornography or other harmful aspects of life which they are not old enough to understand.

(2) The British Board of Film Classification (or Film Censors, as it was known previously) is quite inadequate. Although operating as an independent, self-supporting body, its income consists of fees from distributors when they submit a film for a rating – and it necessarily has one eye on the financial commitments of the film industry. Under the present system, too, its authority is lessened by the fact that its decisions can be overruled. Even when it bans films, local authorities have the power to license them for showing in their own areas. And vice versa. The classification of films is merely an invitation to young people to evade the regulations. This state of affairs is the more deplorable since the majority of cinemagoers today are young people.

(3) The cinema is still popular in places not yet reached by television and particularly in Asia and Africa. Already, untold harm has been done by the caricatures of European and American life shown in films which should have been censored at source.

(4) Television programmes should be more firmly controlled. Violence is depicted too often even in children's programmes – and to a yet greater extent in programmes screened at times when children are still likely to see them.

(5) The Lord Chamberlain's role as theatrical censor was ended in 1968.

Con: (1) It is for the parents and guardians of young people to protect them from damaging influences, or alternatively to influence and educate them so that the effect is minimised. A policy of censorship would deprive children of much in the works of Shakespeare, Chaucer and many other great writers.

(2) According to the type of audience for which they are considered suitable, films are now rated as U, PG, 15, 18 and R18 (meaning, respectively: suitable for all; parental guidance – some scenes may be unsuitable for young children; passed only for people aged 15 and over; passed only for people aged 18 and over; restricted distribution, through segregated premises – e.g. licensed sex cinemas – to which nobody under 18 is admitted.) Similar symbols are used for video material, plus Uc (particularly suitable for children). These classifications give adequate guidance and make any other form of supervision unnecessary.

(3) The peoples of Asia and Africa have had many opportunities to check the accuracy of their impressions of Europeans and Americans in recent years and are by no means so unsophisticated as in the early years of the cinema. Many of the film-shows exported are of a better type and often have to compete with home products nowadays.

(4) It is unrealistic to try to shield children from the facts of aggression and violence altogether. The moral outlook of most television programmes is healthy and, indeed, the main objection to many television programmes is rather that of triviality.

(5) The best managers, the best

But his office was manned by culti-vated and experienced people, and previously the best sort of manager had welcomed their censorship of stage productions as a protection. In latter years, this censorship was usually confined to occasional lines or situations, and no serious subject was denied a hearing altogether.

(6) There is a strong case for censorship of books and so-called 'comics' which appeal to the semi-literate. At present, anyone can air his sick fancies or unsavoury experiences in print and exercise a depraving influence while stopping short of actionable obscenity. In the absence of any guidance, it is left to booksellers, librarians and the police to proscribe works in the light of their own experi-ence and knowledge of literature. This is unfair both to them and to serious authors. Recent court cases have also shown serious confusion over the distinctions between what is obscene and what may be no more than offensive. With proper guidelines from censorship, these doubts would not arise.

playwrights and the best actors were against censorship and, up to 1968, were almost the only people still suffering from it. The Lord Chamber-lain's function of censorship began as a political one and remained excess-ively Establishment-minded (e.g. forbidding portrayals of living or recent royalty). His office banned Hochhuth's *The Soldiers*. It even ordered the deletion of a revue sketch about the sinking of the Royal Barge, despite the fact that no royalty was seen in person – and that the sketch had already been shown on television!

(6) Most of the 'comics' in question are American and can be controlled by import regulations, if necessary. It is quite wrong for librarians and others to exercise a private censorship. If a book is to be called in question, it is better that this should be done publicly in the courts, where balanced views on it can be aired and works of merit can receive fair criticism. Most evil influences are lessened by the fresh air of publicity. Few of our most respected classics would escape the censor, and any risk would be prefer-able to the stultification which results from censorship as applied in Eire or the Soviet Union.

(See also FREEDOM OF INFORMATION ACT)

CHANNEL TUNNEL:
Should the Project Be Scrapped?

Pro: (1) The agreement to go ahead with the Channel Tunnel project which President Mitterrand of France and the British Prime Minister, Mrs Margaret Thatcher, announced at Lille in January 1986 was ultimately inspired by blatant electioneering

Con: (1) The idea of a Channel Tunnel was first conceived by a little-known French mining engineer, Albert Mathieu, as far back as 1802. Napo-leon himself was an enthusiastic supporter. Ever since, the concept had been a source of both inspiration and

motives. Both leaders were desperately anxious to show voters that they were doing something impressive to create jobs — Mitterrand because the northern part of France most directly concerned was the region of the country hardest hit by economic recession, and because his Socialist Government seemed fated to lose the general election two months later . . . Mrs Thatcher because of Britain's horrific rate of unemployment, under her Government, with even the officially admitted total of jobless remaining well over three million (and the real total doubtless a good deal higher), which represented the main threat to her party once she, in turn, went to the polls. An earlier Tunnel agreement between the two countries was cancelled unilaterally by Britain in January 1975 on grounds of the project's soaring cost at a time of inflation and general economic crisis: from an estimate of £846 million two years previously, it was now calculated that the total cost would be £1,200 million (and some other estimates put it as high as £2,000 million). Under the present deal, the estimated cost is close on £5,000 million. Even if this staggering sum is not exceeded, which must be seriously questioned, how can it possibly be held that we can afford the project now, when we couldn't little more than a decade ago?

(2) Never can any big public scheme (let alone one of this magnitude) have been rushed through so hastily. To avoid the certainty of long delay, through the very large number of objectors, it was absolved from the customary planning inquiry. Nor was there the lengthy process of evaluation, between the different schemes on offer, which the Department of Transport would normally have

frustration. What defeated the two previous main attempts to start digging (in 1880 and 1974), still visible on both sides of the Channel, was not the lack of technical skilll but the lack of political will. Throughout the Victorian era until well past the Second World War, British political thinking and defence strategy were entirely dominated on the issue — albeit quite needlessly — by fears of invasion from the Continent, via a Tunnel. It was not until 1955 that Britain's Defence Ministry at last ruled out such fears. Perhaps the most poignant commentary on this is an observation made in 1919 by the great French military leader, Marshal Foch. He expressed the belief that, if a Channel Tunnel had existed before 1914, there would probably not have been a First World War — but that, even if the war had broken out, the Tunnel would have shortened it by two years, thus saving the lives of millions of soldiers. Now that the political will on both sides of the Channel has at last set the project undoubtedly in motion, its potential benefits are already abundantly evident. Between now and 1993, when the Tunnel is expected to open, the construction alone will generate £700 million of work for industry and more than 30,000 jobs — in *each* country. As for financing the project, both governments have insisted that the money must come solely from private investors. This has been the British attitude ever since the previous scheme was cancelled in 1975, and the French conversion to that view was an important factor behind the new agreement. Although the Anglo-French consortium had some difficulty in raising the first tranche of £206 million from the City of London in 1986 (at least, until the Bank of

conducted. The whole operation which led to the final choice, the Eurotunnel and its rail link, was completed in only 35 working days.

(3) Although it barred an inquiry, the British Government promised that it would allow plenty of time for petitions objecting to the project. When it came to the point, though, the matter was handled with what was tantamount to dishonesty. The Department of Transport placed advertisements in five national newspapers, as a reminder to would-be petitioners, only five days before the closing date for receipt of their objections. And even this limited action was taken only because of intervention by the chairman of the House of Lords select committee on the Channel Tunnel, who accused the Government of reneging on its promise.

(4) Because of the late and inadequate notice given, some groups or individuals who had wanted to present petitions were unable to complete them before the deadline. The strength of opposition to the project is indicated by the fact that, even so, no fewer than 1,459 petitions were received in time for hearing by the Lords select committee. When the committee began its sittings early in March 1987, the legal counsel representing the Transport Department still tried to bar a large number of specific objections. Issues which he would object to petitioners raising, he said, included: whether there should be a public inquiry; the effect of the Tunnel on British industry, employment and regional policy; the threat of rabies reaching Britain from the Continent via the Tunnel or of it being used to smuggle drugs; the danger of terrorism or sabotage; the carriage of nuclear waste; the consequent 'fundamental' change to Britain's island

England exerted pressure), earlier fears about raising £750 million more equity by July 1987 were thought likely to be disproved, to judge by investors' growing confidence in the scheme, with reports of strong share-buying interest from places as far distant as Japan. To the financial institutions, it doesn't matter that no public money is going into the scheme (apart from an extra subvention to British Rail); what counts is the two governments' guaranteed political commitment to the Tunnel, and this has been fully borne out.

(2) As so often, the apparent period for the selection process was only the 'tip of the iceberg'. Quite apart from the years of study which some of the contenders had put into the different plans submitted, a group of British and French banks reported some 18 months earlier on appraisals they had made – a report issued in May 1984.

(3) Protests over the apparent 'lack of time' typify the distorted, emotional views of some opponents of the scheme. As would have been customary practice with most public inquiries, everyone affected by the project would have been following the Bill's progress through Parliament and, therefore, the normal expectation is that they should *know* the deadline.

(4) Is it not a telling point that, although the Government hoped the Bill would receive the Royal Assent (i.e. become law) by the 1987 summer recess, the Lords committee still arranged to hear objections from nearly 1,500 different petitioners? Does that sound like an attempt to muzzle the scheme's opponents? In listing the issues which the Government would challenge as not being relevant to the committee hearings, the legal counsel stressed that it was not trying to pre-empt argument

status; the threat of invasion; the impact on public expenditure; and the powers of the French police in the UK. With such a list, might one not have grounds for suspecting the Government of trying to muzzle the opposition – and good reason to wonder why?

(5) Leaving aside the political aspects, there were still an extra-ordinarily high number of purely practical questions which had not been settled when the Lords select committee started its hearings. For example, the Council for the Protection of Rural England pointed out that, up to then, nobody had yet seen any complete design for the enormous, 350-acre terminal serving the tunnel entrance at Cheriton, near Folkestone. Nor, up to that time, had anyone decided the destiny of the four million cubic metres of spoil which would be coming out of the tunnel – although, on the first day of the committee's sessions, the Government did at last publish a statement concluding that disposal of the spoil at the foot of Shakespeare Cliff was 'the most acceptable solution'. They're to be the Brown Cliffs of Dover from now on, presumably?

(6) According to evidence given to Parliament by the British Ports Association (representing most of the country's 160 ports), the Channel Tunnel would destroy as many as 100,000 jobs.

(7) Even if one ignores all the foregoing objections, or the ghastly environmental havoc which the tunnel scheme would wreak, there's still one ultimate flaw in the whole project: neither materially nor economically is there any actual need for it. One cardinal argument advanced by pro-Tunnel people is that conventional ferries would be unable to cope with

about the Tunnel. But, he said, the list covered topics which were not appropriate for private petitioners to raise: they were issues of public interest which it was proper for Parliament itself to discuss. (It should also be noted that, in any case, the select committee indicated that it would not necessarily accept all the restrictions the Government's counsel had called for . . .)

(5) If 'purely practical' matters are being raised, there are a number which Tunnel opponents habitually fail to mention. To cite just a couple, from a parliamentary answer given by the Transport Secretary in February 1987: orders worth £6.4 million for the first two tunnel-boring machines had already been placed with a Glasgow engineering company and £1.2 million for locomotives with another in Yorkshire; and letters of intent placed with the same two firms totalled a further £8.5 million. And that's without mentioning more than £680 million in other contracts, likewise often aiding the northern regions, to be placed for such items as reinforcing steel, tunnel lining, cement, etc. Bear in mind, too, that the Channel Tunnel group's French partner was likely to be placing around the same scale of orders in France.

(6) Apart from the actual construction, the project will create up to 60,000 jobs. This is the figure given by a French film about it, which compared the feat of building the Tunnel with putting the first astronauts on the Moon and described it as the most important project of its kind in the past century or so, after the Suez and Panama canals.

(7) Anyone who has travelled on a Channel ferry in recent years, particularly during the summer season, will know how hideously crowded they

the huge increase in cross-Channel traffic that has been predicted. Back in January 1986, however, ferry operators said they foresaw a need to cope with a 70 per cent rise in traffic over the next ten years – and gave assurances that they would easily be able to do so. With their existing fleets and the larger vessels already on order, they would need only half the number of ships which the Tunnel planners had claimed would be required to handle the traffic. As for the Zeebrugge ferry tragedy in March 1987, all the evidence indicates that it was an isolated accident, in circumstances unlikely ever to be repeated, and that modern roll on-roll off vessels remain safer than a Channel Tunnel could ever be.

can seem – and also, often, how long are the queues of goods trucks waiting to cross. French directors of the consortium have said that there will be up to 20 Tunnel trains every hour, carrying some 7,000 passengers and their cars. A British exhibition has said that, at peak times, the shuttles will leave every 15 minutes and no booking will be necessary. The trains will make the journey in only 35 minutes, reducing the time from London to Paris to only 3½ hours. Even from cities as far north as Edinburgh and Newcastle, through trains will do the trip to the French capital in no more than 8½ and 7 hours, respectively. As for safety, the Zeebrugge disaster has – sadly – served to remind doubters that the Tunnel does have clear advantages. Among them: it isn't affected by fog or gales.

CHRISTENDOM, REUNION OF

Pro: (1) The ideal of Christian reunion is both desirable and necessary if the churches are to stem the present-day flood of scepticism and indifference, or to deal properly with contemporary social problems. It will also be the only solution, in the long term, if the Church is to make any real impression on the non-Christian world.

(2) Minor differences should be sunk or natural allowances made. The Anglican and Methodist Churches have already come within sight of agreement along the road to integration, with churches planned for both forms of worship. Although the proposals have been rejected at the moment, there are many people on each side who are still working for

Con: (1) However desirable, the ideal cannot be realised. Any proposals put forward or supported by the Church of Rome would mean simply the absorption of other churches. There are at present such strong antagonisms between the various sects that we can only wait and try to heal the internal dissensions existing in each body.

(2) The failure to secure ratification of the Anglican-Methodist proposals, even though the gap between these churches is among the narrowest of all, shows how deep-seated are the fundamental objections. Undenominational Christianity would inevitably be colourless and therefore of less value. Few would accept it, least of all the Roman Catholic Church.

them to be accepted and are hopeful that they will be in the foreseeable future.

(3) Modern thought is less interested in theological problems than in the ethical side of religion. Many non-believers could be attracted to the churches if they were to produce a united programme of social reform, based on such views as could be agreed between all sects – and there have been notable advances recently in this direction.

(3) Good works are not the whole of Christianity. Sceptics would still prefer to dispense with the theological doctrines, and people of religions other than Christianity are not impressed by them. But Christianity is concerned with the world after death as much as with this one, and few sects would be prepared to risk eternal error by sacrificing what they believe to be the truth in the interests of temporary earthly advantage.

(See also the next article)

CHURCHES:
Should They Take Part in Politics?

Pro: (1) The churches, as representing the idealist element in the community, are bound to share in its most vital activities, which necessarily involve political questions. When they become directly involved in politics – as, for instance, in Latin America, where many ordinary priests have sided with the workers in protests against oppressive regimes (often in defiance of their own bishops) – it has usually resulted in their moral authority being enhanced, not lessened.

(2) The Christian churches have in the past played great roles in times of crisis. They have a body of ethics and traditions which binds them morally to follow precept with practice and to oppose actively the abuses of the times.

(3) Although church-people may very well differ in their views, it is possible for them to present common policies in accordance with Christian teaching and to exert influence, on this basis, for the problems of the day to

Con: (1) The churches are concerned with religion and private morals. They should remain outside the arena of political controversy and limit themselves to presenting ideals on which all people of good will may draw for inspiration and guidance. They have no business to lay down rulings in political matters which necessarily admit different points of view. The Vatican has warned several times against the growing attachment among some clergy in Latin America and other Third World areas to so-called 'Liberation Theology', whereby local priests either add a strong dash of Marxism to Christian theology or try to synthesise the two in their approach to pastoral work among the poor. Another salient reminder from Rome was that liberation movements can all too easily lead to the replacement of one tyranny by another.

(2) The churches in the past have nearly always been equated with reaction. Despite the increased number of

45

be handled in a humane and Christian way.

(4) Because of their independence of political parties, churchmen of all denominations have been able to take a courageous stand on such questions as nuclear warfare and on racial and other issues involving human rights.

(5) In recent years, the Church of England has published a highly important report, recommending measures to ease the problems of Britain's decaying inner cities, while bishops in the House of Lords have spoken out on issues as varied as the health services and the Strategic Defence Initiative ('star wars'), with individual bishops opposing the abolition of the Greater London Council and speaking in favour of economic sanctions against South Africa. Despite politicians' fierce attacks on the clergy's 'interference', the Archbishop of Canterbury declared in 1984 that the Church had 'an absolute duty to seek out and comment on the spiritual and moral dimension of political issues, to encourage, question and stimulate thought'.

bishops holding liberal or 'progressive' views, in recent years, large numbers of church-people and of those in church government remain highly conservative, and there is no reason to suppose they will be any different in the future.

(3) Members of different churches hold conflicting but equally sincere conceptions of the proper principles of the community's actions and organisation; active intervention in politics by the churches would therefore bring about disastrous quarrels, with serious damage to the cause of religion.

(4) No Government could take the pronouncements of church dignitaries as really representing the feelings of their religious followers on non-religious matters. People who clamour for the churches to enter politics are almost always those who expect it to favour Socialist tendencies. Many of the clergy's pronouncements on such matters are either naive, economically unrealistic, or stem from people with an overtly political rather than religious axe to grind. Perhaps all that needs to be added is that membership of Christian churches in Britain is slumping by 100,000 a year: between 1970 and 1985, it was down by 1.5 million.

(See also the preceding article; BISHOPS: SHOULD THEY BE EXCLUDED FROM THE HOUSE OF LORDS?)

CIVIL DISOBEDIENCE

Pro: (1) In view of the increasingly undemocratic nature of representative government, and in the absence of any really effective provision for the ordinary public to express dissatisfaction

Con: (1) Dissatisfaction with a government can be expressed through voting against its candidates in by-elections, through the organs of popular opinion, and through the

with its conduct of major issues during a government's term of office, civil disobedience is justified as a measure of protest.

(2) Not everybody is willing or able to take the risks involved, but those who do are representing many more of their fellow-sufferers. Civil disobedience has the element of self-sacrifice which is absent from normal forms of protest, and thus adds cogency to a protest.

(3) In India, it did a great deal by proving the devotion and determination of the people to secure independence. Anywhere that the people are suffering under unjust laws, it is justified. We approved not only of civil disobedience but even of terrorism by people resisting oppression in occupied Europe during the last world war. In Northern Ireland in 1974, the form of civil disobedience represented by the so-called 'workers' strike', which brought an end to the power-sharing Assembly, showed how strongly it can work; whatever one's views about the merits of the issue, the fact remains that the protest succeeded because a sizeable part of the population supported it.

(4) The police in Britain are generally tolerant, especially where, as in the case of nuclear disarmament, there is no great argument on the fundamental issue, in the long term. Civil disobedience is generally resorted to by people who are pacific by nature and in intention. Peaceful protest involving deliberate confrontation with authority is often the only way that a cause becomes familiar to a wider public, previously unaware of it.

(5) Refusal to pay taxes for the pursuing of policies of which one disapproves involves no violence or action of Members of Parliament (who can be spurred on by opinion in their constituencies), without disrupting the administration of government.

(2) It is a form of coercion by a minority and is therefore undemocratic. It is displeasing to most people, who object to the disruption of law and order whatever their views on the question at issue. The effects are quickly forgotten, and it is useless as a protest unless it is practised continually and by a majority of the population.

(3) Indian independence was finally secured by her contribution to the war effort in 1939–45, by her strong financial position in relation to Britain and, above all, by the inevitable course of history generally. Other new nations have gained independence without it. War conditions are a special case. So are those in Northern Ireland, where, for anyone not inflamed by sectarian passions, the outcome of the 'workers' strike' can only be regarded as a highly regrettable and retrograde step.

(4) It has a brutalising effect on the police through its provocative nature, and itself easily passes into violence. The Doukhobors in Canada and the British suffragettes resorted at once to arson and destruction generally when they perceived the ineffectiveness of civil disobedience. Prolonged clashes with the police often tend to be counter-productive for a cause – losing it at least some (even much) of the public sympathy it would otherwise have merited. In Britain, the miners' strike of 1984–85, the protests outside Rupert Murdoch's newspaper plant in Wapping, and the drop in support for the women of Greenham Common, are cases in point.

(5) It is impracticable to try to

provocation and is a completely altruistic method of protest.

separate taxes into their components and achieves nothing but the satisfaction of an individual conscience.

(See also DIRECT ACTION)

CLASSICS (LATIN AND GREEK) IN EDUCATION

Pro: (1) The Latin and Greek Classics represent the most important and vital part of our inheritance from the past, both in literature and in social institutions. They have been a great, sometimes the sole, source of inspiration to most of our leaders and teachers of eminence, past and present. Their study need not preclude the proper study of other subjects.

(2) Their literatures have a more permanent value than the generally ephemeral products of contemporary nations, which constitute the staple reading of nearly all students of modern languages except specialists.

(3) The study of the Classics has great disciplinary value, and the prolonged period through which they have been studied and taught has brought the teaching of them to a high level.

(4) Latin and Greek are fine instruments for the expression of human thought. They enshrine the works of the picked intelligences of two great peoples, from whom we still have much to learn. A great deal of their value is lost if they are read only in translations.

(5) Most of the masters of English style have had the Classics as the foundation of their education.

(6) The Classics are a reminder of other values and other achievements, and so prevent mankind from undue

Con: (1) They represent only part of our cultural inheritance. Ancient Egypt, the Middle Ages, and more recent times are quite as important, and are more interesting because less hackneyed. The study of prehistoric and primitive man is of more moment than that of Greece and Rome, which were half-barbarous, half-civilised. Statesmen reared on the Classics have often been ignorant, unprincipled and stupid.

(2) Proper education in other subjects is neglected through lack of time, e.g., modern foreign languages, in which the Englishman is usually woefully deficient.

(3) The disciplinary value of German or Russian syntax is equally great and the practical value incomparably greater. The study of mathematics and science instils habits of logical thought, mental accuracy and regard for truth much more effectively.

(4) 'Classics in Education' usually means Latin crammed for a few years, dropped and forgotten. Greek, much the better language and literature, is less frequently studied. Both are clumsy and undeveloped languages, far inferior in grammar, syntax and vocabulary to English. Only about ten Latin authors from Roman times are worth reading, and no more than a dozen Greeks. Their chief merits are

pride in modern scientific and industrial triumphs. These latter are not of much cultural value. Modern life, scientific, industrial and mechanical, is not satisfying to the artistic aspirations of man, who has had a vastly different environment through almost all his existence; nor are man's recent triumphs over matter likely to create moral and aesthetic values suited to his essential needs and nature. Greece and Rome represent the more permanent values in life. That the teaching of Latin and Greek is increasingly rare in maintained schools and under serious pressure in the independent sector (a 1984 survey showed only one school in 39 still making Latin compulsory at the age of 15), is yet another sign of the deplorable way the curriculum is being levelled down.

visible in translation, and the time saved could be spent on the rich literatures of Europe.

(5) Many masters of English prose have had no such education, and the multitude of bad writers who have studied the Classics for years shows that the benefits are most uncertain.

(6) Modern life is founded on science and technology. Only by concentrating on these, and by treating all problems in the light of current needs and organised knowledge, can we expect to maintain or reach a satisfactory condition. The value of history in relation to current problems diminishes in proportion to its remoteness. Greek and Roman civilisation rested on slavery; ours rests on science. The ending of compulsory Classics teaching is an inevitable side-effect of today's more vocational education (e.g. the pressure on the timetable from such subjects as computers), and the universities were the first to recognise reality when they stopped asking applicants to qualify in Latin.

CLOSED SHOP:
Should It Be Banned?

Pro: (1) While the right of workers to organise for collective bargaining is accepted, in their capacity as producers they are only one section of the community and should not have the right to impose their will on the others. Freedom of conscience is a fundamental right which is being attacked every day in modern society. No man should be deprived of employment because he is unwilling to

Con: (1) The working classes have had to struggle continuously to gain improvements in their wages and working conditions and a reasonable standard of living. Their weapon has been collective bargaining and the unity of their organisations, the trade unions. The closed shop, where only members of specified unions are admitted to employment, is the logical next step in the consolidation and

pledge himself to action which might cause suffering to the community as a whole.

(2) The requirement that only members of an approved trade union should be employed in any industry unduly restricts the freedom of workers to change their occupations and stifles initiative in industry. Such restrictions are unfair to the community and hamper its progress, especially today when new processes and machines have often replaced the craftsmanship required in the old days. In any case, where conditions or new job opportunities offer sufficiently attractive inducement, many trade unionists soon drop traditional restrictions and inter-union rivalries in favour of common-sense advantage (e.g. at the new Japanese-owned factories in South Wales and N.E. England).

(Some) The 100 per cent shop, where new entrants to an industry are required to belong to a trade union during their employment only, would meet the requirements of unity in action without destroying flexibility in industry.

(3) The closed shop system is unworkable where large numbers of new workers are suddenly required, as in the engineering industry in wartime. It then comes into direct conflict with crucial national interests.

(4) Several types of professional work are not amenable to trade union organisation, such as that of welfare and medical workers or people responsible for safety precautions. Even those that have been 'organised' are divided among a number of unions, without much cohesion of aims, and would not accept closed shop conditions.

(5) Workers in closed shops have been able to gain huge concessions, safeguarding of what they have so far achieved.

(2) The principle of the open shop enables unscrupulous employers to introduce new, untrained or semi-trained personnel into industry. This is unfair to those who have had to pass through the stage of apprenticeship and burdens an industry with people who know nothing of its traditions and customs – people, moreover, who may well be prepared to accept lower rates of pay, if the employers can get away with it.

(3) Temporary relaxations could always be permitted to cope with special circumstances, such as war and other emergencies, provided that the general principle is preserved and the unions are consulted.

(4) If all the workers in an industry, including clerical, administrative and professional workers, are not organised in trade unions, strike-breaking becomes easy and union organisation as a weapon for bargaining is rendered useless. In recent years, 'industrial action' by teachers, by social workers, and by doctors and nurses, in withdrawing their labour as a protest, are among several examples proving that professional work is not incompatible with the use of the strike weapon.

(5) Employers have done their best, within the legal limits now allowed them, to combine and exclude competitors from their operations. Employees have no less right to act in this way. Those workers in industries which have already achieved the closed shop are only doing what other sections of workers would do if they had sufficient organised strength.

out of all proportion to those of their fellow workers and at the expense of the community as a whole.

(See also TRADE UNIONS: DO THEIR POWERS NEED FURTHER RESTRICTION?)

COALITION GOVERNMENT

Pro: (1) In time of war, Britain accepts readily enough that a coalition government is the best, perhaps the only way to get full national support for whatever measures may be necessary and to ensure that the widest range of talent is available.

(2) The Alliance, formed by the Liberal and Social Democratic Parties in 1981, established a genuine new third force in British politics. Despite efforts by the two main parties to deny or denigrate the fact, Alliance successes in local government polls and by-elections confirm that it is unquestionably here to stay – and only a matter of time before the Alliance emerges from a general election holding the balance of power or even, eventually, as the largest single grouping.

(Some) In the 1983 general election, the Alliance's share of the poll was only 2.2 per cent behind Labour's.

(3) The Liberal Party had for many years tended to be a powerhouse of ideas and many of its proposals had been adopted as their own by one or other of the two bigger parties. Now, in association with the SDP and *its* many fresh ideas, the Alliance has made this characteristic more evident than ever.

(4) Coalitions have worked successfully in Belgium, the Netherlands and several other European countries, for many years. Nobody

Con: (1) It is relatively easy to sink party differences in wartime, when winning the war is all that matters and every other political issue is subordinated to that one vital objective. But no British coalition has ever been a real success in peacetime – as witness the poor record of the National Governments of the 1930s.

(2) Historically (if not under the Conservative regime initiated in 1979), the two main parties have often, in the past, been in broad agreement over several of the most important policies – notably, for instance, in the field of foreign affairs. Despite a show of differences over detail, therefore, the basic policies on these key issues were effectively bilateral, anyway – thus avoiding any need for a coalition, with all its unwanted compromises. The Alliance's main successes have virtually all been in subsidiary or mid-term elections, where some degree of protest vote against the party in power is always to be expected. It's a very different matter for the Alliance in general elections, when voters decide who is actually to rule the country for the next 4–5 years.

(3) Since the Liberals themselves are so often split, both internally and with their ostensible SDP allies (e.g. over policy on Britain's future defence), this supposed power-house would appear to be founded on

could claim that the first two, in particular, have lacked necessary reforms or otherwise suffered; they are among the most prosperous nations in Europe.

(5) In countries which have quite a number of political parties represented in Parliament, but with the main party groupings fairly evenly balanced, it sometimes takes several weeks or more to agree on a new coalition. Yet this can have its advantages. For, in the process of forming a coalition government which will have majority support, the issues which matter most to a country are thrown up more clearly and subsequently receive more priority than they might otherwise have done.

(6) By their nature, coalition governments usually last only a few years, at the most, before a reshuffle is necessary. But this need not matter greatly, provided there is continuity of administration – as shown by France under the 4th Republic. At that time, coalition governments were considered the only way to prevent the Communists from coming to power. Despite all the political confusion caused by the rapid succession of these coalitions, the broad lines of government did not change much.

(7) When different parties accept membership in a coalition government, they *ipso facto* accept the need to refrain for the time being from demands which their partners regard as too controversial. Equally, though, they will not join a coalition unless demands they consider to be irreducible are included in the programme which all the partners agree as their common platform. A coalition government's initial policies, therefore, reflect each of its member-party's views – and each has equal responsibility for them.

shifting sands.

(4) On the contrary, some European countries have suffered a good deal from the inability of any one of their political parties to win an overall majority. A prime example is Italy, which, for this reason, has had nothing but coalition governments since the last world war – with the result that each in turn, through fear of the political consequences or inability to achieve agreement among the coalition partners, failed to carry out reforms that were overdue years ago.

(5) Can it seriously be suggested that delays of this nature are not harmful? As for throwing up the key issues, no single party forming a government would have won its overall majority unless the biggest proportion of the electorate felt that it had got its priorities right.

(6) The French 4th Republic became notorious for its ever-changing governments because of the chief drawback to all coalition systems: the fact that parties shirk from their responsibility to carry out unpopular measures – if need be, engineering the overthrow of the government and the emergence of a reshuffled coalition in which they still participate but another party has to take the main responsibility for the unpopular measures concerned. It lessens the confidence and trust of other countries when a nation is subject to such continual government changes.

(7) If a majority party is in power and its government makes a mistake, that party has to take the blame. In coalition governments, one party has the opportunity to blame another more easily – and will almost always do so.

(8) That most big parties are them-

(8) Each major political party is itself a coalition. The British Conservative and Labour parties, the American Republicans and Democrats – all have their own left-wing, centre and right-wing strands of opinion, under the broad party umbrella. But, whatever their internal disagreements, that does not prevent them from reaching a consensus on the policies which their party should put to the voters at election times and which duly reflect that party's fundamental attitudes. By the same token, coalition governments formed by a number of parties can be just as effective politically.

selves coalitions is true enough – but irrelevant. It has no bearing on the efficacy or otherwise of coalition governments, as such. The essential difference is that a party, after thrashing out its internal arguments, does not merely hope that members of varying views will accept the ensuing proposals for a limited period, anyway; once it has published its election manifesto, detailing the measures and reforms it plans to carry out, those proposals are advocated by all its candidates during the electoral campaign – and, if the party wins power on the strength of its manifesto, its MPs accept that that is the programme the whole party has undertaken to put into effect. Coalition governments inevitably lack this unity in the long term. Worse still, coalitions are usually formed as a result of post-electoral deadlock – which means that they are set up without consulting or involving the voters and, likewise, that the compromise programme agreed by the coalition parties will not have been submitted to the electorate.

(See also PARTY GOVERNMENT)

CO-EDUCATION

Pro: (1) The mixing of the sexes in education is natural, practical and economical. It was formerly prevalent in Scotland, is in vogue in the United States of America, and has been adopted in an increasing number of private and most State-aided schools in this country.

(2) The feminine mind gains from association with boys and men, and the masculine from association with girls and women. The character

Con: (1) In the early formative years, there is nothing 'natural' about co-education; children between the ages of seven and fifteen nearly always prefer the company of their own sex. Educationally, a number of subjects are necessary for one sex which are not suitable for the other. Some subjects cannot be taught in the presence of both sexes without embarrassment on the part of teacher and class. Co-education tends to diminish the

develops more rapidly and shyness diminishes. Competition is greater between the sexes than between rivals of the same sex, so that higher standards of achievement are reached.

(3) False masculinity was a temporary phenomenon which arose during the struggle of women for emancipation. It now tends to be found only in girls educated in girls' schools. In co-educational schools, it is completely absent; the relation between the sexes falls into a more natural pattern, and the only loss is, perhaps, the ultra-sentimental chivalry which is in any case a survival from the days of women's subjection.

(4) The presence of both sexes together is a wholesome factor in institutions. In all communities where one sex is segregated, e.g., schools, colleges, monasteries, convents, etc., it is more likely that various evils will flourish; women tend to become hysterical, men to acquire unnatural vices, and the whole atmosphere is unwholesome. In colleges and universities, the presence of women raises the general tone both ethically and academically. It says much that more than two-thirds of Britain's public schools now have girls and that, following the success of their first large-scale admission at the sixth-form level in the 1970s, there is now an increasing trend towards admitting them at lower age levels.

(5) Marriages made after co-educational experience are best. If the man and woman have known each other as fellow-students, a surer basis is given for married life than that gained from purely social acquaintance. If they have moved among others of the opposite sex on equal terms, each will have a better appreciation of the qualities and make a fairer

chivalry that is largely the product of early separate education. Co-educational schools in England in the past produced a sizeable proportion of cranks.

(2) The feminine mind assumes masculine characters which are only a hindrance in later life and which actually repel men, while some boys become effeminate and so are disliked by both their own and the other sex. Competition in any form between the sexes should be discouraged. Shyness is a natural stage in the development of youth, which wears off in the course of family life and ordinary social communication.

(3) It has been found that, far from raising the status of women, co-education tends to result in their being relegated to second place and pushed into the careers which have always been considered as belonging to women. The best academic records among women have been achieved by those educated in single-sex schools. Although co-education may be of benefit to the mediocre, it does not favour those of outstanding ability.

(4) Conditions in many co-educational institutions are conducive to undisciplined attitudes. Enforced associations of the sexes at adolescence are likely, in some cases, to make permanent the aversion to the other sex that sometimes exists at that period; in many other cases, it brings about the premature 'growing up' which is so lamentable a feature of Western life today. Public schools admitting girls have done so for reasons of finance and social pressure rather than out of conviction; in practice, except in the classroom, the sexes remain as segregated as ever.

(5) The history of marriage in the USA does not encourage expectations of much advantage from co-

judgment of the short-comings of the other.

(6) Co-education is general in primary schools, and in small schools in rural areas has been so for many years.

(7) In nearly all branches of life, women are becoming more and more the colleagues of men or their rivals on equal terms. They are equally competent as teachers, members of committees, administrators, doctors and research workers. In mixed schools, a greater proportion of headships should be thrown open to them; at present, the most that all but a very few of them have achieved is a kind of assistantship. If it is absurd to think of a woman as head in a school containing boys, it is absurd for a man to be head in one containing girls. Men and women should be placed on the same professional level of conditions and pay.

(8) Co-education enables investigation to be made into the different characters of boys and girls, the different environment and subjects they may need. It offers a field for wide varieties of research that may provide solutions for many of the problems now vexing both education and society.

(9) Most schools are inadequately staffed; many have insufficient material and equipment. The necessary improvements would cost less if provided for co-educational schools than if they still had to be duplicated for separate schools for boys and girls.

education. Nor has the growth of co-education in this country caused any increase in the number of successful marriages. Genuine love (as opposed to temporary infatuation) still needs an element of romance, which is destroyed by too much familiarity between the sexes.

(6) Quite young children may well be educated together; but after they are 9 or 10 years old, boys should be taught by men and girls by women. They need separate training to suit the different rates of physical, intellectual and emotional growth. The two sexes can thereafter mix quite enough in family and social life.

(7) Though men and women may co-operate successfully in their work, children above primary school age usually have a tendency to shy away from the other sex, for some years. One sex gains its experience in a different way and interprets it differently from the other. It can be guided through this stage of life only by someone who has traversed the same path. In single-sex schools, women are more likely to attain the leading positions and responsibilities they desire, as headmistresses and principals.

(8) Such investigations can be pursued with each sex separately. Co-education might perhaps follow – but it should certainly not precede – the conclusions reached by this kind of research.

(9) Mixed schools are more expensive to run than those for one sex only.

(See also PUBLIC SCHOOLS; WOMEN'S RIGHTS)

COMMERCIAL RADIO:
Should It Be Abolished?

Pro: (1) Commercial radio was established at the behest, mainly, of advertising interests who saw it as yet another means of making money. Its inception was legalised by a former Conservative Government in what seemed more than anything a re-affirmation of the party's traditional belief in free enterprise rather than on the merits of the case. Tory MPs themselves had been subjected to prolonged lobbying by protagonists of commercial radio. In the event, the innovation has added nothing to the cultural life of the nation, has made no innovations of note (except, perhaps, for the almost non-stop playing of pop records), and has been an unnecessary and unjustifiable expense in the present adverse economic period – and probably in any other period, for that matter.

(2) Many of the commercial radios have failed to attract the volume of advertising which they need if they are to be financially viable. What advertising they do receive has simply reduced the level of advertisements in such outlets as newspapers, thus compounding the problems of other media. It is highly debatable, in any case, whether any kind of radio 'commercials' should ever have been allowed in the first place. What with commercial TV and the rest, we are submerged in such a flood of advertising that the preservation of one form of communication from its influence would surely have been a blessing. No wonder so many people stick to BBC radio!

(3) The same flaws which marked the first generation of independent

Con: (1) Although commercial radio in Britain has yet to become universally profitable – some of the original franchise-holders have, admittedly, gone to the wall – the claim that there was a demand for it has been abundantly proved. One reason for the objections by its Establishment-minded antagonists is that it has won an increasingly large audience away from the BBC's local radios, which are usually less enterprising in their programmes. In short, commercial radio has justified itself by demonstrating that it fulfils a need. The unique character of the London Broadcasting Company, one of London's two commercial radio services, which puts its emphasis entirely on news coverage, has been a highly successful experiment of which any country in the world would be proud.

(2) There are some kinds of advertisement for which sound is a particularly good medium. That commercial radios provide an inexpensive outlet for local businessmen in their own areas, particularly those for whom national advertising would be unnecessary or too costly, is obvious. In addition, they offer a day-to-day immediacy which can rarely be matched by the local weekly newspapers which serve many provincial areas. The viability of commercial radio is shown by the fact that approval for the launching of new stations, in areas of the country not covered before, continues to be granted to this day.

(3) Commercial radio in Britain is free of undesirable influences because

television have been clearly evident in commercial radio as well. To win more advertisers, it is necessary to show them large audience figures; and this results in lower standards, with the programme organisers pandering to what they suppose to be 'mass' tastes – cheap music, interminable 'phone-ins', cretinous competitions, and the like. All right, it's not always as bad as that; wallpaper music has its place, and local traffic reports are useful. But it was sheer capitalist self-indulgence to set up commercial radio for the purpose. The BBC's network of local radio stations – which would have been even more comprehensive if the Government had got its priorities right and allowed the BBC more money to carry out the original plans – would have been perfectly adequate to meet all genuine needs of the communities it serves. Given the proper backing, it could still do so; and, what's more, without commercialism and without basing its programmes on the lowest common denominator.

it echoes the pattern of our commercial TV programmes, whereby advertisers are not allowed to have any influence on or control of the programme content. Advertising is restricted to certain specified periods and we do not suffer the experience of American listeners, with a 'commercial' breaking into the middle of a piece of music or, excruciatingly, a split-second before an important climax in the plot of a play. Nor do we suffer the results of the US system of sponsorship, under which the nature of programmes is dictated by the advertisers paying for them. Anyone who has had to listen to an average day's American commercial radio will know how fortunate we are! One consequence of the British system is that the intellectual and cultural standards of many of our programmes are a good deal higher than opponents of commercial radio give them credit for. The Peacock committee's proposal that BBC Radios 1 and 2 should be hived off to the private sector was, of itself, a recognition of the merits of the commercial radio system in this country.

(See also BROADCASTING, PUBLIC CONTROL OF)

COMMON CURRENCY

Pro: (1) A common currency, freely usable in every country (or at least, initially, in a number of countries agreeing to it), would facilitate international trade, travel, and many other aspects of relationships between nations. Countries would still be able to use their own currencies as well, internally, and most would doubtless wish to do so – though it's probable that, over the years, the common

Con: (1) It is a Utopian ideal, quite unworkable in present monetary conditions (or any in the foreseeable future). An immediately insuperable stumbling-block is that, as many of the national currencies are 'floating' and their exchange rates thus vary from day to day, it would be impossible to fix a standard value between the common currency and all the others.

57

currency would gradually supersede them. Adoption of the European Monetary System, the so-called 'snake', by most of the leading West European countries, shows that it is quite feasible to keep exchange rate variation within controllable bounds. The participating currencies are defined in notional European Currency Units, or ECUs, currently worth about £1 2/3 – which offer a readymade basis for a future common currency.

(2) The world nowadays is moving more and more towards thinking in international rather than national terms. A common currency, the regulation of which would necessitate close international co-operation, would greatly encourage this trend and eventually be an essential ingredient of it.

(3) Such bodies as the International Monetary Fund already make use of units of account which, although not 'real' money in a tangible sense, have much the same effect as a common currency among the participants. Similarly, under the Common Market's agricultural policy, there are make-believe units – e.g. the so-called 'green pound' – for fixing the level of payments, etc. If artificial currencies like these are used successfully for book-keeping purposes – as already suggested with ECUs, above – it would surely not be all that difficult to transform them into the real thing.

(4) The introduction of a common currency among members of the EEC is one of the key steps foreshadowed under the Treaty of Rome.

(2) A common currency would only be possible, if at all, in conditions of complete economic and financial stability between the participating countries. Otherwise, its valuation would have to be variable, from one country to the next. Instead of contributing to stability, therefore, it would merely aggravate all the present complications. There is already very close co-operation between financial experts of many countries (e.g. the International Monetary Fund); none has ever championed the advisability of a common currency.

(3) Devices which are feasible on paper, to simplify accounting procedures, would not be acceptable in practice for everyday purposes. The units of account used by some international bodies are subject to most of the same disabilities suffered by real currencies (as witness previous devaluations of the 'green pound', made necessary by the effects of inflation). But the chief objection to the idea of a common currency, perhaps, is that it ignores the extremely strong attachment which each country feels towards its own currency, as part of its national heritage and identity. As an example, General de Gaulle's introduction of the 'new' franc, whereby 1,000 became 10 (but without radically changing the appearance of the money), proved to be one of the most important symbols of the re-establishment of French prosperity.

(4) It is one of the Common Market provisions which, because of the practical difficulties, the member-nations recognise as unachievable for years yet.

(See also INTERNATIONALISM; UNITED STATES OF EUROPE)

COMPREHENSIVE SCHOOLS

Pro: (1) At the time of the crucial 1944 Education Act, too much faith was placed in crude intelligence testing (hence the notorious '11-plus'). It has since been discovered that the intelligence quotient is not a static thing but can be altered by environment or nurture.

(2) Secondary modern schools, which were supposed to liberate the less academically-minded from the tyranny of examinations and give them a worthwhile general education, have failed conspicuously in their purpose. The less enterprising have become dreary places in which to mark time until working life begins, and the better ones, under pressure from both parents and employers, have introduced examinations. The fact that some children have passed these, under great handicaps compared with the grammar school child, and gone on to higher education, is further proof of the folly of selection at 11 years.

(3) In spite of the hopes expressed in 1944, grammar schools kept their supposedly superior social status and perpetuated the class division which has always been a curse in this country.

(4) There is no intrinsic reason why the independent schools which merit it should not continue to exist – although, as the basic merit of the comprehensive system eventually reaches full fruition, they must expect to dwindle in numbers. (By 1986, grammar and secondary modern schools had already dwindled to only about three per cent of the system.)

(5) With proper organisation, there is no reason for the more brilliant children to suffer. They can benefit from

Con: (1) Some kind of selection or streaming is essential if the best use is to be made of all levels of intellect. Experience in other countries where comprehensive schooling is the rule has shown this; in the United States, many parents are turning to private schools where streaming is the rule. Some kind of discrimination, however disguised, is inevitable even in a comprehensive school – and streaming does now take place, in fact, within many comprehensives.

(2) One advantage of the 'modern' school is that it allows children to reach the peak of their performance without being overshadowed by their more academically ambitious fellows. Transfers to grammar schools can correct any errors made at the initial selection, and many authorities have colleges of further education where public examinations can be taken. Alternatively, selection could be made at a later age, when abilities and ambitions become clearer.

(3) Education cannot eradicate class distinctions – comprehensives certainly haven't.

(4) The former direct-grant schools, which were to a certain degree comprehensive anyway, and some of the older-established grammar schools built up high reputations for the excellence of their teaching. They gave many brilliant children the chance to develop at a pace suited to them, without upsetting the balance in the ordinary grammar schools. Private schools remain free to develop, and to experiment away from the tyranny of examination and curricular conformity, and have in the past pioneered many changes which are now generally accepted. It would

the extra equipment and libraries needed for advanced work, which previous schools were often too small to provide. Socially, contact with less academically-minded children can give them a broader view of life. By 1984, some 55 per cent of the graduates from English and Welsh universities were from comprehensives, against 23 per cent from grammar schools and 16 per cent from independent schools. Two years later, official university statistics showed that pupils from comprehensives were achieving the same proportion of first-class degrees as those from independent schools – and four per cent more 2-1s.

(6) The curriculum of a comprehensive school can be much broader in scope than that of any of the older types of secondary school. Complaints about over-specialisation in grammar schools are often made by educationists, and a turn to broader education is a feature of university reform.

(7) Though most (but not all) of the earlier comprehensive schools were large, this is not generally necessary or inevitable; in any case, a system of houses and tutoring does much – as in the larger public schools – to mitigate the effects of size.

(8) Thanks largely to the pattern whereby education receives central government funding, though being administered by the local authority in each area, it is generally accepted that the facilities available in comprehensive schools and the results achievable – see (5) above – are at least as good and sometimes even better than those in the private, fee-paying schools.

(9) Whatever the merits of previous systems, there is no doubt that education in this country is not producing enough people with higher education, and that a large reserve of

be suicidal to destroy this store of educational experience and wisdom.

(5) Comprehensives have failed those at the bottom of the heap. They have been too like grammar schools and have not equipped less able pupils with skills they need. The atmosphere of a school where only half the pupils take their education seriously is not conducive to serious study, and academic achievement is likely to be less highly regarded than athletic prowess. The real issue should be how to raise standards for *all*.

(6) Broadening of university entrance requirements is already tending to cure any over-specialisation – a fault that applies not only to grammar schools but equally to the academic streams in a comprehensive school.

(7) One great objection to the comprehensive school is its size, which is fatal to the corporate feeling without which a school cannot prosper. Teachers seldom meet the headmaster, staff meetings take up a disproportionate amount of time, and timetables are complicated, while the group life of the children lacks stability.

(8) Thanks to the cuts imposed under the Conservative Government's policies from 1979, one result of the economies local authorities were forced to seek in consequence has been a growing shortage of equipment and textbooks. By 1985, spending on books per comprehensive pupil had fallen by 12½ per cent in real terms, and many sixth-formers were having to share tattered textbooks that were ten years old or more. While all comprehensives have suffered cuts, it is significant that the ones which have suffered least are those in middle class areas where they have effectively been subsidised by parents – e.g. through

talent is left unused. The universal establishment is a crucial step towards remedying this. It has been estimated that, to meet the needs of the economy into the 1990s, Britain needs 3,000 more graduates per year than the universities can supply. However, a London University report in 1986 stressed: 'The blame must essentially be attributed to an almost total lack of any coherent national philosophy of what is required of the education system ... rather than to the system itself.'

fund-raising for computers and other expensive equipment.

(9) We are failing to produce enough people with higher education simply because the Conservative Governments since 1979 have not been prepared to fund more student places. (In the six years up to 1986, the funding of Britain's universities had been cut by up to 43 per cent.)

(See also CO-EDUCATION; PUBLIC SCHOOLS)

CONTRACEPTION FOR GIRLS UNDER 16

Pro: (1) A ruling by the Law Lords in October 1985 confirmed doctors' right to prescribe contraceptives to girls aged under 16, without their parents' knowledge, in certain limited circumstances. The key words here are 'without their parents' knowledge', because previously a very long campaign had been waged by certain individual and church interests to try to force doctors and family planning clinics to inform parents if an under-age girl sought contraceptive devices from them. In the light of the House of Lords ruling, though, the British Medical Association has now warned that a doctor who informed a girl's parents without her permission would be open to a charge of unethical conduct for breaching the patient's right to confidentiality.

(2) Many doctors faced the problem of dealing with mature girls of 15, say, who had run away from home, were living with a young man

Con: (1) The House of Lords ruling was anything but a *carte blanche*, giving under-age girls unrestricted access to contraception. The Law Lords laid down five conditions that a doctor had to be satisfied were met before he could prescribe without the parents' consent: the girl had to understand the advice; the doctor must be convinced that she could not be persuaded to inform her parents; it was very likely that she would begin (or continue) sexual intercourse, with or without contraceptive treatment; unless she received contraceptive advice or treatment, her physical or mental health was likely to suffer; the doctor must feel sure it was in the girl's best interests to receive advice or treatment without parental consent. As one Law Lord pointed out, no reasonable person could read that guidance 'as meaning that the doctor's discretion could ordinarily override parental right'. And advice issued to

(or were likely to), and refused to give any clue to their family background. How could a doctor possibly contact her parents, in such circumstances? Yet, clearly, the girl was tantamount to an adult and it was desperately urgent to give her contraceptive help, to safeguard her.

(3) Young people are growing up more equal today. If they don't have birth control at 16, there will be a lot more pregnancies. The general mood of present-day mores is that, on an issue of this nature, one ought to respect each person's own wishes. Everyone is entitled to pontificate about what they think is right, in the matter; at the end of the day, though, it's up to the individual to say what she wants. And in these circumstances, if she decides that she wants contraception, then she *ought* to have it.

doctors by the General Medical Council says that they should still try to persuade such a girl to consult her parents and should bear in mind the need to 'foster and maintain parental responsibility and family stability'.

(2) In the period between the Appeal Court ruling, which halted doctors' freedom to provide confidential contraceptive advice to girls they considered most at risk, and the House of Lords verdict which finally ended this bar, a large proportion of hitherto errant under-age girls *did* turn back to their families for advice and support, after all.

(3) Since many of these girls will, by the nature of things, have parents who have opted out of their responsibility or are incompetent to exercise it, the supposed invasion of parental right by medical confidentiality is unlikely to be very severe, in most cases. On the other hand, it would be sad – to say the least – if purported respect for individual wishes were to be abused.

(See also BIRTH CONTROL, VOLUNTARY OR COMPULSORY; TERMINATION OF PREGNANCIES, LEGALISED)

CO-OPERATION:
Compared with Capitalism

Pro: (1) Co-operation, by substituting for the self-interest of an individual or a small group of individuals the interest of the whole community of workers, puts each worker in a position of being, in a sense, his own master, and secures a higher standard of work from him, since he receives his proportionate share of the proceeds in full.

Con: (1) By freedom of contract, or in any case by trade unionism, the worker has already secured fair wages and equitable conditions of work. Co-operation has to face the same labour relations problems with its workers as private employers do and is no less prone to strikes. Every device by which the workers can be made contented, without destroying the

(2) The commercial policy is regulated by the advice of those immediately interested in its success. Unlike capitalism, co-operation does not primarily aim at profits; accordingly, while monetary balances have their due place, as a matter of good business practice, they remain less important than efficiency and service.

(3) Co-operation places the producer in direct contact with the consumer and, by thus saving the expenses of middlemen, reduces costs.

(4) In enterprises where the workers know that they are not making profits for others' consumption, they work better. Private concerns habitually give exorbitant salaries to a handful at the top and pay most of their employees at the lowest rates they can get away with – and these ordinary workers naturally tend to respond in kind.

(5) The co-operative movement has been very successful, not only in distribution but also in production. It has undertaken, with great success, banking, insurance and foreign trade. There is no reason to suppose that co-operation could not be generally adopted.

system, is open as much to capitalism as to co-operation.

(2) Under capitalism, the commercial policy is regulated by a single expert individual or small group of individuals. Uniformity and continuity of policy are better secured than under co-operation, where experts have to be employed but work under harassing conditions.

(3) Middlemen perform important services (e.g. the crucial role of wholesalers in distributing goods to a wide range of retailers); nevertheless, large industrial combines and other later developments of capitalism can dispense with them very largely.

(4) Co-operation keeps all the essential features of the wage system and is therefore of no advantage to the workers; moreover, the dividend, though not of the same origin as profits, has much the same psychological effect on its recipients.

(5) Co-operation has been chiefly successful on the distributive side. Even then, private stores are just as successful in this field. On the productive side, co-operation has been a failure; the Co-operative Wholesale Society is really nothing but a capitalist concern with shares held by unusual holders.

(See also the next article; CO-PARTNERSHIP IN INDUSTRY)

CO-OPERATION:
Compared with Socialism

Pro: (1) Voluntary co-operation, as opposed to State socialism or collectivism, makes self-help the basis of social reform. By banding men together for a common end, it teaches self-reliance and gives independence.

Con: (1) Co-operation benefits only a small portion of the working class, and that the part that needs assistance least. The most optimistic and reliable estimate of the ultimate success of co-operation does not suggest that it

(2) While collectivism would depose the capitalist only to exalt the bureaucrat, thus leaving the worker as dependent as before, co-operation would make him his own master and render impossible such abuses as sweat-shop labour.

(3) Co-operation, unlike collectivism, does not aim at the expropriation of vested interests. It defrauds no man; neither does it cripple the nation with any schemes of wholesale compensation.

(4) The main departments of human effort require special organisations to develop them properly. In the Civil Service, seniority counts far more than special merit; enterprise is stifled; responsibility is insufficiently devolved and immediate decisions cannot be given; and the ordinary citizen is rarely able to obtain reasonable consideration of his complaints or to influence the provision of the services he needs. If things go wrong in a co-operative society, the members can set them right, withdraw, or let them continue, as they please; but in State trading, citizens have to put up with what is offered.

could ever take over more than one-fifth of the national production.

(2) Co-operation simply substitutes competing societies for competing companies. The only other choice would be local monopoly coupled with absolute dependence on the central, quasi-capitalist producing organisation. Sweating and wage disputes are quite common in the co-operative movement.

(3) Co-operation based on the savings of the poorer part of the community has no chance of competing very seriously with capitalism based on profits and credit manipulation. It does not touch such basic wrongs as the land monopoly.

(4) State enterprises are at least as successful as co-operative ones. The weakness of co-operation is shown by the way it is seeking help in trying to overcome its difficulties from people who are committed to collectivism.

(See also the preceding and next articles)

CO-PARTNERSHIP IN INDUSTRY

Pro: (1) By giving the workers a concrete interest in the total efficiency and remunerative operation of industry, much discontent and friction can be avoided and a better spirit be developed, to the great advantage of all parties and of the community at large.

(2) It was very successful in the gas companies which started it, in the enormous concern of Lever Brothers,

Con: (1) Co-partnership is an endeavour to mask the fundamental defects of capitalism by bribing its victims. It makes no attempt to put an end to the vicious principle of production for profit alone. Consequently, it must be condemned as a deceptive and degrading palliative.

(2) It assumes the continuance of good trade and cannot guarantee an income when trade is poor. By

and in many other firms drawn from every section of industry, but chiefly engineering, shipbuilding, chemicals, pottery, and glass. Where co-partnership is in practice, strikes have been almost extinguished and the prosperity of the workers as a whole has increased.

(3) Shareholding gives the workpeople a sense of security, a sense of dignity, and a wider outlook on life and industry. They are thereby raised from the status of mere 'hands' to that of responsible members of a community.

(4) The moral and economic necessity of supplementing wages and salaries by another mode of income is met by these schemes. Workers who are called and treated as 'partners' (e.g. the John Lewis department store group) not only feel that they have a personal stake in their company's welfare but habitually demonstrate this by above-average standards of service to the firm's customers. An independent research report in August 1986, noting that department stores' share of retail sales had declined in every one of the previous five years, singled out the John Lewis Partnership as an exception to this trend – specifying its 'enlightened personnel policy' as one of the prime reasons for its success.

(5) Large concerns, which are unrivalled as exponents of modern commercialism, have adopted the principle on the grounds of commercial expediency.

(6) So well does it accord with modern social attitudes that co-partnership, long a basic tenet of Liberal Party philosophy, has been espoused increasingly by other political parties as well.

increasing overhead charges through the issuing of preference shares, it may actually help to depress trade. The gas companies where it was most successful were quasi-monopolies enjoying peculiar advantages. The Lever concern was a trust, and was consequently enabled to avoid many of the influences which affect other firms. Co-partnership did not save engineering and shipbuilding firms from prolonged depression or their workers from unemployment. The financing of sections of the Lancashire cotton trade by loans from the operatives brought calamity to large numbers of them, even though all the alleged advantages of co-partnership were present in this practice.

(3) Workmen shareholders are kept in a strictly subordinate position and have no real say in the policy of the firms. Whatever lip-service may be paid to them as 'partners', they still have the status of wage-earning employees.

(4) In this context, especially, interest and dividends are immoral. 'He who does not work, neither shall he eat.' It would be disastrous if trade unionists were converted to the defence of parasitism.

(5) Co-partnership is largely the hobby of philanthropists who can afford it.

(6) The kind of co-partnership advocated by other parties is, at best, only a considerably attenuated form of the original concept.

(See also the preceding articles; PROFIT-SHARING)

CORPORAL PUNISHMENT:
Should It Be Retained?

Pro: (1) The House of Commons' vote in favour of abolishing corporal punishment in state schools, with effect from August 1987, was passed by a single vote in July 1986 – some four years after the European Court of Human Rights ruled that parents should be given the right to decide if their children should be caned. An earlier Bill to that effect was rejected by the House of Lords (largely because it would have been unfair, dividing pupils into 'beatables' and 'unbeatables'). Subsequently, the Lords passed a new clause in the Education Bill – this time by only two votes – which proposed turning it into full-blooded abolition. That the move took so long to implement, and then by such a narrow margin, shows the extent to which virtually half our parliamentarians doubted its wisdom.

(2) Corporal punishment for certain offences is most effective, because it is prompt and feared by all. It combines the elements of the remedial, the deterrent and the day of reckoning. It teaches the schoolboy or the convict that the doing of wrong is followed by the suffering of pain.

(3) When inflicted justly and without anger, it does not brutalise the giver. In most of those independent schools where it still occurs, it is resorted to only as a final punishment.

(4) It accustoms the pupil to the hardships of real life. No bitterness is left after chastisement if it has been administered for good reason.

(5) It is impossible always to 'make the punishment fit the crime'. The amount of corporal punishment can

Con: (1) Britain, as a signatory to the European Convention on Human Rights, was obliged to comply with the Strasbourg court's 1982 ruling. That the Government delayed for more than four years before doing so was a reflection partly of its difficulties in placating its own more reactionary backbenchers and partly of the pressure on the parliamentary time-table, but above all of its temperamental reluctance to have its hand forced by other, outside authorities. Even though MPs of the ruling Conservative Party were allowed a free vote on the issue (ostensibly because it was a 'matter of conscience'), the ultimate abolition of the cane was very clearly against the wishes of the Education Secretary and other senior cabinet Ministers.

(2) It is degrading and otherwise harmful to the sensitive victim, while it is no deterrent to the hardened culprit, who often boasts about it to his cronies as though it were a battle honour.

(3) Its brutalising effect is seen when we reflect that those ages when parents and teachers resorted to it most were the most brutal in other respects. It appeals to the strain of cruelty that exists somewhere in everyone.

(4) Children resent injustice coupled with indignity. Were it true that corporal punishment accustoms them to life's hardships, then every boy – but especially the good boys – ought to receive its benefits daily.

(5) It is an excuse for laziness and inefficiency in teachers. By using terror instead of discipline, a bad teacher can

be adjusted to suit the gravity of the misdemeanour.

(6) It is better than other punishments, such as impositions, which are deadening to mind and body. Schools which dispense with corporal punishment, especially for young children, often substitute other methods which are tantamount to browbeating.

(7) Impositions and detentions are harmful because they increase the number of hours a boy is compelled to spend indoors in physical inactivity. His natural restlessness is increased by the enforced restraint, so leading to further offences against discipline.

(8) Judicial corporal punishment should be reintroduced for criminals convicted of violence. It would bring home to them the effect of their crimes on their victims and, since bullies are generally the greatest cowards, be of the utmost value as a deterrent from such crimes in future. Before it was scrapped a few years after the last world war, British prison records from the earlier part of the century showed that hardly any convicts who received corporal punishment ever repeated the offence which incurred it.

continue his work when otherwise the impatience of the pupils would force a change in either the methods or the staff.

(6) Impositions and detentions are more effective because they encroach on the leisure time of the miscreant (which usually worries him far more than physical hurt) and may even give an opportunity for reflection.

(7) In modern schools, there is plenty of opportunity for physical exercise, and it is nonsense to imply that depriving a boy of this for a few hours is physically harmful. Impositions and detentions in girls' schools are not considered to have any bad effect on health. Letting off steam immediately afterwards will always be tempered by a desire to avoid repetition of the punishment.

(8) The infliction of corporal punishment on an already anti-social person who regards violence as a legitimate means of achieving his ends is not likely to have any corrective action; on the contrary, past experience indicates that it will more probably lead to a deeper feeling of enmity towards authority and society.

DEGENERACY OF MODERN CIVILISATION

Pro: (1) The degeneracy of Europe and of European civilisation has been noticeable for more than a century. Literature, journalism and art have more and more laid stress on the sickly and the abnormal. Britain is not exempt, as is proved by the crazes in different classes of society for such importations as lascivious music and dances, and the violence and crude,

Con: (1) Britain and other European countries can be accused of degeneracy only by people who are ignorant of social history or those who idealise the fancied memories of their youth. We often confuse what we do not like with what is evil. Morbidity and sensuality are found in the literatures and art of every country and every age.

67

puerile sentimentalism of many American films and TV series.

(2) A loathsome industrialism has subjected men to machines. Working populations are marked by a mania for gambling, for watching other people, especially professionals, playing games which they themselves do not play, and by an insatiable desire for something new, which shows itself in the endless buying of unnecessary but much-advertised products and the incessant pursuit of machine-made pleasures.

(3) Moral laxness and crimes have been increasing, fed by weak sentimentalism and the flood of pernicious literature and films. The most outrageous forms of immorality are now spreading openly in most countries and are being cynically tolerated.

(4) Mental diseases and neurotic symptoms are on the increase. Faith healers and astrologers flourish. The persistent demand for more leisure-time and longer holidays shows that we are less fitted to stand the strain of life than our ancestors were. Tranquillisers have taken the place of religious consolation. Venereal diseases are widespread, especially in the large towns. Above all, the illicit use of dangerous drugs has become a commonplace – openly vaunted by many 'pop stars' and the like, and an ever more widespread cause of crime, human misery, and lack of even the most cursory sense of morality.

(5) Divorce rates have risen steadily and the institution of marriage is becoming 'unfashionable' among an increasingly large sector of the population. The phrase 'close friend', in newspapers, has acquired a dubious new meaning – such affairs now being publicised blatantly and without criticism. More married women than ever are taking office or factory jobs; while

(2) Industrial progress is steadily improving both physique and intelligence in the areas where it flourishes. The state of mind which made possible the horrors of the industrial revolution was a product of the pre-industrial period. Such evils would hardly be accepted nowadays even by the most reactionary. Gambling and the pursuit of new things are as old as society, and the age which watches football matches and television is perhaps less to be condemned than that where bull- and bear-baiting, cock-fighting and the murder of gladiators flourished.

(3) Immorality is no greater than in previous ages; the reason for its apparent increase is that there is less hypocrisy – it comes under the glare of publicity and is not swept under the carpet. Cases of cruelty and barbarism that now arouse widespread horror would have been part of everyday life, passing almost without comment, some generations back.

(4) Accurate statistics of insanity were not kept in the past and there is thus no real basis for comparison with the present day. But it is certain that new medical treatments have done away with much of the mental and physical invalidism which existed in the last century without being understood. The increased, illicit use of narcotics is admittedly a very serious problem (though there are signs that international counter-measures may eventually start to get on top of it). On the other hand, drunkenness is far less common, venereal diseases are being attacked by the only possible method – medical treatment – and the hypocritical silence which veiled such subjects has given way to a franker attitude.

(5) The increase in divorce has been due latterly to the considerable easing

this may be a good trend, in principle, it should not be at the expense of their children or the proper running of their homes, as is increasingly the case.

(6) Commercial interests are allowed to pander to the young, who have lost all respect for older people and their standards, while parents have ceased to exercise their duties of correction and guidance.

(7) The growing discontent and peevish attitude to the difficulties of life show lack of stamina. Higher standards of comfort bring demands for still more. Suicide as a method of avoiding reality is becoming commoner, as are insanity and nervous breakdowns.

(8) The outbreak of two worldwide wars in one generation proves that Europe has lost its moral standards. The ferocity and stupidity with which war is waged, and the epidemics of frenzy, revolution and braggadocio which accompany it, reveal our degeneracy.

(9) Our political systems are outworn and our statesmen, particularly in the international issues, prove much inferior to such men as Pitt, Canning, Castlereagh, Palmerston and Disraeli, who wrestled successfully with the problems of earlier days.

(10) Our decadence is due to a variety of causes, of which the decline of religion and the older virtues is the chief. Owing to the premature democratisation of our social institutions, power rests with half-educated crowds who are too often directed by experts in deceit and cajolery, whether journalists, politicians or advertising agents; a spirit of small-minded egoism prevails, and loyalty to State and society is replaced by general discontent and skirmishing for greater personal advantages. Children absorb these pernicious doctrines at home; at

of the restrictive laws which previously governed it and may be measured against the suffering, without hope of release, which was the lot of so many people in the old days. Women are just escaping from the serfdom of centuries and are no longer content with the restricted life which was formerly their lot.

(6) Young people have always revolted against their elders' standards. Most parents continue to exercise their duties, but in a less arbitrary and despotic manner.

(7) Our ancestors bore hardships only because they could not circumvent them. For most of our population, higher standards of comfort mean progress, and discontent is a first symptom of moral and cultural advance. In relation to the size of population, it is probable that the incidence of suicide, etc., is actually less than amid the hideous conditions of poverty during, say, the late Victorian era.

(8) War is the result of a complexity of causes, which have little or nothing to do with the moral standards of ordinary people. Never has opposition to war and all its attendant stupidities been more universally pronounced than in our own generation.

(9) Modern problems, owing to the interdependence of modern communities, are much more complicated than those which faced former statesmen. The widespread desire and effort to improve our political and economic systems shows that the ability to make new departures and new ventures is inherent in Europeans today.

(10) If the 'older virtues' are at a discount today, it is because their exponents, the churches, no longer expound a doctrine which corresponds with modern spiritual needs.

the same time, they are deprived of the stabilising influence of religion, and even the most reasonable standards of discipline and obedience are derided.

The newer virtues of co-operation and personal initiative are being inculcated in all modern schools. Universal education and the influence of the better newspapers and the radio have raised the general standard of culture and ended the power which the leaders of society formerly possessed over ignorant populations. The supposed degeneracy of life in other countries, and the inadequacy of democracy in general, was always among the principal propaganda assertions of totalitarian regimes like the Nazis – but it is those regimes' policies which have been thoroughly discredited.

DELEGATION v. REPRESENTATION

Pro: (1) The representative system has broken down in all today's supposedly representative assemblies. Most members no longer represent the general views of their constituents – it may be questioned whether such a thing is even possible. Instead, they tend to serve party, sectional or individual interests. The general feeling that, once an election is over, the successful candidate is free from all effective control by his constituents, has weakened popular faith in political democracy of the old type. The remedy is the principle of delegation.

(2) Theoretically, every elector ought to vote by proxy on every question of government; the nearer the approach to this ideal, the more perfect government is likely to be. An MP, therefore, ought to represent the majority view of his constituents in each vote he gives, and should consult them on every occasion where a vote

Con: (1) A man is elected to Parliament on broad issues, with the necessary understanding that he shall consider and decide on details for himself. His constituents cannot take such decisions for him. The failings found in representative institutions are due to several other causes.

(2) Delegation is unworkable. It entails either complete submission to an elaborate but inelastic party programme, or else futility. In practice, representation is inevitable unless the assembly is purely temporary and deliberative. The mechanical difficulties in the way of getting constituents to express themselves on half-a-dozen main questions are enormous; to get decisions on proposals running to dozens of clauses is impossible. Even to answer a single question, the necessary national organisation entails vast expense – as in Britain's 1975 referendum on Common Market membership. Moreover, experience in

on key policies is involved. The principle of the mid-term re-selection of MPs bears out that this is now the attitude of an increasing proportion of the electorate.

(3) Constant appeals to constituencies would not be derogatory to the dignity of their delegate; consequently, equally good men would offer themselves as candidates. They would, in fact, be protected in a measure from the pressure and influence of parties and sectional interests.

other countries (e.g. France) shows that electors soon get bored if called to the polls at frequent intervals. The Referendum and the Recall (*qq.v.*) are compromise and faulty solutions.

(3) Delegates will always tend to be inferior to representatives in character and ability, for no self-respecting man will act as an automaton without even theoretical responsibility. Under the Delegation system, party domination continues, corruption is not eradicated, and the executive steadily encroaches on the sovereign body. Representation enables many important matters to be dealt with which cannot come within the scope of delegation, e.g. foreign policy.

DIRECT ACTION
(The Use of Industrial Strikes to Affect Political Issues)

Pro: (1) The present system of government reduces the masses of the population to a state of helplessness between elections. As events and situations change rapidly, this has the effect of despotism by the government that has a parliamentary majority. Trade unions comprise the largest organised part of the citizens of the country, and trade union action is the only effective way they have of intervening to show their opinions on critical occasions. A satisfactory government would not be threatened.

(2) In recent times, the British miners' strike of 1984–85 started largely as a protest against threatened pit closures (and the resultant virtual destruction of mining village communities). But it became increasingly 'political' because many strikers saw it as the only way to draw public

Con: (1) Parliament, elected on a very wide franchise, reflects and represents the will of the people as a whole. The government of the day depends on Parliament, and its policy follows the greatest common measure of the wills of the community. It is, therefore, both the constitutional instrument of public policy and the only qualified judge of policy. To attempt to influence its action by extra-constitutional means is wrong and will end in anarchy. Opponents of the trade unions' political demands will inevitably organise their forces to resist direct action and possibly to press demands of their own. Movements have already sprung up in Britain for this purpose.

(2) The illicit, often violent conduct of some of the striking miners alienated many of the sympathisers who

attention to the inequities – in their view – of some of the Government's economic and industrial relations policies.

(3) Direct action can be applied only occasionally and only when the vast mass of the workers approve. The pressure put on Parliament by financial, industrial and newspaper interests is the work of a smaller minority and is more pervasive, more constant and, in many cases, no less unconstitutional.

(4) Direct action is especially to be recommended for securing the ordinary and recognised civil and industrial liberties of the subject. It is then purely in the nature of a demonstration.

(5) Politics are properly the object of such action, since one political development may spell more ruin to trade unionists than half a dozen unsuccessful industrial strikes. Industrial power cannot be gained for any purpose unless there are constant attempts to exercise it.

(6) The ballot box often gives a fallacious result. The constitution, the party system, the machinery of government, the confusion of issues and proposals at election times, prevent the electorate from giving an informed and effective vote.

(7) The 1926 General Strike failed in its objectives through incompetent leaders. As a strike, though, it was amazingly complete.

had previously supported their cause. It shows that direct action is not just counter-productive but (as in this case) can contribute to utter defeat for the strikers.

(3) Direct action, if persisted in, would lead to anarchy. The moral stability of the workers would disappear. It would be resorted to more and more on the most trivial occasions, sometimes by a few unions, sometimes by many, but always by a minority of the community.

(4) Parliament, the law, and the many different organs of public opinion are quite adequate to defend the liberty either of groups of people or of individuals.

(5) It is absurd for trade unions to devote their energy and power to strikes on political issues when they need to settle so many other problems more closely relating to themselves and are too divided to carry through their own modest industrial programmes.

(6) All grievances can be remedied more certainly and much more easily through the ballot box.

(7) Only general strikes are likely to be fully effective and they are in fact a revolutionary weapon. The General Strike of 1926 failed largely because of its leaders' tardy recognition of this fact and their recoil from it.

(See also TRADE UNIONS: DO THEIR POWERS NEED FURTHER RESTRICTION?)

DIRECTION OF LABOUR

Pro: (1) The balance of Britain's foreign trade has always been delicate,

Con: (1) If the balancing of Britain's international trade and the stepping-

owing to her large need for imports. Since the last world war, the dislocation of our economy has made it more important than ever for British industry to expand those essential trades which have the power to earn foreign currency. Canalisation of available manpower into these channels, to the extent needed, can be achieved only by direction of labour.

(2) It is undesirable for the State to have to enter into competition with private employers for available labour.

(3) Workers are traditionally unwilling to leave occupations and places to which they are accustomed, even in those areas where local industry has declined. Even when workers do move, the majority tend to ignore inducements to find new work in the depressed regions and still gravitate to the south-east and other already congested industrial areas.

(4) During the last world war, workers accepted direction without complaint, not only for patriotic reasons but also because it was necessarily accompanied by adequate working conditions and security of employment. Both these reasons are still cogent.

(5) A great deal of the waste and disorganisation which are a natural feature of modern private enterprise systems would disappear if labour were withdrawn from unessential industries and anti-social occupations. Direction of industry and capital expenditure is not a feasible alternative, since the goodwill of the industrialist and financier is essential to the smooth working of the national economy; indeed, its absence can wreck any national plan.

up of national production can be achieved only by coercion of labour, any advantages which may result from it would be nullified by the evils such a method would bring in its train. The national economy should function for the benefit of the nation's citizens and not for some overall concept which overrides the individual interests of large numbers of them. Higher wages, good conditions of work and other incentives have always been sufficient to attract labour into individual industries.

(2) The worker has the right to sell his labour where it will be of most profit to him.

(3) The success of industrial development schemes in hard-hit regions like the north-east shows that it is possible to restore prosperity to areas where the older industries have decayed, without uprooting workers from their homes.

(4) Measures which are accepted in wartime are not necessarily valid in time of peace. Direction of labour interferes with the freedom of the individual and operates, moreover, unfairly. Inducements to employers – such as tax reliefs for new factories established in depressed areas – are more effective and give rise to fewer problems.

(5) The efficiency of industry is seriously hampered if workers are made resentful by encroachments on their rights. Direction tends to operate mainly against the most essential types of workers. Their resentment is further increased if they are conscious that capital is allowed to operate unhindered. Any attempt to operate a scheme which is appropriate only to a Socialist economy is doomed to failure inside the framework of capitalism.

DISESTABLISHMENT OF THE CHURCH OF ENGLAND

Pro: (1) The union between Church and State is undesirable, as they are essentially different in aim. The State deals with the individual as a member of society in his relations with the world, while the Church looks on him as an individual with a soul to save and from the point of view of his relations with God.

(2) In the past, the State knew of but one religion and looked upon those who professed another as scarcely to be counted as citizens. But in Britain this was finally ended when Charles Bradlaugh (Radical MP for Northampton and a professed atheist) was admitted to the House of Commons, in the latter part of the nineteenth century, without taking the normal oath of allegiance.

(3) It may be admitted that Church and State have certain common functions, but it is nevertheless not a wise policy to connect the two, as their spheres and methods differ. Such a union tends to diminish the efficiency of both.

(4) Established Churches create false ideals of religion. Many people who are lukewarm about religion seem to think that religious duties can be done for them by proxy, that the worship of God need make no demand on their life, and that the State, in maintaining an official Church, satisfies the requirements of religious duty and social morality.

(5) The State drags the Church down to its lower level, encouraging worldly prudence and an unreligious tendency towards diplomacy and discretion. Bishops and clergy, for example, through this connection with

Con: (1) While many people in the present day have turned away from the Church, they are not in the majority – whatever the newspapers say – and religion is still an important element in national and social life. It remains a prime duty of the State to countenance religion officially and not be indifferent whether the people hold religious principles or not.

(2) Although the State no longer claims to be the exclusive arbiter of what is religious truth and admits to its counsels persons of many religions or of none, nevertheless the Church of England is historically and psychologically the National Church and should remain so.

(3) Both State and Church exist to improve society and to promote a better life for all. For centuries, no man dreamed that these two institutions for securing such ends were other than two aspects of the same unity. This philosophical principle should still be recognised, and the best form of recognition is by means of an official Church – which no longer entails the condemnation of other non-official Churches.

(4) An established Church, with its social prestige, attracts to itself many who otherwise would have no religion at all. Religious zeal may be stronger in the non-established Churches, but this is because an established Church, while not excluding such enthusiasts, tends naturally to lay less stress on rigid dogmatic beliefs but to combine several elements within it.

(5) The duty of the Church is to import a moral element into our political life. Its ministers are secure

the Throne, are restrained from denouncing evils which the interests of society make it unwise to pass over.

(6) Establishment hampers the Church's efforts to reform itself. Parliament alone can sanction important changes in its rites and ceremonies. The 39 Articles show how this worked in Tudor times; the Gorham judgment and other cases show how it has operated since. Parliament, being composed of people of all types of belief, is manifestly unfit to be the authority in matters of religion. It does not even represent the feeling of the nation on the subject, for members are elected for completely different purposes.

(7) The State's role may oblige it to sanction conduct and pass laws, for civil purposes, which are not in accord with the forward teachings of the Church (e.g. the law allowing the remarriage of divorced persons). Dependence on the State thus exposes the Church to the potential weakening of its own standpoints.

(8) The Church of England can maintain its present relationship with the State only on one condition – that the Crown and Parliament should abstain from any interference in its internal concerns. The Royal Commission on Ecclesiastical Discipline, appointed in 1905, took upon itself the duties of a spiritual court and determined what was or was not consistent with the teaching of the Church. The theory that the State or the monarch should manage the Church was one of the errors associated with the Reformation and Lutheran Protestantism.

(9) The Enabling Act was a recognition that the time had come when churchmen should manage their own affairs. Though it touched only a few points, it was a step in the right direc-

from pressure by the Government because they practically hold office for life and are in no sense of the term either bureaucrats or place-seekers. In recent years, the bishops and leading clergy have even come into direct confrontation with the Government through their denunciation of injustice and social ills.

(6) Parliament cannot alter either the Creeds or a single doctrine. The Prayer Book was drawn up by the Church, not the State, and was then accepted by the latter. For almost all practical purposes, the Church today is effectively self-governing.

(7) No clergyman with scruples need marry a divorced person. The connection of Church and State ensures a broad tolerance in the former, which thus attracts men of widely different individual convictions.

(8) Upon substantial matters of doctrine, the State does not claim to dictate to the Church; but where the internal conduct of the Church is a matter of national importance, it is quite fitting that the State should take a part. State participation has always helped to raise the Church in the estimation of the people. Patristic authority, furthermore, is clearly on the side of monarchical authority, even when it comes to a reform in the status of the Church, so that State Churches are not simply an idea from Lutheran politics.

(9) By the Enabling Act, the Church now has sufficient scope to express its desires without separation from the nation as organised in the State. Complete freedom even to define doctrine need not mean the surrender of the position as National Church. The Church of Scotland is still national, though granted autonomy in matters of doctrine.

tion, and all the steps required to give the Church 'life and liberty' should now be taken.

(10) It is improper that the Government, which may contain a number of atheists, should appoint the chief officers of the Church, i.e. the bishops and archbishops, and that such political dignitaries as the Lord Chancellor, whose only necessary qualification is that he shall not be a Roman Catholic, should have a large number of livings in his gift. Parliament also creates bishoprics at its entire discretion. All religious sects should be treated as equal by the State, though that does not mean that they can be made equal.

(11) Because of its present position *vis-à-vis* the State, the Church cannot insist on its clergy adhering rigidly to its formularies.

(12) Reform has a different meaning in the mouth of each party in the Church, and there are few points on which they can agree.

(13) Some parish clergy neglect their poorer parishioners altogether – and in the big towns, indeed, are not numerous enough to attend to them, or even to all those who require it.

(14) The traditional connection of the established clergy with the landowning class and the well-to-do sections of the community prejudices them in the eyes of large numbers of the working population. Disestablishment would at once tone up the Church and help to remove this feeling against it.

(15) The Church has notoriously misused its very large income. Many clergymen are still living on a bare subsistence; churches of architectural value have been allowed to go to ruin or have been sold off. Much of its income was derived from ownership of slum property which the Church

(10) The Sovereign does not make bishops but (on the Prime Minister's recommendation) merely allocates them to particular posts; they are 'made' by consecration. They are quite as likely to be the most suitable for the dignity as those who would be chosen, after inevitable intrigues and jockeying for influence among possible candidates, within an autonomous Church. Parliament merely sanctions the creation of sees; it neither initiates the demand for new ones nor frustrates that demand when well-founded.

(11) The Church has long been noted for allowing its clergy freedom to teach what they think is right, so long as they keep the main doctrines of Christianity as laid down in the Prayer Book. Heresy-hunting is rarer than among the Dissenting communities, with the happy result that schism is also rarer.

(12) Now that the laity have a recognised position in the organisation and government of the Church, necessary reforms can be carried through with less acrimony and less delay.

(13) If the Church were dis-established, there would be no one in the parish upon whom the poor would have a *right* to call to perform services such as visiting the sick, praying with the dying, or celebrating marriages. For it is in the crises of life that they need and look to the Church most.

(14) Disestablishment would reduce the prestige of the Church, and in consequence the cause of religion would suffer. It would diminish the self-respect of many of the clergy and result in future recruits to their ranks being of inferior quality.

(15) The great inequalities of former days have disappeared and no clergyman is starving today. The

did little or nothing to improve.

(16) Too many of the clergy are now out of touch with the needs and requirements of their congregations.

(Some) An independent priesthood, standing on its own dignity and governing itself without any reference to an external authority, is a first necessity for healthy religion.

(17) The bishops are among the most bigoted, obstructive and useless members of the House of Lords and should be removed from it without delay. (See *Bishops*.)

(18) No Church is stronger for carrying with it a multitude of the religiously indifferent, for these only act as dead weights against true religious life and activity.

(19) The Church of England has undergone vast changes during the last century. These changes have taken it further from both Erastianism and Nonconformity. To a great extent, it has become sacramental and sacerdotal, and even those who repudiate such principles the most strongly have fallen under their influence to some degree. The conditions suitable for its establishment in England have therefore ceased to exist, both as far as its own character is concerned and because the mass of the people are no longer true Church members.

Church has either sold much of its former slum property or spent large sums on replacing it with modern dwellings.

(16) The clergy would be reduced to much greater dependence on the whims and fancies of their congregations, and of the richer members in particular. It would be an evil day for religion if the Church came to be governed by those with the deepest purses, which has often happened in Nonconformist Churches.

(17) The bishops are among the peers who sit by merit and not by the accident of birth. When they intervene in debates, they invariably do so with responsibility.

(18) If disestablishment were effected, large numbers of wavering Anglicans would join the Church of Rome, while others would drift into vague theisms or ultimately into atheism.

(19) Establishment saves the Church from becoming merely the battleground of warring factions. The relationship with the State is a brake on hasty action, giving ample opportunities for reflection and compromise, because action is impossible until the assent of the State is secured. In the Roman Catholic Church, the appeal to Rome is a similarly effective instrument of delay.

(See also BISHOPS: SHOULD THEY BE EXCLUDED FROM THE HOUSE OF LORDS?; THE CHURCHES: SHOULD THEY TAKE PART IN POLITICS?)

DIVORCE

Pro: (1) Though, in the Roman Catholic Church, marriage in theory is held to be indissoluble, in practice this has never held good and some device has been found to circumvent the

Con: (1) In the marriage ceremony, no mention is made of possible divorce. Each party swears solemnly to take the other 'for better, for worse, till death do us part'. Though State

difficulty, e.g. the Pope has always had the power to dissolve marriage, provided it has not been consummated, a plea which has been visibly strained in many instances. In the theology of the Western Church, the doctrine that marriage is indissoluble stands in the closest association with the 'Roman doctrine of intention' – if the intentions of the bride and bridegroom have, in any way, come short of being a genuine 'consent unto matrimony', the marriage is regarded as null and void. A theory of marriage which ignores consent can be defended neither by reason nor by authority. In England before the Divorce Act, as in Ireland now, a long process had to be gone through in each case. Only the rich could afford divorce, therefore; the poor had no hope of escaping from unhappy marriage by legal means.

(2) Marriage is a purely civil contract and should be so treated in law and opinion.

(3) It has always been held that adultery (and, above all, adultery by a wife) is cause for dissolving a marriage.

(4) Divorce for adultery was allowed by Christ; there is no difference between the Greek word *apoluo* (I put away) and divorce. This doctrine was taught by a great many of the Fathers of the Church. The Council of Arles [see Con (4)] has been reported in two diametrically opposite senses.

(5) The denial of divorce never served to deter people from adultery. It merely contributed to increasing laxness, in both public opinion and private conduct, as regards adultery, concubinage and prostitution, and its chief effect was nearly always to victimise the woman rather than the man.

(6) The worst thing that can and Church have erred, they should not continue in error. The indissolubility of Christian marriage is a plain and simple principle, resting on the authority of the whole Western Church.

(2) Marriage has been regarded by nearly every nation as a rite and condition of mystical significance. Its extreme importance for the continuance of the human race makes it imperative to surround it with all possible responsibility and dignity. If we looked upon it as irrevocable, we should enter upon it with more care and solemnity.

(3) When adultery is considered automatically as a ground for divorce, marriage loses its seriousness in popular estimation and opportunity is given for relative promiscuity by a succession of remarriages. Official figures show that, with one in three present-day marriages, either one or both partners has been married at least once before.

(4) Even if Christ allowed divorce for adultery, he never gave sanction to remarriage, which was expressly forbidden by the Church at the Council of Arles.

(5) The knowledge that they were not allowed to separate and remarry nearly always tended to induce husbands and wives to minimise differences which they might otherwise have magnified into occasions for separation. The risk of their agreeing on full licence for each other in sexual relations is not one of which the law can take account, but one against which public opinion should express itself strongly.

(6) Nothing can be worse for children than the legal separation of their parents. A true home cannot exist in the absence of either of the parents, while both are still alive.

happen to children is for them to live with estranged and quarrelling parents or to be brought up in contact with one parent, whichever it may be, who is depraved and worthless.

(7) As the monarch is head of Church and State, the State clergy have no right to debar people who are not breaking the law from being married in church.

(7) The State must not expect the clergy to lend their churches for sacrilegious purposes, such as the marriage of divorced persons. Those who wish to defy the Church's laws can marry in a Registrar's Office.

(See also the next article)

DIVORCE, EASIER
Has It Gone Too Far?

Pro: (1) Although present-day social attitudes regard it as in the interest of both the public and the individual to allow divorce, when a marriage appears to have become irretrievably unhappy, the plain fact remains that the couples concerned are breaking a solemn pledge to each other (and to their children). That Christian marriage should be indissoluble has already been demonstrated in the previous article. However, even if one now has to accept the existence of divorce as an institution, in the prevailing social climate, the massive and alarming increase in the number of broken marriages nevertheless makes it abundantly clear that relaxation of the divorce laws has gone much too far. It also has a perturbing 'domino effect'. A Medical Research Council study, following more than 5,300 babies born in 1946 up to their adult lives in the mid-1980s, found that the children of divorced parents were more likely to make worse parents themselves. A social report published in 1986 also showed that children from families where the

Con: (1) It is injurious both to the State and to the individual that married couples should be obliged to remain together when their relationship has developed such fundamental antagonisms that it has become intolerable to both of them. The atmosphere in such a household inevitably brings out the worst in the characters of those concerned. Previously, when a couple agreed mutually that they wished to divorce, almost the only way they could obtain it was for one party to produce evidence of the other's adultery; this often led to the staging of a fictitious overnight 'affair', for the benefit of a private detective hired for the occasion, which made a farce of the law. Today, the only legal requirement for divorce is proof that the marriage has broken down irretrievably (this being provided by any one of five facts: adultery, desertion, intolerable behaviour, separation for two years if both partners consent or for five years if only one consents). But care is still taken to ensure a wife's continued maintenance, if need be, and there are

father is absent (because of illegitimacy, divorce, desertion or mothers choosing to be single parents) are more likely to do badly at school and become involved in crime and violence.

(2) The figures speak for themselves. In 1867, there were 119 divorces in Britain. By the beginning of the Edwardian era in the 1900s, there were still fewer than 500. The Matrimonial Causes Act of 1937, extending the grounds for divorce to desertion for three years, cruelty, incurable insanity and presumed death, saw a jump of 60 per cent in the number of petitions in the first year of its operation. Between 1951 and 1970, the proportion of divorced people in the population *doubled* (with more than 70,000 petitions in the last year). Then in 1971, when the new Act came into operation (enabling couples to divorce by mutual consent after two years' separation and unilaterally after five years), divorce applications rose by more than half to 110,895. The authorities had expected that the rate would even out after the first upsurge, but it didn't happen – and further impetus came from the 1984 Matrimonial and Family Proceedings Act, allowing divorce petitions to be filed after one year of marriage (e.g. for urgent grounds such as cruelty or other intolerable behaviour) instead of the three-year wait previously required. In the year that Act came into force, the number of divorce petitions in England and Wales rose to a staggering 178,940 – three per cent more than the previous record level.

(3) When couples knew that their marriage could not be dissolved without some difficulty, they often reconciled themselves to the situation, reached the best *modus vivendi* they could with each other and, through it,

particularly strict safeguards for the welfare of any young children of the marriage. This law will be regarded historically as one of the most enlightened steps forward in our social development.

(2) Those figures merely demonstrate the extent of human misery which existed before the progressive relaxations of the divorce laws. Previously, unhappy couples were condemned to stay together, against their wills – or, perhaps, to live separate existences while remaining inexorably bound to each other by law. Such widespread frustration and suffering wreaked untold harm on the community.

(3) It is doubtful if such complete reconciliations were effected much more often than the instances (even today) of couples getting divorced, deciding later that it was a mistake and subsequently marrying each other again. It happens – but pretty rarely.

(4) 'Marry in haste, repent at leisure' still has plenty of force for most people. Since the financial provisions which a man may have to make for his wife's continued upkeep can sometimes be even heavier now than under the previous legislation (depending upon the particular circumstances of the case), he has no temptation to seek divorce without good reason. Equally, young wives may be deterred from walking out prematurely, knowing that they no longer have an easy 'meal ticket' because the same law may now give them only short-term maintenance and will expect them to find a job within a reasonable time. The increase in the number of teenage marriages is due mainly to the earlier maturing of young people nowadays and the greater affluence they enjoy, compared with previous generations who simply

quite frequently ended after a while by recapturing their mutual affection and respect.

(4) If men and women feel that their marriage can be ended easily, should it prove unsuccessful, they will tend to enter into marriage much too light-heartedly and without the deep consideration necessary before embarking on a union that is supposed to last for the rest of their lives. Hence the ever-increasing number of young people who marry in their teens, enjoy a year or two of passionate love, then get divorced in their early twenties.

(5) (Some) Christ's teaching is unequivocal. Our moral and legal codes should be as nearly identical as possible. To claim that the law has been changed merely in response to public demand cannot justify the excessive relaxation that has been allowed. Our social and political institutions have a responsibility to give a lead – and they should at least aim at ideal morality.

couldn't afford to get married at that age.

(5) (Some) Religion, and the morality that is supposedly derived from it, should be kept out of politics. The majority of people are not practising Christians; those who are can keep Christ's law in their own lives, without trying to impose it on everyone else. Christ strove always to help individuals; it is the spirit of what he taught, not the artificial taboos with which it was overlaid later by biased humans, that we should follow.

(See also the preceding article; MARRIAGE AS AN INSTITUTION)

EIGHTEEN-YEAR-OLD MPs

Pro: (1) The present minimum age of 21, for an MP, equated with the former minimum for universal suffrage. Now that the voting age has been lowered to 18, there is no logical reason why that for parliamentary candidates should not keep step likewise. That MPs themselves are aware of the illogicality is shown by the fact that a Private Member's Bill to reduce the age for candidates was introduced as far back as the mid-1970s – without success, though such a measure is bound to be accepted eventually.

(2) Pitt the Younger became Prime

Con: (1) The idea of youth in Parliament doubtless has its attractions, but it is reasonable to maintain age limits aimed at ensuring that candidates can make a practical contribution, based on their own experience. Many professional qualifications cannot be gained below a certain minimum age (often higher than 21, even), for similar reasons; the voting age is irrelevant, therefore. Eighteen-year-olds are unlikely to have much experience or knowledge other than from school education; by 21, many young people will at least have gained wider experi-

Minister – and one of the greatest in British history – when he was only 24.

(3) Britain lost America over the principle of 'no taxation without representation'. Equally, why should there be no parliamentary representation from within their own age group for those who are nevertheless still old enough to be called up into the armed forces, if need be, in time of war? There are not likely to be many 18-year-old MPs, any more than there are MPs still in their 20s, in the present Parliament; a young parliamentary candidate has to be quite outstanding if he is to win enough votes from the mass of electors. But at least the opportunity should be there – ensuring that we do not lose the contribution that could be made by the few 18-year-olds who *are* exceptional.

(4) The chances are that people suited to become MPs at 18 to 21 would either still want to go to university or would not yet have finished other forms of education. But there would be nothing to prevent them from combining parliamentary duty with further study. After all, many undergraduates already do active political work – e.g. for the students' union – without detriment to their academic requirements. Indeed, young MPs of this age (in an echo of the separate parliamentary representatives once returned by universities) might have a particularly valuable role to play in reflecting the thinking of the university community.

ence and knowledge in passing through university.

(2) Apart from the question of earlier maturity in those days, Pitt was the son of a famous statesman, the Earl of Chatham, and had been brought up in an atmosphere of politics and affairs of state since early childhood.

(3) Representation is, indeed, the crux of the problem. An 18-year-old could not be representative of more than a very small minority of the electors in his or her constituency. As MPs, holding 'surgeries' in their constituencies most weekends, they would be called on to give advice and help to constituents of far greater experience than themselves. Few of the older electors would have much confidence in them. The necessary educational preparation is also sadly lacking in this country; very few schools give in-depth teaching about British political institutions (let alone about those of other countries), and nearly all 18-year-olds are inevitably still ignorant on the subject.

(4) How could they hope to put in all the time and effort needed to carry out both tasks satisfactorily? It is inevitable that, to fulfil either function properly, the other would have to suffer.

EUTHANASIA:
Should It Be Legalised?

Pro: (1) We put animals 'out of their misery', rather than let them suffer

Con: (1) A doctor cannot draw up a list of diseases which are invariably

82

intolerable pain; yet we refuse the same merciful release to our fellow men. In spite of all that modern medicine and surgery can do to prevent disease, or abate it, many human beings still end their days by a slow and often agonising illness. Provided that strict legal precautions were observed (particularly as regards the crucial question of consent), a doctor should have the right to give an overdose of morphine to a patient who would otherwise die a lingering and painful death.

(2) Although it may not be possible to draw up a list of diseases that are always incurable, a point comes in each individual case when a doctor knows whether a patient is beyond hope or not. The patient himself should be the best judge of whether life has become, for him, intolerable. If he wishes for release from suffering, it should not be denied. In Britain, suicide ceased to be a crime in 1961. Logically, euthanasia is merely a further step along this merciful path. The number of people recorded as committing suicide in Britain varies very little – averaging about 4,200 a year. It may be doubted whether the number seeking euthanasia would be anything like as much as even this relatively low total.

(3) If the patient is unaware of the hopelessness of his condition, the decision should be taken out of his hands. The family doctor would know best; but to avoid any risk or error of judgment on his part, there should be consultations with a specially qualified medical assessor. If the doctors were in agreement that euthanasia was desirable, the final decision might then rest with the patient's relatives.

(4) If we are to call it murder to take man's life with his own consent, then we must call it theft to take his

fatal. A steadily increasing proportion of cancer sufferers, until recently doomed, can now be cured. People with heart disease may live long and useful lives. It is impossible to make hard and fast rules when medical science is in a state of continual change and progress. The doctor's duty is to maintain life as long as possible by every means in his power.

(2) This argument is tantamount to a plea for the legalisation of suicide. If physical suffering is a valid excuse for cutting life short, then why not other forms of suffering? Unless a patient were aware of his condition and deliberately asked for euthanasia, it would be an act of intolerable cruelty to let him know that such a measure was being considered. A request for euthanasia might easily be due to temporary despondency; a person in great pain is not always responsible for his utterances. It is familiar ground that a high proportion of suicides are people who are 'calling for help' and do not really (in their subconscious minds) intend to kill themselves, but go too far. Among those requesting euthanasia, the risk of (irreversible) error would be even greater.

(3) Doctors do not always correctly estimate a patient's recuperative powers and should not be saddled with the responsibility of making what is, in effect, a decision to murder. It could also be an impossibly heavy burden for relatives to have to be the final arbiters in cutting short the life of one linked to them by ties of blood or affection. On the other hand, legalised euthanasia would be a ready-made weapon for unscrupulous relatives which no amount of legal precautions could entirely guard against.

(4) (Some) The Christian religion

property with his consent, which is absurd. As for pain, no doubt it has its uses, if only as a danger signal. But not many of us would go on enduring a pain we could avoid. And none but a fanatic would advocate the cessation of human effort to alleviate or abolish pain.

(5) In practice, 'mercy killings' by relatives have usually been treated with understanding and a measure of lenience in the courts; even in the past, few of the culprits were sentenced to death, and the sentence was almost never carried out. Many unfortunate people are born who have no hope of ever leading a normal life or of being anything but a tragic liability to their families. Such people should not be forced to enter on a travesty of life, much less to continue it.

teaches that it is wrong to take away human life. 'Thou shalt not kill' is an unequivocal command. Moreover, it is possible that pain itself has a significant place in the scheme of evolution and serves some mysterious moral purpose.

A civilisation based on a high conception of the value of human life cannot countenance the deliberate taking of life where no crime has been committed by the sufferer. A large number of people supported the abolition of capital punishment, even for murder cases, and there was a far better case for it than for euthanasia.

(5) The danger of such cheapening of the respect for human life was seen under the Nazis, who had millions of people put to death for imaginary 'racial defects'. It is better that a few should suffer unwanted life than that the door should be opened, even to the slightest extent, to such ruthless practices.

EXAMINATIONS:
Should They Be Abolished?

Pro: (1) Examinations, as at present organised, test only a certain kind of skill. Some people have a good memory and a special facility which enables them to pass examinations and achieve brilliant results, while completely lacking any capacity for original thought or imagination. Yet such people will continue to be unduly favoured by employers and academic authorities while examinations remain in their present form and are still taken as a criterion of worth.

(2) Examinations are the bane of a pupil's life. They involve cramming,

Con: (1) The ability to pass an examination is currently decried, but it is in reality a valuable quality. It shows a capacity for coping with new problems without the protection of the accustomed environment and for expressing thought in a manner intelligible to others. A *viva voce* examination will elicit any special qualities which the written examination may have passed over, or, equally well, reveal the lack of them.

(2) The mental effect of preparation for examinations is excellent, since even the dullest exert themselves,

depress the pupil, and often rob him of mental vitality at an early age. Subservience to the examination curriculum necessarily frustrates any initiative on the part of the teacher and deadens the atmosphere of school life. Some of the subjects set in examinations, particularly by the older universities, bear no relation to the intended course of study and academic future of the student and merely involve an irritating detour. A report by schools inspectors into a South London borough which still retains four grammar schools said that, although good exam results were achieved, this was at the cost of a 'dull and narrow' curriculum. Because of this limited range of exam-led objectives, the report warned, the schools were failing to develop many of their pupils, including the brightest.

(3) Examinations are set as if all schoolchildren have reached the same mental level at the same age. Medical and educational investigators are agreed that this is not so. Nor does the mental development of boys and girls follow the same course. School records are much more reliable than examinations for the assessment of these differences and adjustments to correspond with them.

(4) Educationists are biased in favour of competition and the brilliantly clever pupil. In consequence, the less gifted pupils who need most teaching are neglected and a specialised curriculum that frustrates the true purpose of education is maintained.

(5) A test of the examination system showed that the same papers, when marked by different examiners, were placed in an entirely different order of merit and that the same papers, marked by the same examiners after an interval of some months, then received widely differing marks. This

while no discoverable harm is done either physically or mentally, except to a handful of unbalanced persons. The curriculum exercises a wholesome restraint on teachers and discourages too fanciful schemes of education. Pupils of schools not subject to examinations sometimes show startling gaps in their knowledge.

(3) The principle of unequal development by age has been recognised at the primary school level by the institution of an exam for 'late developers'. At later ages, the inequality has considerably decreased. Experienced examiners can rapidly assess the general standard of papers they are marking. In national exams, such as the A levels, examining boards can adjust the markings if the general standard indicates that the papers were set at a too difficult level. Indeed, one big advantage of the whole examination system is that it has great flexibility and can be adapted to many varying needs. The new 16-plus GCSE exam is a case in point. Longer term, official studies are now in hand for possible big changes to A levels – putting less emphasis on written papers and more on practical work (e.g. more oral tests for languages, more weight attached to understanding processes than to regurgitating facts, more importance attached to fieldwork in geography).

(4) Teachers are no more to be trusted to give an impartial judgment on a pupil than other people. Examiners have the advantage of being impartial as between pupils. It is a flaw in our educational system that the clever and the stupid have to be taught together, but this should be remedied by better organisation of classes and the provision of more teachers. The difficulty would exist if there were no examinations. It would be equally harmful to the cleverer students to be

clearly proves the danger of relying solely on examinations as a valid basis of judgment.

neglected and have their desire for advancement frustrated.

(5) Modern examiners judge general intelligence as well as book knowledge. An intelligence test forms an integral part of many examinations nowadays. Where intelligence and character are both of importance in a candidate, an examination, supplemented by an interview, remains the best method of selection.

FASCISM:
Should It Be Outlawed in Britain?

Pro: (1) Whatever the divergence of opinions on the cause and nature of Fascist theories, there is no denying that they have in practice caused unexampled devastation and suffering in the modern world and have set back the economic and cultural life of Europe by decades, if not centuries. (In this context, the popular equation of Fascist with Nazi, although they are not actually identical, may be accepted for practical purposes.) As the international courts officially outlawed Nazi ideas during the post-war trials of war criminals, it is anomalous that British offshoots of them should not be declared illegal and similarly outlawed.

(2) Fascism and Nazism, as movements, preach subversion and the use of violence to attain their ends. A peaceful population has no protection against them, and the fate of Austria in 1938 and of the Spanish Republican government in 1936 shows the folly of trying to deal with them without the aid of special legislative measures.

(3) Fascists seek to divide the community against itself by the provocation of racial and sectional hatred.

Con: (1) Many aggressive wars have been fought in the past in the name of movements and ideologies, but their causes have always been a complex of interwoven economic and political factors. The outlawing of Fascism would give no guarantee against the recurrence of war. The increasing horror and devastation of war is due more to the development of new means of killing than to the influence of any ideology. It would be no more logical to outlaw Fascism than to ban Communism (confrontations with which have in fact been responsible for most of the local wars since 1945).

(2) The only certain cure for Fascism is a contented population. Given this, or at the least a government determined to secure it, Fascist ideas would fail to secure anything more than a tiny audience, of no importance or threat – especially in Britain, where the system of government is fundamentally stable, as it was not in Spain or Austria. Violence breeds violence, and coercion in peace-time is undesirable. More harm is done through the publicity given to Fascist movements by their opponents

The inflammatory nature of their doctrines has already led to disturbances and has brought suffering and fear to peaceful members of the community. Among those not directly affected, they create an atmosphere of unrest and instability which leads eventually to disbelief in the stability of government. The influx of Asian and African people since the early 1960s has made it all the more important to prevent the kind of tensions that the Fascists strive to foment. If Fascist-style and neo-Fascist movements were outlawed, they would soon cease to trouble the peace of the community, for underground movements do not prosper in this country. The potential present-day threat from unbridled racialist groups is evident in France, where the resurgence of an ultra-rightwing party has largely falsified normal political considerations in the National Assembly.

than through any influence that Fascist ideas might have of themselves.

(3) The airing of racial questions in public enables the listener to clear his mind of prejudice and provides a safety valve for the upholders of racial doctrines. Prejudices are not the monopoly of Fascists; if everybody holding them were to be outlawed, the liberty of a number of respectable citizens would be endangered. The penalising of people who have not yet committed any crime would, of itself, savour of authoritarian methods and be repugnant to the spirit of English law. The lack of Press publicity received by neo-Fascist movements, in recent years, has been the most effective weapon against them. To drive them underground would not only be more dangerous than allowing them to operate openly but would be an infallible means of ensuring their survival.

FREEDOM OF INFORMATION ACT

Pro: (1) Successive British governments, along with most of the civil servants working for them, have become obsessed with secrecy to an unparalleled degree. So have many bodies in other walks of life (e.g. those representing the medical and other professions). The notorious 'catch-all' Section 2 of the Official Secrets Act makes it a criminal offence for any Crown servant to reveal any information without authority and also an offence for anyone to receive that information. Under this long-outdated Act, therefore, it would even be a crime to disclose the brand of biscuits carried on a Foreign Office tea trolley!

Con: (1) The Conservative Governments of the 1980s acknowledged that the Official Secrets Act is unsatisfactory in its present form. Previous Labour Governments promised to repeal Section 2 (in 1974 and again in 1976), but, for one reason or another, failed to do anything about it. The main problem has always been the difficulty of getting agreement on what should take its place. That was why an earlier liberalising attempt, the Protection of Information Bill, did not get through Parliament in 1979 – and also, in turn, why many parliamentarians feel that freedom of information legislation is still not the right

There is a crying need for more open government, in all spheres, and an essential ingredient is the passing of a Freedom of Information Act, giving the public much greater access to factual data in the possession of official sources.

(2) No reasonable person objects to laws aimed at protecting (say) the nation's foreign policy or defence secrets. But the spurious 'protection' of information on such matters as environmental pollution or product safety is a very different story. People should also have a right, in particular, to look at files kept about themselves or their children – for instance, their personal medical records, notes relating to their status on building society or council housing department waiting-lists, school records, and so on. This would enable them to query or correct details they believe to be inaccurate. As things stand, people rarely get the chance – and then, usually, only by accident – to remedy wrong information which has crept into their files, with the result that they are often unjustly victimised without ever discovering why.

(3) An even more serious aspect of the official obsession with secrecy is the danger that some bodies cloaked by it, such as the security services, may come to think of themselves as also protected from the normal constraints of the law. Hence the profound public anxiety in the mid-1980s about allegations of illicit telephone-tapping by MI5, the infiltration of undercover agents into organisations like the Campaign for Nuclear Disarmament, the keeping of files on admittedly 'non-subversive' bodies such as the National Council for Civil Liberties, and the use of phone-tap material by Government Ministers for purely political purposes. A hurried investi-

answer. Even supporters of such an Act recognise that safeguarding the secrecy of the nation's military plans, and the like, would remain essential. Accordingly, one danger is that, on the pretext of protecting national secrets of this kind, exempted from the normal provisions of any freedom of information laws, some future government might be tempted to introduce measures that were even more restrictive than at present. In short, the supposed 'freedom' legislation could actually prove to be counter-productive.

(2) Whatever the individual's rights in this country, the people most responsible for guarding those rights are, ultimately, his or her elected representatives, the MPs. It is they who must take the lead in challenging any official mistakes or excesses. This explains why the Tory leadership in the mid-1980s opposed any Freedom of Information Act whose implementation would be backed up finally by the courts – because that, it is held, would reduce Ministers' accountability to Parliament. As for passing laws to give greater access to personal files, it would be crucial – but extremely difficult, if not impossible – to ensure that people could not simultaneously find out too much about *others*. (The amount of information which can be gathered about any individual Briton today, by entirely legitimate means, is already quite horrific.)

(3) It is only in spy thrillers that Britain's security services are depicted as acting outside the law. In real life, they are civil servants, obliged to work strictly by the book. Lord Bridge's investigation, for example, found that no British Government since 1970 had issued a phone-tapping warrant which broke the rules. Even so, as an added precaution, the rules were tightened

gation by a former Lord Justice of Appeal, Lord Bridge, appeared to show that all listed phone-taps had been properly authorised – but in fact said nothing of any 'freelance' operations not covered by Ministerial warrant. While some of the accusations may be exaggerated, disclosures made by one or two former civil servants (who 'blew the whistle' because of their concern about alleged breaches) do undeniably give grounds for suspecting that security operations *have* occasionally got out of hand, to put it no higher.

(4) Since the 1960s, the United States, Canada, Australia, France, New Zealand and Sweden have all passed freedom of information legislation. An opinion poll in August 1986 (on the 75th anniversary of the Official Secrets Act) showed that two-thirds of all British voters now favour a Freedom of Information Act, subject to adequate safeguards for national security, crime and personal privacy. Individuals coming out publicly in support of such an Act even included three of Whitehall's most elevated ex-mandarins (Sir Douglas Wass, Sir Patrick Nairne and Sir Frank Cooper – former Permanent Secretaries of, respectively, the Treasury, the DHSS and the Defence Ministry). Also bearing out suspicions that the real opponents of freedom of information are, on the whole, politicians in power rather than civil servants, all the Civil Service unions have likewise said they support the measure, declaring that more open government would lead to better decision-making and fewer 'unauthorised leaks'. In 1986, too, the leaders of three of the main political parties – Labour, Liberal and SDP – each stated that they would introduce a Freedom of Information Bill once they won power. What possible

subsequently through the establishment of new procedures, whereby people now have the right to find out if their phones *have* been tapped. At the same time, it should be pointed out that MI5 and the Special Branch would be failing in their duty if they did *not* keep a check on potential subversives or even just on apparently innocent people known to have fairly regular links with such characters. The fundamental point here, though, is that no Freedom of Information Act could stop abuses, if any, in such specialised areas; the only effective way to do so is still by some form of the existing secrets legislation (albeit rationalised, to get rid of the present anomalies), with accountability remaining vested in Ministers and Parliament at the end of the line.

(4) Experience in other countries, notably the USA, shows that, even when the democratic presumption of a right to know is entrenched in the law, the appearance of greater openness can be misleading. The process of trying to influence or manipulate public opinion, by means of calculated leaks to the media from government or bureaucracy, goes on as intensively as before. As for freer access to documentation, much could depend on whether outsiders (including journalists) knew which documents to ask for – it's not the civil servants' job to make themselves unduly helpful on that score. Despite the crises of conscience which ostensibly led the 'whistle-blowers' to step out of line, the basic dilemma for Whitehall is this: effective government demands that Ministers can have total confidence in their civil servants, so any Freedom of Information Act would need built-in safeguards to ensure that civil servants could go on giving advice to their political masters

excuse can there be for any further delay?

without having their names *unfairly* spotlighted in the newspapers. Since the needs are irreconcilable at present, and in any case the proposed legislation could not be as far-reaching as many people expect, it's not hard to see why such a measure still hasn't been adopted by those who have the actual responsibility of power.

(See also CENSORSHIP)

FULL EMPLOYMENT

Pro: (1) Every member of a community has a right to employment. There will always be a certain minimum of unemployed persons — married women leaving work but remaining temporarily in benefit, seasonal workers, and a small hardcore of unemployables. But any talk of maintaining a permanent 'pool' of unemployed is heartless and immoral, treating the worker as a mere unit and ignoring his moral and material needs as a member of the community.

(2) Unemployment itself, by reducing general purchasing power, restricts production and breeds more unemployment. It is an integral part of the 'trade cycle' which was a feature of the old system of unrestricted competition. This unregulated and chaotic working of the economy is now condemned not only by socialists but also by intelligent supporters of capitalism. The modern trend is towards the proper planning and zoning of industry to correspond with the country's needs, and full employment is quite possible, and is indeed an integral feature, under such a system.

(3) An adequate degree of State control, together with the growth of combination among employers,

Con: (1) Full employment, in the last analysis, is against the interests of the working classes. It makes for a lack of flexibility between industries and industrial areas. The growth of new industries and the decline of others, due to changes in standards and technological advances, must be taken into account. Failure to provide the available labour for the development of new industries adversely affects production and, in the long run, harms the interests of the workers, since it inevitably results in a decline in the world market.

(2) The planning of industry to match available manpower cannot be achieved on a national scale. Such planning does not take into account the constantly changing relations of the different countries in the world markets and their financial interdependence. It could only exist on a basis of complete self-sufficiency, which is difficult for most countries and impossible for Britain. The alternative is for the State to finance unproductive public works in times of crisis in order to provide employment, a practice which would lead to still further distortion of the industrial situation.

(3) The effect of full employment

should curb the anarchic practices of individuals which are the ultimate cause of international crises. The advocates of a large pool of unemployed persons are mainly right-wing politicians who see it as a way to combat inflation (as under Britain's Conservative Governments from 1979 to the mid-1980s) or those big producers who stand to gain by competition between workers in the labour market.

(4) No justification whatever can be made for subjecting anyone to the demoralisation and semi-starvation which was such a blot on our national life between the wars, when mass unemployment was rife. If individual employers are unable or unwilling to cope with the manpower problem by technical advances and improved organisation of production and distribution, then the State must step in and perform its duty to the citizens as a whole. A dogmatic policy which tolerates more than three million jobless, preferring to pay them vast sums in unemployment benefits rather than keep them in productive work (albeit sometimes outmoded), must surely be nonsensical in economic terms.

(5) We have learned enough in the last century or so to insure against the effect of sweeping economic changes caused by new inventions (e.g. automation). Compensation for redundancy is only a stop-gap. A truly effective government could see that new industry keeps pace with invention.

is, in practice, a shortage of labour and resultant competition between employers to obtain manpower. This leads to over-high wages and excessive demands from the workers, which constitute an unbearable charge on industry. The problem would inevitably be solved by the importation of foreign labour which would accept the lower standards (of pay and working conditions) that the maintenance of industry and the export markets would require.

(4) The demand for full employment is a Utopian socialist doctrine which has the effect of robbing the employer of the fruits of his industry. In the long run, it leads to the export of industry and the ruin of the home economy. It is to be noted that Labour governments which have upheld it in theory have never put it fully into practice. Cutting back job openings in industries which are destined to dwindle (or even die out) is the only way to get the workforce to prepare itself for the new, technologically-based industries of the 21st century.

(5) The development of automation was causing redundancies which had already negated the doctrine of full employment, long before the effects of the latest international economic crises would have made this inevitable in any case. Insistence on the employment of unnecessary workers is as reactionary as the attitude of the machine wreckers in the Industrial Revolution.

(See also UNEMPLOYMENT, STATE REMEDY FOR)

GAMBLING, MORALITY OF

Pro: (1) Gambling is a natural human trait and is to be condemned

Con: (1) An evil that is old is not therefore to be condoned. Gambling

only if carried to excess. Its suppression would lead to the emergence of something worse, just as the suppression of alcoholic drinks is followed by graver evils. A recent survey in Britain showed that the stigma once attached to betting has largely disappeared: just over half of those questioned thought it was not harmful in moderation and nearly one-third thought it was not morally wrong at all.

(2) Love of sport is an important national characteristic and is inevitably accompanied by some degree of gambling, because both rest on the same psychological basis. It is part of the average man's make-up to enjoy taking risks, and the taking of risks is the essence of gambling.

(3) When a man can afford to gamble, no harm whatever is done. If he gambles when he cannot afford to do so, the fault is personal to him and does not imply that the same actions by other people are a fault in them. In general, the individual amounts wagered are usually quite low. Of the 14 million Britons who enjoy a traditional bet on the Epsom Derby each year, for instance, the average stake by male punters is less than £3, while women's 'investment' averages only 77p!

(4) Gambling adds an element of excitement to people's lives, which in the conditions of modern civilisation tend to be dull and uninteresting. By keeping alive the hope of personal improvement, which is difficult of attainment nowadays by more austere methods, it helps to prevent discontent and recourse to more harmful activities.

(5) In commerce, an element of gambling is essential and beneficial.

(6) Parliament has already recognised that it would be impossible to

may be a legacy from the animism of primitive man, but civilisation's task is to raise man above the primitive. According to the same survey mentioned opposite, those 'just over half' who thought betting did no harm in moderation still held that it was morally wrong, even so.

(2) True sport is damaged by gambling. The essence of gambling is to get something for nothing. Gamblers actually endeavour to avoid risks (though usually quite in vain) by relying on 'tips', 'exclusive information', 'systems', and other specious devices.

(3) Gambling is mere waste of effort, producing no addition to the community's wealth but increasing its inefficiency, misery and degradation. Its spread among women has had a pernicious effect on home life. As examples of such waste: 43 per cent of adult Britons regularly do the football pools – and an astounding 72 per cent of them buy at least one raffle ticket each year.

(4) The evil of gambling is that it distorts clearness of thought and helps people to avoid facing the more unpleasant realities of life. They would be far better employed in making personal efforts to improve their condition of life than in relying on illusory hopes of unearned wealth to achieve it for them.

(5) Trade which aims at getting a benefit for oneself by doing service to others is quite dissimilar from gambling. Speculation, which is true gambling, should be suppressed.

(6) In countenancing such immoral practices, the Government is abdicating from its proper function, which is the leadership of the people. According to one estimate, Britons now spend well over £6 billion a year on horses, dogs, gaming machines,

suppress gambling and, instead, has made practical use of this universal human instinct by introducing a tax on betting and by establishing lotteries (following the success of the Premium Bond draw). Gamblers thus contribute to the public finances instead of solely supporting bookmakers and football pool promoters.

bingo, football pools and other forms of gambling – almost treble the amount a mere decade or so ago, and now nearly half the total budget for education throughout the UK. One can readily imagine the benefits that money wasted on gambling would bring if devoted to more productive purposes.

(See also LOTTERIES)

HOMOSEXUALS, SOCIAL RECOGNITION OF:
Has It Gone Too Far?

Pro: (1) Since the 1967 Sexual Offences Act, which decriminalised certain sexual acts between men under certain conditions, homosexuals have benefited from liberal public attitudes which have conferred an unprecedented degree of social acceptance. But this acceptance has encouraged militant homosexuals to make demands for special treatment, tantamount to privilege, in such fields as education, employment and housing. Heterosexuals do not demand special treatment or privileges. Nor should homosexuals, who should be grateful for the tolerance extended to them.

(2) It is ridiculous to expect a perversion to be treated as normal. It goes against the natural order and, while we should have some sympathy towards these people, it is the gift of a tolerant society, not a right. In return for tolerance, homosexuals should cease their onslaught on traditional family values and recognise that their militancy is counterproductive and their proselytising distasteful, a corrupting force on

Con: (1) The 1967 Sexual Offences Act made only a limited reform affecting men over 21. There remains a differential in terms of the age of consent, which is 16 for heterosexuals, and in legal definitions of privacy, which place restrictions on homosexual men that do not apply to heterosexuals. This in turn informs public policy, whereby recent legal judgments have been held to indicate that homosexuality, both male and female, is only tolerated in law, not accepted on equal terms. This means that the level of social acceptance at any one time is dependent on the whim of public opinion, an inadequate safeguard.

(2) Homosexuality *is* normal – a naturally recurring feature of the spectrum of human sexuality, present in all societies, in all classes and in all centuries. In the same way that a majority of people will always be heterosexual, a minority of perhaps 10 per cent will be homosexual. That is the natural order, and gay men and lesbians are part of it and should be

93

young people and a destabilising factor in society.

(3) One of the prime purposes of marriage is procreation, which obviously cannot apply to homosexuals. There is no longer any legal bar on them living together, if they so wish. But to treat homosexual couples as if they were married is absurd and an insult to normal married and family life. Although so-called marriages have taken place between homosexual males in the Netherlands, for example, such ceremonies are hideous travesties that devalue the basic unit of society, the family. The handicap of childlessness shows that homosexual relationships cannot be treated on a par with heterosexual ones. The legal status of marriage was developed to safeguard the family, not to legitimise odd relationships based on a bizarre sexual quirk.

(4) The drive to include homosexuality in the curriculum in schools and treat it as on a par with heterosexuality is particularly pernicious. It exposes young children to immoral and dangerous ideas and could corrupt them into an unsatisfactory and warped way of life. And to promote gays and lesbians as suitable foster parents, which a number of local councils have tried to do, is to court disaster and open the children to exploitation and a bad upbringing.

so treated. Homosexuals are already members of families, who should accept and value them. It is rejection of a minority that is socially destructive, not its integration.

(3) Childlessness is no barrier to love and no criterion by which to value the depth or sincerity of a relationship, as many married couples who cannot have children (or choose not to) will confirm. There is no need for homosexuals to ape heterosexual conventions, although a public affirmation of love is a stabilising factor in any relationship. From a more material point of view, it is also important to ensure the rights of partners in the event of death or illness. Bereaved partners have lost their homes, for example, because relatives have refused to recognise the bond between the couple and have claimed the legal ownership of property, or because local councils have given no weight to the surviving partner's rights.

(4) Sexual orientation is generally fixed in advance by the time a child has reached the age of about four. Children are not corruptible, in the sense that they can be turned into homosexuals. But for that 10 per cent or so who will grow up homosexual, it is important that they should know they are not freaks and thus avoid an unnecessarily painful adjustment in late adolescence. It is equally important for their heterosexual peers to know that homosexual people exist as full human beings. And studies have shown that children brought up in homosexual households turn out no different from others.

IMMIGRATION:
Should The Present Restrictions Be Lifted?

Pro: (1) Britain always prided herself in the past on holding her doors open to the needy and to victims of oppression from other countries. Protestants from France, Jews from most European countries, refugees from Poland, Hungary and other parts of Eastern Europe, and workers from every Commonwealth country . . . all these have already enriched our economy and our social and cultural life. Since the early 1960s, successive restrictions have been imposed to stop the big post-war increase in the influx of immigrants. But experience has proved that most of the fears which led to these restrictions were ill-founded, and we should now get rid of the injustices they have brought in their wake.

(2) Beginning with Malaysia and Singapore in the 1950s, Tory administrations offered British passports to minorities which might be discriminated against when former colonies became independent. By 1968, as a result, there were 400,000 Asians throughout the world who had the right of entry to Britain as full British citizens. Through our ensuing legislation, however, we have reneged on our promise to many of these people. We have a moral obligation – and should keep our word to them.

(3) The 1968 Commonwealth Immigrants Act was pushed through Parliament in less than a week. Two years later, in a case before the European Commission of Human Rights, the British Government admitted that this Act was racially discriminatory in 'intention and effect'.

(4) Recent history shows that

Con: (1) The welcoming of immigrants was reasonable when the population was relatively small and industrial opportunities were increasing rapidly. Britain has now reached a stage when the population is already too large for comfort. Even before the economic recession of the mid-1970s, industry had ceased to expand at anything like its previous rate; and, in the pressure for jobs, it is inevitable that recently arrived immigrants find it difficult to get work or are among the first to be laid off, swelling the unemployment burden. Employment statistics published in 1986 showed that ethnic minorities in Britain had grown to about 2.5 million people. Whereas the unemployment rate for all males was then 11.5 per cent, the rate for the non-white population stood at 21.3 per cent. Yet the number of immigrants accepted for settlement in the UK the previous year was 55,360 (about 4,400 more than in 1984). In the circumstances, surely, this is still a generous rate.

(2) The chief motive for the legislation in this earlier period, slowing down the immigration rate, was not so much to ease the pressure on space and resources, caused by the huge increase in the preceding 2–3 years, but more because the uncontrolled influx presented too great a risk of straining race relations. Subsequent legislation against race discrimination, as well as the work of the Race Relations Board and the efforts of local community officers, serve to show that the original concern about the size of the problem to be tackled was well founded.

Britain is perfectly able to take a higher rate of Commonwealth immigration, if the political will is there. We did so in 1972, when we accepted some 25,000 additional Asians, expelled from Uganda – virtually doubling the previous annual immigration rate. In terms of any extra strain on jobs, accommodation, schools, etc., the higher intake caused far fewer difficulties than had been anticipated – proving that we *could* successfully absorb a bigger total each year, on a regular basis, than the numbers allowed in at present.

(5) It took years to persuade the British Government to remove such anomalies as the double standard for male and female immigrants, whereby husbands allowed entry were entitled to bring in their wives with them but, previously, wives were not entitled to bring in their husbands. Other ideas arousing justifiable complaints include the use of 'virginity tests' by immigration officers at Heathrow airport, as well as blood tests to determine a child's parentage. Several more injustices remain. For instance, in India, Pakistan and Bangladesh, dependants seeking to join heads of families already settled in Britain are having to wait up to two years for a first interview with British officials. Even then, the red tape of documentary proof and checking frequently results in delays of three to four years, all told, in the processing of applications. There have also been complaints that some of the questions asked by immigration officers are misleading or irrelevant – even dealing with such unlikely topics as chickens, oxen and string beds. All this has been described as 'intolerable' by the Commission for Racial Equality, in a report declaring that the immigration rules operate unfairly and unjustly against coloured families

(3) This particular Act was introduced to reduce the sudden huge increase in the flow of East African Asians – particularly from Kenya, which had just embarked on 'Africanisation', thus depriving many of the Asian inhabitants of their former means of livelihood. As with all other British legislation on the subject, however, the purpose was not to bar the door completely to immigrants – merely to cut the rate to a level we could cope with. That precaution remains necessary to this day.

(4) The Ugandan Asians were a special case. Victims of political blackmail, they faced danger not only to their property but possibly even to their lives (which had not been the case in Kenya, for instance). But their reception, on humanitarian grounds, necessitated the establishment of special camps and many other costly and difficult arrangements which could certainly not become a regular feature of our immigration procedure. Even though there was a specific campaign on the Ugandan Asians' behalf, the task of resettling such a big additional influx took a good while longer than had been hoped.

(5) Steps have now been taken to hasten immigration procedures in these countries (and to revise the list of questions asked). One cause of the delay is the need to sort out fake applications from the genuine. Many supposed 'dependants' turn out to be no relation of the person concerned (i.e. the immigrant already in Britain). There have also been many cases of couples arranging to become engaged, at long distance, to permit one to join the other over here; then, once the formalities have thus been circumvented, the engagement is broken off. ... In some areas, immigration officers have reported that *90 per cent*

attempting to be reunited. The rules, it said, are far more likely to keep out genuine applicants than to let in 'bogus' immigrants.

(6) Another disturbing fact revealed by the Commission for Racial Equality report is that, at UK ports of entry, the average length of time taken to interview an African visitor on arrival was nine times longer than for an EEC citizen. In similar vein, it found, black people were always more likely to be refused entry. One in 140 visitors from the New Commonwealth and Pakistan were refused, compared with one in 4,100 from the Old (white) Commonwealth countries.

(7) Both the Labour Party and the Alliance promised in 1986 that they would repeal or ease many of the present immigration rules, if they won power. Labour called for everyone born in Britain to have the right to citizenship automatically and also pledged to do away with rules stopping people from using marriage as a way of entering Britain and to relax the rules governing the admission of elderly parents or other relatives. The Alliance, putting the spotlight on one particular problem which will become increasingly urgent in the 1990s, has reminded everyone of the obligations that Britain has (or ought to have) towards the British Dependent Territory citizens in Hong Kong.

(8) The contribution made to the British economy by Commonwealth immigrants in recent years has been invaluable. They have filled the least popular jobs in public transport, industry, public health services and many other fields. A large proportion of doctors and nurses in our hospitals are of Commonwealth origin – and without them, many hospitals would have had to close. Transport authorities often claim that they are obliged

of the applicants 'could be expected to be lying about some aspects of their applications'. The plain fact remains that the Government has undertaken to admit all *genuine* dependants – and, despite the many difficulties posed by the fraudulent, the queue of applicants awaiting a decision on their case has already been practically halved.

(6) From some (mainly coloured) Commonwealth countries with particularly poor economic prospects, there is greater pressure to immigrate than from others. A closer check on the much higher number of arrivals from such countries is therefore both inevitable and essential.

(7) According to a Conservative Minister responsible for immigration matters at the Home Office, Labour's promises would open the door to tens of thousands more immigrants each year, while the Alliance (he alleged) was promising right of abode in Britain to no fewer than 3¼ million people from Hong Kong. The Minister, Mr David Waddington, added: 'It is a simple but undeniable fact that there is a limit to the number of newcomers any society can absorb, and we could not possibly accept all those who want to come.'

(8) Without dwelling on the aggravation of housing problems, the creation of bad feeling in communities where it was previously almost unknown, and the allegations of a sizeable immigrant contribution to the rise in crime, one fact is salient: in multi-racial Britain today, almost three per cent of the population was born in the New Commonwealth or Pakistan. In other European countries which have won praise in the past for their 'enlightenment' in accepting large-scale immigration from their former colonial territories – notably, France and the Netherlands – the equi-

to run fewer bus or underground services than in former years because they cannot get enough staff. That is just one example of Britain's national needs which a sensible easing of the immigration restrictions would help us to fulfil.

valent percentage is nothing like as high as ours.

(See also BRITISH COMMONWEALTH: IS IT A REALITY? CAN IT SURVIVE?)

INDETERMINATE SENTENCES FOR PROFESSIONAL CRIMINALS

Pro: (1) There is a small class of prisoners, the professional criminals, who consist of formidable offenders, men who are physically fit, who take to crime by preference, decline all normal work and, unlike the habitual criminal whose offences are of less gravity, are not amenable to reform. They should be sentenced to an indeterminate period of imprisonment (i.e. no date being specified for its conclusion, within the criminal's probable lifespan).

(2) These offenders should not be released until they have given satisfactory proofs of such an improvement in character as would make it safe to the community for them to be at large again. They can be observed by competent experts, who could arrive at accurate decisions. There is no need to detain them in prisons proper; penal colonies would be suitable for the purpose.

(3) Whether the aim of punishment is the protection of society or the reformation of the criminal, there is no justification for keeping a man in prison after he could safely be released. The indeterminate nature of the sentence would be maintained only as long as it were not safe to free

Con: (1) Except, perhaps, in the degree of their offences, there is no real difference between the habitual and the professional criminal. Provision has already been made for incorrigible offenders to receive long sentences (8–10 years) after a certain number of convictions, even if their ultimate crime was relatively minor, and this has been undeniably successful as a deterrent. The cry for indeterminate sentences is mainly an endeavour to avoid thoroughgoing social and prison reform. In extremely serious cases, judges can already impose a lower limit on a convicted man's jail term – ordering that he should serve (say) a minimum of 25 years of the sentence before being considered for release. In effect, therefore, a more practical form of indeterminate sentence already exists.

(2) Conduct in prisons affords no proof of reform; most professional criminals show exemplary behaviour while in jail. Indeterminate sentences would give an impetus to religious hypocrisy. Jail conditions render psychological examination difficult; freedom is the only condition under which we can accurately judge of character.

the man. Preventive detention gives greater scope for education and remedial training than penal servitude or hard labour, which it replaces.

(4) To prevent abuses, a maximum period could be fixed. This would probably be desirable, anyway, while the system is in the experimental stage.

(5) The criminal of this type should be treated exactly as persons suffering from epidemic disease, who are isolated to prevent them from injuring society.

(6) Where tried, as in some parts of the USA, it has worked well. One advantage is that it prevents criminals from making plans with fellow prisoners to participate in the commission of new crimes on the expiry of sentence.

(7) Prisoners under indeterminate sentence could still be released provisionally, on parole. A system of after-care should be developed to deal with these, as other cases.

(3) The indeterminate sentence would, in practice, always become a long-period sentence, thus robbing the criminal of hope, if he does reform, and lessening the chances of him being willing to reform.

(4) Such sentences infringe the liberty of society and good government. Men serving indeterminate sentences would be put entirely at the mercy of a few officials, without check or criticism from the community.

(5) There is no analogy between disease and criminal acts; disease is not punished. Society must be just even in protecting itself.

(6) The indeterminate sentence in the USA is imposed, more often than not, on the less professional of criminals, who are still thought to have a chance of redeeming themselves.

(7) This would be an unfair risk for the community. There are already Discharged Prisoners' Aid Societies.

(See also PRISON REFORM)

INDUSTRIAL EXPANSION

Pro: (1) A steady increase (overall) in industrial output, and thus in trade between the nations, is necessary for the world's economic survival and for raising the living standards of all the world's peoples. Cyclical ups-and-downs are inevitable, but the general trend must always be towards expansion. The economic crises caused in the Western world by the actions of the Arab oil-producing nations, after the Middle East war of October 1973, demonstrate the chaos which can result when this trend is thrown out of balance by abnormal factors. Nevertheless, it was only a matter of time before industry began to adapt

Con: (1) Ever since the Industrial Revolution, expansion has been pursued for its own sake and there has been wide acceptance of the erroneous belief that industry and national economies alike would collapse unless they continued to grow. But there is clear evidence that, in many cases, the need is for contraction rather than expansion. As a result of the oil crisis, for example, it is doubtful if the motor manufacturing industry will ever be the same again, either in the rate of growth of its volume of production or in the nature of the vehicles it turns out, which will have to become generally more economic in fuel consump-

itself to the new conditions and resume its former progress.

(2) At the present rate of increase, the world's population is expected to reach 6,130 million by the turn of the century, a rise of 50 per cent on United Nations estimates of the population level in 1977. (See *Birth Control*.) Only by expanding the production of industry – notably, for example, in such fields as housing, transport, textiles, and all the farm machinery, chemicals, and so on, for the necessary growth in agricultural output, as well as future undersea farming – can we hope to meet the essential requirements for this huge populace. The process of industrial expansion will also be crucial, in itself, for providing the extra inhabitants with enough jobs.

(3) To husband the world's natural mineral deposits, scientists have long been investigating alternative materials in place of various metals, etc., and new methods of creating energy, which, similarly, will not use up existing resources. Without industrial expansion, in its broadest sense, such alternatives cannot be developed adequately to fulfil even our present needs. Moreover, it is the only way to ensure that the benefits are shared among all peoples. If the level of world industry remained comparatively static – not merely in manufacturing but in related fields such as energy supply and communications – the inevitable consequence would be simply to widen still more the existing gap between the rich and poor nations.

(4) Increased trade among nations with otherwise deeply opposed political and social systems is always conducive to the maintenance of peace between them. It was crucial in helping to end the East–West 'cold

tion than hitherto. Far from being undesirable, such a rationalisation of the industry heightens the possibilities of reducing pollution, reversing the continual worsening of traffic congestion, making better use of existing resources, and forcing the introduction of a proper, comprehensive transport policy.

(2) The real problems to be tackled are over-population and the stark fact that the world's natural resources are *finite*. Even though recession has helped to slow the rate of increase in consumption prevailing up to the end of the 1970s, all known oil deposits could still be exhausted within the 21st century, as could those of important metals such as copper. Instead of the spendthrift industrial expansion now encouraged, we should be seeking new ways to lessen the scale of demand, as a deliberate policy – before the pressures of over-population bring it about in any case. With increasing automation certain to reduce the overall proportion of jobs, in the long run, one of the big tasks for the future will be to educate people into using the greater leisure made available to them.

(3) The search for alternatives is all too often along the wrong lines. In Britain, for instance, there could be few more obvious examples of illogicality and waste than the long-standing rivalry for custom between the two nationalised energy suppliers, gas and electricity. It is a prime illustration that – quite apart from the future possibilities of harnessing inexpensive new sources like solar energy – the expansion of these particular industries, to meet anticipated consumption levels, could not only have been avoided (by a coherent joint energy policy) but was actually unnecessary. The heedless acceptance

war'. Any industrial expansion which permits a growth in this trade, thereby facilitating the improvement of relations between the power blocs, is surely to be welcomed – it's to everyone's advantage.

(5) In modern conditions, 'biggest is best' – greater efficiency, a wider range of products made available to more people, and cheaper prices.

(6) (Some) The biggest drive for the creation and building up of industry nowadays is in the Third World – the developing nations striving to achieve economic self-sufficiency and to start remedying the pernicious imbalance between themselves and the major industrialised powers. Are we to deny them that right?

of supposed 'progress', for its own sake, bedevils fields like transport, too. Instead of hideously expensive jet planes, it would be much cheaper and less pollutive to use airships for international freight-carrying purposes – indeed, the first successful efforts in this direction are already well under way. Internally, similarly, we could make far greater use of our inland waterways for transport between industrial centres, rather than continue to despoil the dwindling countryside with new motorways for the benefit of the juggernauts. If the pace of industrial production becomes somewhat slower and we have to make do with less as a result, then that is – quite simply – the price we must pay for mankind's survival.

(4) When a nation exports some of its skills, products or raw materials (exchanging them, in effect, for others it lacks), these are usually surplus to its domestic requirements and do not necessitate any expansion of its existing industry for the purpose. In some cases, notably in 'planned economy' countries, emphasis on foreign trade is at the expense of consumers at home; certain governments would do better to concentrate first on meeting unfulfilled demands within their own countries.

(5) On the contrary, many big industrial concerns are now recognising that a return to smaller units produces greater efficiency and is often the best way to satisfy local needs.

(6) (Some) It is only natural that developing countries should wish to end the economic dominance of their former colonisers. But attempts to make an immediate, massive increase in their own manufacturing industries are not necessary to achieve this. Usually, the principal wealth of such countries lies in their raw materials –

which, in colonial times, were acquired by the capitalist nations at the cheapest possible prices. The first priority should be for the developing countries to be guaranteed higher (and stable) prices for their raw materials in world markets.

INDUSTRIAL PSYCHOLOGY, APPLIED

Pro: (1) The essential idea of Scientific Management – that the processes and conditions of production (including salesmanship) are capable of being improved by systematic study – is a sound one. Industrial psychologists have realised the shortcomings of the generality of so-called efficiency experts and the great advantage of their work is that they look upon the problems chiefly from the human point of view.

(2) Industrial psychologists aim first and foremost at improving the conditions under which workers operate, so that unnecessary strains, whether due to physical fatigue, mental boredom or emotional antagonisms, e.g. between foremen and workers, may be eliminated. They take no side in disputes between employer and employed; all they are concerned with is that the knowledge at the disposal of the community which relates to these problems shall be applied and extended. In doing this, they have achieved excellent results, though the study is still incompletely developed. Even in a Communist State, industrial psychology would be needed.

Con: (1) Industrial psychologists are merely scientific managers and efficiency experts under another name. They are aiming almost exclusively at making the worker more efficient within the capitalist system. They expect to increase 'productivity', i.e. more output per man. In the long term, though, the net result will be a reduction of working staffs and more unemployment.

(2) One of the most important factors in industry is the question of incentives. The supporters of this movement rely on it to save the industrial system from the consequences of its imperfections. Industrial psychologists necessarily have to work under the conditions imposed by these flaws, heightening the suspicion with which they are regarded by most of the employees for whom they prescribe. The beneficial results are therefore likely to be small, but industrial psychology's semblance of concern for the welfare of the workers no doubt consoles those who believe that, with trifling adjustments, the present system is satisfactory and likely to be permanent.

(See also SCIENTIFIC MANAGEMENT)

102

INTELLIGENCE TESTS

Pro: (1) Tests of the capacities of children and adults, where used, and decisions as to the kind of work for which they are most fitted, formerly depended entirely on unscientific and stereotyped examinations. It is now generally conceded that such examinations are inadequate, and intelligence tests have been widely adopted to supplement them. There is a strong argument for abolishing written examinations altogether, at some stages, and for using intelligence tests in their place.

(2) For schools purposes, IQ tests have the advantage of being short and therefore convenient – an assessment can be completed in less than half an hour. It is almost impossible to falsify the results through prior 'swotting' because there are so many different versions of such tests – and copies of most of those used in schools are restricted to people authorised to carry out the testing. For ordinary exams, it is well understood that a pupil who appears to have an average of 50 per cent, for all his papers, may in fact have scored 70 in some subjects at which he excels and only 30 in others at which he is poor. In like vein, this is one reason why many supporters of IQ tests now reject a single composite score from the test results and, instead, prefer new-style tests which produce what they call the 'profiling of abilities'. Among advantages of such a profile are: first, to pinpoint those areas where a pupil may need particular help (perhaps without the difficulty having been apparent previously); and secondly, to give a pointer to where the pupil should begin the next steps in his or her educational programme.

Con: (1) The use of written examinations is admittedly limited, but no adequate case has been made out for their abolition, especially in the higher levels of education. They are the only method of testing the acquisition of knowledge, the possession of which is even more important than the capacity to react quickly to situations where experts are required. Many intelligence tests have no conceivable relationship to the problems of school or of life.

(2) In recent years, new findings in educational psychology and remedial techniques have discredited the concept of fixed ability. It is surely crucial to draw a distinction between the hypothetical assessment of a child's development on a very wide range of skills and the appraising, as happens in practice, of only a narrow group of skills in a 'one-off' test. Without a series of tests over a prolonged period, how could the measuring of one type of skill have any validity, in the long term, as a guide to the complex functioning of the human mind on a broader plane? It must be doubted, too, whether IQ testing takes adequate account of the extent to which children's performance may be affected by such factors as motivation and cultural bias – not merely as regards the tests but also in their entire prior attitude to the educational process. Nor can one have much confidence, despite the faith many parents and teachers still have in IQ 'scores', that the testing is able to distinguish the fact that a child may have got an answer wrong but nevertheless arrived at a concept which showed that he or she had exercised their intelligence creatively.

(3) In adult life, manual dexterity, memory, reasoning powers, swift reaction to sensations, etc., are required to varying degrees in many different occupations. The crude guesswork on which employers have had to rely in the past for information about their work-people has put many square pegs in round holes, with unfortunate results to both employer and employed. Intelligence tests have been used with great success in the armed forces to determine the kind of jobs for which men are best suited.

(4) Intelligence tests do not claim to be character tests, but the fact that they do not deal with every side of life is no reason to ignore their application to the sides they do test.

(5) That intelligence tests are remarkably accurate is proved, for example, by the fact that the results of the tests applied to the American Army by Columbia University examiners gave a grading of the soldiers almost identical with that given by the officers who had had the same men under them for many months.

(6) There is a strong case for their being included in entrance tests for all universities. This would eliminate the wastage arising from the admission of students who are capable only of cramming.

(3) Trial and error, and experience, are the soundest tests for vocational suitability. Putting square pegs in round holes is almost always due to the rigidity of our economic system and labour market, whereby a young person entering one occupation is too often obliged to remain in it for the rest of his life. The result of an intelligence test may be rendered futile by the lack of jobs considered suitable for the examinees. Since production can never be correlated with the capacities of potential workers, promotion on the basis of the employer's judgment is the only satisfactory method of exploiting intelligence.

(4) These tests have the great shortcoming that they cannot test character – the qualities of initiative, hard work, determination, honesty, etc., which are more important in life and business than mere cleverness. Neither can they provide a fully reliable test of the all-important quality of power to grasp new ideas.

(5) They frequently break down in practice, because, for a start, they set questions to which the examinee must answer yes or no, though the only intelligent answer should often be long and qualified with all sorts of reservations. The testers often encounter resistance in adult examinees because of the apparent absurdity of the questions. Intelligence testing of soldiers ignores the qualities of endurance and courage which may be their most important assets.

(6) The wastage of university students is usually due to much more complex social or psychological causes.

INTERNATIONAL AUXILIARY LANGUAGES

Pro: (1) In areas such as the Mediterranean and India, common languages for communication between people speaking different tongues became widely accepted in the past to satisfy an obvious need. Latin was the international language of Europe for many centuries (and, within the Roman Catholic Church, is still used freely as a means of communication between church-people from different parts of the world). Commercial, political and social relations would be made easier by the adoption of an international auxiliary language.

(2) Esperanto and Ido are scientifically constructed languages, with flexible structure and the simplest grammar. They can be learned with ease by nearly everybody, arouse no national jealousies, and are not without literary possibilities.

(3) Basic English (consisting of a vocabulary of about 800 essential words with which any ideas can be expressed) is eminently suited to become an international language. It has obvious advantages over an artificial language and can be learnt in a very short time even by those ignorant of English.

(4) That Basic English should replace good normal English is not suggested. But there is no gainsaying its value where a good working knowledge of English is required, without a great expenditure of time. Basic English has been used in schools in Denmark, Poland, Rumania and Czechoslovakia, and is making headway in the East.

(5) In international affairs, the use of an international language would

Con: (1) Enough people are able to learn the one or two other languages besides their own which enable the business of the world to be carried on successfully. The newspapers and news agencies already spread, through translation, more information about the world than can be properly assimilated. It is erroneous to argue that the ability to communicate with people of other lands will promote international understanding. For example, many French people are well acquainted with English, and many English with French, but they have rarely been able to comprehend the psychology of each other's country.

(2) For many purposes, English and French are international languages already. They have acquired qualities, in the course of centuries of growth, far superior to those which any artificial language could have.

(3) If only its absurd spelling were rationalised, English would rapidly become accepted as the world's prime international language, even by those nations which do not regard it as such already. Its grammar is less complicated than that of most other languages. In its excessive simplification, Basic English has lost most of the vigour of the true English tongue.

(4) Basic English can no doubt be learnt with ease. But language has a dual function. It should enable us not only to express our own thoughts but also to understand those of others. Students of Basic English may express themselves adequately in English but would be lost in trying to understand an Englishman who used a vocabulary going well beyond the 800 or so essen-

save an enormous waste of time and expense involved in the use of interpreters and translators. It would also tend to avoid many of the disagreements and irritating misunderstandings between statesmen and diplomats, a good proportion of which are certainly due to their insufficient knowledge of one another's languages. Now that diplomacy has become world-wide in its scope, and so highly publicised, the old-fashioned closed corporation of diplomatic exchange is out of date. Accordingly, a language in which all speakers have the same standing, thereby ensuring that none can suspect collusion between others speaking an alien language, is more than ever necessary.

tial words of Basic English.

(5) The value of an interpreter is that he understands the idioms and turns of speech of a language as well as its more academic conceptions. Misunderstandings between statesmen would continue even if a common language were used, since they arise more from fundamental antagonisms in philosophy and interpretations of the meaning of words – and at times also from a clash of temperaments – than from any mechanical language difficulty. Many words are capable of different interpretations: for example, 'democracy', 'freedom', 'honour' – all words which occur frequently in international discussion. An artificial language would be equally unable to establish a definitive meaning for such words.

INTERNATIONALISM

Pro: (1) Despite the upsurge of nationalism that marked the period between the wars of 1914 and 1939, it is clear that the struggle of the future will be between classes and ideologies and not between nations. Nationalism has become obsolete as a basis of political organisation, since the development of communications has begun to render the whole world an economic unit.

(2) The nation is not eternal. It has existed for only a few hundreds of years, originating in response to the economic needs and development of the time. It will probably remain always as a reflection of differences in culture and custom, though these are tending to lessen with the increase in international communication, but its part in the world will sink to that

Con: (1) National rivalries and nationalism are more accentuated than ever. They transcend the class war, just as they destroy international agreements.

(2) The nation is a fundamental fact, and national patriotism is a persistent virtue. Nations may well form associations for their mutual economic benefit (for instance, the EEC), but each insists on retaining its individual identity.

(3) The international organisations mentioned, especially those of labour and political groups, cannot become of really major importance until their members control all the nations to which they belong, which is impossible. International combines often operate by making agreements to respect national frontiers. The UN is an

106

which the province, the county or the clan now plays in relation to the nation.

(3) The economic problems of most nations are similar. Hence, trade unionists and capitalists alike have been led to establish their own international organisations. The UN is a public recognition that isolation is an anachronism.

(4) A beginning has already been made in Europe with the EEC. Its first fruit, and probably the most important, was the abandonment of former national antagonisms between France and Germany. Now further stages are well under way with the admission of more countries to the Community, and with the proposed moves towards a much greater degree of decision-taking by majority vote (and, consequently, fewer occasions when member-countries could still use their power of veto).

(5) One example of the inevitability of internationalism is provided by the new African nations. They were mostly formed from territories arbitrarily thrown together by the economic needs of their conquerors, and their alignments are bound to be fluid.

(6) The advent of Socialism in some form or other, if only because all alternatives break down, will see the triumph of internationalism. General prosperity and culture will overcome the narrowness of nationalism.

(7) Internationalism is a noble creed to which all religions pay at least lip service. It must be the basis of world organisation if civilisation is to be saved from destruction by war and human folly. National differences are in reality no greater than those which often cause regional antagonisms within a country, and mutual tolerance can smooth them out.

(8) Internationalism is compatible

organisation of sovereign States and could not exist otherwise.

(4) The history of the EEC provides all too many examples of its membernations fighting principally for their own economic interests. Their attitude to nations outside their own organisation has often tended to be restrictive and mistrustful; it is only very recently that they have evinced the least sign of anything approaching true internationalism (and even then, the professed intentions have yet to be borne out). When General de Gaulle talked originally of the Community's eventual path towards greater European political unity, he still envisaged it only as a 'Europe des patries' ('Europe of the fatherlands') – not, in short, as an international body in which member-countries would have to give up any crucial aspects of their sovereignty.

(5) That separatism and not association is fundamental is proved by the new African countries, several of which were split by separatist demands within a short time of gaining independence.

(6) It is by no means certain that Socialism will triumph. Nevertheless, if it does, the national divisions and national peculiarities will survive. This is recognised even by the Communists, whose gospel is internationalism. A series of Socialist or Communist societies might not even be so closely allied as to form a federation.

(7) Internationalism postulates an unprecedented change in human nature. Most religious sects are limited by national frontiers, and their adherents, while they might aspire to internationalism, do not generally attempt to practise it.

(Some) Internationalism is bad because it implies the continuance of national divisions. Cosmopolitanism –

with true patriotism. It is only objected to by the 'my country, right or wrong' type of person.

a single World State – is a preferable objective.

(8) Internationalism in practice means anti-patriotism, and propaganda in its favour should be stopped.

(See also UNITED NATIONS ORGANISATION; UNITED STATES OF EUROPE)

IRELAND:
Should Ulster Join Eire?

Pro: (1) Despite the sectarian violence and near-civil war in Ulster since the late 1960s – stemming from the Protestant majority's fears and the Roman Catholic minority's grievances – it is almost inevitable, historically, that the whole of Ireland will eventually be reunited. Recent events have set back progress towards this, obviously; whatever time it takes for passions to cool, though, some form of agreed reunion will be the only commonsense solution in the long run.

(2) Since Northern Ireland's Stormont Parliament was abolished in 1972, the broad thrust of the British Government's policy has been to try to persuade the Ulster Unionists that they should reach an accommodation first with their Roman Catholic fellow-countrymen and then with the Dublin Government. In this light, it's worth noting that recent moves to introduce 'positive discrimination' in public sector employment for Catholics in Northern Ireland, i.e. giving them preference for job vacancies, aroused relatively little protest from the Unionist side. Equally, the Anglo-Irish Agreement reached in November 1985 (under the aegis of the two Prime Ministers, Dr. Garret FitzGerald and Mrs Margaret Thatcher) has already shown signs of producing measures –

Con: (1) The rest of Ireland is different in religion and race from the majority of Ulstermen. Northern Ireland's Protestants are implacably hostile to the dominating role played by the Roman Catholic Church in Eire. Their belief that persecution, due to religious and political bigotry, would be their lot if they joined the Republic is reinforced by Eire's refusal to grant such elementary rights as facilities for divorce and its often absurd but rigid censorship of literature and culture generally.

(2) British policy has been based on the optimistic assumption that the Irish Republic was moving, slowly but surely, towards becoming a pluralist society in which the civil liberties of the North's Protestants could be guaranteed. The removal of Eire's constitutional ban on divorce was to have been a crucial symbolic step along that path. In the event, the crushing defeat received by Dr Fitz-Gerald's Government in a referendum on the divorce issue, in June 1986, bore out that the reactionary influence of the Roman Catholic Church in the South is still virtually irresistible. The Protestant militants had no need to step up the level of violence – the South's referendum result had argued their case for them. It is now self-

in certain specific fields – for closer cooperation between North and South than at any time since partition. It may be significant that threats of violence tantamount to civil war made by Unionist extremists, in protesting against the new Agreement, did not in fact materialise.

(3) The north-eastern part of Ulster was responsible in large measure for the disastrous history of the Irish nation after 1913. The Covenanters committed treason before the Nationalists and set an example for unconstitutional proceedings. Today, clearly, reunion would be impossible until law and order has been restored in the North; but this does not preclude measures aimed at progress towards it – with power-sharing as the first step, until mutual suspicions have been proved groundless.

(4) The existence of two governments in such a small island is absurd. Partition cannot be a permanent solution.

(5) If Ulster is as superior in wealth as its protagonists claim, it would naturally have the dominant economic role in a united Ireland rather than be despoiled and dominated.

(6) All Ireland was an economic unit before political exigencies of the time led to what was then intended as a temporary official separation; neither side can be assured of future prosperity until they form such a unit again. The thousands of workers who now leave Eire to work abroad in England could be retained to build up the country's industry if the economy of Ireland as a whole were reintegrated.

(7) The Unionist question kept Ulster's industrial workers years behind the industrial workers of Great Britain, in conditions and ideas, and imposed a near-authoritarian rule on

evident that Northern Ireland's full integration with the UK, coupled with a reform package to improve conditions for working class Catholics in the province, has become the only feasible 'solution' (if there is one).

(3) Ulster has deserved well of England, which it supported throughout two world wars with Germany – while Eire, by its neutrality in the last war, provided a home for enemy activities. Notwithstanding the fearful strains of recent times, the great majority of Ulster's people remain deeply loyal to the United Kingdom – and the strength of this emotional attachment must not be under-estimated as a factor in their opposition to joining Eire.

(4) Hard facts dictated partition in the early 1920s. They have not really changed.

(5) Ulster would remain in a minority, unable to resist the extirpation of the things it cherishes. It would also be looked on as the milch cow for reviving Eire's flagging economy.

(6) The nature of its industries differentiates Ulster from the rest of Ireland, connecting it more directly with Glasgow, with the textile and engineering districts of England, and with England's international trade. Despite the EEC-inspired establishment of more multinational factories, the South is still predominantly agricultural and has nothing to offer which would compensate for the cutting of Ulster's industrial links to the mainland.

(7) Ulster's comparative prosperity was due to the steadiness and efficiency of its workers and traders – legacies of their Protestantism and Scottish extraction. Union with Eire would mean the levelling-down of Ulster, not the levelling-up of all Ireland. Alleg-

the country. With a united Ireland, Ulster's workers would soon be in the van of reform and playing a key part in the maintenance of political democracy.

edly undemocratic forms of government in the province, before the outbreak of the present troubles, were Ulster's only protection against subversive propaganda from Eire and the terrorist means used to secure its ends. This is borne out by the fact that, even though measures had already been agreed to iron out inequities of which the Catholic minority complained, the extremists gave them no chance to take effect before resorting to armed violence.

JURY SYSTEM:
A Serious Need for Reform?

Pro: (1) The protection formerly represented by the jury system is no longer necessary, now that the judiciary's independence of the state is accepted as sacrosanct and that there are, in any case, so many checks and balances against legal abuse. In nine cases out of ten, innocent people would prefer to be tried by a judge than by a jury, because they know their defence would be weighed up by a better, trained intelligence.

(2) In all but the most straightforward cases, juries are likely to be influenced by one dominant personality among their members and also (particularly in very complex proceedings) by the impression they pick up from the judge's summing up, rather than solely from the facts presented to them during the hearing. It is well known that a judge's summing up, however impartial in appearance or intention, will often indicate his own views between the lines.

(3) Whatever the merits of the jury system in criminal cases, they do not apply to anything like the same extent

Con: (1) People have a right to be tried by their peers; the 12 ordinary men and women who comprise a jury, under the British system, are more likely to arrive at the truth than a single judge, however capable. The system should certainly not be abolished – and even any reforms of it should be introduced with the greatest possible care – because it is the chief bulwark of the common man against abuse by the State or by individual members of the legal profession.

(2) The system, thought to have been established in England originally during the Norman period, developed to its present form and status because of the crucial role it played in abolishing abuses. A classic example was the Old Bailey case in 1670, when '12 good men and true' suffered fierce browbeating from the bench, were locked up for two nights without food or warmth and heavily fined (causing four of them to be kept in prison for several months afterwards), but still refused to convict two Quakers – William Penn (later the founder of

in civil proceedings. Some verdicts delivered by juries in civil cases have been notoriously unjust, usually as a result of sheer prejudice or ignorance among the jurors.

(4) Although what goes on in the jury room is supposed to be strictly secret, there is abundant subjective evidence to show that the great majority of juries, in trying to weigh evidence, are more swayed by superficialities and by evidence given orally in the witness-box than they are by documentary evidence. Equally, they are more susceptible to those appeals to emotion which are part of some barristers' stock-in-trade. Judges are harder to move and pay more regard to facts.

(5) For these and several other reasons, reform of the jury system is seriously needed. In cases where it is deemed that juries should now be dispensed with, three principal alternatives put forward are: trial by a single judge; by a bench of three judges (as in many appeal court hearings); or by a mixed tribunal of professional judge and two appropriately qualified lay judges. This last was proposed by the committee under Lord Roskill for the hearing of the most complex fraud cases. (The 'appropriately qualified' assessors recommended in the Roskill report, published at the beginning of 1986, would have been laymen with the special business knowledge fitting them to understand sophisticated financial ramifications.) Although the Government subsequently rejected this particular recommendation, it did indicate its intention to introduce other changes in the system – notably, abolition of the defence right, in criminal trials, to challenge (i.e. veto) up to three of the people being empanelled for the 12-strong jury.

Pennsylvania) and William Mead – who had been accused of 'preaching to an unlawful assembly'. It was only after this that the Chief Justice of the day delivered the opinion confirming 'the Right of Juries to give their Verdict according to their convictions' – a ruling which, ever since, has protected jurors from any fear of reprisal if their opinion contradicts that of Authority. As for suggestions that many juries are nevertheless unduly influenced by the judge's summing up, misdirection of a jury by the judge is dealt with by the appeal courts and any errors can be corrected there.

(3) In all cases where the credit of either party to a lawsuit is at issue, a jury is still the best tribunal because its members usually have more first-hand qualification than any judge to form a valid opinion upon facts connected with the daily life of ordinary people. The great widening of the pool for jury service in recent years – in terms of social class, sex, age, colour and so on – has removed earlier cause for criticisms (e.g. when only people who owned a certain amount of property were called as jurors).

(4) On the contrary, there is even more evidence – from the verdicts they hand down – that juries are not so easily beguiled by rhetoric as certain lawyers may imagine. The jurors are the sole arbiters of the facts, upon the evidence laid before them. That they may reach a view on the basis of someone's demeanour in the witness-box, therefore, is not a fault; frequently, it can be an essential feature of assessing the validity of the evidence.

(5) Trial by a single judge in criminal cases would be no less subject to controversy (*vide* the Diplock anti-terrorist courts in Northern Ireland). Where could enough experienced

Objections first arose partly because a defendant or his lawyer did not have to give reasons for the challenge: somebody might be rejected merely because he had a neat hair-style or was wearing a collar and tie. In recent years, as a result, there have been increasing complaints of abuse of the right, through attempts to 'pack' a jury with people thought likely (from their appearance) to be more favourable to the defence. Another reform decided by the Government, raising the previous age limit for jury service from 65 to 70, was aimed similarly at providing some counter-balance to the alleged 'anti-authority' bias of certain younger jurors.

(6) Juries represent public opinion, but this – alas! – can often turn out to be ill-informed, wrong-headed or unfairly prejudiced. Despite the traditional belief that they have made a priceless contribution to British justice, specific instances are, in fact, few and far between. Juries, for example, notoriously failed to check the horrific increase in death sentences, often for very trivial offences, that were imposed in earlier centuries. Judges, in contrast, *have* frequently contributed to social progress by their rulings.

lawyers – and finance – be found for the number of three-judge benches that would be needed? The Government's rejection of the Roskill committee's proposal for a mixed tribunal in fraud cases rather suggests that official sources still have more faith in the jury system than some policemen or politicians would claim. However, both with these and the other announced reforms actually being implemented, it is significant that the demand for each such change followed some case in which the jury delivered what certain people regarded as a wayward verdict – for you will note that none of the proposed changes seems designed to produce anything but *more convictions*! The one aim of a criminal trial should be to ensure that the guilty are convicted and the innocent walk free. It is not the jury's fault if the police and the prosecution fail to provide adequate evidence to enable it to decide correctly.

(6) At times when legislation lags behind the social conscience, the jury system enables ordinary citizens to force the legislature's hand by refusing to find a verdict in accordance with unjust laws. That is how abolition of the death penalty for stealing was first achieved. In our own day, that is also how juries have hastened the scrapping of the infamous 'catch-all' Section 2 of the Official Secrets Act by defying evident Government wishes to convict people under it, despite official admissions that the accused had not harmed national security (e.g. the case of Clive Ponting). Do we really want to trammel the wonderful common sense that British jurors have so often manifested, notwithstanding official displeasure, over the centuries?

LAND, NATIONALISATION OF

Pro: (1) Land differs totally in kind from all other kinds of property, inasmuch as its value is not the result of human labour, which alone constitutes a valid claim to property of any sort.

(2) Land is limited in quantity but is essential to all.

(3) Land is still concentrated in the hands of a relatively small proportion of the population who constitute a near-monopolistic body, having undue economic, political and social power. They exact ever-higher prices for use of their land but spend as little as possible on behalf of their tenants. Although official figures are not entirely clear, it is estimated that about 70 per cent of the land in Britain is held by only one per cent of the population.

(4) The private ownership of land (other than owner-occupied land, of reasonable size) is a menace to the health, comfort and prosperity of the community. There is no such thing as an incontrovertible right in property.

(5) Most of the country's largest landowners today have done nothing to earn the land for themselves. Often, their ancestors stole it from the common people and previous owners.

(6) The present land system is the ruin of agriculture. It militates against the most efficient large-scale farming and equally against peasant proprietorship. The agricultural worker is without hope and the farmer without real independence.

(7) The countryside has been depopulated because of the inadequate pay and living conditions imposed on agricultural workers.

(8) Rural depopulation leads to overpopulation in the towns. But the

Con: (1) Land has no value unless human labour has brought it into cultivation or built on it or exploited it.

(2) Land is no more limited or essential than capital or food. All commodities are limited. Land plays a less important part in the country's economy than it did a century ago.

(3) The landlord monopoly is not so complete as is imagined. There are many small owners, especially since the practice of buying houses and land on mortgage from building societies has become general and since the post-1979 Conservative Governments made it easier for council tenants to buy their dwellings, at beneficial prices. (It was estimated that, by the end of 1984, some 61 per cent of British families were now living in their 'own' homes, in this sense.) The large estate is more generously managed than the small one, and tenants are treated better.

(4) Land nationalisation is a gross interference with the natural right of private property.

(5) The enclosure movement laid the foundation of England's prosperity. The origin of the property is irrelevant. Where an institution is well established, those who benefit from it do so without incurring blame and should not be made to suffer unjustly on account of alleged historic injustices.

(6) Merely to transfer land from private owners to the State would not increase the farmer's or the labourer's interest in the land. Post-war legislation has helped to ensure a certain security to the tenant farmer.

(7) The countryside has always been undergoing depopulation. The chief cause nowadays is a distaste by

chief cause of urban overcrowding is the extortionate cost of privately-owned land for housing schemes, and the consequent soaring prices of both freehold and rented property. It has been estimated that, in the 'boom' years of the early 1970s, the huge profits made by property speculators far exceeded those of such crucial industries as ship-building and aircraft.

(9) The Labour Government's Community Land Act of the mid-1970s set about curbing unbridled property speculation by giving local authorities not merely the right but, after a transitional period, the statutory duty to acquire all land needed for private development. Its provisions were aimed at ensuring that ultimately, perhaps over 10 years or more, virtually all development took place on land that was in, or had passed through, community ownership. Then, in 1980, the Conservatives' Local Government and Planning Act provided 'powers of direction' to force local authorities to sell unused or derelict land by auction. Up to 1986, fewer than 20,000 acres had been sold voluntarily. Of the 115,000 acres then remaining on the land register, nearly 60 per cent were owned by local authorities – and, as they could be forced to sell, the Government had already embarked on a campaign to make them do so. Besides reflecting the Tories' general political dogma in favour of 'privatisation', this was also another of their expedients for raising money without having to raise taxation. The next stage will be to compel nationalised industries, similarly, to sell their 26,000 acres of unused land. For opponents of Tory policy, the fear is that it could lead finally to even more harmful property speculation than in the 1970s – which, in their view, makes the need to

the younger generation for the supposed dullness of rural life and a desire for the (equally supposed) excitements of town life.

(8) Urban overcrowding is due to overpopulation. Far less than the price of land, it is the soaring cost of labour and raw materials, in the present inflationary period, which has aggravated housing shortages by slowing down the rate of new building and redevelopment. Earlier legislation showed that it is quite possible to prevent large-scale property speculation without nationalising land.

(9) Some of the original provisions of Labour's legislation were held to be either unworkable or contrary to elementary principles of justice – for instance, it was alleged, the implication that people could have their land taken under a compulsory purchase order, without being told why and without the right to an inquiry. Labour's land nationalisation proposals were introduced mainly to placate the party's left-wingers. Local authorities would have needed many thousands of new staff to implement them. In contrast, the campaign launched by the Conservative Government in November 1985 was aimed at relieving the pressure to build on precious Green Belt land and at improving the lot of the decaying inner city areas – shifting the urban balance by bringing new housing, shopping developments, business and light industry back to the inner cities. It is a programme designed to transform the shape of urban Britain over the next 25 years – one that could be implemented efficiently only by private enterprise, certainly not through any form of nationalisation. The scale of derelict land in urban Britain is much greater than most people realise; in some parts of

nationalise land (except for that of owner-occupiers) more urgent than ever.

(10) Mainly because of onerous taxation, many large landowners in recent years have been driven to split up their estates among a number of purchasers or to sell them outright to companies, which are concerned solely with profit-making. Land nationalisation, as now mooted, is the only way to retain what was good in the old system while ensuring a more equitable distribution of wealth and power.

London alone, it amounts to more than 13 per cent of available land. Whatever the critics may say, calling on the resources of private builders and developers, to tackle the problem, is not a matter of political dogma but of plain efficiency.

(10) Public interest would be served best by a fair system of taxation which allowed the land-owner enough incentive to develop his land and left the developer with sufficient freedom to carry out the tasks at which he is more expert than anyone in either central or local government.

LIQUOR LAWS:
Should They Be Relaxed?

Pro: (1) The restrictions imposed by Britain's liquor laws, notably as regards the permitted opening hours for public houses, are a legacy of the Government's (needless) fears about the sobriety of munitions workers during World War I and of undesirable social conditions in earlier ages – accentuated by the puritanism of that Nonconformist conscience which has long had undue influence on British affairs. The present laws no longer reflect the prevailing social conditions of the day.

(2) In May 1986, the Home Secretary, Douglas Hurd, said the Government gave its support in principle to the case for reform, which had been urged by the tourist industry and up to 200 MPs of all parties. A pledge to allow all-day opening of the 69,000 pubs in England and Wales was expected to be included in the Conservative Party's next general election manifesto. After the Government's failure to win the day for the

Con: (1) As the law stands, public houses can serve alcoholic liquor for at least nine hours a day, in most areas. Drink can still be consumed with meals at other hours, in restaurants and clubs, and it can be bought from 8.30 a.m. on normal weekdays in the wine departments of supermarkets, etc., for consumption in one's own home whenever one wishes. Surely that is more than adequate provision for all normal needs? Do we really want to return to the days of Hogarth's Gin Lane?

(2) There was still no Government commitment to introduce early legislation. Nor is the nature of any changes yet decided. Most publicans would prefer flexibility – the freedom to choose their own opening hours within officially prescribed limits (say, between 11 a.m. and 11 p.m., much as the Scottish model). But this would not necessarily entail each pub staying open longer. With all the daily restocking, cellar work and document-

115

liberalisation of laws on Sunday shopping (*q.v.*), Ministers were understandably chary of proceeding with a somewhat similar kind of liberalisation until they were certain they had majority support for it. Mr. Hurd also emphasised that care will be taken, under the eventual reform, to maintain adequate and effective controls, 'given the concern which exists over alcohol misuse'. Nevertheless, this does not alter the fact that the Cabinet as a whole *had* come round to the view, at the time, that the licensing laws were now out-dated.

(3) It is well known among travellers that abuse of alcohol is in inverse proportion to the strictness of a country's liquor laws. France, which has the most liberal laws in this respect, probably has the least amount of visible drunkenness in public (except, perhaps, among some tourists!). The very tough restrictions in parts of Australia, on the other hand, gave rise to the notorious 'six o'clock swill', in which many men drank a vast amount in a very short space of time, because the bars were closed at the early hour of 6 p.m. It became so bad that the restriction had to be eased, by extending the hours to more reasonable limits. Opening hours in England and Wales, though slightly less restricted than they were, still present a similar problem – of people trying to consume a few more drinks quickly before 'time' is called. In contrast, experience in Scotland is that both alcoholism and drink-driving convictions have fallen significantly since opening hours were extended there in 1976 (according to a recent independent research report from the Adam Smith Institute).

(4) When pubs or bars have longer permitted hours than are now the rule here, the result is if anything a tend-

ation, it's already quite usual for licensees to work from 10 a.m. to past midnight. Many of them would naturally be disinclined to take on a heavier burden of hours than they have already. So, even assuming a Bill to allow greater flexibility were introduced some time after the next general election (which is by no means certain), it might not actually change things very much. And the setback to a Private Member's Bill to allow more flexible opening times – it failed to get a second reading in the Commons, in January 1987 – must have considerably lowered the priority given to such a measure in any of the political parties' election manifestos . . .

(3) The appearance belies the facts. Drunkenness may be less visible in France, but the overall problem there is actually far more acute than in Britain. According to official statistics published in Paris, an average of 21,955 French people die from alcoholism every year and France has more cases of cirrhosis of the liver than any other country. Britain's current liquor laws, by allowing an extra ten minutes' 'drinking up time' after the official hour of closure, have largely ended the indecent haste previously exhibited by some drinkers in the last minutes before closing time. In Scotland, specifically, the licensing laws previously applied there were perhaps unduly severe and had thus tended to become self-defeating. An official survey in 1984 showed that, since the introduction of longer opening hours, there has been a rise in the number of women drinking alcoholic beverages – and that, among all adults, the *time* spent drinking has increased by more than an hour a week.

(4) Even if longer hours had the paradoxical effect of leading some

ency towards lower rather than higher consumption, overall. Because people are not under the pressure of time, they are more inclined to make a drink last over a longer period and thus often end by drinking less than they would have done if their hours were restricted.

(5) When something is forbidden or unobtainable, human beings always tend to want it much more than they would have done if it were readily available. Prohibition in the USA, for instance, certainly led many people to become regular drinkers who, but for the restriction, would probably have remained only infrequent drinkers. Station buffets, small café-restaurants and so on, which are in any case open for very long hours, would have no objection to serving liquor throughout that time, and there is no logical reason why they should be barred from doing so.

individuals to drink less (though it's to be doubted if they'd do any such thing), the tendency would be more than outweighed by the availability factor. As a parallel, look at gambling; many people have always liked to bet, but the number has grown out of all recognition since betting shops were legalised. In terms of total consumption, it would inevitably be the same with drinking.

(5) Nothing exceeds like excess. . . . Over-strict measures will always produce a backlash, human nature being what it is. But Britain's liquor laws are not unduly strict; within the framework of the State's responsibility to protect people from themselves to a certain degree, the present laws are if anything fairly generous.

(See also PROHIBITION)

LORDS, REFORM OF THE HOUSE OF

Pro: (1) As an institution, the House of Lords is an anachronism and out of sympathy with the modern democratic spirit. It is the only institution of its kind persisting in the modern world.

(2) While the House of Commons has been made representative of the whole nation, the House of Lords has stood still. Its members – even those translated from the Commons as Life Peers – are unelected and represent no one.

(3) The attendance of peers is notoriously small; in fact, a great many attend only to vote on party

Con: (1) The House of Lords has grown up with and forms an integral portion of the British Constitution, and, consequently, is much more adapted for its purpose than any new Second Chamber could be. Far from being out of sympathy with modern attitudes, the Lords were the first to admit Hansard (the daily parliamentary reports), the first to install electric lighting instead of gas, and, latterly, the first to allow TV cameras into the chamber – this last still rejected by the Commons in November 1985, for the eighth time in 19 years.

117

measures or those affecting their private interests. It is desirable to relieve peers from parliamentary duties when such work has come to them solely by inheritance but they are ill-suited for it or find it irksome.

(4) The majority of the peers are, inevitably, Conservative and largely opposed to the programmes of both the Alliance and Labour parties. When enlightened legislation is needed urgently to meet serious situations, the Lords often tend to oppose it. Even the reducing of their veto period to one year has not curbed the power of the Lords, since they can still hold up nearly every measure brought forward in the final year of a Government's term of office, in the hope that electoral changes will prevent them from being brought forward again. The only solution is for the function of the Lords to become purely consultative.

(5) If the Upper House is to function as a body of elder statesmen and act as a bulwark against over-hastiness on the part of the Commons, it should be reconstituted on an elective basis. We do not object to a son inheriting his father's title, but we object to his making or unmaking *our* laws.

(6) The House of Lords is an irresponsible body. It should, like other Second Chambers, be a body responsible to the people in whose interests it is supposed to exist. Accordingly, it should be elected by them, or at least by their representatives.

(7) It is possible to have a reformed Second Chamber which, while consisting entirely of people qualified to deal with a nation's affairs and responsible for its acts, will yet be free from party ties. As a logical extension of this thought, an Alliance party policy paper suggests that, in future, *equal* numbers of men and women

(2) It thoroughly represents the material and intellectual wealth and culture of the nation and expresses those aspects of national life more fully than the Commons. The House of Lords has already undergone one of the most important reforms in its history: the policy of creating only Life Peers – of all parties, or independent – from men and women who have shown exceptional ability in their professions. These new peers, experts in their fields, have brought added authority to the Lords' parliamentary contribution – and they are much less subject to the powerful party machines which have helped to lessen public regard for the House of Commons.

(3) The House of Commons also gives examples of small attendances and of voting in obedience to party orders without necessarily hearing a word of the debate. The peers who do attend are at any rate keenly interested in the topics discussed, and important subjects draw a large attendance.

(4) The Lords have always had very good reasons for their opposition. If their policy is conservative, it is not without advantages, for from 1914 onwards it is the House of Lords which has championed the traditional liberties of the subject and resisted the growing power of the Executive. The period during which the Lords can exercise their veto is now dangerously short.

(5) If the House of Lords is put on an elective basis, it will either be subject to the operations of the party machines and lose its independent character, or, if its party majorities are markedly different from those of the Commons, be in a continuous state of conflict and rivalry with the Commons.

(6) The House of Lords is respon-

should be recommended for life peerages.

(8) There is no scheme of reform which, while adding greatly to the moral strength of the Second Chamber, would reduce the particular value it has as a predominantly conservative body. This has been the universal experience in other countries, where the Second Chamber is always to the political right of the Lower House.

(9) The peers themselves have been the first to put forward proposals for reform of the Upper House, recognising the need for change in keeping with modern thinking, but so far it is the Commons which has failed to have any of these reforms implemented.

sible because it is independent. All Second Chambers should be removed as far as possible from the transient gusts of popular control. It is noteworthy that several of the most progressive laws enacted in recent years were initiated in the Lords.

(7) It is difficult to see on what basis such people would be selected. If they are to be chosen by the Government, endless opportunities for packing the House with their protégés would arise; if various sectional interests are to be represented, there would be no concession made to democratic practice. Election by popular suffrage would certainly not bring forward the most suitable people, as experience in the Commons has shown.

(8) Reforms which strengthened the role of the House of Lords would incur the risk of placing the forces of reaction in a stronger position than at present.

(9) If the peers have suggested reforming themselves, it is only to try to pre-empt those who want the Lords to be abolished entirely.

(See also SINGLE-CHAMBER GOVERNMENT; BISHOPS: SHOULD THEY BE EXCLUDED FROM THE HOUSE OF LORDS?)

LOTTERIES

Pro: (1) Through legislation passed in 1975, permitting local authorities to run relatively small lotteries for their own benefit, Parliament at last recognised that there is a definite public demand for lotteries and that it was unfair for the puritanism of the few to hinder the harmless enjoyment of the many.

(2) A lottery in itself is a quite

Con: (1) Members of the public already have only too much opportunity for gambling, which is a national evil, involving loss of time and money and creating misery for the families of those who waste their substance on it.

(2) A lottery, like all gambling, is an immoral attempt to gain something for nothing and can never be entirely

innocuous amusement and provides a modicum of excitement in many otherwise dreary lives. It involves no destruction of wealth but merely transfers money from one pocket to another, with the consent of both parties to the transaction. The new legislation restricts the prices of lottery tickets to levels which do not encourage excessive gambling. Even if a few gambling addicts were to stake more than they could afford to lose, that is no reason why the moderate gambler, any more than the moderate drinker, should be penalised.

(3) A law which cannot be enforced and which is systematically evaded should be removed from the statute book. That has been the case with lotteries for years. Many local charities and sports clubs have long depended on small lotteries for survival. Despite legal technicalities about the use of skill, football pools are also lotteries, in effect – and the Government has recognised this by imposing a tax on winnings.

(4) A well-organised lottery is an excellent way of raising money. The Irish hospitals are now wealthy and well equipped on money raised by this method, and most foreign countries find lotteries a useful adjunct to taxation. One of the leaders of the now-defunct Greater London Council once pointed out that a London lottery alone could provide a £5 million profit annually, which could be devoted to the arts and other amenities now of low financial priority.

(5) The local authority lotteries allowed by the Government do not, in fact, go far enough. At present, the top prizes permitted are £2,000 for weekly lotteries and £4,000 for larger quarterly lotteries. But earlier experience with Premium Bonds soon showed that, to retain public interest

harmless. It encourages idleness and waste of time. Moreover, a sudden change of fortune through sheer luck rather than merit, such as is occasioned by the winning of a big prize, often brings unhappiness by placing the winner on a different social level, where he tends to lose his former friends but is not accepted by his new financial equals.

(3) The law in this connection admittedly needed revision, but it should have been tightened up, not relaxed. The tax on gambling profits effectively sanctions immorality; since it was imposed, the gambling 'industry' has expanded out of all recognition.

(4) State lotteries may be useful in countries where the citizens habitually resist direct taxation and the bulk of revenue has to be raised through indirect taxes; but this does not apply to the British public. Even if one accepts official lotteries as the least harmful form of gambling, the gain in revenue will be a drop in the ocean against the volume of official expenditure; the Government has stressed that they will not be a substitute for the rates or an alternative method of financing local government.

(5) Even in this betting-mad country, there is a limit to the money available for gambling. The officially-approved lotteries, despite their relatively restricted size, doubtless cream off some of the cash which people would otherwise have spent on small raffles and similar ventures in aid of such worthwhile causes as local charities and sports clubs.

and ensure no drop in revenue, the prize levels had to be raised.

(See also GAMBLING, MORALITY OF)

MARRIAGE AS AN INSTITUTION:
Is It an Outmoded Concept?

Pro: (1) In the present-day social climate, there has been a clear and continuing increase in the number of couples who no longer feel any need to get married in order to establish a stable relationship – one that most of them usually intend to last for the rest of their lives. By the same token, those who do decide to live together without marrying are no longer subject to anything like the stigma they would have been a generation ago.

(2) Even among couples who do marry, a high proportion nowadays – nearly one in three, according to the Office of Population Censuses – have had a 'trial marriage' first. In most cases, it seems, they have eventually decided on the real thing only because they wanted to have children and/or because, under prevailing mores, it is still 'tidier' legally.

(3) It used to be said that one of the most cogent arguments in favour of the formal marriage bond is that, without it, any children of the union would be illegitimate, in law, and could face many complications or embarrassments in later life. This applied notably to such matters as inheritance, citizenship, financial support and property rights. But the problem no longer arises under new legislation aimed at giving such children similar rights to those whose parents are married. Alarm over a steep rise in the numbers of so-called

Con: (1) Every religion underlines the prime importance of marriage, and sanctifies it. Quite irrespective of the Church, so does every major moral and ethical code. Ultimately, the very survival of mankind depends on couples being able to come together to propagate the species, and to rear the offspring to adulthood, in the knowledge that they can do so under a system that has the full protection of the law.

(2) Despite the apparent advantages of a 'trial marriage' – particularly in enabling couples to make sure first that they do get on with each other, over a reasonable period, before agreeing to legalise the bond – the fact remains that, *in the long run*, it is probably no more successful in cementing a permanent relationship than the process of a good few months' formal engagement which used to be the traditional prelude to marriage. Many teenagers today, when asked about it, say that they regard living together as 'an easy way out' and that they would still prefer to make it an agreed bond. Apart from mere legal convenience, one important reason why marriage remains more popular among young people is (paradoxically, perhaps) the very fact that it entails responsibility: in getting married, you are making yourself responsible to and for somebody else.

(3) As regards the relevance of the

121

illegitimate babies (and of those conceived before their parents married) has been exacerbated by a misunderstanding of the underlying facts. Among teenage girls who become pregnant, far fewer marry while in that condition than was the usual case up to the mid-1970s. Among young people aged 20 or over, an increasingly high proportion of illegitimate births – as many as 65 per cent in 1985 – is now being registered by both parents, resident at the same address. This is abundant proof that, with the parents taking joint responsibility for its welfare, the baby had been born of a stable union. The great majority, in short, were not unintended births. The couples had deliberately chosen to have them out of wedlock and to care for them in a loving family, without the ties of marriage.

(4) That more and more people have concluded that there is no longer any point in 'holy wedlock' has probably stemmed, at least in part, from the dwindling of religious belief and an equivalent growth of opinion that the Church has become largely irrelevant in present-day conditions. At the same time, and perhaps above all, those who hold that the formal marriage tie has become an anachronism are not motivated by anti-religious sentiment, as such; rather, it is a reflection of that frankness of outlook, that unwillingness to be hypocritical about observing customs one does not really believe in, which is such a refreshing facet of the modern-day generation.

(5) In Nature, animals have no need of any formal piece of paper or primitive tribal rite – or, of course, some animal equivalent of such – for their 'pair bond' to be duly recognised by their fellow-creatures. (What

illegitimacy problem to any debate on marriage as an institution, the statistics speak for themselves. In the decade from 1971 to 1981, there was a 71 per cent rise in the number of single-parent families; about 1.5 million children were involved (and up to one in three children in inner cities). By 1985, nearly one-fifth of all babies born in England and Wales were illegitimate – 14 per cent more than the previous year and more than double the number a decade earlier. Similarly, one-third of all babies were conceived before marriage. The following year, 1986, it was estimated that, altogether, some four million people in Britain were illegitimate in the eyes of the law. The horrific size of such figures simply can't just be shrugged aside. To decry marriage, in this context, is – if nothing else – unbelievably callous.

(4) Other figures from the Office of Population Censuses confirm that, except among teenagers, the number of couples marrying is actually rising. From 1983 to 1985, the annual average showed an increase of nearly two per cent. Moreover, the reason teenagers do not figure in this trend is, encouragingly, that couples are generally waiting longer before marrying: the average age of those getting married for the first time is now the highest since just after the Second World War (when large numbers of servicemen returned home). As for the Church being regarded as 'irrelevant', the trouble with many such charges is that, while they may echo the views of a section of supposedly 'sophisticated' people in the big cities, they are rarely if ever an accurate reflection of opinion in other parts of the country, representing an appreciably bigger proportion of the population. A survey conducted by *Wedding Day*

ceremony there may be is solely between the prospective partners themselves, when deciding whether or not to set up shop together.) This does not affect the permanence of the union. Many species, once they form a pair bond, stay with the same partner until they die. (Swans are one familiar example.) Surely mankind is no less capable of doing so?

magazine showed that more than 80 per cent of Britain's present-day brides still want a white wedding in church!

(5) A great many more species either change partners every year or, when the time is ripe, procreate with as many different ones as they can. The almost anthropomorphic attempt to equate mankind's social arrangements with those of other species, irrespective of the latter's widely varying needs and conditions, is as muddle-headed as nearly all the other arguments put forward opposite.

(See also DIVORCE and EASIER DIVORCE, HAS IT GONE TOO FAR?)

MILITARY TRAINING, COMPULSORY:
Should It Be Restored?

Pro: (1) Nations should rely on their whole manhood for defence purposes and not on a limited professional class. It is the moral duty of everyone to take part in the service and defence of his country and to be trained so that he can do this effectively. In Britain, the only answer is the restoration of National Service – and this time, perhaps, with young single women also conscripted, for training in non-combatant jobs. A Gallup Poll in September 1986 showed that two out of three people in Britain now support the return of National Service for 18-year-olds.

(2) After every war in the past, British governments have neglected the national defences, only to find themselves unprepared when the next crisis arose. Witness the frantic haste with which preparations had to be

Con: (1) The moral argument is misleading: the real national service that we owe is the fulfilment of the duties of everyday life. This is the most effective way to strengthen the nation's moral power and financial resources. Conscription in peacetime is in any case not really efficient, militarily, because of the lack of continuity and the difficulty of training conscripts adequately in today's complex weapons before their period of service ends. With the passage of time since National Service was ended in Britain (in 1963), people championing its return have forgotten just how unpopular it was – the huge resentment at young men having to waste two years of the most formative period of their careers.

(2) Immediate conscription in wartime, as carried out after 1939, is

123

speeded up after the Munich fiasco in 1938. This danger would be greatly reduced if every citizen received basic military training.

(3) The training and discipline received by young National Servicemen makes them better citizens. Physically and morally, the benefit is enormous. The voluntary associations can still be used for refresher courses and for the training of older men.

(4) The mingling of young people from many different backgrounds, during National Service, promotes respect and comradeship between them and inculcates a spirit of teamwork and mutual toleration which has a beneficial effect later on their return to civilian life.

(5) Modern warfare demands intensive weapon training, which can be given to large numbers only through the method of conscription for peace-time service. Unless a large number of combatants is available at once, an aggressor might well overwhelm his victims before they can be mobilised for defence. Brief annual periods of reserve training, after National Service, will help to keep the ex-conscripts reasonably abreast of new weapons and methods.

(6) In times of peace, a citizen army is much the cheapest form of military establishment, and any extra expenditure on it should be regarded as insurance.

(7) A citizen army is a valuable check on the policy of a government, as it must be persuaded of the rightness of acts it is asked to carry out.

(8) Compulsory training enables the responsibilities of citizenship to be realised by all. Those less fit physically are assigned to light duties, while conscientious objectors can do hospital or other useful work for the same period of service.

adequate. For peace-time purposes, especially now that Britain's overseas commitments have been reduced, the regular army can meet all normal needs. Britain's main problems in 1940 arose from shortage of materials, not men. Even in the First World War, a time came when Britain had more conscripts than the armed forces could usefully absorb.

(3) To take young men away at a crucial moment in their civilian training is unfair and, for those studying for professional qualifications, might actually unfit them for their future work. Military training in peace-time necessarily involves long periods of demoralising idleness or futile occupation.

(4) Despite recent reforms, the preservation of class distinction is probably still stronger in the armed forces than in almost any other sphere of life today.

(5) Weapons are continually changing and only those who have recently been under arms will be up-to-date in their training. The main things to be learnt in peace-time military service are discipline, team-work and smartness, and these could be learned just as well from other, non-military forms of service. Reserve training after National Service, even if for only a couple of weeks annually, would involve increasingly large numbers – and industry simply could not afford to lose so many workers, however briefly.

(6) The expense of maintaining a huge conscript army was prohibitive for a small country like Britain. It is all the more unnecessary now that we have abandoned the large military presence 'East of Suez' which was a legacy of our imperialist past.

(7) The existence of a large army encourages a government to be reckless

(9) Whatever air and sea successes a country's forces may achieve, no war can ever be won decisively without a large army to follow them up on land.

(10) Strength and numbers of military personnel remain the fundamental basis of military effectiveness. This was proved conclusively in the Second World War. Israel and Switzerland provide two examples of small countries where the military pool resulting from a period of conscription, for all, is (or would be) absolutely vital to their survival in the event of war. Both recognise, too, that it is useless for training purposes if the basic conscription period is too short and if it is not followed by regular refresher training thereafter.

in diplomacy and to take on commitments which increase the risk of war.

(8) Compulsory military training, as formerly operated in Britain, left a large part of the population without this reminder of their civic responsibilities. Moreover, it actually had a demoralising effect, since many young men decided to avoid conscription by emigrating and were thus lost to the country.

(9) In these days of nuclear arms and missiles, our only hope of defence lies in highly trained regular forces, enlisting voluntarily for long terms.

(10) Military effectiveness depends less than ever before on the mere weight of numbers of armed men. The building up of aircraft and munitions industries to war strength is a much lengthier and more complicated business than the elementary training of recruits, and it is on this that a country should concentrate for preparedness against war.

(See also SOCIAL SERVICE CONSCRIPTION)

MINORITIES, RIGHTS OF

Pro: (1) Ever since the remaking of Europe after the First World War, it has been recognised that national minorities have a right to a certain autonomy. Such oppression as took place under the Austro-Hungarian and Tsarist Russian regimes is discredited today, but not all national minorities have been liberated, while some of the new countries which arose as a result of such liberation have been guilty of oppression in their turn. The attempt to solve the problem quickly by the summary ejection of foreign communities, such as that of the Asians from Uganda in 1972, offends

Con: (1) People who settle in a foreign country have no right to remain in it as an organised separate community. They should assimilate themselves with the community which has received them; otherwise they are liable to become nurseries of unrest and can be used by unscrupulous aggressors as outposts, just as the Sudeten Germans in Czechoslovakia were used by Nazi Germany.

(2) The whole idea of artificially fostering separatist feelings in a community abroad is absurd and unreal. Left to itself, the second generation normally becomes part of the

125

against the principles of justice.

(2) The fact that some members of national minorities have abused their privileges is not an argument for depriving others of them. Subversive elements in a foreign country are not necessarily organised in compact national communities; indeed, they may prefer to permeate the indigenous population. The only logical consequence of this argument is the expulsion of all foreigners, which is repugnant to civilised countries.

(3) Not all minorities are formed by immigration. Some of them are communities and nations which have been forcibly annexed in the past to suit the economic needs of conquerors, as in the former Belgian Congo; others were summarily attached to another country, as in the creation of Czechoslovakia. Justice demands that they should be given full rights; failure to do this always leads to conflict and, in the end, the offending governments are usually forced to concede what they would not grant willingly.

(4) Separation by proper agreement would involve provision for possible economic problems. International bodies have usually concerned themselves with minorities only in so far as these affect the interests of the Great Powers. The cause of justice would be immeasurably strengthened by some provision which was incapable of misinterpretation and by United Nations action to implement it.

indigenous population, as seen notably in the USA. The preservation of national festivals is harmless and may enrich the cultural life of the foreign minority's host country, but that does not give minorities the right to try to elevate such national expressions into the political sphere.

(3) The linking of different communities together into nations was usually inspired in the past by considerations of economics; the agriculture of Slovakia complements the industry of Bohemia. In the same way, Zaire would probably be bankrupt without the mineral wealth of Katanga. In modern economic conditions, the creation of small units amounts to economic suicide; the whole trend is towards ever larger units. The political and economic *rapprochements* of the Western European countries are examples of this tendency. For small minorities today, the only possibility is a form of independence which is politically meaningless.

(4) Separation by agreement, while it might be desirable, is not feasible in the case of the few minorities which are left. A better solution, and one more likely to allow for economic difficulties, would be a painless transition – perhaps via 'Dominion status' – for such minorities as are recognised as having a right to independent existence, with the option of eventual federation.

MOTOR TRAFFIC:
Should It Be Restricted?

Pro: (1) The first car appeared on British roads in 1888. By 1914, there

Con: (1) Attempts to limit the ownership of cars are as absurd as the

126

were 140,000 vehicles on the road. In an island the size of Britain, there is hardly enough room for the more than 20 million vehicles we now have – yet, before the economic situation began to cause a temporary slow-down in 1974, statisticians were predicting an increase to 29 million vehicles by the year 2000. Motor cars have already become a menace to amenities of town and country, through noise, air pollution and the disfigurement of towns with a chaotic collection of signs and bollards. Parked cars fill every available space. It is high time to call a halt to this erosion of our amenities by restricting either the ownership or the circulation of cars.

(2) Since it would be impracticable to forbid car ownership, taxation could be used to restrict it. In any case, private motor traffic costs the country far more than it yields in revenue.

(3) All towns and cities, even large villages, have had to impose parking restrictions, and a system of tolls to restrict entry into central London has been proposed. Commuters, in particular, should be discouraged from bringing cars into city centres. Public transport should be improved, and subsidised out of taxation if necessary, with free or cheap parking at the termini for long-distance commuters. It has been estimated that traffic congestion in cities costs, in various ways, more than £2,000 million a year. It is absurd that a machine capable of high speeds should be used for journeys which, because of traffic congestion, average barely 11 m.p.h., as in London.

(Some) A ban on non-exempted heavy lorries in certain key London streets at nights and over the week-ends – brought in by the former Greater London Council – has been maintained since the GLC was abol-

so-called Red Flag rule which tried to curb their speed in the early days of motoring. The motor car is valued because it has enriched leisure, performs a public service and has increased the pace of economic advance. It is regarded almost as an extension of the personality, and any further attempts to restrict it would certainly arouse fierce resistance. Damage to amenities arises only because the development of the motor car has outstripped the development of towns and town life.

(2) Motorists are already heavily taxed, and wholesale evasion would be the immediate result of excessive taxation. This kind of restriction is a form of rationing by the purse, and as such is undesirable.

(3) No sound scheme for taxing circulation in cities has yet been found, for the expense of enforcement and possibilities of evasion are formidable. Similarly, the problem of discrimination between users, in the granting of exemptions, cannot be solved on a basis that all would accept as fair. Bye-laws to ensure the provision of parking space with new buildings and a more imaginative approach to the parking problem generally would enable us to take advantage of the door-to-door service which is an essential part of town life. Many people are forced to use cars precisely because of the inadequacies of public transport, but it would take many years (and vast sums) to improve the latter sufficiently to overcome the problem.

(4) While railways performed a great public service in their time, they are unsuited to the increased mobility of modern populations, owing to their natural inflexibility and the inevitable delays involved in the transfer of freight. Passengers have made clear

ished in 1986 because it had already cut such traffic by 20 per cent and most of the public clearly favoured it.

(4) The railways, which have been allowed to run down owing to our shortsightedness, are much more suitable for traffic between cities, being both faster and safer than motor transport. Failure to develop rail freight facilities adequately is largely to blame for the continual, unwanted increase in the use of 'juggernauts', those huge lorries which aggravate traffic congestion and wear out road surfaces.

(5) There is a limit to the building of new roads in an island the size of Britain. Not only is all available land needed for housing, agriculture, and open spaces for recreation, but motor roads are themselves unbeautiful, and too much road-building would destroy the countryside, the enjoyment of which is the main ambition of many car owners. A system of junctions and fly-overs at the edge of towns can create a nightmare landscape as bad as anything produced by the Industrial Revolution. In 1984, Britain had 60 vehicles for every kilometre of road – or one for every 17 metres!

(6) The accident figures have reached appalling levels. During 1984, nearly 5,600 people died on the roads and the number of injured totalled 318,715. These figures alone should be an unanswerable argument for restriction of motor traffic.

(7) In the attempt to ease congestion, towns have built – at great expense – by-passes and ring roads of doubtful value. Re-routing of traffic is destroying the amenities – and roads – of once-quiet suburbs. Pedestrian precincts in town centres are of limited size and application. Ambitious schemes for new towns ban

their preference for door-to-door transport.

(Some) The London ban on lorries over 16 tons is largely falsified by the high number of delivery vehicles exempted from it. At the same time, the ban has created uncertainty for the freight transport industry over the vital task of keeping the capital supplied. Yet there is no evidence that this somewhat cosmetic ban has actually brought about a substantial reduction. Much of the drop in the volume of lorry traffic in London is, in fact, due to the opening of the M25 orbital motorway.

(5) The building of motorways and the improvement of the older trunk roads have concentrated a great deal of the increased traffic of recent years. A well-made and landscaped motorway, or an imaginatively conceived junction system, can be architecturally beautiful and even give interest to some kinds of landscape. It is certainly fortunate that not all the available vehicles are out on the roads simultaneously ... However, the potential pressure does underline the need for a carefully-judged programme of further road building and widening.

(6) The fact that the USA, with more motor cars than any other country, has an accident rate per car less than half that of many European countries shows that the cause of accidents must be sought elsewhere. Better roads, better training in the driving and maintenance of vehicles, and perhaps more frequent replacement, could do much to improve accident figures. It took many years of invention and legislation for railways to reach their present level of safety. The present emphasis in car design is above all on new safety features. While any number of road deaths is

pedestrians from ground level altogether, as if motor cars had the prior claim to existence. The planners seem to have lost all sense of proper priorities.

(8) It took only a short time for society to curb individual enterprise on the railways a century ago. Motorists permit themselves to deface beauty spots with their vehicles, to break speed limits, to carry dangerous loads in inadequate vehicles, or to drive while unfitted by drunkenness, physical incapacity or lack of judgment and knowledge, powerful machines of whose internal workings they often have only the vaguest idea. The permissive attitude to motoring is out of step with more urgent present-day needs.

too many, the fact remains that the ratio of accident figures in Britain is actually being lowered. In the mid-1970s, more than 7,000 were being killed each year – and this when there were some three million fewer vehicles on the roads than today.

(7) Road improvements in and around cities have been tackled piecemeal and too cheaply in the past. Bolder planning could remake our older city centres on more dignified lines and remove many of the worst atrocities of nineteenth-century building. Many new towns have shown the way, by incorporating pedestrian precincts and environmental areas, with distributive roads away from the main arteries. Travelators, chair-lifts and monorails are among other ideas suggested. Either old or new city centres could be completely replanned on split-level lines, with through traffic, parking and pedestrians completely isolated from one another.

(8) It is unconstructive to draw inferences about the behaviour of motorists from the actions of a comparative few. For every delinquent car owner, there are a thousand or more law-abiding ones.

(See also PUBLIC TRANSPORT, FREE)

MULTI-NATIONAL FIRMS

Pro: (1) The growth of multi-national firms has arisen naturally from the economic structure of the free world as it has developed in the past century, coupled with the tremendous improvement in communications and transport facilities between all parts of the globe which has occurred during that period. Often from small

Con: (1) The growth of multi-national firms stems basically from the misconception that 'biggest is best' – a traditional belief of the capitalist economies which more and more experts are now beginning to question (see *Industrial Expansion*). By their very nature, these huge corporations tend to be monopolistic and to squeeze

beginnings, the firms concerned have become very large corporations with branch companies or subsidiaries in dozens of places abroad, far from their own home bases. It has been fashionable in some quarters to criticise these companies and to suggest that their power and influence is undesirable. But whatever their faults may have been in earlier days, these have long since been outweighed by the benefits which the firms now bring to the economies of their own and other countries – for instance, through creating new industries in under-developed countries and providing the local inhabitants with more jobs, and through bringing a vast number of products and services within reach of peoples who could not otherwise have hoped to enjoy them.

(2) Their supposed influence has been exaggerated. A United Nations report listed only 650 firms which it classed as multi-national corporations (divided mainly, in origin, between the USA, Japan and Europe). Big though the companies are, that total cannot be enough to give them complete or undue dominance. Nor are they restricted to industry and manufacture, as many people suppose; companies of this scale are also found in commerce, mining, transport, banking and other services – which, again, shows that their role is a long way short of monopolistic.

(3) An official French report recognised that foreign investment in the country has been beneficial because the companies concerned have improved the employment situation in regional industry, because they offset economic recession and 'because foreign companies behave like good citizens'. In one region alone, Alsace, almost half the work force, in the last thirty years, obtained their jobs

out competition wherever they operate, thus enabling them to fix arbitrary price levels for their goods and services. With their world-wide networks, they are able to employ artificial transfer prices between various subsidiaries as a means of reducing their tax payments. Because of the size of their operations, they are able to indulge in very large-scale currency manipulation, which has undoubtedly harmed the economic interests of the countries concerned. Many of them have also been guilty of political interference, particularly in developing countries.

(2) The extent of their invasion of rival industrialised countries, quite apart from the under-developed nations, is shown by the fact that about 400 multi-national companies (mainly Japanese and American) now have bases in Europe. Today, some 30,000 Americans work in Brussels alone, where more than a third of the 400 companies have their European headquarters. France has 50 such companies on her soil. The American General Electric company's takeover of the French firm Machine Bull in 1966 effectively deprived France of her own computer industry, obliging the Paris Government to set up a new French data processing and computer concern, in association with German and Dutch firms. The wide range of activities carried out by the various business giants ranked as multi-nationals merely serves to emphasise just how all-pervasive the spread of these companies has become.

(3) When a multi-national firm installs a new factory in another country, creating more jobs locally, the government of that country may well welcome it. All too often, though, these big corporations merely buy up an existing local company. This not

through foreign companies. The establishment of a large multi-national firm in a provincial locality has also brought indirect benefits to the area, by helping to encourage the regional development of various services needed by the company itself, such as communications, tourism, banking and insurance.

(4) In many of the world's under-developed countries, multi-national firms can take much of the credit for the discovery and subsequent development of natural resources (e.g. oil, minerals and other raw materials) which are now the principal elements of wealth in those countries' economies. Usually, the existence of such resources was previously unknown to the local inhabitants, who in any case had neither the technological nor financial means to exploit them. Besides introducing the necessary production techniques to these countries, the multi-nationals have also added immeasurably to the local wealth through the scale of the export earnings they have facilitated (by virtue of the world-wide marketing and distribution techniques they employ).

(5) Of the 650 multi-national corporations in the United Nations list, 74 are Japanese. Internally, Japan's early post-war domination by American multi-nationals has led to a policy whereby foreign companies are now allowed to operate in the country only if they do not disturb the development of local industries. Externally, the Japanese have learned from this domestic experience that their factories abroad cannot prosper if they ignore the public interest – for instance, by causing pollution or by failing to make a social as well as an economic contribution to the communities where they are located.

only makes little or no extra contribution to the economy of the host-nation but may actually have a negative effect. To combat the practice, France now insists that any foreign investment of 20 per cent or more in a French company must first be approved by the Finance Ministry. Among other measures to keep a firm hand on the multi-nationals, the French Government has imposed rigid control over the prices charged by foreign oil companies in the country.

(4) The production techniques of most multi-national companies are determined first in the industrial countries and then transferred to the developing countries. But the techniques are not always appropriate for the purpose. They tend to be capital intensive and labour saving, whereas nearly all developing countries have a shortage of capital and a surplus of labour. Many of the companies ignore this and continue to operate in ways contrary to the local people's best interests – particularly in some Third World countries where the governments are still too much in need of foreign investment to be able effectively to control and channel the activities of the multi-nationals on their soil.

(5) The normally aggressive attitudes of these huge enterprises have been tempered mainly by the awareness that Japan is vitally dependent for its very survival on the goodwill of other countries, both for its markets and for its raw materials (a lesson brought home particularly by the oil crisis of 1973–4). In short, the behaviour of the Japanese multi-nationals remains motivated by self-interest and not by the altruistic paternalism which seems to be implied opposite. Indeed, Japan's *internal* policy on the issue has set a pattern for other nations to

In short, Japan is keenly aware that the behaviour of the multi-nationals can make or break the development of a harmonious world economy, and the 'good neighbour' policy of its own big corporations reflects the present-day attitude of the great majority of multi-national firms in general.

(6) Whatever may have been the position in the past, no single multi-national company is powerful enough to bring about radical political changes for its own ends nowadays, even in the most newly independent of the developing countries. Alleged instances in the past attracted such adverse publicity later that it is doubtful whether a multi-national firm would so much as contemplate any attempt of this nature today. While there is some truth in allegations that foreign companies have made gifts to politicians in various countries with a view to gaining favoured treatment, it should be borne in mind that such practices are part of the local way of life in many Asian and African countries, and they cannot be classed at the level of attempted interference in government policy.

(7) The top managements of most multi-nationals are not merely among the most skilful in the world but also among the most far-seeing, particularly in anticipating the responses necessary to long-term trends. Accordingly, the nature and philosophy of many of these companies have already changed greatly. They recognise that, rather than merely exporting their own goods to foreign markets, the main impetus in future will have to be, increasingly, on providing the means for local manufacture in other countries. At the same time, as management from the centre becomes ever more complex, there are the first signs of a trend towards the devol-

follow in protecting their own interests against the multi-nationals – and the policy is already being copied by some of the developing countries, such as Indonesia and South Korea. While it is true that Japanese multi-nationals have helped to develop the economic resources of other Asian countries, there have been undesirable side-effects socially. The gap between rich and poor has grown larger, and the increased urbanisation resulting from industrialisation has disrupted traditional values and ways of life.

(6) To suggest that multi-national corporations would no longer try to interfere politically in countries where they operate, if they thought they could get away with it, is regrettably naïve – and disproved by events. The notorious case of ITT, the giant American conglomerate, and its role in helping to engineer the downfall of President Allende of Chile in 1973, is a matter of public record. Even more recently, major US oil firms have had to admit publicly that their local companies in two different countries (one Latin American, the other European) had made sizeable 'political contributions' to parties in the areas where they were based. Though not stated explicitly, it was clear that the level of these 'contributions' was a good deal higher than any routine form of business insurance in such countries.

(7) Because of their sheer size, multi-national companies are able, if they so decide, to eliminate virtually all competition in any of the smaller countries they care to enter. Indeed, this has even happened in some of the larger industrialised countries. The danger is particularly acute when multi-nationals are overwhelmingly dominant in areas of high technology. It is often claimed in defence of these

ution of authority and eventually it is likely that, while the skeleton of a multi-national may remain, the individual parts of it abroad will be much more autonomous than at present.

industrial giants that size is necessary for economic efficiency, in present-day conditions; but this is readily disproved by the example of China, which, with about 25 per cent of the world's population, has managed very well without the assistance of the multi-national companies in its determined progress towards becoming an advanced industrial power.

NEWSPAPERS:
Should They Be Reformed?

Pro: (1) The Press in Britain has travelled very far from the days when periodicals were read by the cultured few and broadsheets contained the only comment on the events of the day for the unlettered many. In these days of almost universal literacy, the Press has become a great power that can make or break governments and systems of government and change the fortunes of a country, and it is time that more control was exercised in the interests of the public.

(2) As newspapers grew in size, they fell in number. Through amalgamation and the buying up of bankrupt competitors, a situation was reached where a handful of national daily newspapers were read by almost the whole population. The fortunes made from the sale of popular newspapers created a class of 'Press barons', some of whom had no real interest in anything but the profits from the newspapers they controlled. The true function of a newspaper, the dissemination of information, was distorted by the pressure of financial interest. Today, apart from the few 'quality' papers, most newspapers resort too

Con: (1) The influence of the Press on the general public has been greatly exaggerated. The election of a Labour Government in 1945, and that of President Roosevelt for his second and third terms of office in the USA, took place despite opposition beforehand from an overwhelming majority of the newspapers – thus proving readers' ability to form their own judgments. People are, in fact, far less credulous now than in the days before compulsory education and national newspapers existed.

(2) The amalgamation of newspapers and the tendency towards monopoly were merely examples of the general trend of world economy today. Yet small newspapers continued to flourish in the provinces and suburbs – and this has been accentuated by the huge increase in 'freebies', the weekly papers (many with six-figure print runs) which are delivered free to homes throughout the country, their production costs being met solely by the advertising they carry. Under the system of private enterprise, there are enough newspapers of different political views to

133

readily to sensationalism and superficial entertainment to bolster their circulations – and their presentation of news can still be subject to the personal predilections of the proprietor or the interests which he openly or otherwise represents.

(3) The last danger has been vastly increased by the wider adoption of new computerised technology for newspaper production in the 1980s, because a daily paper can now be economically viable with a circulation of only a few hundred thousand (instead of the seven-figure print runs needed previously). As a result, the number of newspapers is again on the rise – and, with it, a potentially greater need for safeguards against the eccentricities of any maverick owners.

(4) Because of the predominance of advertising as a source of revenue, the interests of advertisers influence the policy of a newspaper – not in suppressing news items, perhaps, but certainly in the nature of its efforts to achieve a bigger circulation (when higher rates can be charged for advertising space). A newspaper which is prepared to risk the loss of advertising custom can scarcely hope to survive, or even to be started.

(5) The popular press is guilty of gross errors of taste, both in the kind of news it prints and in the methods used to obtain it. Unwarranted intrusions on privacy have had to be condemned by the Press Council in all too many cases.

(6) Journalists themselves have complained of their servitude to financial interests. The power wielded by the great editors of the past, who built up the reputations of our best known national newspapers, is virtually unknown today. It is a traditional dictum that 'news is sacred but comment is free'. However, many

cater for all main interests, and the effect of a proprietor's influence is no more undesirable than would be that of a Government monopoly. In the past, the reading of newspapers was confined to a leisured minority; the presentation of news in easier-to-read form and the inclusion of items of general interest are the very reasons why newspaper reading is now indulged in by the whole population.

(3) Ultimately, it is the law of the market place that prevails. No amount of public control would change that. Any paper accused of going beyond the bounds can be brought before the Press Council and would be constrained to publish its judgments, however condemnatory. Despite criticisms of the Council's supposed 'lack of teeth', its moral force should not be underestimated. Nor should the power of advertisers to withhold their advertising – or that of readers to stop buying the paper.

(4) Advertising is a legitimate occupation which has naturally grown in extent with the growth of industry and trade generally. Advertisers do not influence the policy of newspapers directly in the pushing of their products, and there has been no evidence for many years (except, possibly, on some of the very smallest local papers) of advertisers trying to get specific news items modified or suppressed.

(5) While some reporters err through excess of zeal or lack of scruples, the Press generally does its duty of informing the public without unwarrantable intrusions. Far fewer people than might be supposed object to the publicity they are given, and many even find that they have benefited from it.

(6) Journalists have the remedy in their own hands to a large extent. No journalist who objects to the policy of

papers today 'angle' their news so that it supports their own views.

a newspaper need work for it. Comment on and interpretation of news do not necessarily amount to falsification, and most facts can be interpreted in more than one way. The existence of rival newspapers, and of the radio and television news services, gives the public adequate protection – and, as indicated above, the Press Council has proved an effective deterrent against any really serious excesses.

NUCLEAR WEAPONS:
Should They Be Banned Completely?

Pro: (1) Nuclear weapons are not merely more deadly weapons than any before but are of a completely new nature, in that they interfere with the very structure of the Earth and its atmosphere. Apart from the horrific destruction caused by their explosions, they can contaminate whole areas of the Earth by radioactivity which may last for hundreds, even thousands of years.

(2) Nations become more cautious about the use of weapons only if both sides in a dispute possess them. That was why neither side used poison gas in the Second World War – but Mussolini's Italy was prepared to do so in 1936 against the Abyssinians, who could not retaliate. Hence, the greatest danger from nuclear weapons lies in the possible temptation of a nation possessing them to employ them against another which does not – a danger accentuated by the fact that more and more countries already have or are in sight of nuclear capability.

(3) The belief that wars can be won by these weapons alone is a fallacy. The Japanese had already been effec-

Con: (1) The invention of new weapons has been a consistent feature of mankind's history, from the sling and the club onwards. The first use of gunpowder was probably met with similar protests. There is a good case for reducing the existing stocks of nuclear weapons, both to save the crippling cost and as an insurance against any of the present prolific stocks falling into the wrong hands. But there is an even better case for retaining an agreed minimum of such weapons, as a mutual deterrent.

(2) The very horror aroused by nuclear weapons has made the superpowers determined not to go to war with each other and to abstain from using them in a war already begun. Hence, the USA refrained from the use of even 'tactical' nuclear weapons in the Korean war and Vietnam. It was the world-wide fear that nuclear weapons might be used which brought the Cuban crisis to a speedy end in 1962. The natural course of history is thus more effective, of itself, than any attempts to impose a formal ban.

(3) The use of nuclear weapons

135

tively defeated before Hiroshima and Nagasaki in 1945; the bombs merely hastened their surrender. No war will be won without the occupation of territory by troops on land. But the perils of radio-activity could postpone large-scale occupation indefinitely, while the scale of destruction on both sides in a nuclear war would render any normal political or governmental control virtually impossible. The super-powers' present weapons systems have long since out-moded the 'first strike' idea, whereby one nation would hope to get in first with such a lethal blow that its enemy could not retaliate in kind. Accordingly, the only hope of mankind's survival is to abandon all these utterly destructive weapons, for all time.

(4) Because previous attempts at prohibiting weapons have failed, it must not be assumed that they always will. Clearly, while the major power blocs still mistrust each other, it can only be achieved step by step. But progress *has* already been made: the partial test ban treaty of 1963; the nuclear non-proliferation treaty (1970); the first strategic arms limitation pact between the US and the USSR (1972), and their 1974 agreement to restrict their anti-ballistic missile systems and the size of underground nuclear tests. Following the successful conclusion of the European security conference in 1975, the big powers all expressed the hope that this would give a new impetus to the negotiations on the mutual and balanced reduction of armed forces, previously deadlocked. Vast difficulties and suspicions remain to be overcome; but, essentially, the will is there.

(5) So far from benefiting by the discovery of nuclear weapons, the development of the civilian, industrial use of atomic power has been crippled

would tend to shorten war and thus, in the long run, to save life — as, indeed, happened through their employment against Japan. While it may seem callous to make a balance-sheet of human lives, particularly those of civilians, the dictates of overall strategy nevertheless require it; and the plain fact is that, because nuclear weapons are delivered by air, from missiles or bombs, the loss of combatant lives would be minimised. The knowledge that armies would still be in existence to fight each other, despite the use of nuclear weapons, is thus another deterrent factor. That being said, no government would willingly countenance the huge potential loss of civilian life; so a nuclear balance between the powers is the best guarantee against any use of such weapons.

(4) Apart from the argument over whether it would actually be wise to ban all nuclear weapons, were that possible, it is unrealistic to imagine that the latest gradual disarmament moves will be any more successful than previous such attempts, for the necessary degree of mutual trust is still sadly lacking — and likely to remain so for the foreseeable future. Since the SALT 1 agreement, for instance, various American authorities have privately alleged that the Russians, if not actually violating the terms of the pact, have pushed close to the limits (on such matters as jamming and the use of silo covers to impede the agreed satellite surveillance of strategic systems). And how can agreements like the non-proliferation treaty succeed when, even now, more than thirty important nations have not signed it? Those countries, moreover, include the two other nuclear powers, France and China, as well as India (which has exploded a nuclear device

by the priority given to war research. No way has so far been perfected for using the thermo-nuclear process for peaceful purposes. A situation has arisen where only those countries which cannot afford the bombs are able to pursue civilian research satisfactorily.

(Some) Whatever their potential side-benefits, research and discoveries which might end in destroying the earth or the human race could very well be dispensed with.

'for peaceful purposes') and other near-nuclear nations such as Argentina, Brazil, Egypt, Israel and South Africa.

(5) Research for purposes of war usually has a beneficial effect on civilian progress, and so it has been with the atomic bomb. Radio-active by-products are used in hospital work; much progress has been made in the production of electricity from nuclear power stations. Civilian and military research projects have proceeded side by side, to their mutual benefit. Without the incentive which produced nuclear weapons, this would not have been possible.

(See also ARMAMENTS, LIMITATION OF CONVENTIONAL; WAR: IS IT
DESIRABLE?; WAR: IS IT INEVITABLE?)

OLYMPIC GAMES:
Back to Square One?

Pro: (1) When Baron Pierre de Coubertin re-created the Olympic Games in 1896, they enshrined the amateur ideal that what matters is not winning but taking part. Nowadays, this is more honoured in the breach than the observance. Many countries set out blatantly to gain prestige through their athletes' achievements at the Games. To that end, they provide likely prospects with well-paid but undemanding jobs and other facilities which, if difficult to prove as contravening the letter of the law, are clearly contrary to its spirit. (The athletics scholarships provided by some American universities are not much better.) Many if not most of the athletes are now professionals in all but name. All this has made the modern Games particularly vulnerable to political blackmail,

Con: (1) Although too many countries do indeed flout the Olympic spirit, treating the event primarily as an opportunity to enhance national prestige, even this cannot destroy the essential benefit of the Games – the sight of many hundreds of young people, from scores of different countries, getting to know and understand each other a little better, in completely friendly rivalry. There is nothing in the least starry-eyed or illusory about that impression: it is borne out at every successive Games, quite irrespective of the variegated political interferences each time. Whatever governments may think, the young people themselves know that it is an honour merely to have been selected for the Games – and no matter if they don't get beyond the first heat!

137

e.g. the US 'Black Power' demon-strations in Mexico in 1968; the attack by Arab terrorists on the Israeli team at the 1972 Munich Olympics; some Western nations' boycott of the 1980 Moscow Games in disapproval of the Soviet invasion of Afghanistan; the Soviet counter-boycott of Los Angeles in 1984; the withdrawal of some African countries for anti-apart-heid reasons, as a protest against those alleged to be supportive of South Africa. Action is urgently needed to restore the original Olympic ideals.

(2) Although individual cities vie fervently for the honour of staging the Games, reckoning that the huge cost is more than justified by the world-wide publicity a host city receives, the expense is so enormous that it can cripple the municipality concerned for years after. Montreal will be paying off its £130 million debt for the 1976 Olympics until the year 2030 – and that sum was probably only a tenth of the amount other host cities have spent since. Clearly, some means must be found to ease this enormous burden.

(3) The best answer to all these problems could lie with a 'Back to Square One' offer made by President Karamanlis of Greece in 1984 – the offer of a permanent home for the Olympic Games in the country from which they originated. They would need to be on a smaller scale and with cast-iron guarantees against contra-vention of the fundamental ideal. One subsidiary suggestion, for instance, is that each participating nation should make a capital investment in the permanent facilities to be established in Greece and should also make a deposit before each Games of (say) $1 million for every 100 competitors it entered. If this deposit were forfeitable in the event of political withdrawal,

(2) Some cynics have suggested that the only cities that can afford the Games nowadays are ones with a political axe to grind. But, except perhaps in terms of Spanish domestic politics, that could hardly be said of Barcelona, the city which has been awarded the 1992 Olympics; and it certainly doesn't apply to Birm-ingham, one of the other contenders for that year. The fact that these and several more cities were each prepared to spend three or four million pounds, or even more, merely in presenting their case to the International Olympic Committee, speaks volumes about the esteem in which the Games are still held and the continuing belief in their fundamental validity, whatever the extraneous problems. While the exuberantly capitalist exploitation of the 1984 Los Angeles Olympics prob-ably made them the only ones to show a clear profit in recent times, virtually all the other host cities have derived real if unquantifiable benefits: not merely world-wide publicity for the city but also a legacy of increased trade, an extra stock of accommo-dation (from the Olympic Village built to house the athletes), new arenas and other modern sporting facilities. Add in the direct cash benefits for the host country's sporting bodies, plus the inspiration which the event gives the country's youth to try to emulate the star athletes, and it's easy to see why the Olympic Games are likely to retain their present general format for the foreseeable future.

(3) Generous though the Greek offer may seem, it has several distinct snags. Even assuming that the perma-nent host country could solve the enormous logistical problems that would still be posed, the smaller scale envisaged for the Games would prob-ably rob them of some of their world-

and such countries were automatically excluded from the ensuing Olympics, they might well think twice about it. Another idea is that the Games should be confined to individual athletes and that, as in the original Olympics, there should be no team sports, since these tend to be the main focus for undesirable nationalistic rivalries. What with the present astronomic costs and the harm caused by relentlessly-mounting political intervention, these proposals may represent the only way of getting back to what, up to AD 394, the original Olympic Games were supposed to be all about.

wide interest (and thus of crucial revenue from TV coverage), especially as a number of team games are often among the most exciting events. At the same time, confining the Olympics to individual athletes would plainly do nothing to remove nationalistic rivalries between countries seeking to bask in reflected glory (however spuriously) from their own sporting 'heroes'. Forfeiture of a $1 million deposit would be most unlikely to deter a government determined to use the Games for political ends; many have already lost (or spent) a great deal more than that, in the past, in pursuit of political gestures. Nor should the value of one present organisational trend be underestimated: the allocation of successive Olympics between East and West bloc countries and the Third World (e.g. Moscow 1980; Los Angeles 1984; Seoul 1988). That undeniable benefit would be lost if the Games returned to Greece alone – and a good number of countries, still hoping to stage the event themselves one day, would assuredly resist the idea.

PACIFISM

Pro: (1) Pacifism is a belief which reflects the noblest aspirations of man. Throughout the Gospels, Christ enjoined it on his followers, and all the so-called Christian nations, however much they may backslide in practice, profess lip-service to it. The early Christians survived and flourished precisely and only through the practice of passive resistance to persecution. It is also an essential article of the Buddhist faith. After a brief period of domination, the Moslems were forced to abandon their

Con: (1) It is disputable whether Christ was as pacific in outlook as pacifists suppose. Many of his sayings can be quoted to illustrate a more militant attitude. Countries adopting Buddhism have survived in a warlike world only by mutilating their doctrine beyond recognition. A third great religion, Islam, had holy war as an integral part of its beliefs and established itself by direct military conquest. The Christian sects in general have abandoned passive resistance, recognising it to be unpractical.

aim of conversion by conquest, and many surviving Moslem communities exist contentedly under alien domination.

(2) That a pacifist attitude was not unpractical was shown by William Penn, who established peaceful relations with the American Indians and was enabled to build up the colony of Pennsylvania, whereas other colonists encountered bloody resistance.

(3) The charge of cowardice is made against pacifists in times of national hysteria and for propaganda purposes. Men volunteering for non-combatant service, such as driving ambulances, have saved many lives in wartime at the constant risk of their own, and absolute pacifists who refuse to take even this limited part in war have shown by their fortitude under violent persecution that they are as brave as any soldier, perhaps braver than those whose fear of the herd drives them into battle.

(4) The results of all wars prove the error of expecting progress to follow the use of force. Especially in a modern war, there are no true victors among the peoples as a whole, and the issues for which the war is fought are never settled by it.

(5) War gives rise to vice, cruelty and meanness, and there is no one taking part in it who is not demoralised by it. The so-called warlike virtues arise simply from herd instinct. Pacifism represents those emotions which lift man from the animal level. Women, who are concerned with the propagation and nurturing of children, are particular sufferers from war and are natural pacifists.

(6) The stage which modern weapons have reached, with the invention of the H-bomb and the possibility of complete annihilation for the

(2) Penn's pacifism had no lasting influence on the Indians and was suitable only to the early stages of contact with them, before they realised the intentions of the colonists. Pennsylvania very soon abandoned its Quaker form of government and became like other colonies. Pacifist communities, from those of earliest man onward, have been short-lived and limited. The course of history is against their survival as such.

(3) Pacifism is a refuge for people who, for physical or emotional reasons, cannot adjust themselves to the rigours of life in the community. A case can be made, perhaps, for people who, out of genuine religious conviction, refuse to risk taking human life but are willing to work in helping to save it. But it is illogical in the modern world that other pacifists who refuse to fight in defence of their countries should decline even to contribute some form of humanitarian service.

(4) That professed aims are not always achieved by a war is not relevant to the argument, since these aims are not necessarily identical with the situations and stresses which are the real causes of the wars. Thus the First World War, although not fought for that purpose, brought about the liberation of many nations and classes of people from reactionary domination.

(5) The waging of war can also bring out the best instincts in people, who often discover an idealism, brotherly love and willingness to co-operate with one another which tend to atrophy in peace-time. Even if war is a deplorable way of stimulating such virtues, it remains true that there is no inspiration in the pacifist creed for the mass of people, and this is no less true of women than of men.

(6) The existence of new weapons,

human race, makes pacifism more than ever the only possible creed consistent with our survival.

however horrific, does not change the situation, and a pacifist nation would merely be tempting others to use such weapons against it.

PARLIAMENT, REFORM OF:
Devolution

Pro: (1) The chief cause of the present inadequacies of the parliamentary machine, with the consequent loss of its prestige throughout the country, is the enormous pressure of business. Since 1874 at least, Parliament has been overworked. Lack of time has sometimes resulted in important legislation failing to be passed; money has been paid away for matters the Commons could not discuss; Scotland and Wales have had insufficient attention paid to their special interests; the power of Whitehall departments has increased to an alarming extent; and efficient government is possible only if the Cabinet practically ignores the Commons. Worst of all, foreign affairs have passed out of the Commons' control. The system of committees for dealing with particular questions, which can occupy up to 90 per cent of an MP's time, is too often used to support party interests rather than for objectively constructive study.

(2) All the main parties have paid court to the principle that, in one form or another, local affairs should be handed over to local Parliaments. It is immaterial whether, as some wish, Scotland, Wales and England should have a Parliament each, or whether, as others wish, a less grandiose form of regional autonomy should be chosen. Such a federal system would not destroy the main principles of the

Con: (1) The internal problems of Parliament are due to more fundamental causes than physical insufficiencies. The party system has wasted enormous amounts of time. The shortsightedness of members will, eventually, ruin even sectional parliaments. It is an exaggeration to say that matters of importance have been neglected. Scotland and Wales have had all the important Bills they wanted. No reliance can be placed on statistics which purport to show that these parts of the British Isles have received inadequate attention, because one Bill for Scotland may be more important and beneficial than twenty Bills for England.

(2) The removal of all local affairs would mean the inanition of the federal body, since the electors would not be enthusiastic over foreign, economic and other business that did not appear to concern their own region. There would be constant bickering between the various parliaments, as no system of devolution would prevent the adoption of different policies on matters that seem local but really affect the whole country.

(3) Devolution would have little or no bearing on any moves for European political union – a dubious prospect in the foreseeable future, anyway – since in this context Great Britain would have to remain a whole unit.

(4) The devolution issue has been

United Kingdom, since the federal or central government would retain its supremacy. MPs might sit part of the year at Westminster and part in the local Parliaments.

(3) Federal devolution would provide Britain with valuable experience for her participation in the EEC's eventual progress towards European political union.

(4) After a rebuff to Scottish devolution proposals in the March 1979 referendum, when Westminster politicians decided that the 52–48 per cent vote in favour was too narrow to justify implementing the move, what Scotland and Wales perceive as central government neglect of their areas has led latterly to a marked revival of local interest in the issue of devolution. It is now, once again, a 'live' topic in those regions.

seized on by 'national' parties in Scotland and Wales as part of their efforts to revive their otherwise flagging fortunes. But opinion polls indicate that, politically, it is still a 'dead duck' – that most voters in these regions no longer believe that some form of autonomy is either achievable or even relevant at present.

PARTY GOVERNMENT

Pro: (1) Government by one party holding a clear majority, with the other parties in opposition, is desirable and beneficial, and in some form or other inevitable. Only if the government is directed by a coherent group with a settled policy can progress be made or public business be done.

(2) Coalition experiments have generally been a failure. A national coalition is particularly inefficient in peace-time, because its pace is regulated by the most conservative section. If a government receives its mandate from a sufficient majority of electors, it has no right to abdicate from its position of supreme responsibility in attempting to share the burden with its defeated political opponents.

(3) Party government ensures a thorough discussion of all important

Con: (1) On many questions before Parliament, there is a general measure of agreement. Yet, to maintain the prestige of the party, unimportant points are frequently used for purposes of obstruction. Proposals cease to be judged on their merits but are judged on their supposed influence on the party fortunes.

(2) Coalition government was eminently successful during the Second World War, when the complexion of the government had ceased to correspond with the country's wishes in some ways but a general election was impracticable. There is no doubt that it called forth an immeasurably increased amount of devotion and hard work from the people.

(3) Debate is reduced to a farce. A

topics. There is no possibility of collusion to rush controversial measures through without publicity.

(4) The group system has failed repeatedly on the Continent. It is a synonym for unstable Cabinets, intolerable intrigue and failure to carry out much-needed reforms.

(5) There are only two real parties in the House of Commons today – the Labour Party and the Conservative Party. These correspond with the only two real forces in the State. In the course of time, the Liberals and Social Democrats are bound to disappear; any success they may be enjoying is ephemeral and is due only to voters' temporary dissatisfaction with the other parties on particular issues.

(6) It is impossible to prevent the growth of parties under a representative system. Any such devices as *ad hoc* coalitions, formed mainly to pass one specific reform and then dissolved, are futile (as shown by experience in Italy and pre-Gaullist France). All the disadvantages that are put down to party systems are inherent in political life of any kind.

party government can always use its majority to enforce its will and can stifle discussions by use of the 'guillotine' and other parliamentary devices. The net result is that the Cabinet is master of Parliament.

(4) The group system ensures a greater elasticity of policy and greater responsibility for the individual members.

(5) Three party groupings in the House of Commons are now an established fact of life, and the long-term trend will be for them to approach approximate equality of numbers. Despite the machinations of the two main parties, the Liberal/SDP Alliance has consistently maintained support of at least one-fifth to one-quarter in the opinion polls and has made very big advances in the municipal elections (taking local power, in some instances). In the 1983 general election, votes received by Alliance candidates, nationally, were only some 676,500 fewer than those for Labour (approx. 7.8m. against 8.5m.). If Alliance candidates' share of seats in the Commons represented even half their share of the poll, they would already hold the balance of power – and they seem quite likely to do so after the next general election or the one thereafter.

(6) Party systems are full of dishonesty, dubious mutual-aid deals among politicians, secret influences and other undesirable practices, which destroy the uprightness and independence of the individual and bring politics into disrepute.

(See also COALITION GOVERNMENT)

PAYMENT BY RESULTS IN INDUSTRY

Pro: (1) The workman paid by results is rewarded according to the energy, efficiency and initiative which he puts into his work. This is more just than the time-work system by which lazy and active, efficient and inefficient, get the same. Where payment by results is adopted, the morale of workmen goes up and they take greater pride in their work.

(2) Production is stimulated; machines and plant are used to the fullest extent and most economically; the workman gets higher wages and the employer higher profits; and the consumer benefits by lower prices. This is particularly so in the export industries and in building, where a high rate of production will be needed for many years to come. Fears of victimisation are groundless when a guaranteed minimum wage is also secured.

Con: (1) The important thing in industry is the general standard of the workers and not nice discrimination of merit. Indeed, the inefficient worker may be just as hard-working as the most efficient. All piece-work systems sooner or later result in the cutting of prices for work done and are more for the benefit of the employer than the worker. The logical outcome of dealing according to results is the turning of the inefficient adrift.

(2) While production may increase in quantity, it can equally prove harmful to quality, which is harder to measure. In the building trade, it is likely to lead to scamped work and the decline of honest craftsmanship. In many trades the work is non-repetitive and cannot be paid in this way. Wherever payment by results is applied, though, it has the effect of setting worker in competition with worker, to the detriment of team-spirit and morale within the factory.

POLLUTION OF THE ENVIRONMENT:
Are Tougher Laws Needed?

Pro: (1) The Royal Commission on Environmental Pollution, in its tenth annual report, defined pollution as: 'The introduction by man into the environment of substances or energy liable to cause hazards to human health, harm to living resources and ecological systems, damage to structures or amenities, or interference with

Con: (1) The existing legislation is much tougher than many people seem to realise. What counts is to implement it properly. Once improved economic conditions permit all the present provisions to be carried out in full, the introduction of stronger measures would be unnecessary. The Royal Commission report cited

legitimate uses of the environment.' That was in 1984, a decade after the Control of Pollution Act became law. A year later, the Commission complained that the puny sentences imposed for infringements were still often leaving offenders 'laughing all the way to the bank'. In many cases, it said, the penalties for the illegal dumping of waste were far lower than the saving that guilty parties had made by ignoring the proper procedures. Under the current legislation, the maximum fine for a first offence is still only £400 – a derisory sum, compared with the enormous amount of damage the offender may cause.

(2) Although the 1974 Control of Pollution Act did strengthen previous legislation, it has yet to be fully implemented, even now. There was backsliding from some of its provisions, right from the start, on the grounds of the cost entailed in carrying out the necessary improvements. If the authorities seriously intend to combat pollution, the provision of adequate finance for the purpose is essential.

(3) The danger of well-meaning measures failing to be implemented properly is illustrated, notably, by what happened after the Water Resources Act was passed. In theory, it gives water authorities wide powers to act against pollution; in practice, the authorities come under the Department of the Environment – which has told them to withhold action, because of the financial problems involved. These cash difficulties do not apply only to water pollution stemming from industrial companies or farms. Even more critically, they affect the regional water authorities themselves – because these, too, are now serious polluters, as a result of taking over the responsibilities of the

opposite also appraised the progress made in the ten years since the new Act came into force. While expressing concern about many issues – e.g. motor vehicle exhausts, 'acid rain', some farm practices, use of the North Sea as an industrial waste dump – it did also find that a number of apprehensions were unjustified. In the home, for example, the risks from white asbestos, the use of formaldehyde in cavity wall insulation, and various other substances potentially contaminating the air, were all (with the exception of tobacco smoke) much lower than many people had feared and there was no need for the new legal controls that some had called for. Above all, the Commission did *not* see any need for further legislation on nuclear energy. Reaffirming that it favoured 'an energy strategy that offers the prospect of least environmental harm', the report supported 'a modest increase in nuclear power'. And, notwithstanding understandable public concern about minor mishaps at Sellafield, Sizewell and Dungeness (an anxiety naturally accentuated by the Chernobyl disaster), the fact remains that the Commission *praised* the overall safety record of the UK nuclear industry. So, although there can never be room for complacency, it does seem that the present law has opened the way to pretty effective monitoring and control.

(2) The 1974 Act contained a new code regulating the deposit of waste on land and laying down conditions for the regulation of waste disposal sites. Local councils in England and Wales were constituted as waste disposal authorities and were required to carry out a survey of all the problems. On the Government side, the Environment Secretary was also given wide-ranging powers to make regu-

various, fragmented bodies formerly in charge. One such responsibility is for a number of sewage works which are producing effluent that is not up to standard, but the water authorities are unable to put the situation right simply because they do not have enough money for the costly remedies entailed. Bearing in mind the untreated sewage pumped into so many of Britain's coastal waters (not to mention industrial waste and controversial muck from nuclear power stations), it is doubtless significant – unhappily – that the average number of dolphins and porpoises sighted offshore each year, from Britain's coastal holiday resorts, has dropped by well over half in the past 30 years.

(4) The current legislation appears to have been framed on the assumption that industry is the most serious polluter. In the opinion of many independent experts, though, agriculture is now the chief culprit. The decline of heavy industry in Britain, as a result of economic factors, has had a decisive influence on the abatement of industrial pollution in our rivers and the transformation of that problem from one of essentially urban industrial 'black spots' to one of generalised rural pollution throughout river valleys, especially in the vast arable zone of Eastern England. Modern agricultural methods (e.g. the vast use of inorganic fertilisers, over enormous areas, and the concentrating of livestock for intensive rearing) are infinitely more pollutive than those of traditional agriculture. According to the Nature Conservancy Council, the incidence of agricultural pollution has risen every year since 1980. Plainly, therefore, this is another sector in which much stricter legislation is urgently needed. Mainly because of water pollution from farms, though

lations to deal with dangerous or intractable waste. The law re-enacted and reinforced, almost in their entirety, the previous Rivers (Prevention of Pollution) Acts 1951 and 1961, the Clean Rivers (Estuaries and Tidal Waters) Act 1960, and parts of the trade effluent legislation. In addition, it applied to certain underground, tidal and coastal waters not covered before. In short, it was – and is – extremely comprehensive. Even if financial strictures have delayed its full implementation, as yet, no reasonable person could possibly doubt the Government's determination to tackle pollution.

(3) The same economic difficulties have applied to the Water Resources Act – a measure which, incidentally, has not only imposed much more severe penalties than before but has also expanded the number of offences (for instance, now bringing estuaries under protection). Despite the delay in implementing some provisions, it certainly hasn't happened in all cases. Equally, despite the financial constraints, extra money *is* still found for projects regarded as essential. For example, with more than half of Britain's beaches so polluted that they failed to meet standards set by the EEC, the Environment Minister announced in the House of Commons in July 1986 that £300 million would be spent over the next five years on cleaning up the beaches and coastal waters. This expenditure, covering 80 schemes to improve sewage treatment and outlets, was roughly *double* the amount spent on such projects in the preceding four years.

(4) One feature of the legislation which should not be underestimated is that the Environment Secretary is now entitled to take precautions to *prevent* pollutive danger; formerly, he

also partly because of huge cuts in spending on sewage treatment between 1974 and 1981, the success in cleaning up Britain's rivers has been set back again for the first time in more than a quarter of a century. A report published in January 1987 revealed that more than 500 miles of rivers, canals and estuaries in England and Wales became more polluted during the first half of the 1980s. In that period, clean-up efforts improved 3,028 miles of water – but 3,506 miles became filthier, marking an abrupt reversal.

(5) The particular problem of nitrate pollution in some areas, through the over-application of fertilisers, was highlighted when new EEC standards for drinking water came into force in July 1985. These standards control the amount of nitrates, as well as lead, aluminium, pesticides and other pollutants, in drinking water. At that time, the water authorities told the Department of the Environment that no fewer than 600 of their sources of water supply could not meet the new rules. (As examples of individual regions: 26 of the Anglian authority's water supplies and 20 of those in Severn-Trent failed to meet the EEC standards for nitrates. Towns served by the biggest ones included Scunthorpe, Wisbech and parts of Leamington, Warwick, Lichfield and Sutton Coldfield.) Government scientists are reported to have warned privately that nitrates represent 'the biggest environmental time-bomb ticking in Britain'. Getting to the root of the matter, excessive use of fertilisers, it would be perfectly feasible to start reducing the problem by making the practice much more expensive, even downright uneconomic. Some countries, such as Sweden, already put a special tax on fertilisers

could do nothing until an offence had occurred. This power of prevention rather than attempted cure can be an extremely important weapon – against agricultural as well as industrial pollution. In pleading 'good agricultural practice', the burden of proof is on the defendant; in the present climate of opinion, he could sometimes find courts less easy to convince than he might have anticipated.

(5) Under the EEC directive, a government can ask for a delay in applying the new rules to specific water supplies, provided it submits a programme for cleaning them up. Britain did just that. What counts, though, is that the Government also announced that it intended to meet the EEC standards by 1989 ... Hardly a case of shilly-shallying! Moreover, it should be stressed that Britain is ahead of most European countries in collecting data on its water supplies and in starting to implement the directive. As with so many of the other objections raised opposite, we draw down an unmerited opprobrium on our heads precisely because we *are* more prompt than others to expose our failings publicly, in deciding what can be done to remedy them. From what the critics assert, you might almost think officialdom was unaware of the problems caused by over-use of fertilisers. In fact, the Ministry of Agriculture has geared itself to give farmers very good advice about fertilisers and farm waste management. The Ministry also provides grants for silage clamps. However, the farmer would still have to find a fair amount of money to store and dispose of animal wastes, silage effluent, and so on. On this score, therefore, it has to be a matter of 'softly, softly'. Whatever may be feasible over a period, there's a limit to the immediate cash

for environmental reasons. Why not here?

(6) Among other environmental issues where British officialdom has been dragging its heels, and on which there is now a crying need for much firmer legislation, are: (*a*) the 'acid rain' menace; (*b*) the cutting of sulphur emissions; (*c*) the reduction of air pollution by motor vehicles. Taking them in order . . .

(*a*) Britain has long emitted more sulphur dioxide, the main contributor to 'acid rain', than any other country in Europe. The Central Electricity Generating Board alone, through its power stations, puffs out more than most European nations. However, with 70 per cent of the emissions leaving our shores, blown north-eastwards by the prevailing winds, the CEGB has consistently refused to admit the harm it is causing. This is not greatly appreciated in such countries as the Netherlands, where 40 per cent of the forests show signs of damage, or (above all) Sweden, where about 18,000 of the lakes have been poisoned by 'acid rain' and some 4,000 of these are now virtually without fish.

(*b*) In an initiative led by the Scandinavian countries, nearly all the main European nations, including the Soviet Union, have joined the so-called '30 Club' – committing themselves to a 30 per cent cut in sulphur emissions by 1995. Britain has steadfastly refused to join, arguing – lamely, one might think – that no action should be taken until further research had clarified the problem. But surely even this pretext should not preclude new regulations to ensure that at least there's no *increase* in such emissions?

(*c*) The West German Government has decided unilaterally that all new vehicles in the country must be fitted

demands you can impose on anyone.

(6) What with the widely publicised reports of the Nature Conservancy Council, Friends of the Earth and many other bodies and individual scientists – what, too, with the threat to wildlife, the stone decay in ancient buildings and the damage to trees, at home in Britain as well as abroad – it is nonsense to suggest that the British authorities are complacent about 'acid rain'. Equally, though, it is quite unfair to attribute most of the blame to this country. In Switzerland, one-third of the forests are dying; in Austria, 1.5 million acres of forests have been damaged; in Czechoslovakia, more than half a million acres of forest have been destroyed and a further two million acres are dying. One only has to look at the factories of the Ruhr, the hideous pollution of the River Rhine, or, on an individual plane, the disastrous escape of noxious material from a Swiss chemicals factory in the autumn of 1986, to realise that Britain is by no means the prime source of 'cross-border' pollution in Europe. To tackle the problem properly requires a concerted assault on *all* the sources. In like vein, on the issue of sulphur emissions, there may be sound sense behind Britain's argument that pollution from motor vehicles is at least an equal, if not greater, environmental hazard than power stations. The obvious solution is to curtail *both* sources of pollution – but first, you do, indeed, need to be sure about the facts. This also applies to the question of vehicle emissions . . . an issue on which the British Government could hardly be accused of being obstructive, given its introduction of unleaded petrol. There is no space here to go into all the highly complex technicalities. Broadly, though, the motive for

with anti-pollution devices from January 1, 1989. This is six years earlier than the date from which the EEC had proposed making the measure compulsory for all member-nations. But even that has been resisted by the British Government, which has sought to dilute the EEC standards – to have them set higher so that they could be met by other means, without using the expensive catalyst technology now proposed. The Government has also intimated its intention of not complying with the EEC proposal (which it is free to do, since this is only a *voluntary* directive). Sooner or later, though, Britain will find it impossible to carry on ignoring the measure. In the interim, moreover, the directive may well be tightened, in response to any further large-scale deterioration in the European environment. Faced with these prospects, would it not make sense for Britain at least to lay the groundwork for eventual legislation?

(7) Until the early 1970s, incredible though it may now seem, pollution offences in Britain were covered by the Official Secrets Act! The ostensible reason for this extraordinary restriction was to protect the confidentiality of industrial processes (it being just a coincidence, of course, that the restriction also happened to have the convenient effect of protecting the anonymous bureaucrats involved). Since the 1974 Act, this ban no longer applies and offences may now be given full publicity. Experience shows that, while a good proportion has indeed come under the spotlight, there are still a number of cases in which one may suspect that, because of the habitual reluctance of civil servants and local government officials to disclose any information unless they have to, great vigilance remains

Britain's stance is that West Germany wants limits which require the use on all new cars of expensive three-way catalysts, which can operate only at a fixed air/fuel ratio, whereas British car manufacturers are developing a generation of engines which operate at a *thin* air/fuel ratio – the so-called 'lean-burn' engines, which will be able to comply with the very tough US emission standards. A compromise has since been reached within the EEC whereby large cars would use three-way catalysts and medium-size cars would combine leanburn engines with simpler, much cheaper oxidation catalysts. So the justification for Britain's supposed 'obstinacy' – and for the lack of need for any draconian new legislation – has been amply borne out.

(7) It is highly probable that the unfavourable publicity received by polluters will have a cumulative and ever greater impact in deterring other potential offenders. Most people today are so perturbed about the pollution problem that it is increasingly likely there would be a public outcry if civil servants or officials were caught trying to cover up breaches of the law. The force of public opinion is the all-important factor in the fight against pollution. It brought about the present, much tougher laws against offenders; it will ensure that there is no let-up in the struggle; and it remains far more effective than proposing yet another batch of laws which would be more honoured in the breach than in the observance.

(8) It has become all too fashionable to deride governments or other official bodies for trying to 'cut their cloak according to their cloth'. Yet the plain fact is that initiating an anti-pollution measure (or any other, come to that), when you know you may not

necessary to ensure that they comply. Accordingly, new regulations ought to be introduced to compel them to publish regular reports on all cases of pollution, within the area for which they are responsible, and on the action taken in each instance.

(8) Time and again, the British Government gets out of actually having to *do* anything by asserting that some project or other may be very desirable, but that we simply do not have the money to pay for it. However, an opinion poll conducted in 1985 by the Organisation for European Cooperation and Development showed that 62 per cent of Americans and 59 per cent of Europeans gave environmental protection a higher priority than economic growth. Perhaps it's *governments* that ought to amend their order of priorities, then?

have the finance to complete it, is far more undesirable and dishonest than to admit candidly that lack of cash obliges you to delay some desired action for the time being.

(See also PRESERVATION OF BEAUTY SPOTS, ETC.)

PREMATURE BURIAL:
Are the Safeguards Inadequate?

Pro: (1) Owing to the absence in most countries of completely foolproof laws governing the disposal of the dead, to hastiness in burying victims of epidemics, and to uncertainties arising in certain cataleptic and other morbid states which counterfeit the appearances of death, the danger of living burial is a very real one. In Britain during the last twenty-five years, several dozen cases have been officially recorded in which undertakers or mortuary keepers detected signs of life in people who had been certified as dead. If such mistakes are known to this extent, is it not probable that even more terrible mistakes

Con: (1) The present laws and regulations are sufficient. Premature burial may occur, but it must be exceedingly rare in Europe. The essential point which must be borne in mind throughout all these arguments is that, in cases where people have shown signs of life after being taken to mortuaries, the signs have been relative in the extreme and the victims were moribund to the point of no return; despite immediate treatment in intensive care units, their deaths have always been established finally within a matter of hours, or a day or so at the most.

(2) Premature burial is a very good

150

have been made at a later stage, by the premature burial of still-living bodies?

(2) The first safeguard it is essential to tighten concerns the issuing of death certificates. At present, if a doctor has seen a patient within fourteen days prior to death, he can sign the certificate without examining the body. Only a few years ago, a Home Office pathologist reported that, of five bodies taken to a London mortuary, all certified by doctors as natural deaths, one was in fact due to multiple injuries, another to disinfectant poisoning and a third to gas poisoning. Clearly, the law should be changed so that doctors should not sign a death certificate without having seen the dead person.

(3) Another important safeguard should be the provision of up-to-date testing equipment in mortuaries. This is needed especially for avoiding the danger of mistakes in one ever-increasing category: people in drug comas. The risk is heightened in such cases because the victim's pulse and breathing may be slowed down to an extraordinary extent while in the coma.

(4) The controversy over transplants led the Department of Health to plan setting up an advisory panel – its members including a neurosurgeon and a neurologist, as well as heart, liver or kidney specialists – to decide when a brain was technically dead. The fact that such experts were considered necessary, in this special situation, suggests that there must also be room for doubt over the precautions in determining 'ordinary' deaths (when the extra care required for transplant operations is not called for).

(5) Obviously, a panel of consultants, as described in the previous paragraph, would be neither necessary nor

subject for newspaper scare stories, but none has ever yet been proved true. In the vast majority of cases, it is relatively simple to establish that a person is dead, with complete certainty. When subsequent signs of life showed that mistakes had been made, special circumstances usually applied. Outside his hospital or surgery, a doctor can do little more than look for evidence of heartbeat and breathing. Both may be undetectable in a cold, unconscious patient without special tests being made. But, precisely because he is fully aware of the possibility, a doctor will normally try to delay issuing a death certificate in these circumstances until such tests have been carried out.

(3) Equipment of this nature already exists in some mortuaries. Mainly as a precaution in drug cases, for instance, Sheffield mortuary installed an oscilloscope machine which can detect the slightest movement of the heart muscle – and its lead has been followed by others. It is admittedly desirable, perhaps, to require all municipal mortuaries to have such equipment.

(4) Transplant operations are, indeed, a special situation, involving public emotion to a very considerable degree. But it would be quite impossible to take such elaborate precautions for all deaths. There simply aren't enough specialists available; the number of bodies awaiting burial would very soon become intolerably large; and, in any case, such precautions would be absolutely unnecessary for all but a tiny handful of deaths.

(5) The rule that at least two doctors must examine a body before it is cremated was brought in at the turn of the century mainly to meet early fears that cremation might be

feasible in most cases. It is not being argued that stricter safeguards should be applied other than in circumstances where it is recognised that these are clearly advisable – and there is a precedent for this. Prior to cremation, rather than burial, it is still a rule that more than one doctor must certify the cause of death. Reasonably, therefore, the two-doctor rule could be instituted for all deaths in categories where doubt is liable to arise (a very small proportion of the overall total).

(6) Among other proposals which have been made are: (a) that a doctor, even though he has already issued a death certificate, should examine the body again on the day before the funeral; and (b) that a bottle of chloroform with a loose stopper should be placed in each coffin, as a general practice. (It is understood that most crematoria do, for this reason, inject formalin into corpses before incineration.) The depth of many people's anxiety about premature burial must not be underestimated.

used to conceal evidence of crime. The precaution is no longer necessary, if ever it was. The early fears have proved groundless, and the Cremation Society has long been pressing for parity with the regulations for burial. Another reason for the two-doctor rule originally was to guard against premature burial (or incineration), and this has been equally groundless.

(6) The scaremongering about premature burial is neurotic and quite unjustified. In Western countries, the possibility is so remote as to be virtually non-existent. Even if it did happen that an apparently dead body were placed in a coffin before the moribund victim was completely dead, the act of shutting the coffin would presumably ensure speedy and painless death by suffocation.

PRESERVATION OF BEAUTY SPOTS AND SITES OF SPECIAL SCIENTIFIC INTEREST:
Are the Laws Inadequate?

Pro: (1) Far too many flaws have become apparent in the laws currently supposed to give protection to recognised beauty spots and to sites declared of special scientific interest (which embrace areas of unique plant growth, of uniquely important geological formation, or harbouring rare and threatened wild life). Much banging of drums accompanied the

Con: (1) Since the National Parks Act of 1949, ten national parks have been created which cover some 5,228 square miles, or close on 9 per cent of the total area of England and Wales. The idea was not to change the character of these territories but to control their development in accordance with two main principles:

(a) to preserve the characteristic

152

introduction of the 1981 Wildlife and Countryside Act, an immensely complex measure which was vaunted as providing a comprehensive environmentalist solution to such issues. But so far, despite achieving a few individual successes in detail, it has largely failed to do so in overall terms.

(2) Here are some of the losses suffered by Britain's countryside since the last world war: 80 per cent of the chalk downland; 60 per cent of the heathlands; more than 50 per cent of the wetland; 40 per cent of the traditional broadleaf woodland; and 125,000 miles of hedgerow – equivalent to five times round the Equator. Most of these losses have been caused by the introduction of modern farming methods, particularly intensive cereal production, and others by the building of motorways and new towns. Even conceding that by no means all the features cited were necessarily beauty spots, as such, nor sites of special scientific interest, the threat to Britain's wild life has been unmistakable – the corncrake, sand lizard and red-backed shrike typify species once comparatively common but now on the verge of extinction due to habitat-loss. And the plain fact remains that, in just under 40 years, an area of prime habitat *the size of the Lake District* has been destroyed. Faced with problems of this magnitude, claims that the latest legislation has taken the measure of the difficulties, as heard from some complacent MPs, just won't wash!

(3) It was not until some five years after the 1981 Act that plans were announced for new controls on farm and forestry buildings and roads in Britain's national parks. These were needed to close one glaring loop-hole whereby, because of the statutory delays for negotiations and appeals, a

beauty of the landscape within the park area; and (b) to ensure that the public has ready access to the parks and facilities for recreation and enjoyment. The Countryside Commission also has powers to designate areas in England and Wales, other than the national parks, as 'areas of outstanding natural beauty'. Existing legislation already covered a wide range of contingencies to reinforce the necessary protection for these places – and, if properly observed, was quite adequate for the purpose. The same applies to the 1981 Wildlife and Countryside Act, which, in the fullness of time, seems likely to become recognised as the most comprehensive environmentalist law yet instituted by any nation in the world.

(2) It is all too easy to select statistics which appear to indicate that all is for the worst, in the worst possible of all worlds (whether on environmental or any other controversial issue). Were it not that such matters are inevitably a question of subjective judgment, it would doubtless be possible to produce equally impressive figures for those features of the countryside which have been saved from destruction. Just within the wildlife field, for example, one case in point is that superb raptor, the peregrine – once dwindling in number with alarming rapidity, brought to the point of extinction in England and Wales by excessive use of permanent pesticides. It has since been rescued from that fate by farmers' voluntary agreement to take the welfare of this and other threatened bird species into account by restricting and refining pesticide use. One factor that conservationist militants tend to overlook is that, whatever undoubted mistakes have been made in the past, the issue can never be one-sided. A balance has

farmer whose land lay within a national park, for instance, could still sidestep control. If he went ahead and completed his desired building while the above procedures were still in progress, there was nothing the national park authority could do about it. The insensitive visual damage caused by some farmers during this period has been almost beyond belief. (As examples: an unsightly modern farm building, utterly inappropriate for the surroundings, or a new path scarring a hitherto untouched hillside and now glaringly visible for miles around.)

(4) Among numerous other inadequacies: attempts to protect rare geological features such as limestone pavements (found in only a few limited areas of N.W. Europe) involve such lengthy procedural delays that only a very few orders have been sanctioned – in relation to the size of the problem, a mere fraction of those needed. Similarly, Ministers have powers to protect moor or heath from being converted by agricultural or forestry operations, but the orders they may make under the Act are limited to only 12 months – so the potential despoiler could simply wait for it to expire and then go ahead and plough up or convert the moorland, as he'd planned. The limitation, clearly, should be for a much longer period. Another example: land drainage, in the interests both of local agricultural improvement and avoiding downstream flooding, is a water authority responsibility. Carried out insensitively, it does great damage to the capacity of water-courses to harbour attractive flora and fauna, whose protection is *also* a water authority responsibility. Traditionally, land drainage departments have a powerful voice, and a history of resistance to

to be struck between each party's legitimate needs. Neither can nor should be implemented at crippling expense to the other.

(3) The new order provides certain local planning authorities, including all those responsible for the national parks, with a discretionary control over the siting, design and external appearance of various farm and forestry developments. Prior notification now has to be given, to enable the planning authorities (when they deem it appropriate) to regulate some of the detailed aspects of the development concerned, in order to help conserve and enhance the natural beauty of the countryside. Far from being a belated measure, it was based on procedures which had operated in parts of the Lake District, Peak District and Snowdonia since 1950. Its wider application – as with so many other environmental measures – depends to a large extent on establishing much better cooperation with the farmers, landowners and other parties concerned. National park authority representatives now meet farmers on their own ground, for instance, to talk in very practical terms about land management and conservation; a great deal of mutual understanding has been built up, as a result, and many farmers have willingly amended their original development proposals once valuable features have been pointed out (often of which they were not aware) and alternatives discussed. This voluntary process is bound to be more effective in the long run, and certainly more so than the unilateral imposition of restrictions which, overnight, could drastically cut farmers' legitimate earnings and plunge many of them even further into debt than they are already. Despite the powers given to the Countryside

interference. There is no statutory requirement to prove the cost-effectiveness of 'drainage improvement' operations (usually financed in part by the Ministry of Agriculture) to the satisfaction of any outside body. This is manifestly anomalous.

(5) Similar snags apply to many of Britain's sites of special scientific interest (SSSIs), of which there are now more than 4,000, offering a completely representative cross-section of habitat types in this country. According to the Nature Conservancy Council, between 10 and 15 per cent of the SSSIs suffered 'significant damage' in the year before the 1981 Act and a further 156 were damaged over the next 3–4 years. Their two main protections are through the notification procedures introduced by the Act and through development control. But the latter, regrettably, does not cover the activities most likely to harm an SSSI, because many operations on land used for agriculture or forestry (e.g. converting countryside to intensive agricultural systems, ploughing moorlands or growing coniferous plantations) are not subject to control by the local planning authority. Moreover, in cases where action *can* be taken, it often depends on local authorities deciding whether or not to exercise their discretion to do so – a decision against which conservationists have no effective means of appeal.

(6) The present penalties for the destruction of 'scheduled' ancient buildings, or of trees on which a protection order has been made, are trifling in comparison with the financial gain which is usually to be made by the infringement. These blatant defiances need to be made thoroughly unprofitable by the insti-

Commission, the law still requires it to have 'due regard to the needs of agriculture and forestry and to the economic and social interests of rural areas'.

(4) Many of the above considerations apply equally to the problems of protecting geological rarities, moorland, marshes and so on. As just one example: the case of a limestone pavement in Cumbria, under consideration by the Countryside Commission and Nature Conservancy Council for a protection order, has been complicated by the fact that the area involves common land and commoners' rights to gather stone. However desirable the ultimate objective, you cannot simply trample on people's age-old rights, without due process of discussion and persuasion.

(5) Some critics query whether the protection of SSSIs is at the expense of other parts of the countryside; they also hold that there are parts of the country where the existence of too many SSSIs seriously affects the rural economy. Yet these sites, while only part of a package of measures to protect wildlife habitats, are frequently regarded as the key symbol of nature conservation in Britain. Moreover, the criticisms fail to note the importance of a parallel step, the designation of Environmentally Sensitive Areas (ESAs). Farmers in these areas will qualify for special payments from the Ministry of Agriculture if they volunteer to continue, or adopt, specific farming practices which will safeguard the characteristic landscape, wildlife and archaeological features of the locality. In August 1986, out of 14 sites put forward as candidates by the Countryside Commission and Nature Conservancy Council, the Government chose six to be the first ESAs – among them, the Broads and the

tution of realistic penalties, reviewed at frequent intervals.

(7) The two officially-sponsored bodies most closely concerned, the Nature Conservancy Council and the Countryside Commission, have stated quite frequently that they have agreed on a joint method of working the various conservationist measures open to them, under the current law, but that neither has sufficient staff available to do such work in a comprehensive manner. In short, making the law work properly is a matter of more money. The only valid conclusion from this is that the undoubted shortcomings are less the fault of the agencies on the ground than of the politicians behind them, who at present seem very unlikely to cough up more cash because they put conservation far down their list of priorities (except for a brief vote-catching flurry prior to elections!) But pleading adverse economic conditions is no longer an adequate excuse – not when you're spending untold billions on new nuclear weapons, without any certainty that a situation will ever arise in which a small island nation would dare to employ them. Large or small, though, *all* nations have environments to preserve which are of astonishing fragility. The issue is not at root just a cultural one (although there are cultural connotations). Environments are first and foremost life-support systems, subject to fatal damage by mismanagement. Political priorities require adjustment so that it becomes seen as far more important to devote large sums to the preservation of our environment than to the insatiable military appetite.

Somerset Levels. In these areas, official agricultural policy and conservation interests go hand-in-hand and it now makes good financial as well as environmental sense to farm the land with sensitivity. More ESAs will doubtless follow. Hardly a case of inadequate legislation, surely?

(6) A just balance has to be struck with the requirements of agricultural and urban development. It is neither desirable nor possible for a landscape, urban or rural, to be subjected arbitrarily to paralysis. A landscape is a dynamic entity, not a fossil. (Although, unhappily, it also has to be recognised that arguments of this character are now in the shadow of growing mountains of foodstuffs which may eventually be burned or dumped in the sea, for want of any other feasible disposal.)

(7) The effectiveness of the 1981 Act was first tested at a period when local authorities were under severe financial and manpower restrictions and were thus reluctant to use some powers which entailed long-term financial obligations. This reluctance will disappear as economic conditions improve again. In like vein, one argument put to the EEC is that European agricultural policies and regulations should incorporate conservation objectives and that money should be available for this purpose under the EEC's Common Agricultural Policy, e.g. to maintain or improve farm incomes without necessarily increasing agricultural output. Here again, the essential finance seems bound to be forthcoming eventually.

(See also POLLUTION OF THE ENVIRONMENT: ARE TOUGHER LAWS NEEDED?)

PRISON REFORM

Pro: (1) The principal objects of imprisonment are the protection of society and the reclamation of the criminal. On the second count, to reform the offender, our present prison system still does far too little – hence the high proportion of recidivists, particularly among the young. Even the Youth Custody system (replacing the former Borstals), though an advance on previous methods, can still be criticised for aping too closely the ideas of the English Public School, with its emphasis on loyalty, patriotism and team spirit – ideals so remote from the young offenders' former experience that the response tends to be hypocrisy rather than honesty and independence. The 'short, sharp shock' of the new Detention Centres, for the youngest boy offenders, simply has not worked; statistics indicate that a large majority of the boys commit new crimes within months, if not weeks, of their release.

(2) Every prisoner should be regarded as mentally sick and given the special psychiatric treatment appropriate to his case.

(3) The present system has several serious defects. Although the strict discipline has been made more sensible in most (though not all) prisons in recent years, there are still too many pettifogging restrictions which have the effect of needlessly 'institutionalising' some prisoners and making them unwilling to face up to the responsibilities of independence. Some of the work given to prisoners is futile and the machinery used out of date. Creative activity, even for the more intelligent prisoners, is insufficiently encouraged. In consequence, the prisoners are not fitted to find work or

Con: (1) The State has a duty to the public as well as to the individual. Advocates of 'pleasanter prisons' tend to forget that a term of imprisonment *must* do more than merely reform the criminal. It is of prime importance that the sentence should act as a deterrent, not only to the criminal in question but also to others who might be tempted to follow his example. At the same time, the prison system has, in fact, been humanised and transformed by administrative measures, so that the old strictures no longer apply. The expedients of Detention Centres, Youth Custody, Community Service, probation and suspended sentences are all aimed at making prison a last resort – giving those whose characters are capable of reform a chance to make good before 'the clang of the prison gates' becomes the only way of dealing with them.

(2) Much of the reformatory system is completely unrealistic. It leads to blatant hypocrisy on the part of the prisoners, whose sole aim is to escape proper punishment and obtain release (all too often in order to commit further crimes).

(3) Many of such conclusions have been drawn from observations made by criminologists on subjects who were (understandably) nervous. When prisoners are allowed too much freedom from discipline, the risk of them corrupting one another is greatly increased. Many men have been taught a trade in prison, enabling them to earn a respectable living in the outside world for the first time in their lives.

(4) Under Government plans costing £360 million, 16 new prisons are due to be opened by the early

resume a normal life in society; instead, many of them develop mental disorders which render them a misery to themselves and a menace to others.

(4) Within the general European sphere, only Turkey jails more offenders, proportionately, than Britain does. Our prisons are now grossly overcrowded. Figures published in April 1986 showed a total of 46,600 inmates – whereas the maximum number these prisons are designed to accommodate should (in theory) be 37,000. Probably about a quarter of the prisoners, therefore, are having to sleep three to a cell. Worse, some are having to spend up to 23 hours in their cells each day, because financial cuts have resulted either in there being no work for them to do or in a shortage of staff to supervise them. Similarly, accommodation arrangements are utterly inadequate for prisoners on remand (i.e. still awaiting trial) and for petty offenders who ought to be segregated from hardened criminals. In Britain's 25 local prisons (as distinct from the main establishments), about 45 per cent of the inmates are remand prisoners. Waiting times between committal and trial still greatly exceed the eight weeks recommended in an official report more than 25 years ago; in London, the average waiting times are nearly 24 weeks. While that is the fault of the judicial rather than the prison system, it does not alter the basic problem. All the statistics cited here serve to show, incontrovertibly, the crying need for reform. As for the prison building programme, it is estimated to take up to ten years to build a large new jail, and a parliamentary committee report published in June 1986 expressed serious doubt whether the target of ending overcrowding by the 1990s would be met. The MPs were

1990s. By 1993, too, an even larger number of extensions to existing buildings should have been completed. Altogether, this building programme will add 11,500 places to the system, which should result in the elimination of over-crowding (according to the former Home Secretary, Mr Leon Brittan). The problem should also be eased by current efforts to get the courts to make more use of fines for indictable offences and thus to send fewer people to prison (and for shorter periods than before). On average, it costs £250 a week to keep an offender in prison. The total annual cost of running all the prisons in England and Wales is put at £700 million, of which 72 per cent goes on staffing. That the authorities are prepared to spend such a large extra sum on the new building programme, therefore, particularly at a period of financial stringency, must surely confirm the efficacy of our prison system. Once overcrowding and other temporary problems are removed, it is a system which has been shown to work perfectly well. At the same time, the overcrowding is of itself proof of another salient factor: when it is generally accepted that severe measures are necessary to combat the sharp increase in criminal offences – and above all, crimes of violence – life in our prisons is no longer sufficiently rigorous. If it were, many more men would avoid a life of crime rather than risk jail terms which, under present-day conditions, they tend to regard with some equanimity.

(5) Incorrigible offenders should be shut up for life, as dangerous to society. It must be recognised that there are some criminals whom no amount of educational work can reform – and that high-security jails will always be needed for them.

also critical of inadequacies in the plans – pointing out, for example, that by 1991 there would still be almost 20,000 cells without integral sanitation.

(5) Educational work in prisons, voluntary or otherwise, needs extension and development. Those jails which are in too remote places to make this feasible should be done away with.

(6) Most law-breakers offend through economic pressure. Others are physically degenerate and therefore fitted for occupational or education centres, or else suffer from obsessions and mental weaknesses which it is the proper function of the psychiatrist to treat. Recent advances, notably in connection with psychoanalysis, now give real hope of such treatment succeeding. A few moral degenerates who are past hope should be kept in mental hospitals. The handful who are deliberately and so to speak inexcusably, habitual criminals, ought to be sent to a penal colony. The present system deals adequately with none of these several classes.

(7) The Elmira State Reformatory in New York, Sing Sing Prison under Osborne, the Neudorf Convent Prison near Vienna, and other such places, have been successful in their humane methods of dealing with their inmates. The success of Britain's open prisons shows how much can be achieved from a less restrictive regime.

(8) Prison diet is badly balanced and inadequate for health, and most of our prisons are grossly deficient in sanitary conditions and general health and cleanliness. Prison officers suffer from low pay and status, and not enough officers of the right calibre can be recruited under present conditions.

(9) In past ages, when punishment was savage, crime was more rampant

(6) Most of the psychological theories of crime rest on shaky foundations and have yet to be convincingly proved. The treatment suggested tends to be objectionable in itself and would be very difficult, tedious and expensive. The criminal code is concerned not with antecedents, causes and expectations, but only with the facts of crime.

(7) Elmira was long a by-word among prisoners who had a much better life inside than outside its walls. New York State declined to support it. Sing Sing also has since been reorganised on the old lines. Many experts consider that, except possibly for the type of prisoner who is not normally a criminal and would be unlikely to repeat his offence, it is doubtful whether open prisons in Britain are any more successful than other forms of detention in terms of reducing recidivism.

(8) Punishment must be to some extent retributive, to satisfy the sentiments of the community and of the criminal's victims. Much of the concern for the criminal is due to a perverted sympathy which forgets the suffering of those he has wronged.

(9) If prison is to be reformed, let it be made more unpleasant. For several classes of criminal, guilty of offences against both person and property, jail conditions are at present quite inadequate as a deterrent and bear no relation to the damage the criminal has inflicted. Many inhabitants of our deprived inner-city areas have to endure harder conditions than men in prison.

than it is today – which proves, yet again, the ineffectiveness of drastic methods.

(See also INDETERMINATE SENTENCES FOR PROFESSIONAL CRIMINALS; CORPORAL PUNISHMENT)

PRIVATE MEDICINE

Pro: (1) All people should have the right to choose the doctors they prefer and, within reason, the timing most convenient to them for medical treatment, operations, etc. In theory, the National Health Service does allow people to change to another general practitioner, if they wish; but in reality, because many overworked NHS doctors already have full lists, it is often difficult to find another doctor in your home area who is willing to accept you as a Health Service patient. As for the timing aspect, the NHS allows for no freedom of choice at all.

(2) Envy of people with money is a root cause of the opposition to private medicine. It may be argued that, whether under a capitalist or a socialist economy (or a mixture of both, as in Britain), one universal reason for trying to earn higher incomes is to be able to buy things one could not afford before. Even if one ignores that point, as part of another, broader issue, the fact remains that it is financially possible for the great majority of people to secure the advantages of private medicine. There are several thriving medical insurance schemes, which enable subscribers to meet the charges of treatment as private patients. Subscribers still pay their normal National Health contributions, which thus benefit other people. In 1984, the NHS in England treated 450,000 more in-patients than

Con: (1) It is quite wrong that the few should take precedence over the many. For all its flaws and problems, Britain's National Health Service represents an ideal which has been achieved by no other nation and which must rank as one of the greatest social advances in history. Its object is to make the best possible medical and surgical treatment available to the whole population, without favour. While it may not always achieve this, its shortcomings are due mainly to inadequate finance, in the adverse economic conditions now prevailing, and will be remedied in the fullness of time, when the economy improves. It would still be possible to get much nearer to the ideal, even now, if all members of the profession gave the NHS their whole-hearted support.

(2) The belief that opposition to the buying of privilege is raised mainly from those who cannot afford that privilege is held, typically, by moneyed people themselves. It ignores the real cause: the present-day trend towards an increasingly egalitarian society, not by lowering standards but by enabling everyone to have access to higher standards. The commercial horrors of private medicine are illustrated by the USA, where many people are ruined financially by an unexpected spell in hospital – and where the poor, unable to afford medical insurance, may well die because they cannot pay for the

in 1978, and there were nearly 2.5 million more out-patient attendances – proof positive that, in a period when health authorities were cutting jobs, improved productivity and efficiency within the service were quite unharmed by any increase in private hospitals. According to a 1985 report, consumers were spending £1 billion on private health care, as against £17 billion then being spend on the NHS.

(3) Most of the important advances in medicine have been made by private doctors, working on their own, or by privately financed research organisations. Many consultants maintain private practices, where their earnings are high, so that they can afford to devote several days a week to working in public hospitals or free clinics.

(4) Waiting lists at NHS hospitals are so long that some patients are having to wait up to four years for any but emergency operations. No less serious is that, due to the shortage of NHS beds, patients undergoing operations regarded as relatively minor are being sent home the same day they were under the knife. Similarly, because of staff shortages and the pressure on hospital beds, elderly patients who might 'block' beds for a lengthy period are sometimes refused admission in favour of younger patients – a hideous dilemma for the doctors, who know that their decisions may well condemn old people to an earlier death. Lack of money for the facilities they need is fast destroying morale among NHS staff and has led increasing numbers of young doctors, who can ill be spared, to decide to emigrate. In these deteriorating circumstances, the public's need for the services of private medicine has become more acute than ever.

(5) An aspect of private medicine

treatment necessary. Since the Conservatives returned to power in 1979 and unemployment rates began to soar, the health gap between rich and poor has grown sharply. Wives of men in the lowest two socio-economic classes are now up to 70 per cent more likely to die young than those of men in the highest two classes. Death rates among semi-skilled and unskilled workers aged 25–44 are more than twice as high as those for professional men and managers in the same age group.

(3) The latest developments in heart surgery and many other advances in surgical technique were all perfected at NHS hospitals. Only through the NHS has such expensive equipment as the kidney machine been made available to patients, even in their own homes, who could not have hoped to buy them from private sources. Similarly, NHS doctors are able to give out prescriptions for extremely expensive medicines, etc., which their patients obtain for only a nominal charge. Before the NHS was established, such medicaments would have been beyond most people's reach.

(4) The problems of the NHS are not denied, though it should be stressed that the overall picture is by no means as serious as asserted opposite; some regions are worse hit than others. The fundamental difficulty, as stated earlier, is the Government's inability or unwillingness to provide more finance (that is, in *real* terms, ahead of the inflation rate). The Conservative Government began cutting back funds for the NHS as long ago as 1973. Since then, the shortfall in cash actually needed has become progressively more critical. In short, governmental policy is to blame and not the essential structure of the Health Service itself. That being said, it is all the more important

which should not be underestimated is its importance for business companies and their employees. It is recognised practice for many firms to pay for their staff to have free medical treatment – which has the further advantage of ensuring continuity of contact, through telephones in their private rooms, etc., and is thus mutually beneficial. The right of companies to pay for private medicine in this way is sound common sense. It is an attractive inducement when recruiting staff; it relieves employees of many anxieties and obviates delay before they receive treatment; thereby, in turn, it makes for greater efficiency overall. Large companies habitually provide a sick bay on their premises, which is open to all the workers without charge.

(6) It is not suggested that the NHS should be done away with and that all medicine should return to the private sector. That would be neither feasible nor desirable. But the reverse is equally true. There is room – and need – for both private and public medicine.

that the existing facilities should be shared fairly and that such anomalies as private beds in NHS hospitals should be abolished.

(5) Private firms have no more right to buy privilege than do private individuals. As long as a private sector exists, however, there is one constructive solution that they should adopt. If a company wishes to offer its staff facilities of this nature, it should get together with other firms to establish a clinic of their own, with all the companies involved paying jointly for the staff and equipment. That way, while priority could still be given to their own employees, they would at least have created a new medical facility which other people could use as well. Many of the larger trade unions have long run convalescent homes, for the benefit of their members, to supplement NHS facilities but without cutting across them.

(6) Some countries already have an entirely public medical service without any private sector, and this has not prevented them from being among the most progressive in the medical field (e.g. the Soviet Union). One of the principal objections to private medicine is that it leads to a diversion or dilution of medical skills from the public sector. When the two are still accepted side by side, as in Britain, the existence of one should not be at the expense of the other.

(See also STATE MEDICAL SERVICE)

PRIVATISATION

Pro: (1) The process of 'privatisation', as generally understood, entails selling back to the public a majority share-holding in enterprises which

Con: (1) The nationalised industries were brought under State control originally in accordance with the Labour Party's commitment to the 'common

have been nationalised under previous governments or in which the Government of the day still has the largest share. It is a form of 'popular capitalism' (as Prime Minister Margaret Thatcher once described it), which not only spreads share ownership throughout society but also, and perhaps above all, gives ordinary people a direct stake in the nation's means of production and distribution.

(2) Among numerous advantages of privatisation are: (a) it frees those responsible for the industry concerned from the constraints imposed by State ownership, including governmental intervention in day-to-day management, and protects them from fluctuating political pressures; (b) it releases them from the restrictions on financing which public ownership imposes (i.e. they could now raise money in the City instead of only from the Treasury); (c) access to private capital markets makes it easier for them to pursue effective investment strategies for cutting costs and improving standards of service; (d) the financial markets would be able to compare the performances of individual sectors of a privatised industry against each other and also against those of other sectors of the economy, thus providing a financial spur to improved performance; (e) a system of economic regulation would ensure that the benefits of greater efficiency were passed on to the public in the form of lower prices and better service. In the process, industries thus unshackled would be able to contemplate raising their standards with the aid of such incentives as higher salaries, profit sharing, and so on.

(3) Equivalent measures in other countries have been undeniably successful, e.g. the 'property formation' strategy pursued in West ownership of the means of production, distribution and exchange'. It follows, therefore, that to claim privatisation gives ordinary people a direct stake is entirely spurious. In effect, it is simply selling back to people what was already their own property. At an individual level, false pretences of this nature would normally make someone liable to criminal charges!

(2) Most, if not all, of the advantages cited opposite could be achieved perfectly well without privatisation. The one big exception is governmental intervention – a factor which would continue to loom large, through economic, legislative and other controls, even if the Government decided against continuing to hold a minority stake (as in some cases hitherto) but sold off its holdings completely. Were the Government to allow the managements of nationalised industries a genuinely free hand to run them on proper business lines, there would be no need to privatise them. One problem is that, in initiating its sell-off programme after returning to power in 1979, the Conservative Government of the day continually (and falsely) equated privatisation with deregulation. No less misleading was its failure to point out the consequences of two other aspects of its policy. On the one hand, by dangling only the *profitable* bits of nationalised industries as bait for private investors (otherwise, of course, there'd be precious few takers), the remaining bits were made much more vulnerable to eventual cuts and reduced services – facilities which, even if financially unprofitable, had still been fulfilling a public need. On the other hand, as a corollary, the dogmatic insistence on State industries making a profit took no account of the fact that there are

Germany, resulting in fewer strikes and higher productivity (benefits equally evident in Sweden). Even Communist Hungary now sells shares to its population.

(4) An essential feature of privatisation is that employees of the industry concerned are given a direct stake in it (as with the long-standing Liberal policy of Co-Partnership, q.v.). For example, the flotations of the Trustee Savings Bank, British Telecom and British Gas all gave preference to share applications from their own staffs.

(5) There is nothing underhand or undesirable about a government's use of the proceeds from privatisation to help ease the strain on other sectors. In the summer of 1986, for instance, it was revealed that the then Government was aiming to raise £4.75 billion annually from privatisation, over the ensuing three years, to help pay for its proposed tax cuts. If that seems unduly high, it need merely be borne in mind that, as of 1986, the Government's remaining 31.7 per cent shareholding in British Petroleum alone was valued at nearly £3 billion (having already realised some £819 million from earlier sales of two tranches of its holdings, in 1979–80 and 1983–84). Similarly, it was pointed out that, from April 1988, the Government would be free to sell its remaining 49 per cent holding in British Telecom, previously estimated to be worth £7 billion. Given the Conservative Government's stated intention of following the sale of British Airways with other privatisations it had postponed until after the ensuing general election (e.g. the delayed sales of the dockyards, the Royal Ordnance factories and, above all, the 10 water authorities in England and Wales), then the projected target for meeting tax cuts is perfectly feasible.

some which probably never will but which ordinary people still *expect* to pay for, because it provides a service they want. To cite a Continental example: no rail network could be more efficient than the SNCF, France's nationalised railways; yet the French have always recognised that the SNCF simply could not do the job demanded of it without a huge State subsidy each year.

(3) There is not the slightest evidence that widening the number of people owning shares has any effect on political attitudes or labour relations. In reducing strikes or raising productivity, such factors as better management and better arrangements for collective bargaining, over pay and conditions, have far more relevance.

(4) The true weight of this supposed 'co-ownership' is exemplified by British Aerospace, which sold three million shares to its workers. Sounds a lot – until you learn that, in fact, it's a mere 1.3 per cent of the total shareholding. As one financial writer observed: If all these worker-shareholders decided to sell their entire stock on the same day, 'it is doubtful whether it would even register on the Stock Exchange'.

(5) Quite apart from the highly dubious morality of the process, cited earlier, it may be questioned whether 'selling off the family silver' – as privatisation was described by the late Earl of Stockton (the former Tory Prime Minister, Harold Macmillan) – has any more economic validity than the wholesale wasting of revenues from Britain's now-dwindling North Sea oil resources. These revenues, similarly, have been largely used to avoid raising taxes, instead of as a heaven-sent opportunity to build up new capital investment. Yet opinion polls have consistently shown that,

(6) Far from 'selling the silver', privatisation is simply transferring the silver from the politicians and civil servants *to* the family. It avoids the monolithic snags of monopolies and opens up such industries to the invigorating breezes of free competition. Nor is there any question of it being intended mainly to help finance tax cuts. On the contrary, Ministers arguing in favour of such measures have often pointed out that the sale of State-owned industries and assets would support a substantial programme of new public investment in roads, housing and hospitals.

(7) At a more local level, the drive to get hospitals and local authorities to put certain key operations out to competitive tender – e.g. hospital cleaning services, refuse collection and school meals – has reaped very big benefits: either the internal labour forces of the authorities concerned, in competing for the tenders, have greatly improved their own efficiency and productivity; or the private sector companies which have succeeded in winning some of the contracts have enabled the authorities to achieve substantial savings.

rather than tax cuts, a clear majority of Britons would prefer better public services, even if it entailed having to pay more.

(6) Privatisation is supposed to increase competition, yet the British Gas monopoly remains intact, just as British Airways has been allowed to keep some key routes to itself. When Britoil was State-owned, the Government stopped it prospecting for oil, on the ground that this would increase its borrowing – but then privatised it, to let it do just that. Similarly, it forced British Gas to sell off its oil discoveries – which, after privatisation, could then be resumed once more . . . The only conclusion to be drawn from these illogicalities (other than the fact that the proposals hadn't been thought through properly, anyway) is that the Tory Government responsible for initiating the policy had no interest in public and private companies competing in the market on equal terms: in reality, as a matter of political dogma, it wanted to remove every trace of public enterprise it could.

(7) What happens when a private company, having put in an artificially low bid to win a contract, reduces the level of service or re-hires the former labour force for poorer wages and conditions? When the money from North Sea oil and from privatising national assets starts running out, would Conservative Ministers fill the gap by tax increases, more public borrowing or renewed cuts in public spending? Somehow or other, there seems to have been a deafening silence on all these points.

PROFIT-SHARING

Pro: (1) As the worker creates to a large degree the profits pocketed by the capitalist, it is only right that he should be allowed a share in them. Though he cannot directly contribute to losses in bad years, he may do so indirectly by the establishment of a reserve fund and by forgoing bonuses in good years. A 1986 survey by the Department of Employment showed that more than one in five of British companies now operates profit-sharing schemes for its employees. Employers believe that such schemes do enhance a sense of 'belonging' among their workers and a greater commitment to the company.

(2) Under the present system, many employees have no interest in the success of a business or in the prevention of waste or of damage to machinery. Profit-sharing improves the quality and leads to an increase in the quantity of the output.

(3) It has generally succeeded very well where it has been tried, especially when there is some provision for the workers to take up shares in the company. Failures have been due to employers' attempts to use the system as a weapon against trade unionism.

(4) Profit-sharing brings worker and capitalist together. Strikes are prevented, industrial unrest avoided, and all sides benefit. Before the gas industry was nationalised, the old South Metropolitan Gas Company introduced a scheme of this nature — and enjoyed more than a quarter of a century of industrial harmony. An independent research report in 1986, noting a decline in retail sales by department stores, singled out one group as an exception: the John Lewis stores, in which all employees are

Con: (1) As long as workers have no share in losses as well as in profits, any scheme for profit-sharing amounts to charity on the part of the employer. The employee has no claim beyond the competitive value of his labour; profits depend on the wisdom and skill of the employer in using his capital. It is surely significant that more than half those with profit-sharing and share-option schemes, according to the 1986 survey, were public companies. Among private companies, the proportion was only 11 per cent.

(Some) Profit-sharing is a concealed form of paying wages and is unjust in that it is not reasonable to invite men to receive more or less remuneration for their services in consequence of causes entirely beyond their control. The details and rates are generally at the mercy of the employer, who may sometimes try to use them to depress standard wages.

(2) It is only occasionally that workers get a sufficient share to interest them. Payment by results is a much more efficient method of encouraging increased production.

(3) Its success is greater where labour forms but a comparatively small part of the costs of production, e.g., ship-building. At least half the schemes initiated have failed, and most of them are intended to isolate the workers from trade union influences.

(4) Profit-sharing is no cure for the ills of our industrial system. It merely puts a section of capitalists and workers in league — usually to the detriment of price stability for the consumer.

(5) Agriculture has proved, in the event, as susceptible of trade union

'partners'. The report said unequivocally: 'John Lewis's policy of having profit-sharing partners leads to high staff motivation, low staff turnover and good customer service.'

(5) Profit-sharing is especially suitable for agriculture, where regulation by trade union methods is difficult owing to the variation between local conditions. It incorporates many of the advantages which are claimed for a co-operative system, but without involving any new departures in management or changes in habit.

(6) Profit-sharing could be organised nationally, with a Government Ministry to pool and distribute the profits. It would be a suitable arrangement for the kind of industries which might once have been considered for nationalisation – those in which some sense of wider public involvement is still desirable.

organisation as other industries. Agricultural conditions can also be improved by industrialising farms. Profit-sharing is least applicable, because labour is such a large item in the cost of production, and it lacks the element of individual independence which is fundamental to a co-operative system.

(6) The difficulties are too complex for any such national scheme to work. Profits are best shared on a national scale by means of a special tax on them, whereby the revenue returns to the country as a whole.

(See also CO-OPERATION; CO-PARTNERSHIP IN INDUSTRY)

PROHIBITION

Pro: (1) Where liberty in the consumption of drinks containing alcohol leads to licence, and licence to such evils as are apparent, the State should carry out its duty of protecting the public by prohibiting all intoxicating beverages.

(2) It is erroneous to suppose that the suppression of one evil leads to the creation of others to replace it. That has not been the case in history when great social advances have taken place.

(3) Prohibition has been a success time and again. It increases a country's industrial efficiency and the prosperity of the working classes. Many leaders of industry and of religion support it.

Con: (1) Prohibition is a gross attack on the liberty of the individual. The existence of a small proportion of admittedly harmful results is no excuse for victimising the bulk of the population, any more than cases of gluttony or unsound habits of diet would justify the State in saying what people shall and shall not eat.

(2) The imposition of near or total abstinence by force would suppress much good with the evil and replace one evil by others which might be worse. Prohibition is a symptom of an unsound view of sociological problems: drunkenness is less a cause than an effect of bad social conditions.

(3) Prohibition in America has been

PROPORTIONAL REPRESENTATION

In a country such as Britain, with an
efficient police force and a traditional
respect for the law, evasion would be
negligible (once political consent to
the measure has been given).

(4) To impose the will of a minority
on the majority of a democratic
community is quite common in this
and other countries, and the results
are rarely serious under modern
conditions. Nevertheless, the imposition of the will of the majority on
the minority is the established rule in
most States today, where serious
issues are at stake. Prohibition, therefore, will come only with the general
consent of the electorate. However
desirable one may believe the measure
to be, that consent will take time to
secure. But it is by no means a remote
or improbable prospect. As formerly
in America, many more people in
Britain now advocate prohibition than
is usually realised.

(5) Palliative measures, which have
now been adopted by anti-prohib-
itionists only because they fear defeat,
are not adequate to deal with the
colossal waste and suffering due to
alcoholic indulgence.

tried and abandoned (1919–33). It
was the product of a neurotic Puritanism, which attained its ends by
highly dubious means. It led to an
increase in the use of other drugs,
encouraged defiance and mockery of
the law, produced widespread corruption in the ranks of public officials,
and weakened belief in other, quite
separate moral issues. It removed or
distorted a whole group of social
habits without putting anything in
their place, while its effects on the
generation growing up were
thoroughly bad, for they were
surrounded by an atmosphere of
contempt towards public authority.

(4) Elsewhere, too, prohibition has
been put into practice only by underhand methods, which have enabled a
minority to dictate to the majority.

(5) All the evils which constitute
the alleged justification of this policy
can be removed, and in fact are being
removed, by education, by improvements in social conditions, and by the
efforts of the manufacturers of
alcoholic liquors, who are no more
enamoured of excess than are their
opponents. Often their proposals are
thwarted by the fanaticism of these
opponents.

(See also LIQUOR LAWS: SHOULD THEY BE RELAXED?)

PROPORTIONAL REPRESENTATION

Pro: (1) Britain's present electoral
system produces unrepresentative
Parliaments and may even reverse a
national verdict. On several occasions,
one of the main parties has polled
fewer votes than the other but has
obtained appreciably more seats in the

Con: (1) On the whole, the present
system is fair, and its shortcomings
affect all parties about equally. The
weight of public opinion is reasonably
reflected in the Parliaments elected,
and any undue predominance which
the present system appears to give to

House of Commons. Equally, a party gaining an overall majority may obtain much more than its fair share of seats (and thus of power), so that representation in the House of Commons is dangerously one-sided. In the 1983 general election, the Conservative Party received just over 13 million votes – roughly two-fifths of the poll – but won by a landslide majority, with 144 seats more than Labour, which polled just under 8.5 million votes. The Liberal/SDP Alliance was in quite a close third place, with more than 7.75 million votes, but gained only just over a score of seats – a bare one-tenth of those received by Labour. In the 1984 elections for the European Parliament, West Germany's Green party and two extreme-right parties in France and Italy won seats with 8, 11 and 6.5 per cent shares of their national polls, respectively. Yet in Britain, where the Alliance received more than 2.5 million of just under 13 million votes cast, near enough 20 per cent, it didn't get a single seat. The British Government's insistence on keeping the first-past-the-post system, even though it made us the only EEC country out of step, in this context, produced a palpable electoral injustice.

(2) Under proportional representation, the House of Commons would represent the nation fairly. The majority party would have a majority of seats, while substantial minorities would be represented in proportion to their share of the poll. When three main party groupings, plus minority nationalist groups, have seats in Parliament, as now, and when it is clear that this will remain the broad picture henceforth, the anomalies of our present system seem more acute than ever; yet the need for reform was apparent, and such reform was duly

one-party government is offset by the influence of other manifestations of public opinion.

(2) Under proportional representation, minorities would still be at a disadvantage in by-elections, which often have an influence on policy much greater than their immediate bearing on the state of the parties in the Commons. The difficulties of the present system might be met by adopting the less radical method of the second ballot (q.v.).

(Some) Present tendencies indicate that we shall eventually return to the fundamental characteristic of British political opinion – that is, of being roughly divided into two parts, broadly labelled Left and Right.

(3) The House of Commons has lost prestige in recent years for quite different reasons – the parties' internal squabbles being among them – and its position is not to be restored by any mechanical devices such as proportional representation. It is significant that, in the debate on the Representation of the People Bill in 1948, the Conservative Opposition did not speak in favour of proportional representation, even though the operation of the present system had lost them many seats only three years earlier.

(4) Proportional representation would cause a great increase in the number of candidates and members whose programmes were limited to special hobby-horses. This would make a farce of Parliament – and it would still be unrepresentative, for the more entrenched it became, the more certainly it would turn representatives into mere delegates.

(5) The 'single transferable vote' may work reasonably well in a strictly Irish context, though its relative simplicity for the voter is counterbal-

demanded, even when there were only two main parties.

(3) Today, if the House of Commons is not representative, if it is weak in personnel, it loses respect. The House will retain its authority only if it is truly representative of the nation. The excessive powers exercised by the party machine tend to diminish the prestige of Parliament. With proportional representation, MPS would have greater freedom from the control of the party whips; they could, without giving up their main principles, take independent action when they deemed it in the national interest to do so, and yet secure re-election.

(4) One scheme submitted to Parliament provided for constituencies returning some five members each. Such constituencies, would overcome the limitations of the present system and permit a broader scope of representation. Those returned would be the ablest of the party politicians, plus other candidates known and approved by virtue of their personality or previous public service.

(5) The PR system known as the 'single transferable vote' already operates most successfully in Eire and has also been adopted in Northern Ireland, except for elections to the Westminster Parliament. It has proved that, in a multi-party democracy, proportional representation is the only way to avoid freak victories and undeserved defeats. The Westminster system, in contrast, enabled a leading figure of Provisional Sinn Fein to win election to Parliament with only 37 per cent of the votes.

(6) Under proportional representation, MPS would to a great extent continue to be associated with parties, and parties would in general form the basis of government. Governments would, where necessary, be formed by

anced by some highly elaborate mathematics for the people who count the votes. Even so, this is not enough for the Alliance parties, the main advocates of proportional representation; they want to add frills to the Irish-type voting system which would make it even more complex. The drawbacks of poor PR systems are readily visible abroad. Those used in Israel and the Netherlands almost seem designed to ensure that they never get stable governments. The West German variant does produce governmental stability, but at the price of having half the Bonn Parliament filled with people nominated by party headquarters.

(6) The independent men would in practice represent local interests. Everyone with good qualifications for political life can enter it through one or other of the major parties, for their bases are broad. If proportional representation were to succeed, the House of Commons would come to resemble France's Chamber of Deputies under the 4th Republic, when a stable government with a settled policy was almost unknown, because there were so many groups and sub-groups which could be got to work together only after much horse-trading and intrigue. This state of affairs was undoubtedly responsible in large measure for the French voter's temporary abdication of his constitutional rights in 1958.

(7) While petty bribery might vanish, subtler forms of currying the favour of constituencies would be developed. There would be a general campaign to obtain the votes of small sections which ran no candidates. The wealthy or astute man would be at a greater advantage than before in being able to canvass a huge area. Expenses, already prohibitive for all but the chief

a frank co-operation of parties in respect of policies held in common. That is, they would be less partisan and more national in character. The Scandinavian countries use proportional representation in all their elections, with the result that, while their governments can be, and are, changed democratically, they usually enjoy stability. In France, which is again using the second ballot and not proportional representation (after a brief try with the latter in the 1986 general election), the need for inter-party bargaining between the two ballots, to gain other parties' support for remaining candidates, inevitably entails compromise on many issues.

(7) The greatest corruption occurs in small single-member constituencies in which the result can be turned by those electors who, seeking their own sectional interests, are influenced by demagogic promises. The adoption of proportional election by New York City is considered to have diminished the corruption which formerly reigned there to a startling degree.

parties, would increase. Not mechanical devices but education and a better spirit are the cure for political evils.

(See also COALITION GOVERNMENT; SECOND BALLOTS)

PSYCHO-ANALYSIS

(The three main schools of psycho-analysis are those of Freud, Jung and Adler. Other people have proposed a combination of the teachings of these three. The common doctrine of them all is that many of our states of mind and many of our actions, if not most, are largely determined by 'unconscious' wishes and memories. The Freudians have stressed the importance of our love and sex relationships, Jung and his followers man's need to discover meaning in life, and Adler the instinct of self-preservation and self-expression, which, when thwarted, produces an 'inferiority complex'. Needless to say, the whole subject is difficult and technical, but there are several general arguments worth mentioning.)

Pro: (1) Many of our actions and emotions cannot be accounted for by

Con: (1) Though we may grant the importance of the 'unconscious'

171

causes of which we are aware. They are clearly influenced by other things unknown to us consciously. Psycho-analytic technique shows that there is an active part of our mind of which we are not aware, and that this affects even those of our actions for which there appears to be adequate motive in our conscious life. This 'unconscious' mental activity comes out in a confused form in dreams, symptoms, etc., and from these we can get back to it and learn *how* it acts.

(2) 'Unconscious wishes' which are out of control or unintegrated are potent causes of mental instability and even insanity. By applying psycho-analytic technique, they can often be made 'conscious' to the patient, so that he can face them squarely and often be cured of his affliction. A large number of cases have been successfully treated by this technique.

(3) The principle of determinism, i.e., that everything that is or happens is a result of a series of causes which can be discovered, at any rate in theory, is a successful hypothesis in physical science, of which it is, indeed, the foundation; it is also true to a significant extent of psychological occurrences and phenomena. If it were not true, then there could not be any systematic psychology at all, for we should be quite unable to say that one thing will always follow something else, other things remaining the same.

(4) The main theses of psycho-analysis are supported by a worldwide examination of the myths, customs, beliefs and practices of primitive and other peoples. In these we see the results of unconscious forces on a larger scale.

(5) The discrepancies between the psycho-analytic theories are partly due to the fact that it is still a new discipline, with its data being collected

activities of our minds, they are not to be regarded as *determining* our character and actions. Psycho-analysts are wont to find what they set out to find, especially in dream-interpretation. This is shown by the different interpretations that different analysts put on the same dreams and the same symptoms.

(2) Psycho-analytic treatment has upset the mental balance of quite a number of people. The cures might have been obtained by other methods, especially by suggestion or via spontaneous improvement. In fact, though psycho-analysts claim not to use suggestion, the prolonged treatment the most eminent of them employ cannot but be suggestive. A great deal of ordinary medical treatment depends for its success on suggestion, a phenomenon which cannot be avoided, however much we desire it.

(3) There is reason to suppose that psycho-analysis is based on the unprovable assumption that mental phenomena occur in a deterministic fashion. It is not at all certain that they do.

(4) If we adopt the theory that the various cultures in the world grew up independently of one another, the argument from anthropology might hold. But there is a growing school of thinkers who argue that they are causally related one to another. If their arguments hold, the anthropology of Freud, Jung, and their followers becomes untenable, as the facts on which they rely will prove to have definite historical causes, and so cannot be the product of the 'collective unconscious'.

(5) Psycho-analysts do not agree among themselves over the most essential points of their theories. The majority concern themselves with the abnormal. Psychology as a science

only gradually, and partly because the theories are often incomplete and stress one side of the matter.

(6) Psycho-analysis aims at establishing man as more aware of his own mind and character. This is a perfectly moral and wholly admirable purpose. Those who attack psycho-analysis often have a vested interest in keeping man the slave of ignorance and prejudice. The analyst is a well established professional and his services are constantly used by such bodies as the Forces, the school medical services and universities, as well as in clinical psychiatry.

would make better progress if more effort were directed to the study of the normal and the perfecting of experimental technique for that purpose.

(6) By exalting the importance of the unconscious, psycho-analysis aims a blow at the idealism of mankind and tends to undermine morals by making it appear that men are automata. Many so-called analysts are charlatans.

PUBLIC OPINION POLLS

Pro: (1) The public opinion poll or 'straw vote', in which selected samples of the public are invited to give their opinion on questions of public policy and interest, and the results are analysed statistically, has become an important feature of present-day life. Run on scientific lines, these polls are capable of yielding very accurate results, and most of those taken prior to general elections in Britain have proved, in the event, remarkably near to the actual result. There is no reason to suppose that the findings of polls on general questions are any less accurate.

(2) Inaccuracies are rare enough to be of little importance and can in general be allowed for by statistical adjustments based on mathematical principles. It is possible to get a broad picture of the majority view of a subject and also the prevailing view of a particular section of the population – according to age, sex, social standing, etc. The degree of importance which the public attaches to a

Con: (1) It is a fallacy to suppose that public opinion on general matters can be ascertained with complete reliability in such a mechanical manner. The system is subject to considerable inaccuracies, resulting from such factors as the inadequacy of some of the questioners, the nature of the questions asked and the way they are framed. The only answers possible are generally 'Yes' or 'No'. Qualifications and reservations have to be ignored. There is thus a risk that they may reflect the conscious or unconscious prejudices of those who formulate the questions, even to the extent of being 'angled' to produce a desired answer. In some cases, further questions have revealed that the original question was entirely misunderstood.

(2) A vague or undecided answer might well indicate that the person questioned has not had time to make up his mind. It is not possible for most people to give snap judgments on every question, and the practice of

given issue can often be judged from the number of undecided answers.

(3) Any changing trends in opinion, on any question, can easily be established by a further poll. At present, the public's only opportunity to express its views on many questions is at elections, which may be at up to five-year intervals. The questions then presented for its consideration are often more susceptible of misunderstanding and inaccuracy than those in a poll. Since referenda (*q.v.*) are not normally used in this country, opinion polls can even serve as a safety valve – far more desirable than political strikes or other disturbances – by giving members of the public an outlet whereby their views on crucial issues are brought home with immediacy to the powers-that-be.

(4) The only doubt now raised by politicians against public opinion polls is whether they should be banned just before elections, on the ground that their findings might influence voters unduly. It is argued by some that, if the polls show one party to be well in the lead, supporters of that party might become complacent and not bother to vote. Alternatively, supporters of a party which is trailing in the opinion polls might be led to make more effort than they would otherwise have done. But such arguments cancel each other out and there is no evidence at all that opinion polls have ever had any real effect on an election result.

trying to make them do so is one of the main flaws of opinion polls. Considered opinions are based on a variety of causes, not all of them purely intellectual; an opinion may be changed overnight by some new argument or event, and the record will become completely inaccurate.

(3) Owing to the method of sampling on which public opinion polls are based, very few members of the public have the chance to express themselves in person. (The number of people questioned, even by the best polls, is rarely more than 1,500 or so.) The value of such polls as a safety valve is therefore negligible. The use of opinion polls by aggressive or unscrupulous bodies might lead to the lobbying of legislators which is one of the curses of American political life. Most questions of national importance can be settled at elections.

(4) That anxiety on this score cannot be so lightly dismissed is emphasised by the ruling that no public opinion polls may be published later than 24 hours before an election. Even at this last-day stage, the polls have had some notorious failures: for instance, President Truman's re-election in 1948, when all of them forecast his defeat; and similarly, the British general election in 1970, when only one out of the many opinion polls caught a faint hint that there had been a last-minute swing to the Conservatives. Rather than risk any such potentially misleading influences on the voter, it is surely better that all opinion polls should be barred throughout the official election campaign periods.

PUBLIC SCHOOLS

'The term 'public schools', in Britain, denotes educational establishments which are anything but public. They are private, fee-paying schools, which until recent years were nearly all of single sex. The Public Schools Act of 1864 listed these nine: Eton, Harrow, Rugby, Winchester, Westminster, Shrewsbury, Charterhouse, St Paul's and Merchant Taylors. There are now about 200 recognised public schools in the country, the term being applied to schools financed by bodies other than the State, the headmasters of which belong to the Headmasters' Conference. Several of the boys' public schools date back to the fifteenth century, and one – King's, Canterbury – to the year 600. Most of the leading public schools for girls were founded in the nineteenth century.)

Pro: (1) The British public school system has been the source of many of our country's most valued traditions and reputation for high standards of honesty and service in public life. It is a unique institution, without which our social and cultural development would be infinitely poorer.

(2) Among the many advantages of public schools are the high academic standards of the teaching staff they are able to attract and the relatively small size of their classes – much smaller than in State schools – which thus have something of the beneficial character of tutorials at university, permitting more individual attention to each pupil.

(3) The fact that so many parents still make considerable sacrifices to ensure that their children get a public school education is proof that they consider it well worth while. If people did not believe that public schools gave their children benefits unobtainable at State schools, the economic difficulties prevailing nowadays would have long since ended the existence of most public schools. The crux of the matter is whether people who can afford it, or who make strenuous efforts to do so, should be entitled to give their children the best that is available. Since we live in a free enter-

Con: (1) Public schools represent one of the last bastions of class and financial privilege. Despite a few marginal reforms, they are completely out of keeping with majority opinion today and should be abolished or absorbed into the State system.

(2) It is now widely accepted that all children should have equality of educational opportunity (i.e. that each capable of reaching the highest levels should have full facilities to do so, irrespective of parents' ability to pay), and the trend of official policy has moved increasingly towards achieving this. In the past, the financial resources of the public schools gave them an undoubted edge. Today, though, the academic records of public school pupils are, in general, no better than those from the upper reaches of the State schools – and, in some cases, it may be doubted whether their facilities are now even as good.

(3) People with money will always use it to try to buy things which, they think, give them (or their children) an advantage over others less fortunately placed. It makes no difference whether such things are not actually superior to those generally available, so long as they believe them to be so. The crux of the matter is whether, in a supposedly egalitarian society, people who can

prise society, the answer must be Yes.

(4) Although most public schools take day boys (and a few, in fact, have hardly any boarders), the great majority of them are boarding schools. From the community feeling thus engendered, the children acquire an instinctive awareness of how to live more easily with their fellow-men in the larger community of the adult world.

(5) The majority of public (boarding) schools, again, are situated in the country and have facilities for sport and country life generally which exist only in the more privileged homes. This is one reason why public schools remain in great demand, particularly among middle-class parents. Another is that public school education is concerned not only with academic standards but with developing the children's characters as future citizens. Both work and leisure time are used constructively to foster physical and mental health and to produce young people with wide interests, a sense of service to the community, and a well-rounded, balanced attitude to life.

(6) Only a very few public schools are co-educational at all ages, but the level of demand shows that there are enough of them to meet the requirements of parents who prefer this system. Although some people criticised the single-sex nature of most public schools which was the general rule until recent years, it did in fact reflect the overwhelming demand. Indeed, at the age they go to public schools, many children themselves would rather be without the society of the opposite sex – in school surroundings, anyway. The total seclusion once customary at public schools no longer applies, since older pupils at most

afford it should be entitled to buy privileges not open to everyone else. Where the education of the nation's children is concerned, the answer should be No.

(4) All too often, the cloistered life of boarding schools is out of touch with the realities of day-to-day existence in the outside world and engenders its own artificial values, the disillusionment of which comes as a rude shock when the children leave to take their place in adult society.

(5) The privilege enjoyed briefly by public school pupils – merely because their parents have been able to pay for it – presents the danger of them acquiring snobbish attitudes of the worst kind (especially if the leisure facilities of the school are of a nature unknown in their own home lives). Without discussing the issue of boarding *v.* day schools, which is another argument, the fact remains that day pupils at public schools tend to be less 'snobby' than boarders. Their comparative freedom to explore the world outside school gives them mental and emotional advantages which make them more immediately fitted for adult life.

(6) Children in their very young teens will nearly always prefer the company of their own sex, but those from the mid-teens onwards need to learn how to comport themselves naturally with the opposite sex, without silly self-consciousness. Many public school boys, when they leave, are still far too immature in this respect. The argument for single-sex schools has in any case been partially shattered by the fact that increasing numbers of well-known boys' schools, in recent years, have accepted girl pupils as well – in the sixth forms, at least. Nearly all the State schools are co-educational, and their children

boys' schools nowadays have a modicum of association with girls' schools – through dancing classes, orchestras, joint dramatic productions, etc. – or through the advent of girls into more senior classes.

(7) The first and perhaps the most important lesson learned by any child entering public school is the practice of mutual tolerance. From this, in turn, develop the qualities of loyalty, decision and natural leadership – which explains why most of Britain's national leaders (of whatever political party!) have usually been educated at public schools.

certainly emerge with much more understanding and recognition of the opposite sex's attitudes and natures than do those from public schools.

(7) The impossibility of escaping from school influence and atmosphere, during term-time, frequently entails the stifling of individuality. The regimentation imposed by public schools is overtly inimical to independence of judgment. Against the highly dubious advantages of the 'old boy network' – the implicit favouring, in later life, of people who went to the same school – must be weighed the fact that too many products of public schools are instantly recognisable by their dull uniformity and lack of initiative.

(See also COMPREHENSIVE SCHOOLS; CO-EDUCATION)

PUBLIC TRANSPORT, FREE

Pro: (1) Nationalised road and rail transport undertakings suffer from governmental demands which are incompatible. On the one hand, they are obliged to run many uneconomic routes and services, while being restricted in the charges they may make; on the other, they are still expected to show an overall profit. Experience proves that, in those circumstances, they are almost certain to register heavy losses. It would be more realistic if the State recognised that passenger transport should be a public service, in the fullest sense, and therefore met all the costs. Free public transport would not apply to freight, nor to long-distance travel, but it would be appropriate for the bus, underground and suburban commuter services used by the great majority of

Con: (1) Even if a very limited form of public transport could be operated without payment of fares, which is highly doubtful, its costs would still have to be met – and that means extra taxation. No new tax burden for the purpose could be fair, since people who normally need to use public transport rarely, if at all, would be helping to pay for those who use it every day. Why should people who live on or near their place of work, as in the country, meet a similar share of the costs, in tax, as suburban commuters? Clearly, the only equitable system is for each traveller, like any other consumer, to pay *pro rata* for what he or she uses. This is borne out by the nationalised airlines, which do frequently show an annual profit because they are able to set their fare

the public – and it would enable those undertakings to provide the standards of service which people want.

(2) 'Pilot' schemes for free public road transport have already been tried abroad, with some success.

(3) Public service is a misnomer unless travel is free. While encouraging greater use of public transport, it would permit savings in other ways. Since booking-office clerks, ticket collectors and the like would not be necessary, such staff could be transferred to more productive functions. As a result, operating costs per mile would be lower if public transport were free than under the present system.

(4) (Some) Other ideas for improving transport facilities, such as the pool of battery-driven bubble cars for city centre travel in Amsterdam, usable on a co-operative subscription basis, have failed to catch on. Existing means of public transport are more efficient, and there would be far greater enthusiasm and support for them if they were turned into a free service. This would also help to solve traffic congestion problems, because there would be a corresponding reduction in the number of people using private cars to take them to and from work each day.

and freight charges at realistically high levels.

(2) The schemes concerned, from all accounts, were one-day wonders and resulted in chaos; little more has been heard of them since.

(3) This takes no account of the increased fuel costs, nor of the basic problem that recruitment of the extra staff needed, even now, is hamstrung by the high costs of living and accommodation in the towns. Bus and underground services are already running at much lower frequency than in the past because, with cheap housing unobtainable, they cannot attract enough new employees for their present requirements.

(4) (Some) Many people regarded the Amsterdam scheme as an admirable, idealistic experiment, but concluded that it was impracticable and unbusinesslike. It was opposed not only by the local taxi drivers (predictably) but also by the police, because of the traffic problems caused. Even if such schemes were taken over by the authorities and operated without charge, they still wouldn't succeed.

(See also MOTOR TRAFFIC: SHOULD IT BE RESTRICTED?)

RATING REFORM

Pro: (1) The English rating system has been altered only piecemeal since it arose from the Poor Law of the seventeenth century, and a thorough overhaul is long overdue. It has been said that 'taxes are paid in sorrow but rates are paid in anger'. This almost

Con: (1) Piecemeal alteration to allow for changing conditions is a feature of all English legal and administrative systems and has the advantage of permitting greater flexibility than the systems applied in other countries. Uniformity of assessment is

universal resentment stems from the inequities and anomalies of the present system – not only the ever-increasing burden on rate-payers, aggravated by inflation, but the lack of uniformity in assessments from one local authority area to another (whereby, for instance, a property in one district can be rated three times as high as a similar property in an adjoining district).

(2) Expenditure by local authorities has risen so rapidly that their total budgets have become ever more dependent on the annual grants they receive from the Exchequer. It is estimated that, on average, Treasury grants now meet 46.4 per cent of local authority spending. While well down on the 60 per cent average which prevailed a decade ago, this continued dependence on Whitehall, intrinsic to the inadequacies of the present system, inevitably entails a decline in the independence and vitality of local government.

(3) One basic reform which has been proposed is that the rates should be replaced by a system of local taxation, enabling authorities themselves to raise *directly* a much higher proportion of the money they need to spend. This could take the form of a percentage levy on incomes, similar to National Insurance contributions and payable by employers, employees and self-employed people. The British Labour Party, in its manifesto before the October 1974 general election, stated: 'Public services have to be paid for by the public – the only argument is about how to share the costs, not how to avoid them'. The Conservatives' manifesto said they would abolish the domestic rating system 'and replace it by taxes more broadly based and related to people's ability to pay'. Both parties, therefore, recog-

impossible in a country with such a wide variety of communities, and the idea takes no account of the widely varying benefits and public services enjoyed under different local authorities. One way or another, such services as education, road maintenance, public health facilities, and so on, have to be paid for; and despite prolonged study of other ways to raise local government money, no one has yet been able to find a fairer method than the present system.

(2) The cost of maintaining local government services has increased to a much higher level than anyone would be willing to finance solely out of local property taxes. Yet the financial limits imposed by the central government, as part of its drive to combat inflation and revive the national economy, still leave local authorities with very considerable freedom of action. Far from undermining that freedom, the Government took an essential step towards allowing the authorities greater exercise of their own initiative, by its reform of the local government structure so as to create fewer (and bigger) local authorities.

(3) Experts have been studying alternative methods of local taxation since before the last world war. If any had been able to devise a new local tax which conformed to certain essential criteria, it would have been adopted long ago. Among the necessary conditions for such a tax, it would have to be: available to all local authorities; capable of being both levied and collected locally; relatively cheap to administer; appropriate as a local tax; and socially acceptable. In addition, local authorities' freedom to fix and vary the rates of the tax would need to be set within limits acceptable to the management of the national

nised the need for rating reform. The suggested percentage tax on incomes could meet the ideas of each, from their different standpoints, and would be fairer and more rational than the present system.

(4) In the event, the reforms eventually outlined in the Government's 1986 Green Paper were for domestic rates to be phased out over 10 years and replaced by a Community Charge, payable by *all* adults. Business rates would be paid at a standard level throughout the country and redistributed to the various local councils from the central government.

(5) Given the time lag before these reforms could be implemented, it is still possible to consider other specific measures. Among them, immediate steps could be taken to remove the cost of some local authority services from the rates, with the central government taking over full financial responsibility for them. A prime candidate for this is education, which is by far the biggest single local government expense. Relieving them of the burden would cut local rates by nearly half.

(6) Further ways to relieve the rates include: (a) crediting the proceeds of capital gains and land development taxes to the locality in which they originated; (b) giving local councils, rather than central government, the right to levy stamp duty on property transfers and to raise extra revenue by such means as planning fees, taxes on animals, and possibly even a 'bed' tax on tourism; and (c) giving councils most of the revenue from the existing motor taxes, i.e. vehicle and driving licence fees (which are already collected locally anyway) and the duty on motor fuel (which could be collected at bulk storage depots).

economy. No new tax proposal has succeeded in meeting all these criteria (nor, perhaps, is ever likely to). It is significant that the pledge to abolish the rating system made by Mrs Margaret Thatcher, first when she was Opposition spokesman on housing and the environment, and then repeated in the Conservative Party's ensuing election manifesto, did not even reach the stage of a Green Paper (outlining proposed reforms for discussion purposes) until 1986.

(4) According to some authoritative estimates, the Community Charge would cost each person over 18 between £100 and £200 in shire districts and £400 or more in some London authorities. The TUC attacked it as 'an anti-democratic poll tax which will bear hardest on those on low incomes and be extremely problematic to administer'.

(5) Local authorities cannot expect to 'have their cake and eat it'. Even if they remained the agents for implementing educational policy, the price for transferring the cost burden to central government (i.e. to national taxation) would be the loss of their present relative freedom to control education in their own areas.

(6) The revenue produced by such expedients would still be inadequate to meet the full bill for essential local government spending. Measures of this kind would also tend to worsen the imbalance between local authority areas, widening the gap in the quality of public services provided in different areas – higher in some, lower in others. As an example, a less well off local authority could not collect enough from its own motor tax revenues to pay for the costs of new national motorway construction cutting across its area. In general, there would be a continued need for

(7) The methods cited in the previous section are already employed by some European countries, most effectively, in raising money for local services. In West Germany, the main burden of local taxation (about 80 per cent) is borne by business and industry rather than by householders. The local tax is levied on all businesses, from a hot dog stall upwards. Local authorities are also empowered to levy a tax on land sales, on dogs, and on bars and places of entertainment. Compared with their British counterparts, most German cities are well off financially. In France, all the financing is centralised. A citizen is liable to pay several of hundreds of varied taxes, depending on his job and social position; but every centime paid through the local tax collector's office goes to the State, which decides how and where to allot the money.

(8) (Some) Several reformers urge the introduction of a system of partial rating, under which people would not be compelled, as now, to pay for public services they do not use, such as education or public libraries.

centralised finance to even out differences in local authority resources, to stimulate the provision of certain services and, when necessary, to provide for national standards.

(7) Population densities and other conditions differ so greatly, from one country to the next, that methods used successfully in some would be a failure elsewhere. Because of the aversion to direct taxation and the high rate of tax-dodging in several Continental countries, their governments have to rely much more on indirect taxation than is necessary in Britain. Hence, for instance, the wide variation in the VAT rates imposed. The same factors apply to local revenue raising. Eventually, the EEC aims at the harmonisation of indirect taxation, and this will pose other member-countries with far greater problems than will the present British system.

(8) (Some) Such a device would be contrary to the fundamental principles of all taxation, including rating – and it would be virtually impossible to administer efficiently.

RECALL OF REPRESENTATIVES

Pro: (1) The Recall of Members of Parliament is a necessary complement to the theory that Parliament should be subject to the will of the people. If it were possible for re-election to be forced on Members at the petition of a certain number of the electors, politicians would become more responsible and more serious. (On a lesser plane, the mid-term re-selection of their MPs carried out by constituency Labour parties exemplifies just such advantages.) If the Recall were adopted as a readily available part of

Con: (1) The doctrine of the Recall is wrongly based. It applies properly to delegation, whereas representation is superior. Unless representatives are given a measure of responsibility, only inferior candidates will come forward; these will indulge in the wildest demagogy, and no coherent public policy will be advanced. The Recall might too often be exercised on trivial grounds and could lead to incessant elections.

(2) The Recall would not be an occasion for manifestations of popular

our political system, elections would be conducted in a better spirit and a distinct check would be given to the operations of party machines and unscrupulous election propaganda.

(2) The Recall would give opportunities for showing the feelings of the country towards Government policy. At present, between general elections, this depends solely on the fortuitous occurrence of by-elections. It would also enable voters to deal with MPs who, once elected, repudiate the view of their voters, or of the party on whose programme they were elected, and thus in effect disfranchise their electors.

(3) The Recall is very popular in the USA and the USSR, where it is held to be a necessary item in the machinery that expresses the sovereignty of the people.

(4) The principle should be applied more widely. Not only elected representatives but semi-elected people – officials, judges, and important functionaries – should be liable to it. Only thus can satisfactory public service be assured and the likelihood of corruption be eliminated. It should apply to both State and municipal affairs.

feeling on general policy. There are always enough by-elections during the life of a government to show the trend of public opinion, and a hundred other ways of expressing it.

(3) The Recall was instituted in the USA to satisfy people who had little faith in their local political leaders. But it does not secure its ends: for example, in Oregon it was made a weapon by which corrupt interests got rid of their opponents on public bodies. In the USSR, where the individual candidates are chosen beforehand by the Party and only one list is presented to the voters, the procedure more closely resembles the dismissal of an official for inefficiency than the public's expression of disapproval of a political policy.

(4) The Recall is a desperate measure. It is not conducive to the development of a responsible, trustworthy public service. Judges would lose their independence. Corruption would still prevail, and the work of officials acting with care and foresight could be imperilled by public criticism that was both inexpert and uninformed.

(See also DELEGATION v. REPRESENTATION; and the next article)

THE REFERENDUM, MORE USE OF

Pro: (1) More use of the Referendum would be a check upon hasty legislation; it would ensure that vitally important measures could not be passed by a government against the wishes of the majority of the electors; it is the last step in the process of

Con: (1) Checks on hasty legislation are abundant. In general, legislation is years behind the times, and the Referendum, which tends to appeal to conservative tendencies, usually puts off the day of reform. It is impossible to prevent the Government from

making the voice of the people effective. The efficient operation of Britain's Referendum on Common Market membership proved that the system would work well in this country.

(2) The compulsory Referendum would be the greatest possible safeguard against sudden tampering with the constitution. It would be chiefly applied to questions of constitutional change and so would not involve serious changes in the routine of government. In America and elsewhere, it has generally been used in this way.

(3) The representative system has largely broken down. British statesmen, though professing to serve their constituents and the will of the people, are becoming more and more independent and out of touch with ordinary people, except at elections. They can hardly object to becoming more subject to popular control. Under the Referendum, it is not necessary for a Minister to resign when one of his department's schemes is rejected. The system thus permits able men to remain in office even if the public votes against them on a particular policy issue.

(4) The heart of a whole policy is often contained in some single resolution or law, and if the doctrine of the mandate has any place in democratic theory, it is applicable on these pivotal occasions.

(5) The electors would have to vote for measures and principles, not men. This they are perfectly competent to do. At present, they are asked to decide between two or three complicated policies, which touch every foreign and domestic interest of the State, without a chance of exercising a critical selection between the good points and the bad. They can surely

deciding which questions are to be considered important and which not. The most important measures are not necessarily those most talked about. Britain's Common Market Referendum was mainly a political manoeuvre to overcome the Labour Party's internal dissension and cannot be regarded as a valid precedent.

(2) The British constitution has the advantage that it is largely unwritten and thus flexible and open to change whenever needed. The Referendum is normally workable only under a written constitution, and all written constitutions grow out of date and harmful long before anyone dreams of changing them.

(3) The central theory of the constitution is the responsibility of Ministers to the House of Commons. The Referendum would seriously affect that position. A true democracy is representative and does not depend solely on the counting of heads.

(Some) The British constitution is too democratic already. Final decisions should not be placed in the hands of the populace, which is too often uninformed and swayed by passing whims and emotions.

(4) It treats policy in fragments. When a law is one part of a policy, to submit each part for separate acceptance or rejection is to present the issue artificially and out of perspective. The more intelligent electors would still refuse to accept an individual measure they disliked, even if it were part of a larger policy of which they approved.

(5) The disadvantages of the Referendum are similar to those of voting for individual party candidates. It is possible to accept or reject, but not to select or amend. The advantage lies with voting for a candidate, in fact, because other influences may afterwards be brought to bear on him; like-

decide on the advantages or disadvantages of a single legislative proposal. The merits of voting for 'men, not measures' are disproved by the steady degeneration of the type of candidate elected. The reason why voting is so small in many referenda is that the considerations of party and personal passion and prejudice are absent. Those who do not vote are presumably indifferent to whatever happens, and so those who are concerned are rightly allowed to decide.

(6) It would be politically educational and would free people of the habit of thinking on party lines. Measures would then be considered from the point of view of the community and not of the interests of parties, creeds, sects or classes.

(7) The House of Commons would still deal with everyday measures and would have to draw up each measure to be referred, settle all the details connected with it, and finally present the best result it could reach.

(8) The adoption of the Referendum would lessen the evils of the party system, because the certainty that party support meant party victory would vanish.

(9) A partial or trial application of the Referendum might be made. As stressed earlier, it would not be feasible for Britain to use the Referendum on a regular basis – only on key issues involving drastic change, which necessarily occur at infrequent intervals.

(10) The Referendum would put more vigour into political life and would give the electorate the sense that they really controlled their own destinies.

(11) In some states of the USA and in Switzerland, it has been tried with great success. So far from being an un-English institution, its origin was

wise, it is easier to weigh up the merits and demerits of a number of items taken as a whole than of one item consisting of various closely related parts. The unsatisfactory nature of the Referendum is shown by the fact that, in very many cases, the total vote for and against a policy has been less than one-third of the total vote for and against the advocate of that policy.

(6) Political education must be gained less expensively and more thoroughly. The Referendum would not abolish the party or the section. Rather, it would unite discontented and dissatisfied parties of every sort into an unnatural alliance *against* any measure. The Referendum is the great and fatal device for maintaining the *status quo*.

(7) The House of Commons would become even more an object of disrespect than it is now, as its debates and amendments would have an air of futility. It would labour in committee over every clause of the enormously complicated measures which are now the usual form of legislation, knowing quite well that the electorate would presently have to say Yes or No to the whole without proper consideration of the parts, because it is mechanically impossible for a Referendum to sift the good from the bad.

(8) The party system would remain; the mass of voters would follow one party or another, for in most cases one party would be identified with adoption and another with rejection of the measure. Each side would make the usual promises as the price of support, and voting would still be swayed by the popular idols of the day.

(9) A partial application would not prove whether the system would be appropriate in its complete form. When voters are called to the polls

English (seventeenth century). When used in America, it has served as a substitute for the veto, which is a cardinal feature of English constitutional theory. Although British monarchs still have the power of the 'royal veto' in theory, it is no longer applied; nevertheless, it remains necessary that some form of a sovereign remedy should exist. No fewer than 1,600 instances, at the least, are known in America; if the system had been a failure, it would have been dropped. It is a common enough feature in trade union constitutions in Britain, and has worked well; decisions to call strikes are nearly always subject to it, and those in which it is not used very often fail because of the discord which follows lack of agreement about the policy adopted.

(12) It keeps the legislature and individual members in touch with opinion in the country during the interval between one general election and the next. It helps to ensure that a government cannot carry through, unchecked, a policy different from that for which it was elected. It would also serve as the decider when the two Houses were in head-on disagreement over a measure.

(13) The expense need not be greater than the Government wished. If a simpler organisation were adopted, it would cost much less than a general election.

(14) Laws thus sanctioned receive greater respect than otherwise. They could not be said to be the result either of party or of class legislation.

more often than for normal elections, they soon get bored (as experience in France showed under de Gaulle).

(10) It would make political life more dependent on mechanical devices and lead to a further decay of popular interest in politics. Elaboration and complication in political institutions is both a symptom and a cause of apathy.

(11) In Switzerland, the results have usually been ambiguous, while in the USA the Referendum has been confined to simple state issues. Trade union experience has not proved its great superiority to other methods, but rather suggests that it gives freer play to the transient whims of the moment. A strike is a simpler affair to decide on than an Act of Parliament.

(12) By-elections are sufficient to keep the House alive to popular opinion. Shorter Parliaments would be preferable to this device. The Referendum would give the House of Lords an excellent excuse to block every measure it disliked and, for this and other reasons, the already unduly slow parliamentary procedure would become even slower.

(13) The expense of this succession of minor general elections would be excessive, probably even prohibitive.

(14) Each Referendum would be accompanied by an outburst of all the worst features of political campaigning in the Press and by the parties.

(See also the preceding article; DELEGATION v. REPRESENTATION; PARLIAMENT, REFORM OF; WRITTEN CONSTITUTION)

REGISTRATION, NATIONAL, IN PEACE-TIME

Pro: (1) Britain is one of the few countries which in normal times has no registration system and thus no continuous record of its citizens. National registration served to increase the flexibility of administration in wartime and was useful particularly in the management of rationing. It can be used at any time for such practical purposes as the revision of voting lists, and avoids much cumbersome procedure.

(2) Identity cards help to prevent crime, to catch criminals or to detect illegal immigrants or undesirable aliens. During the Second World War, one mass inspection of identity cards was apt to give the police more information than weeks of searching.

(3) In these days when there is so much necessary regimentation and recourse to documents, an identity card is a much simpler means of identification than the set of documents which would otherwise be necessary to establish an individual's *bona fides* at any time. Impersonation becomes impossible; the identity card was found very useful as a means of preventing Post Office frauds, for instance. No innocent citizen need object to carrying his papers with him; they are, in fact, a convenience, since they may avoid lengthy questioning. They are no more a threat to liberty than passports, the necessity for which is now generally accepted.

(4) The French, long renowned for their love of liberty and independent-mindedness, are among the nations which have used identity cards for many years, without regarding them

Con: (1) Registration is only one more example of the increasing regimentation that is threatening the liberty of the British public today. While it may have some value in a police State, in a democratic country in peace-time there is no excuse for it. Machinery already exists for dealing with voting lists and census-taking, and rationing is not a feature of peace-time life in Britain – not normally, anyway.

(2) They are utterly useless for catching criminals, for, when identity cards are introduced, the forging and stealing of them becomes an industry. Only with the addition of fingerprints could they be completely reliable as a means of identification; but the use of such documents, and especially the finger printing of innocent citizens, is repugnant to a free community. A false identity card is otherwise accepted without question and police investigations have often revealed that it is quite possible for a man to get away for years without possessing one at all.

(3) Since ordinary identity cards are no danger to the criminal, their main effect is the harassing of the respectable citizen, who can be required to produce them at any time, even where there is no shred of evidence that he is involved in crime. The same applies to passports, which, so far from being accepted, are generally detested and have been the subject of repeated governmental promises to abolish them.

(4) The French are so liberty-loving that all their policemen carry guns on everyday duty . . . As a nation, in fact,

186

as irksome or an infringement of individual freedoms.

they are far more regimented and bedevilled by petty bureaucracy than the British people have ever been.

RELIGIOUS TEACHING IN SCHOOLS

Pro: (1) One dictionary definition of religion is: 'Belief in a personal God, controlling the universe and entitled to worship and obedience; the feelings, effects on conduct, and the practices resulting from such belief'. It is surely incontestable that this is a subject which it not only appropriate but a duty for schools to teach. Even the advocates of strictly non-denominational teaching will recognise that religion, in this context, is a fundamental part of human knowledge – and therefore an essential ingredient of education, *per se*.

(2) Except in specifically denominational schools (e.g. those for Roman Catholic children), religious teaching is not simply about worship, nor does it centre on any one particular faith. Its purpose, above all, is to instruct children, in their most formative years, about morals and the code of conduct to be followed by self-respecting people in adult society.

(3) Young children themselves, without any prompting, nearly always feel a desire for a religious 'anchor'. In later years, the perspective offered by lessons in religious history gives them a better understanding of the way mankind has developed over the centuries and, thus, a better understanding of humanity as a whole in our own day. At whatever age, indeed, all of us need yardsticks by which to judge our own and other people's actions. Religious teaching is by far

Con: (1) The principal objection to religious teaching in schools, even those which are supposedly non-denominational, has been that these lessons were usually made obligatory for all pupils (up to a certain age, anyway) and there was, equally, compulsion in attending morning prayers, etc. While the increasingly multi-ethnic nature of our society has largely put an end to this at day schools, children at many boarding schools may still have to attend prayers up to three times a day, plus compulsory church attendance on Sundays. This is contrary to the spirit of the times, which leans increasingly towards freedom of choice, both socially and educationally. Whether for religious lessons or observance, all children should have the right to decide – initially, through their parents, if need be – whether they wish to take part.

(2) One of the most important functions of school life, as a community in miniature, is to lead children to follow a social code which will stand them in good stead throughout their lives. They learn more about this from the everyday experience of how to co-exist tolerably under school conditions than from any amount of Bible stories.

(3) Guidelines of this nature – as, indeed, the morality imparted by religion – are all embodied in the legal code. It is not necessary to learn them

the best source of such guidance.

(4) All religious faiths aim to improve human society, to help alleviate social injustice and to express ideals from which, sooner or later, necessary social reforms emerge. Accordingly, when schoolchildren receive a basic grounding in religious knowledge, their horizons are broadened and they are introduced to issues which are crucial to society in general. It follows that religious teaching in schools will not only combat the scepticism and indifference which afflicts so much of the world today but, morally, can help to counter the pernicious attitudes of the so-called 'permissive society'.

from religious lessons. Teaching children an understanding of the law, with an appreciation of how its past development reflects man's social progress, would be much more practical.

(4) This confuses the role of religion, as such, with the question implicit in the present debating issue: whether religious teaching in schools should be compulsory. Some people hold that the Church is no longer relevant because it is out of touch with present-day needs – but that is another, bigger argument. The plain fact remains that awareness of the problems of society can be imparted to children quite effectively enough without any dependence on religious knowledge.

SCHOOL-LEAVING AGE:
Should It Be Lowered Again?

Pro: (1) Even though childhood may be recognised as a privileged state, a time comes when most children are tired of learning in isolation and begin to feel a desire to take part in the working life of the community. Except for those who wish to acquire higher qualifications or to make the pursuit or imparting of knowledge their life work, education after that time should be carried on as an adjunct to paid work in factory or office, or by evening study. Raising the school-leaving age to 16 led to increasing frustration among a majority of children who, maturing earlier these days, derive no real benefit from the extra year's enforced schooling and, waiting ever more impatiently to enter the adult world, often cause serious problems for the overworked teachers. The

Con: (1) It is now generally recognised that a child has not finished his or her development even at the age of 16. At one time, it was thought that children of 5 or 6 were sufficiently mature to work a full day in factories! The descendants of those who held this view are the kind of people now most in favour of reducing the school-leaving age again. Although changes in school population levels and new trends in educational systems have caused some problems, raising of the leaving age to 16 proved highly beneficial overall. Many children receive technical training in their last year or two which helps them to get better jobs, in fields that interest them, once they leave. Many others have suddenly spurted ahead educationally in their final year and have been able to go on

age should be reduced to 15 again. Children aiming for higher academic levels would stay on anyway.

(2) The increasing need for technicians goes hand in hand with a need for mass production workers who may be unskilled or semi-skilled. Moreover, many children have neither the capacity nor the inclination to reach a high level of technical efficiency. Allowing such children to leave school at 14 need not be a bar to them reaching whatever standard they are capable of, since most progressive firms now sponsor day-release courses for their young workers.

(3) The present school-leaving age is unpractical and harmful to industry, because young people need to begin technical or industrial training as soon as they are capable of it, especially now that older people are tending to retire earlier from working life. A child of 15 is sufficiently developed to start such training, without physical or mental strain. In the prevailing conditions of very high unemployment, the sooner young people acquire qualifications – under their employer's aegis – for more skilled levels of work, the better for their future prospects.

(4) Improvements in technical education and equipment at school have not yet been carried out as fully as planned, through lack of money for new buildings, etc., and through inconsistencies in the supply of teachers – too many in some years, shortages in others. (Or rather, shortages in some areas, like London, because young teachers cannot afford the high prices for accommodation.) Raising of the school-leaving age to 16 greatly aggravated such problems and put extra strain on what facilities do exist.

to higher education, even university – which would not have happened if they had left school at 15.

(2) If the country is to acquire the advanced technicians it needs in ever greater numbers, they must be freed as children from the disability of having to leave school before their capabilities are truly known. At present, the majority of children who wish to continue their education after the age of 16, but are unable to remain at school to do so, are forced to undergo the strain of working by day and studying by night. Reducing the leaving age to 15 would aggravate this situation immeasurably – and would be a retrograde step for which later generations would find it hard to forgive us.

(3) Many children fail to take advantage of the present facilities for higher education because of economic stress in the family. Before the universal leaving age was raised, there was always a temptation for parents with low earnings to sacrifice their children's education for temporary economic advantage. Because of Britain's horrific unemployment problem, there are already far too many young people who have never had a job since leaving school at 16. How much bigger the 'scrapheap' would be if they'd left a year earlier!

(4) Modern theories of education need a longer period of school life to be successfully worked out in practice. Without this, any scheme of improvement can remain only a pious hope, sketchily applied. Raising of the leaving age also increased the supply of children willing to qualify for teaching, and thus, once more normal economic conditions return, will be self-balancing in the long run. The popularity of colleges of further education and similar institutions

shows that there is an undeniable demand for more prolonged schooling.

SCHOOL SPORT, COMPULSORY

Pro: (1) Schools have a duty not merely to educate their pupils in an academic sense but also to lay the foundations for them to become rounded individuals in adult life. Sport is a valuable, even essential ingredient of this process. Apart from its obvious advantages in maintaining and improving young people's physical fitness while they are at school, it provides implicit lessons in the importance of teamwork, initiative, imagination, the need for hard work and continual practice to achieve higher standards, and many other qualities which contribute to good citizenship.

(2) Schoolchildren who are unwilling to take part in sports, at first, often discover to their surprise that they are above-average at a particular sport – and it ends by becoming a lifelong enthusiasm. Even among the ultra-devoted athletes who reach Olympic Games status, quite a few started this way.

(3) Children are naturally energetic and need plenty of activity to let off steam; but adults also require a certain amount of physical exercise to ensure their well-being. It doesn't have to be strenuous, nor a team activity; plenty of walking in the fresh air (rather than motoring everywhere) will suffice! Sport at school helps to inculcate the habit of exercise, so that it becomes second nature to try to keep reasonably fit.

(4) Children have the habit of obedience at school – or, at least,

Con: (1) Most people have a tendency to resent any activity which is compulsory rather than voluntary, especially if it impinges on their spare time (as school sport frequently does). In these circumstances, sport is as likely to produce an excess of frustration and aggression as to encourage any theoretical spirit of good citizenship. The advantages claimed for it can equally well be gained in other ways – and more effectively so, above all, when the activity is undertaken by young people of their own free will.

(2) Those responsible for running school sporting activities have a tendency to concentrate unduly on children who are good at them. A competitive spirit is right and natural in games; but some teachers' desire for their school's success – particularly in matches with other schools – can be so excessive that it sets a thoroughly bad example.

(3) Adults, particularly those in sedentary jobs, are fully aware of the probability that they will start getting out of condition and make up their own minds about the extent to which they try to keep fit – or not. But they're much more likely to maintain interest in a sport they chose for themselves originally than one with memories of being reluctantly compelled to take part in it at school.

(4) Acceptance may be automatic among young children; as they grow older, though, they are supposed to be taught increasingly to think for themselves. More enlightened schools give

automatic acceptance of the curriculum drawn up for them. In this sense, therefore, few pupils regard organised sport as any more unfair than, say, lessons in history or maths; it is simply part of the scheme of things. Moreover, the point should not be overlooked that, for the great majority of children, a games period provides a welcome break from classroom lessons.

older pupils, at least, the right of choice – and this is the crux of the matter. The opportunity to choose between a number of available activities is a key facet of modern educational trends.

SCIENCE:
Is It a Menace To Civilisation?

Pro: (1) It is more than doubtful whether the advantages of scientific progress are not counter-balanced by the harm that it does. In particular, scientific research as applied to mechanical inventions is fast becoming a menace to the world. We travel at continually increasing speed in our trains, motors and aeroplanes; yet, on the roads alone, the number of people killed in this country in a single year exceeds that of all the British soldiers killed in the whole of the Boer War. In terms of economic loss, the estimated cost of the 5,165 road deaths in 1985, and of the 855 other casualties every day, was put at a staggering £2,800 million.

(2) Science has enabled us to manufacture engines of destruction for use in war – tanks, submarines, high explosives, poison gas and atomic bombs – which are so devastatingly effective that very little of our civilisation is likely to survive if another war between the big powers were to break out.

(3) In industry, scientific inventors are continually improving the

Con: (1) In some respects, obviously, the risks of modern life are greater than those of a few generations ago. But it is by no means certain that the proportional accident rate is any higher. There are more people in the world, and there are more vehicles on the roads. Life is less static than it used to be. Besides, against some 5,000 deaths in road accidents in Britain each year, scores or even hundreds of thousands used to die in epidemics before science had taught us the laws of health and hygiene or in famines before science had been applied to communications and transport – and this at a time when the population was much smaller in any case.

(2) It is not science that is to blame for this, but man's evil nature. There would be no war but for the greed, jealousy, fear and quarrelsomeness of man. The scientist rarely has an axe to grind. He works disinterestedly to increase the sum of human knowledge, because he feels the urge of the quest for truth. If his discoveries are seized upon by politicians and by governments and used for harmful

machinery of production, with the result that fewer and fewer men are required to do the same amount of work. Thus the advance of science is one of the main causes of unemployment, because the rate of increase of productivity is so great that reorganisation cannot keep pace with it. At the meeting of the British Association in 1934, Sir Josiah (Lord) Stamp seriously advocated that attempts should be made to slow down the rate of scientific progress and invention because society could not readjust itself sufficiently rapidly to the changing conditions.

(4) One of the greatest dangers of science today is the opportunity it offers to those in power to create a race of robots. Not only can they subdue their victims by force. They can subdue their minds by radio and television propaganda, by control of the Press, and by a subtle use of the knowledge of psychology in education and public affairs. There is a growing and sinister gulf between the rest of the world and those scientists who, for example, have the knowledge to build space ships and atomic reactors.

purposes, that is not the fault of science or the scientist.

(3) The improvements in methods of production certainly enable fewer men to do the same amount of work, or in other words to produce the same amount of wealth. Therefore, the same number of workers can produce far more wealth. If this increased wealth were satisfactorily distributed, as it might be by rational reorganisation, the general standard of living could be raised and hours of labour could be reduced. The chief obstacle to this is not science but capitalism, which blocks the way to the necessary reorganisation.

(4) Against these possibilities we must set the effects of science in the past on the human mind – the liberation of thought due to the work of Galileo, Copernicus, Darwin and other pioneers of learning. Science has changed man's outlook from superstition to an enlightened understanding and has substituted the concept of natural law for a state of ignorance in which, for instance, a comet was thought to be a sign sent by an angry god.

SCIENTIFIC MANAGEMENT

Pro: (1) Scientific management eliminates grounds of contention between workers and employers by giving an independent standard to which disputes can be referred. It determines, through accurate analysis, the proper task, wage and working day for each individual, the results being calculated according to the laws of human nature and in a spirit of fairness and liberality. It introduces a positive teaching that harmony and mutual understanding should be cultivated between

Con: (1) The essence of scientific, or, as it is sometimes termed, psychological management, is that men are to be treated purely as productive machines, completely dependent on the expert. Management and men might agree, provided they were the only parties in industry, but the policy of industry still remains controlled in the interests of profits by outsiders. Trade unions are necessary to protect the less efficient workers from a low standard of life, reflecting their low

management and men. Trade unions become superfluous and strikes are prevented. Suitable men are raised to posts of responsibility.

(2) It greatly increases output by systematising piece-work, by setting tasks based upon time-and-effort study, by encouraging the standardisation of tools and equipment, by careful choice of managers, foremen, etc., and by greater opportunities for specialisation. In some cases, the increase in productivity is 100 per cent, and the workers are not fatigued because suitable rest-periods are allowed. With the general adoption of scientific management, production would be increased so as to provide enough for all, without increasing cost.

(3) In firms where it has been adopted, the results all round are excellent. The best possible working conditions are provided, the men are contented, and the industrial problem may be considered solved. Though there may be certain divergencies between labour opinion and management principles, co-operation and reasonable compromise have enabled both to operate together in some plants. It will restore the morale which all observers declare is deserting the industrial world.

industrial worth. Their policy is for a high level, not a fluctuating standard. In practice, only a few 'efficiency engineers' have any real responsibility or independence.

(2) Scientific management cannot be applied on a national scale to all forms of industrial activity. In practice, it tends to overwork employees and turn them into automata, for it is most successful in fields of work that can be resolved into repetitive processes. The reduction of the need for skill is an insult to the best tendencies in the workers' nature. At the level where scientific management itself operates, it is incapable of increasing or rationalising the activity of a man's brain.

(3) It is usually an excuse for union smashing, and its introduction serves to break up the natural association between men working in the same shop and industry. No matter how benevolent it may appear, a powerful concern cannot be allowed to get free of all restrictions put on it by unions, or cease to have them as potential checks on its actions, without grave dangers to the liberty and welfare of the workers; for power, even more than profit, is the aim of the industrial overlords. It is a device to perpetuate and make the most of an evil system.

(See also INDUSTRIAL PSYCHOLOGY, APPLIED)

SECOND BALLOTS

Pro: (1) Candidates frequently and notoriously are returned by minority votes (i.e. out of the total poll in a constituency). Second ballots would always elect the candidate most favoured by the constituents as a whole.

Con: (1) This is not so frequent as to make the system seriously at fault. The candidate preferred by the majority of electors in any given constituency is produced just as often by the present system.

(2) Taken on the whole, the people

(2) The system of second ballots, by requiring the successful candidate to have a clear majority of the votes polled, would lead to a truer representation of the people.

(3) They would destroy the arguments against third-party or independent candidates which now embitter political life and lead to caucus manoeuvres on a large scale.

(4) The greater the number of candidates, the greater the choice of the electorate, while the deposit system checks 'freak' candidates.

(5) They would reduce the power of party managers and break up hidebound parties. Candidates could afford to be more independent.

(6) In France, where second ballots have long been the practice (and have been brought back after a brief excursion into proportional representation for the 1986 general election), the system requires a candidate to win an overall majority (i.e. over all the other candidates in his constituency) to gain election in the first ballot, which normally happens in only a few instances; but in the second ballot, he merely needs a simple majority over the other principal candidate(s) remaining in the field. The outcome, therefore, is a genuine reflection of the predominant views of the entire electorate.

are fairly represented; if accuracy is wanted, second ballots are inadequate.

(3) Intrigues for support in the second ballot would give rise to the same phenomena.

(4) In Parliament, we would have a multitude of parties and splinter-groups, with all the inevitable intrigues and confusion they cause. The deposit introduces a property qualification which has ruled out excellent candidates already; second ballots would add to the already heavy cost of candidature.

(5) Party discipline is a valuable factor in stabilising our political life. Independence of candidates would vanish at the second ballot. Where it has been tried, the results are not encouraging.

(6) One of the most dubious features of French politics is the inter-party bargaining in the period between the two ballots, whereby one party agrees to support another party's man and withdraw its own less successful candidate in one constituency, in return for a like favour in another constituency. This is bound to entail compromise over policies and the soft-pedalling of plans for needed reforms. And the system still motivates against some parties (e.g. the Communists need roughly twice as many votes as the Gaullists for each parliamentary seat they gain).

(See also PROPORTIONAL REPRESENTATION)

SINGLE-CHAMBER GOVERNMENT

Pro: (1) The tendency of all modern governments is to centre on one

Con: (1) Wherever democratic countries have tried the single-Chamber

Chamber. The only result of having two Chambers is a pendulum swing between the obstruction of any reforming government and what is tantamount to single-Chamber government (since Second Chambers are always conservative and give almost unquestioning support to governments of like view).

(2) There is no danger of a single Chamber prolonging itself in power indefinitely under a democratic electoral system. The single Chamber is elected by the people and is therefore always under their control. The bicameral system is a slow and cumbrous way of conducting public business and is unjust to the electorate.

(3) No Parliament which represents a people like the British, predominantly averse to sudden change, is ever likely to be guilty of precipitate legislation.

(4) The House of Lords has often been responsible for the withdrawal of men from useful public service in the Commons, especially where progressive governments have seen the need to strengthen their power in the Lords, and has thus ended many a promising political career.

(5) No other country besides Britain has a Second Chamber assembled on such haphazard principles – in many cases, with no regard to intellectual or physical fitness. New Zealand manages her affairs without a Second Chamber, and so do the Socialist countries of Eastern Europe. In Norway, the Second Chamber is chosen from members of the Lower House already elected.

(6) If a Minister is a member of the House of Lords, he is rendered less amenable to criticism than if he were a member of the Lower House; this is especially felt when the Minister is of Cabinet rank.

system, the Second Chamber has almost always been restored subsequently. The consensus of educated opinion in Great Britain is in favour of a Second Chamber.

(2) A popularly elected government is not proof against the temptations of absolute power. Many tyrants have rested their tyranny on the people. The only safeguard for the State is a balance of power among the different organs of government.

(3) The chief value of a Second Chamber is to provide security against over-hasty legislation; it gives an opportunity for reflection and further, more objective consideration.

(4) The House of Lords has secured for the nation the continued service of men who, for various reasons, would be unable or no longer wish to take part in contested elections, but whose experience entitles them to a voice in the national councils. If the Lords were abolished, the House of Commons would lose much of its own distinctive character.

(5) Conditions prevailing in other countries are not necessarily applicable to Britain. New Zealand is a small country with a homogeneous population and without the extreme conflicts of interest which give rise to ill-considered legislation. Russia has her Soviet of Nationalities, but in any case the extent to which her single Chamber and those of the satellite countries actually govern is severely limited, and so no comparison is valid.

(6) A Minister in the Lords will always have a No. 2 in the Commons, who has to deal with questions about the department concerned – and criticisms made there about the Ministry's conduct of affairs are fully effective as criticisms of the Minister himself.

(7) Any existing institution, especially if it can point to an ancient

(7) No institution ought to be allowed to continue in existence unless it can be proved to fulfil a useful purpose. The value to be put on the Lords is shown by the relatively scant attention its proceedings receive from the public and from the majority of its own members – notwithstanding the advent of TV cameras.

(8) Reform of the Lords would not meet the chief criticisms against it, unless such reform were so radical as to involve a complete break with our constitutional tradition and procedure.

(9) In the past, Conservative-minded peers have used their power of delay in the interests of the section of society which they most reflect, to nullify measures for which a Labour Government had duly received majority backing from the electorate. Although the degree of confrontation has lessened in recent years, and the increase in Alliance and cross-bench peers has made the Lords more independent in its decisions, the fundamental conflict still exists. On issues the Tories regard as particularly important, their party managers still summon up the 'backwoodsmen' – the unelected, hereditary peers, who otherwise rarely attend the Upper House – to ensure themselves of a majority. Hardly a good example of democracy at work!

and honourable career, has *ipso facto* an argument for its continuance. The vitality and importance of the Lords have been demonstrated frequently.

(8) It is undesirable to abolish the Second Chamber, even if we do not approve of the present one, because the increase in the scope and volume of business dealt with by the State renders it impossible for one body like the Commons to cope with it all. Reform, or a new type of Second Chamber, is necessary to prevent the Executive from becoming supreme.

(9) The Lords stand for a more permanent element in the country than a Commons majority and, consequently, are entitled to be cautious about approving proposals that might well be countermanded after the next general election. Many of the amendments to parliamentary Bills proposed by the peers (e.g. on recent transport and legal reform measures) have subsequently been 'taken on board' by Ministers in the Lower House. Even though governments with a big majority could ride roughshod over the Lords, the wisdom of the Upper House's counter-proposals usually becomes self-evident.

(See also LORDS, REFORM OF THE HOUSE OF; PARLIAMENT, REFORM OF; DEVOLUTION)

196

SOCIAL SERVICE CONSCRIPTION
(FOR BOTH SEXES)

Pro: (1) It is well known that the majority of young people, of both sexes, have a deep-seated desire to do work of benefit to their fellow-humans. That desire could be put to more effective use, for the general good, if all young people underwent a limited period of social service conscription. They should be given the choice of various kinds of social work, should have the assurance of being able to find a place in one or another of the fields most of interest to them, and could also be given the opportunity to decide whether to do their service here or abroad.

(2) Although peace-time military conscription (or National Service) was unpopular, it did have its advantages for the development of young men's characters. Few would wish the military aspect to be restored, but its beneficial effects could be fully equated by conscription for social service. Young people would accept this much more willingly than military service. An important reform should be to make social service conscription applicable to girls as well as boys. Most girls are just as willing – often, even more so – to devote themselves to useful work of this kind, and they would welcome the wider opportunities for it which an official scheme would offer them. (The only necessary difference would be that the conscription of young women would have to be restricted mainly to single girls, with married women entitled to obtain exemption, if they wished.)

(3) The period of social service conscription would not cause such interference to young people's careers

Con: (1) This commendable trait in young people normally finds expression in their late teens or early twenties, when many of them do in fact seek voluntary social work. Unhappily, the desire is all too often stifled or made impracticable, before long, by the pressures and responsibilities of adult life. To harness it to the machinery of official conscription would even more quickly stifle the spontaneity of young people's desire to serve. The very act of formalising it would make their contribution less effective.

(2) It is doubtful whether many young people would welcome any form of service that is imposed rather than voluntary. Nor is there any proof whatever that more than a small proportion of girls would be glad of this particular equality; a greater probability is that there would be a sharp increase in the number of girls getting married in order to avoid conscription. If young husbands are to be called up (as they were for military service), usually obliging their wives to manage on lower earnings than before, why should the wives be entitled to exemption, anyway? Unless they are bringing up babies, such differentiation would merely add to the resentments in these egalitarian times. Illogicalities of this nature serve to demonstrate just how unpractical the whole idea would be.

(3) Non-interference with young careers could be only a pious hope. Most would find social service conscription just as much of an interruption as military service was. Even among those who had just qualified,

as National Service did, because its timing could be more flexible. Those training for professional or technical qualifications would either be able to complete their studies beforehand or, in many cases, regulations could be amended to permit their social service to be incorporated as part of the practical work required before they qualify. Since full-time social workers need considerable training – as, of course, do the teachers, medical staff and many others involved in various fields of social service – the proposed arrangements would help to ensure higher standards among the conscripts. Moreover, once they had completed their 18-months or two-year period of service, many might well be motivated to carry on with it of their own accord.

(4) A period of obligatory social service could become regarded as payment by students for the university or technical college education they had received. This would mollify public opinion at large and silence most of the present, ill-informed criticism of students.

few would yet have the necessary skills for some of the often difficult and diplomatically delicate work entailed (particularly in the developing countries). Much of this work requires continuity, and the endless turnover would be harmful in that respect. Moreover, only a small proportion of those conscripted would have reached the level of acquiring professional or technical qualifications; the majority would have to be used for less skilful work. But if these were obliged to spend 18 months or two years doing social service at a lower level (e.g. painting old people's homes for them, reading to the blind, playing with mentally handicapped children), they would not be fully engaged and would soon suffer the frustration of feeling that much of their time was being wasted or inadequately used. Another snag: the logistical difficulties of providing enough accommodation for the conscripts (especially the new residential centres necessary for the girls) would be almost insuperable – and far too costly in present economic conditions.

(4) Should students be expected to pay, anyway? Doesn't the nation have a duty to educate its children?

(See also MILITARY TRAINING, COMPULSORY: SHOULD IT BE RESTORED?)

SOCIALISM AND COMMUNISM

Pro: (1) The fundamental fact of human life is that men are drawn into association with one another. It is to take the fullest advantage of this natural characteristic that a Socialist society should be established. It is not to be denied that individual and sectional interests have been dominant of necessity at various periods in the

Con: (1) The evolution of society does not move in the direction of the Socialist State. The self-regarding impulses are more fundamental than the associational. The only way in which advantage is likely to be taken of the latter is by putting everything under the despotism of the State.

(2) True individuality and freedom

past, but human history is a long succession of changes leading up to a general reconciliation of the interests of the individual with those of society at large. The State is not necessarily the organ of integration.

(2) Men are not entirely selfish, nor entirely altruistic. In the past, however, society has rested its conscious policy solely on the first impulse, with the result that excellent moral codes have existed side by side with the triumph of the strong, the brutal and the cunning. If freedom, or rather the power to do whatever one wishes, is limited by society, the interests of all are enhanced and freedom is much more secure and much more extended.

(3) The alternative to Socialism is chaos or a slave State. The present system is breaking down in the spheres of morals, economic efficiency and culture.

(4) The economic development of capitalist production has divorced the producers almost entirely from all property in or control over the instruments of production, creating a proletariat on the one hand and a non-working capitalist and propertied class on the other. The surviving independent craftsmen are an unimportant exception to this general rule and have an increasingly difficult task to maintain themselves. Peasants and farmers are very often only nominally the owners of their holdings, exploited unmercifully by mortgages or in the hands of transport or distributing agencies. Peasants manage to maintain themselves only by exploiting their families. Though idealised by some people, they are, in fact, physically, morally, intellectually and culturally inferior even to the town proletariat. Shop-keepers are rarely independent; they are tied down to the wholesale

can obtain only where the individual is left as much freedom as is consistent with the safety of the State. Humanity has no collective mind; human progress is due to the free play of rivalry between man and man.

(3) The main spur of economic and social progress in the past has been individualism. The same force is the only one capable of carrying mankind forward in the future. Civilisation always depends for its cultural development on a small class, which is supported by the profits of individualism. That class has also been the standard-bearer of freedom in politics and morals.

(4) (Some) The trend of development does not divorce the worker more and more from the means of production. Side by side with the big factory, there constantly occur chances for small people to start independent trades. The peasant proprietor in most parts of Europe is as strong as ever. It has been shown that small-scale production can secure practically all the advantages of large-scale and, in terms of relative efficiency, is often superior to very huge organisations.

(Some) Even if it were possible to put an end to the economic and social process of differentiation, and to all its causes and effects, such a consummation would not imply an advance in human culture.

(5) The capitalist could not exist without the labourer, nor could the labourer without the capitalist, who supplies the sinews of industry with which the former produces a commodity. Besides this function, the capitalist often performs that of directing production. Most of the profits are the earnings of managerial ability. The distinctive feature of capitalism today is the complete with-

firms, whose paid agents they often are. The only places where independence survives are in the interstices of big industry.

(5) The measure of individual wealth should be the amount of work done by the individual; this being impossible to apply, the best maxim is: 'From each according to his ability, to each according to his needs.' The present system secures a distribution that approaches neither principle. The capitalist exploits the labour of the producers by hand and brain, from the unskilled labourer right up to the manager, not by virtue of his transcendent services but because he has inherited stock from an ancestor or can limit production, or secures a mortgage, or can maintain prices – in fact, by means of any successful application of the principle of obstruction between the production of goods and their distribution to those who need them. A 'pull' is more certain of gaining wealth than great genius or singular powers of organisation.

(6) Lack of an assured purpose breeds despair; hence the inefficiency of the chronically casual worker. Man loathes boredom to such an extent, and has such an instinctive aversion from futility, that in a properly constituted society, where a few men could do the work with the machines to hand, there would be competition to get work rather than to avoid it.

(7) The luxury of the rich increases faster than the comfort of the poor. Though better off than his great-grandfather, the worker has not received a proportionate share of the vast increase in the country's wealth. Terminologically, the theory that wages sink to the level of 'bare subsistence' may need restatement: its substance – that the workers receive only enough to keep them efficient –

drawal of the men of exceptional intellect from the business of performing or directing any labour of their own and the concentration of their powers in organising the labour of others, with the result that the mental capacities of the few, instead of being confined to the task of guiding their own muscles, lend guidance to the muscular operations of the many. The profits of the capitalist employers have their origin in the fact that, in this way, commodities are multiplied to an extent they never were before, their individual values remaining unaltered in proportion as this multiplication is general; and the sum of the values thus added to the general product forms the funds from which profits are drawn.

(6) Socialism, by guaranteeing to all a livelihood, takes away the chief incentive to exertion. Saving becomes useless. Private enterprise has been the best prerequisite of progress everywhere; wherever there are traces of Communism, it is only as men get away from it that they become energetic and progress is possible.

(7) The labourer has shared proportionately in the increase of wealth; he has shared very probably to a greater degree than the capitalist. He also now has shorter hours and better conditions. The statistics magnifying the disproportion of the wealth of different sections of the community are fallacious. If the national income were shared out equally, the addition to the workers' wages would be negligible. Under a free, individualist social system, none has a fixed status; the same men are both capitalists and workers. To a large extent, men reputed to be the possessors of great wealth are simply its distributors.

(8) There is no universal tendency

remains fundamentally true. This is the latest scientific wage theory of capitalism – the economy of high wages. All the advances the workers have made have been gained despite capitalism, not because of it.

(8) Individualism is a theory that does not fit the present facts. The industry of the country is passing rapidly into the hands of a few men, as great firms diversify their interests. Smaller concerns are usually helpless in the face of takeover bids. Interlocking directorships are held everywhere. The shareholder has to have blind faith in two or three of the board of directors. Financial and industrial magnates influence the stock, produce and raw material markets in their own interests. The result is a nation of serfs on the one hand and a few industrial and financial overlords on the other.

(9) The creation of a great body of unemployed is an invariable accompaniment of capitalism. When advances in invention or foreign competition render an industry obsolete, whole regions are left high and dry, with no prospect of better times, and nothing is done to help them beyond pious exhortation. The men affected are neither idlers nor wastrels, though constant disturbances may turn some of them into black sheep. It is only in times of war, when weapons of death are produced in vast numbers and immediately consumed, or in the period after war when the devastation it has caused gives rise to a demand for all kinds of goods for the rebuilding of normal life, that workers can be temporarily assured of steady employment. In a Socialist society, the very few who were unwilling to work could be dealt with by disciplinary measures as a last resort. Socialism demands no 'change

to eliminate the small capitalist and businessman; a small, ably conducted business has a very good chance of success. Co-operative enterprises and limited liability companies secure a large field of investment for the small capitalists, who are necessary to the captains of industry. Takeover bids are an essential weapon of the market, either to improve efficiency in viable companies or to eliminate hopelessly inefficient ones. Even a Socialist economy must find some means of doing this.

(9) Socialism would not solve the problem of the unemployed because that problem is as much moral as economic. In every community, idlers and black sheep will always be present, yet Socialism assumes an ideal state of society in which all men will be equally good.

(10) All Socialist systems mean the minute regulation of life by statute and bye-laws, probably administered by officials. These would be so numerous that the manual workers would become impotent. All spontaneity or self-expression would cease or, eventually, escape from repression into revolution. Bureaucrats tend to develop the 'red tape', obstinately conservative habit of mind. Their conduct becomes high-handed, as they feel bound to support the dignity of the administrative machine of which they are part. The general standard of efficiency of the industries nationalised in this country since the last world war has not been impressive and has strengthened many people's determination to resist any further nationalisations. In many countries, wholesale corruption would be inevitable, and here we should not be immune. The German official in the old days used to be incorruptible and intolerable; with the coming of the Third Reich, he lost

of heart', only the enlightenment of self-interest.

(10) Society is at present minutely regulated, openly but unobtrusively, by Government officials in part, but mainly by capitalists. Socialism will endeavour to reduce regimentation and set people free individually in groups to manage their own affairs. Socialism does not mean necessarily the aggrandisement of State departments. Devolution by area and function is possible, and Guild Socialism and the Soviet system are examples of other schemes. The British official is efficient and not corrupt, and can be trusted to work in the interests of the community.

(11) Crises which render everybody's existence insecure are inherent in the capitalist system, arising from the fact that production for the world's markets cannot gauge the limits of consumption and that production is continually outstripping the effective demand. The conditions under private property have become too narrow for the constantly growing accumulation of wealth. Malthus's law of population is now obsolete. It is not the population that presses upon the means of subsistence but, on the contrary, the means of subsistence that press upon the nation. Hence the feverish race for new outlets, new consumers, profitable investments. Hence also the deliberate destroying of goods which would have been of use to the community, in order to maintain the level of prices at times when purchasing power has fallen. Under Socialism, such crises would be avoided, for production would be adapted to national consumption, and the needs of the nation could easily be ascertained. The mere production of great wealth is no test of social and industrial well-being; distribution is the real test.

much of his incorruptibility but little of his overbearing behaviour. Nor would these dangers be avoided if some other form of organisation were adopted. For every large organisation develops the same habits; trade unions, industrial conglomerates, the Soviets and the Church can be cited as instances. Here, numerous incidents involving the Post Office, the Treasury and the Ministries responsible for health, insurance and agriculture can all be cited as showing how the jack-in-office afflicts the supposedly free citizen and enfranchised constituent. Our aim should be the reduction of administrative machinery and the freeing of choice and initiative in as great of degree as possible.

(11) The primary question which presses for solution is not the unequal distribution of wealth but the production of the wealth to be distributed. The wealth of modern nations depends upon international credit and trade. Under capitalism, the two virtues necessary in the accumulation of capital – thrift and industry – are encouraged, and the rewards for the effective and punishments for the non-effective direction of labour are automatic. Under Socialism, the detection of the mis-direction of labour becomes a practical impossibility, and thus capital must waste away while the primary cause of its waste is unknown and therefore not remedied.

(12) The management of the entire production would force the Socialist State, in order to prevent overproduction, to abolish the right of the worker freely to choose his profession. Everyone would have to act in accordance with orders. Otherwise, everyone would flock into those professions which afforded the pleasantest way of life.

(13) The regulation of consump-

(12) The regulation of production is not incompatible with freedom of choice of profession. If it were found that too many people were turning in any one direction, it would always be possible to increase the inducements in other directions by offering more favourable conditions of work, e.g. increased remuneration, shorter hours or other privileges. The dirty work would be remunerated in proportion to its unpleasantness. Short hours, long holidays and generous treatment should be accorded to those who do it.

(13) No regulation of individual consumption would be necessary, for modern labour is so productive that it could satisfy all needs of a civilised society. Moreover, Socialism, by broadening the basis of consumption, would give individual freedom also to those classes which, under the present conditions, are poor and obliged to limit very strictly their individual consumption.

(14) Socialism would have no need to abolish competition, but would leave men free to compete not only for 'service' but for high salaries, for position, for authority and for leisure. Socialist competition is a well-known feature of life in the Soviet Union. Under capitalism, while competition among workers for the means whereby to earn their daily bread becomes keener, competition among capitalists gives way day by day to co-operation. The more production gets into the hands of the big companies, the easier do capitalists find it to form rings, etc., to keep prices up. No legislation can prevent secret agreements. Again, the practice of advertising warfare and misleading half-truths condemns the competitive system. Dishonesty is an essential part of present-day competition. The

tion destroys all freedom of choice and enslaves everybody; only through regulation can production be made exactly to meet consumption – otherwise, the old difficulty must recur. Moreover, everybody would want the best things, which, by their nature, are limited.

(14) Socialism would abolish competition and establish a huge monopoly, which would soon be that worst of tyrannies, a mob tyranny. Free competition is the only real freedom in industrial matters, as well as the only guarantee to the consumer that he gets what he wants. The law should make and enforce regulations to ensure that fraud is not perpetrated on the consumer, but that is the only way legislation should intervene, in this context. Honesty pays in the general run. Given a number of labourers equal in productivity, working for an equal number of hours, and receiving as their rewards equal shares of the total product, no single group of labourers could augment their own gains in any way except by a successful attack on the gains of all the others. However much an individualist community might be socialised, all the elements of industrial conflict would survive in it. The only way in which the position of any group of labourers could be improved would be by the advent of some exceptional man. He would demand his special bargain. The bargain which a Socialist State would, in the interests of the majority, have to strike with its exceptionally efficient citizen would be, in its essentials, the same as that made under a system of free exchange and competition.

(15) Socialism would involve wholesale confiscation, which would inevitably create universal mistrust and prevent all progress. Theoreti-

consumer is not in a position, under the complex conditions of modern life, to know a genuine article, or to know what is compatible with health in food, dwellings, etc. He cannot be a universal expert. Such measures of inspection and regulation as have been taken are insufficient to deal with those whose intention it is to defraud or mislead.

(15) There need be no such thing as confiscation. The tendency nowadays, especially in Britain, has been to give compensation to the former owners of nationalised industries, generally in the form of State bonds. Although this involves a charge on the State, the curbing of the practice of investing in subsidiary industries or abroad should provide sufficient funds for improvements in working hours and conditions, as well as wages. The large, near-monopolistic industrial groups have shown how enormously production can be raised, and the great difficulty of the capitalist – how to limit production so as to sell the products at a profit – would disappear. In a transformed society, when all the private capital of production and exploitation has been socialised, the compensation that former capitalists have received will enable them to buy the products of social activity but not to control their production.

(16) The existence of idle classes is a direct social evil – whether the idle rich or the idle poor. The so-called services of the former to society are for the most part the merest dilettantism, and their social influence is pernicious in every way. Their artistic taste, even when sincere, is based on false values and is often mere ostentation. Inclined strongly to superstition, belief in luck and so on, and to barbarism in their amusements, blood sports, etc., they speedily

cally, the State might confiscate all such resources as exist at any given moment, but no one, if it aimed at making this confiscation permanent, would ever accumulate any such resources again. The idea of buying out the whole property-holding class would spell bankruptcy and, moreover, bring no advantages. It would simply have the effect of turning active workers into pensioners of the State. Socialists would soon find that people would not work if assured of a living; hence production would soon fall off. Destroy confidence in the future and the great driving forces of the economic processes are paralysed. The continued progress of Socialism, if translated into a national policy, must drive the owners of liquid capital to domicile elsewhere. On the other hand, the owners of fixed capital and the population who live on their own personal labour would suffer from the consequences of excessive taxation and the attrition or flight of capital in abnormal quantities. As ninety-five per cent of the industries of Great Britain are conducted by credit, any interference with that confidence which is the basis of credit necessarily drives the injured industries to foreign countries which are our competitors in the world markets.

(16) The so-called idle classes do much valuable social and philanthropic work, which could not be done by any paid official with the same disinterested love. They are, moreover, the upholders of culture and patrons of art. From these classes our greatest statesmen have sprung.

(17) Socialism, by stopping the competitive struggle for life, puts an end to the process of natural selection for the elimination of the unfit, and thus brings progress to a standstill.

degenerate. The political leadership of the propertied classes tends more and more to fall to men whose social origin is different from theirs. Their philanthropy, where felt, degrades the proletariat, as their patronage degrades art. It is not denied that this class has in the past performed a certain social function, though badly; but it has now become superfluous and noxious.

(17) Social progress and social evolution are different from natural selection and natural evolution. The present system has produced an inferior population out of a sound stock. The successful men are the cunning men, those with a commercial instinct. Given economic and social equality as far as may be, the best types would come to the front. The type of person who has a talent for prospering at the expense of others is not necessarily the 'fittest' human being.

(18) The present marriage system is still a reflex of the property system. Socialism would determine whether monogamy suited humanity by making everyone freer than he or she is at present. Recent trends in the USSR, with tightening up of marriage and divorce laws, suggest that monogamy would be found to be the best system; the example of the USA, on the other hand, suggests that monogamy is not an essential feature of capitalism. Socialism is in any case an economic doctrine which bears on the sex question only where it is complicated by money matters.

(19) By making work obligatory for all, Socialism would reduce work to a minimum for all alike and would set free the worker to enjoy his leisure, to develop his cultural equipment, or to express himself in more personal methods of work. The culture that

Those who fail are less desirable types of humanity than those who succeed, since they are physically, intellectually and even morally inferior. The growth of medical science reinforces this tendency. Socialism encourages the survival of the unfit.

(18) The Socialists teach that existing marriage relations are simply the outcome of property. Property in children under Socialism would soon cease to exist, and marriage would be an association terminable at will by either party. Thus the family would disappear. If society guaranteed subsistence to all its members, it must regulate the number of citizens for whom it would have to provide.

(19) Socialism would have no leisured class; and since we owe a great deal of our art, literature and science and the refinements of everyday life to this class, cultural progress would cease. The Socialist society would maintain a constant level of dull materialism.

(20) It is almost impossible to conceive how work is to be remunerated, save on a competitive basis. Under Socialism, all kinds of work would have to be valued on a common basis, which could only be the amount of time spent in the production of commodities. Socialism would be possible only if all men were not just equally good but equally gifted. One of the chief incentives to labour would be removed if parents were deprived of the wish and ability to provide for their children's advancement. The Christian doctrine of the equality of man is an ideal, not a working system. Character must be the mainspring of the State; an atmosphere of potential inequality gives free play to all the passions and active powers of man. Socialism presupposes men not only more perfect but of an entirely

depends on a leisured class and is the monopoly of the few cannot be very valuable.

(20) The competitive reward of labour is a fiction in present-day society. The worker was never rewarded in proportion to his toil but only as allowed by the market rate, determined by factors outside his control. Collective bargaining by trade unions has ended the theory. The best work has never been done out of consideration for money. Though inequalities may persist as between different classes of workers until society has achieved a sufficient abundance, ultimately equality of income will be general. Socialism would secure free play to the better side of humanity, i.e. pride in one's work. Socialism is designed for a humanity that has not been repressed and thwarted by economic serfdom.

(21) (Some) Socialism is the social interpretation of Christianity, and though some individual Socialists may be atheists, there is no connection between atheism and Socialism.

(Some) Socialism has nothing to do with religion, which is a personal affair. It is a sociological programme. Capitalism has equally little to do with religion, though its theories and practices are repugnant to most of the leading religions of the world and some of them have been specifically condemned by the Church. Socialists are generally anti-clericals because most of the clergy, especially in the higher ranks, have always been on the side of their enemies in the past.

(22) Socialism will abolish war by mitigating the frenzies of nationalism and preventing the capitalist developments which make for international competition for foreign markets and resources. The patriotism of a Socialist society will accord with justice and

different nature from what they will ever be.

(21) Socialism is atheistic. This is clear, not only from the doctrines and philosophy of the leading Socialist thinkers but also from their policy and action when in power. Marx and Engels said that religion was 'the opium of the people'. Socialists everywhere desire the secularisation of the schools and the educational system.

(22) The international doctrines of Socialists are absurd. The real causes of war are nationalist ambitions and over-population. Socialism might well be intensely nationalist. The main driving force of Russian resistance to German invasion in the Second World War was the desire to drive out the foreign aggressor, and many British Socialists today have shown themselves to be excessively nationalist (e.g. the left-wing opposition to Britain's membership of the EEC). Socialised industries would have to enter world competition and, as the whole might of the State and political machine would be brought into play to support them in their struggles for markets and the sources of raw materials, the danger of international rivalries and feuds would be as great as under the most rapacious private capitalism. The class war provokes even more bitterness than international war and, on a world-wide scale, could cause even more harm. Socialists often condemn strife between nations and at the same time extol strife between sections of a nation.

(23) The horrors of Socialism in practice are illustrated by Russia under the Bolsheviks. The cultured classes were extirpated, production as a whole fell off enormously after the Revolution, and distribution was poor. As time went on, the Soviet

benevolence. No Socialist regards the class war as desirable, though some believe it to be inevitable; all strive to gain their ends by the constitutional methods of modern political democracy. The conflict of classes is recognised by Socialists as inevitable until economic democracy has supplemented political democracy.

(23) The Bolsheviks were not typical Socialists; nor are present-day Russians. The state of the country at the end of 1917, after the Russian Revolution, and the widespread hostility it has had to face since, for most of the time, are largely responsible for the special features of Socialism as now practised in the Soviet Union. In each country, indeed, the form of Socialism would be modified by the economic and cultural development of that country.

leaders found themselves obliged to abandon more and more of their original doctrines, in practice if not in theory.

SOFT DRUGS, LEGALISATION OF

Pro: (1) There is no legal bar on the purchase of alcoholic drink and cigarettes, though both are often addictive. No logical reason exists, therefore, for the continued ban on soft drugs, which, despite assertions to the contrary, have not been proved to be addictive.

(2) The open availability of soft drugs would help greatly to reduce the incidence of alcoholism and addiction to hard drugs. It could also lead to a reduction in cigarette consumption, thus lessening the incidence of lung cancer from tobacco, since the smoking of soft drugs has far less harmful effects on the health than cigarettes.

(3) Public alarm has been stirred up more by the undesirable side-effects of the illicit trade in soft drugs than by

Con: (1) There is no proof whatever that soft drugs are non-addictive. On the contrary, the evidence points entirely the other way. That alcohol and cigarettes are available to all, despite their admittedly harmful effects, is no reason for the legalisation of soft drugs as well – merely an argument to restrict the sale of alcohol and cigarettes.

(2) Even if irrefutable medical evidence were eventually to prove that the majority of soft drugs are not addictive, which is highly unlikely, this would still not overcome the greatest danger in these drugs – the likelihood that they will lead on to far worse substances. When people find that soft drugs are no longer giving them as much satisfaction or pleasure as before, the first reaction is usually

any knowledge about the drugs themselves. Since the law bans them, it is inevitable that a black market should have grown up to meet the considerable demand that exists. If their sale were made legal, at officially-controlled prices, the black market would disappear overnight – and with it would go the theft, blackmail, drug-pushing and other evils which surround it at present. In view of the widespread, albeit illegal trade in drugs (soft and hard), fully effective control of this illicit market is in any case currently almost impossible, in practice – seizures by police and Customs amount to only a tiny fraction of the whole. In the Netherlands, toleration of soft drugs has not led to a massive rise in consumption, as critics feared, and the police have found it much easier to keep an eye on the trade.

(4) Soft drugs merely induce a sensation of being mildly 'high' – much less so than with alcohol – and a pleasant feeling of well-being. The predominant characteristic among people taking such drugs is their peaceful attitude to all fellow-humans; violence is abhorrent to them.

to increase the intake (which can be serious enough); but the most probable outcome is that they will progress to hard drugs, which are killers. That this tendency has become all too common is shown by the ever-increasing number of young people dying in Britain each year from the effects of drug addiction.

(3) Since the word side-effects has been used, it should be mentioned that among those known to result from addiction to soft drugs (and not just hard drugs) are impotence and sterility. One of the most pernicious social effects of drug trafficking is that addicts, particularly the young, are led into crime in order to obtain the drugs for which they crave. They may commit thefts to get the money required; they may break into a pharmacy or doctor's surgery to steal drugs; when unable to pay the trafficker on whom they rely for supplies, they may well be enrolled as 'pushers' themselves. All these cases figure frequently in the drug trials one can hear in the courts every week. Legalising the sale of soft drugs would not end the problem. Addicts unable to pay for them would still resort to crime.

(4) The process of 'coming down', as the effects of the drug wear off, can be anything but pleasant. Drug addicts have a tendency to live in a sub-culture world utterly removed from the realities of life. Indeed, their refusal or inability to face the real world is often the reason they resorted to drugs in the first place.

SPACE EXPLORATION:
International Only?

Pro: (1) Two main forms of space exploration are now in prospect: (a) the unmanned probes, pushing ever farther outwards into the universe (and including attempts to discover whether any hint of elementary life exists on other planets); and (b) the closer study, from space, of the Earth's resources and environmental problems (notably through 'space laboratories' – into which other craft can dock – and also, it is hoped, a new American 'space shuttle'). To ease the huge and ever-growing costs, to avoid wasteful duplication, and to prevent future political confrontations, the time must come when all such explorations cease to be conducted unilaterally but are carried out on an international basis.

(2) As a first step, an International Space Agency should be formed, its members comprising not only the two super-powers but all nations which already have a lesser scientific role in space exploration (like Britain) or are likely to make an increasing contribution to it in future (like China and Japan). The initial purpose of the Agency would be to co-ordinate all space activities, but ultimately it would become the controlling body.

(3) Proof that space co-operation is entirely possible, given the political will, was provided by the Apollo–Soyuz project in July 1975. It did not represent any significant advance in the technology of manned space flight; its greatest achievement was one of organisation, in overcoming new, different kinds of problems – language, getting the control centres and tracking networks opera-

Con: (1) The two super-powers, the USSR and the USA, have hitherto been the only countries with the resources to embark on large-scale space programmes. But their motives were not altruistic, nor even a matter of simply trying to gain prestige over each other. The principal spur behind their space exploits has been militaristic. (One has only to think of the large but unpublicised number of space satellites now in orbit for intelligence and other military purposes, as well as the furore over President Reagan's Strategic Defence Initiative – the so-called 'Star Wars' programme). Until the powers achieve such mutual trust that all threat of war is removed at last – and with it, the potential instruments of war, wherever they may be – there can be no hope of anything but relatively limited co-operation between them in peaceful space affairs. International space exploration is a fine ideal; so is the concept of World Government; but conditions are unlikely to be ripe for either of them in the foreseeable future.

(2) Such a body would have all the defects of present UN agencies in other fields. It would inevitably be dominated by America and Russia, and thus still subject to the political strains and rivalries between them – with the customary undesirable line-up of their respective supporters behind them. No measures envisaged by other members, however wise, could be enforced unless both the super-powers agreed. It should also be recalled that China, now a nuclear power, has refused to sign any of the treaties

ting closely together, making the two spacecraft compatible in many various ways. In short, it was an important first step towards true space co-operation, though only a first step. As an example of the immediate possibilities arising from it, one result of this initial collaboration was agreement that all Soviet and American manned spacecraft in future would use the compatible docking system developed for the Apollo–Soyuz link-up.

(4) The financial savings which could be effected by pooling resources for space exploration are indicated by the fact that the Apollo–Soyuz project was one of the cheapest in American space history. It is estimated to have cost the USA only $250 million. In contrast, it was estimated initially that the cost of replacing the ill-fated Challenger shuttle would be $3 *billion*!

(5) There is already one area of the world, Antarctica, where the nations have kept their word to reserve the territory solely for peaceful purposes, to co-operate in scientific investigation and research, and to preserve the *status quo* with regard to territorial sovereignty, rights and claims. Now, Apollo–Soyuz has proved that in space, too, nations with political systems widely different in values, outlook and purpose *can* co-operate in a peaceful project. There has long been international co-operation as well in such fields as communications satellites and the obtaining and sharing of information for purposes like astronomy and climatology. In short, precedents have been set, and the gap between individual national and general international operations in space will be much easier to bridge than many people imagine. That the two super-powers are at present following divergent lines in their space planning does not lessen but, rather,

restricting nuclear tests or weapons; how long would she decline to co-operate in space affairs, too?

(3) Despite its world-wide impact as a symbol of *détente*, the Soyuz–Apollo project merely underlined the enormous gulfs to be bridged before international space exploration could even begin to seem a practical possibility. For instance, Soviet and American engineers did not develop the compatible docking mechanism jointly; they agreed on dimensions and on how the system would work, etc., but built their own mechanisms quite separately – and along completely different lines (hydraulic for the Americans, mainly mechanical for the Russians). Technologically and psychologically, the USSR derived most from the project. The Americans provided the bulk of the know-how – the Russians had little or nothing to offer, technologically, that was not already known to American scientists.

(4) The cost was so low (comparatively!) only because the Americans used a starter rocket and an Apollo capsule which were already in existence (and which would otherwise have been scrapped). As witness the huge cost of merely replacing Challenger alone, the design and construction of the new material which would doubtless be required for any major joint space exploration might well be even more expensive for each nation than its own space programmes.

(5) In Antarctica and the other examples cited, the co-operation is relatively superficial and each nation continues to go its own sweet way in its researches, etc. To give an analogy: two car manufacturing companies might agree to standardise tyres, but this is very different from jointly producing a car. In practical terms, the main thrust of each super-power's

would enhance the advantages of cooperation between them in whichever areas of research it was feasible. For a start, it might have averted at least some of the postponements (or eventual cancellations) of future American deep-space missions, including the launching of the 94-inch space telescope, resulting from the Challenger tragedy.

space programme is now developing on very different lines, with the Americans still looking to reusable shuttles and the Russians talking about putting very big space stations into orbit round the Earth.

SPECULATION, SUPPRESSION OF COMMERCIAL

Pro: (1) Gambling in goods, shares or land disturbs ordinary trade and business.

(2) Dealers and investors are thereby exposed to more risks than need be, while an army of parasites does nothing useful and gets rewarded for doing it.

(3) Prices fluctuate and expenses increase, and for both it is the general public that has to pay.

(4) Trade, inevitably, is full of risks, but the gambler increases them. He excludes much talent from legitimate commerce.

(5) 'Rigging' markets is made easier by the liking of many traders and investors for deals with a prospect of excitement (and of big profits almost overnight), and this tendency provides ready opportunities for unscrupulous businessmen.

(6) During the world's present precarious economic conditions, commercial gambling is one more obstacle to reconstruction on sound lines.

(7) The so-called 'Big Bang' on the British Stock Exchange, in October 1986, was brought about – in effect –

Con: (1) Speculation is inevitable in commerce, for nothing else brings the present into connection with future needs and supplies.

(2) Middlemen are a necessity for securing efficient distribution. Without readiness to take large risks, large results cannot be obtained. All business has an element of gambling in it.

(3) In the long run, the free play of business brings about the lowest possible level of prices.

(4) There is no way of making, in a business context, a clear distinction between what is gambling and what is not.

(5) 'Rigging' would occur anyhow, and steadiness might even promote it.

(6) Free opportunity will bring about the results desired more quickly than red tape and restriction. Beyond a certain point, efforts to make trade conform with rigid systems result in far more harm than good.

(7) The so-called speculator is an essential part of the market's price-steadying mechanism; and for any one speculator who is very successful, there are many whose fingers get burnt

by the realisation that certain restrictive practices (e.g. the division between the functions of jobbers and brokers) were inimical to the interests of a genuinely free market. But it is significant that the change was accompanied by very strict measures to protect members of the public from the machinations of dubious speculators trying to cash in on it.

– and this at no ultimate cost to the public. In the past, on the contrary, great suffering *has* been caused to the public by wild market fluctuations when speculation was banned or restricted.

(See also GAMBLING, MORALITY OF)

SPELLING REFORM

Pro: (1) The spelling of English, which became finally fixed by pedants only as late as the eighteenth century, bears little relation to the spoken language. It is a logical absurdity. Its substitution by a phonetically consistent method would be of enormous value.

(2) Correct spelling is looked upon as a *sine qua non* for an educated person, so that an enormous expenditure of time and effort is involved in teaching it to children and to foreigners – who, on the average, take five times as long to learn to spell reasonably well as they would if the language were spelt phonetically.

(3) The time taken to learn to read is similarly extravagant. Because of the difficulties, many people lose all interest in reading as soon as they leave school, and thus remain inefficient workers and citizens. The form of phonetic spelling taught in some junior schools in recent years has been very successful; the children learn to read much more quickly and they have had little or no difficulty in coping with conventional spelling at a later stage.

(4) The superiorities of English as

Con: (1) The present spelling of English is an integral part of the language. Few languages have phonetic spelling, and there are sufficient rules for English spelling to make it reasonably easy to master adequately.

(2) Phonetic spelling would not make it any easier for the child or the foreigner to learn English. Our alphabet contains five vowels. At least twenty symbols would be required to represent the various ways in which those vowels are pronounced in spoken English. Would this simplify the task?

(3) Those who want to read will surmount the difficulties. The remainder would not be any more interested in acquiring ideas through reading under a new spelling system than they are now. Reformed spelling would mean that children would have to learn two schemes until all our literature could be reprinted, at the risk of being cut off from the great writings of the past. Many adults would not learn the new system at all. That the recent phonetic spelling experiment at some schools has fallen short of success is proved by the fact

a language, on the scores of grammatical ease, logical syntax, expressive idiom and magnificent vocabulary, warrant an effort to relieve it of its quite inessential difficulty. If this were done, English would be accepted without question as the world language for purposes of international communication.

(5) Phonetic representation would be unnecessary, though not unduly difficult if the international phonetic symbols were used. The use of a conventional but sensible system, employing simply the ordinary letters, would meet all requirements. American is already so different from English as to be ranked in several countries as a separate language. In any case, if we wish to take American English into account, it has already set us an example in spelling reform.

(6) The aesthetic argument against spelling reform is merely a plea that what is novel is ugly, what is old is beautiful. The meanings of words are by no means usually to be discovered from their derivations. Many words give no obvious clue to their origin and history.

(7) There is no real difficulty in choosing which pronunciation to use. The accepted pronunciation is given in any standard dictionary. Local dialects and variations of pronunciation would continue to exist, as they do now, independently of spelling.

that it has not been adopted generally.

(4) As the Basic English experiment showed, English is too rich a language for fully satisfactory 'rationalisation' and is thus unlikely to become the unanimously accepted world language; nor are national susceptibilities likely to permit this. An International Auxiliary Language (q.v.) is much more hopeful for the purpose.

(5) Spelling reformers are not agreed on what system to adopt. The only sensible one, a phonetic system, would be extremely difficult to apply to English, with its many vague sounds and numerous diphthongs, and would cut us off from writings in other varieties of English, such as American, which differs dramatically at times from our own language in pronunciation as well as spelling.

(6) The NU Spelling is incurably ugly. To see the English classics transliterated into it gives our aesthetic sensibilities a shock. It also largely obliterates the indications of the derivation of words which the present spelling gives, and so weakens the interest we take in them and the understanding of their true significance.

(7) If spelling is to be made to fit pronunciation, whose pronunciation is to be chosen? Would the Scots, the Irish or the northern English accept the decision of a committee of English dons? They would more probably prefer to set their own standard pronunciation.

SPIRITUALISM

Pro: (1) Mankind has always believed that death was not the end of human existence and that the dead

Con: (1) The belief in spiritualism has not been universal; even if it were, that would be no proof of its truth,

were sometimes able to communicate with the living. Many religions are based on this belief.

(2) In history, there are many authenticated instances of spiritualistic phenomena which cannot be dismissed as baseless or given any 'normal' explanation.

(3) In modern times, multitudes of sober and reliable people have witnessed marvels. Though sometimes they may have been mistaken or deceived, it is incredible that they should all have been deceived all the time.

(4) Eminent public men and, more especially, eminent scientists, such as A. R. Wallace, Lombroso and Sir William Crookes, have conducted impartial and scientific investigations, which gave conclusive results. Many people who have made themselves famous for intellectual qualities and sound judgment, such as Sir Oliver Lodge and Sir Arthur Conan Doyle, and certain shrewd journalists with no axe to grind, have been convinced of the truth of spiritualism. We may have confidence in the conclusions of a variety of people of first-class intelligence.

(5) There is good evidence for the occurrence of otherwise inexplicable physical manifestations. The phenomena (including levitation) attributed to the famed Victorian spiritualist, Daniel Dunglas Home, were unexceptionable. He courted investigation, he was never detected in trickery, and the witnesses are numerous and of the highest standing. Stainton Moses was, for years, the centre of phenomena recorded at the time by people with no motive for deception. The Boston medium 'Margery', the Belfast Goligher circle, and the Austrian mediums Rudi and Willi Schneider are cases in point. An

as men have always believed firmly in things that were baseless.

(2) Most of the historical evidence is untrustworthy and is based on incorrect observation or prejudiced theories. Much of it refers to happenings which would now be ascribed to disorders of the subjects' minds, while the best of it contains indications that the original story has since been elaborated.

(3) Mediums work under the most propitious conditions, as they choose the time and circumstances, e.g. darkness, and their audiences come in an excited frame of mind, prepared to accept any occurrence as the work of spirits. Some years ago, members of the Magic Circle staged a 'seance' at which they reproduced many of the reputed phenomena of spiritualist seances. Although people in the know were allowed to search the demonstrators at each stage, beforehand, they did not discover any of the methods used – and, until afterwards, not one of the ordinary spectators present knew that the seance was in fact spurious!

(4) Only a few investigations can properly be described as scientific, and they give only negative results. The scientists commonly cited were not investigating their own subject-matter under their own conditions, and a physicist is no more qualified to investigate problems involving psychology and conjuring than a psychologist is to investigate physics. Their evidence shows the same gaps and faults as other people's. The scientific specialists most fitted for the task, the psychologists, include hardly any adherents of spiritualism.

(5) Nearly all mediums in whose presence physical phenomena have occurred have been detected in fraud when sufficiently shrewd observers

enormous body of evidence about the paranormal exists, which conventional scientists have refused to consider simply because it does not fit in with their own current dogma.

(6) Numerous messages have come from the dead, giving information for the living that no one else knew.

(7) Spirit photographs give permanent and objective proof of survival. The conditions generally preclude fraud, as sitters are unknown to the medium.

(8) It is not sufficient to cavil at items in the evidence, as the mass of witnesses and the multitudes of separate instances establish a solid case. Evidence for spiritualism is much more abundant and of better quality than that for the origins of the Christian religion.

(9) Mediums, as a class, are as good as the average man or woman. A few black sheep are not sufficient to establish a general charge of fraud. Even then, it is not impossible for lax morals to go with psychic power; geniuses are not noted for moral perfection.

(10) Spiritualism gives mankind a great hope, and more than hope, at a time when traditional religion is decaying and unsatisfactory. It is morally uplifting, does not promote nervous disorder and, indeed, is much healthier than fervid religion.

(11) The marvellous in spiritualism should not excite incredulity, for it is no more astounding than the ordinary phenomena of human life, or such discoveries as wireless telegraphy and telephony. Much has been done to advance and prove its cause in the past, and much more will be done in the future.

(12) There is nothing in spiritualism which makes it hostile to Christianity on either the moral or the

have sat with them. Home's career is not free from suspicious events, and it is to be noticed that he always chose his audience carefully. It is quite possible that he had the power of causing hallucinations in his sitters. The evidence in his case is so incomplete and unsatisfactory that it cannot be properly appraised. Moses was undoubtedly a pathological character in some ways. His phenomena took place in a very select circle and were reported only by himself and his friends. In reporting or discussing other people's phenomena, he was credulous to the last degree. 'Margery' has been declared fraudulent by certain experts of weight, and the Golighers would never accept the presence at their seances of Psychical Research Society investigators. The Schneiders survived a number of tests, but judgment on all such cases must be suspended until the mediums involved have been subjected to investigation under the strictest scientific control. Perhaps the most striking feature of the 'evidence' proffered by spiritualists is its sheer banality. So much purposeless table-lifting, so many vague messages about how happy people are on 'the other side' ... If a medium can levitate himself, why doesn't he do it in Trafalgar Square instead of in a darkened room? And why doesn't Uncle Henry tell us, in his message, where he hid those valuable antiques he'd promised to bequeath us?

(6) Messages from the other world are generally incapable of verification. Those which seem most promising usually turn out to be guesses or derived from hints thrown out by the sitters. The state of mind of the bereaved sitters must be taken into account.

(7) No spirit photographs have yet

theological side. Many earnest Christians have been convinced of its truth, but remained Christian. The established churches believe it threatens *their* prerogatives and oppose it just as they have always opposed what they thought would damage their worldly position. The Roman Catholic Church does not deny the phenomena of the seance room but holds that they are the work of devils or evil spirits.

(13) (Some) It is well to keep an open mind and pursue investigations. Indubitable data of supernormal phenomena are still not available in sufficient quantity to permit of a scientific or logical examination. Spiritualism has at least the advantage of a ready hypothesis, which we should not reject merely because we are used to scientific phenomena which demand more mechanical and materialist theories.

been accepted as genuine scientific proof, because conditions lend themselves to deceit. It is a proof of the credulity of believers that the very evidence of double exposure, etc., is passed over without remark. It is significant that the best known 'spirit' photographers insisted on using plates and avoided using roll films, which can give just as good photographic results but are nothing like so susceptible to fraudulent manipulation. The most famous 'spirit' photographers have been exposed one after another.

(8) A multitude of bad links will not make a strong chain, and the accumulation of bad evidence does not prove a good case. Evidence of the trends in human thought which led to the foundation of Christianity (as distinct from documentary evidence about Jesus Christ himself) is substantial and irrefutable.

(9) Spiritualism is the great arena for fraud, and the majority of professional mediums are deceitful – some to a small extent, perhaps, but others on a large scale.

(10) Spiritualism promotes insanity and minor nervous disorders, and encourages a disastrous indifference to the affairs of this life.

(11) Analogy is not proof and does not make up for the absence of definite and conclusive evidence. Great progress was expected when the Society for Psychical Research was founded. Except for a wider knowledge of the abnormalities of the mind, no progress has been made since then.

(12) Spiritualism's beliefs go too far to be compatible with Christianity. Its teachings simply give what the teachers think their followers want.

(13) It is precisely the need for keeping an open mind in the present state of our knowledge that should lead us to reject 'ready hypotheses'

based on such inadequate observation. A section of mankind is as ready now to accept assurances of communication with the other world as it was in former ages to believe that objects of daily use buried with the dead in their tomb would be made use of after death. Desire to believe in spiritualistic phenomena can be simply explained by the desire for personal immortality.

STATE MEDICAL SERVICE

Pro: (1) In a State Medical Service, members of the profession would receive salaries in accordance with their qualifications and abilities, without having to worry about boosting the size of their practices or hospital lists. The present system, under which doctors are still paid according to the number of patients on their lists, reproduces the evils of the old, since they are obliged to attract custom just like any other tradesmen.

(2) Enthusiasm which varies with a money incentive is valueless in a profession which is supposed to have as its aim the service of humanity. It is often regrettably true that, at present, a financially successful doctor has no time to give adequate attention to his patients. Under a salaried service, he would be relieved of the burden of overwork without suffering financially.

(3) The public authorities already maintain a salaried service in the county and borough health departments and in the hospitals. No one in either of these branches of the profession complains of lack of freedom or incentive, and the service given is often better because of the greater facilities, which individual

Con: (1) The present system is intended to ensure that doctors give satisfaction to their patients or lose financially by it. Under a salaried service, there would be no such incentive and the attitude of slackness which is notorious in the Civil Service would prevail. Doctors with full lists (notably when they are the only GPs in the area) have become so busy that many can give only two or three minutes' time to each patient visiting their surgeries. The need is for more doctors – and State control would worsen rather than remedy the situation.

(2) Both doctors and patients would object to any further regimentation. Both complain already of the excessive formalities involved in the National Health Service, but at least the patient has at present the right to change his doctor and the doctor an equal right to refuse a patient.

(3) While it is possible that hospitals may benefit from national or regional control, the case is different from that of a general practitioner, who usually has the whole work of diagnosis, treatment and after-care in his charge. In many instances, doctors have found themselves obliged to refer more and more cases to the hospitals

217

doctors usually cannot afford. Hospitals have been freed from the degradation and distraction of begging for funds and, through the reorganisation resulting from complete control, have improved the scope and performance of their work.

(4) A State-salaried service is alone able to practise preventive medicine on a wide scale, and does so very successfully both in school and maternity clinics and in the armed forces. It is not disputed that, through the work of the maternity and child welfare clinics, recent generations of infants are the healthiest ever produced in Britain.

(5) There is little freedom at present for the newly qualified practitioner, who cannot even settle in an area without the permission of his potential competitors. Under a salaried system, he would at least be assured of an income and be freed from the financial anxiety involved in starting a business. Doctors' sons are still given preference in the succession to their fathers' vacated practices, and tend to be trained with this end in view, sometimes in disregard of their own preferences and capabilities.

(6) Under a properly graded system, a young doctor would have prospects of promotion, possibly to more rewarding and responsible types of work. At present, a general practitioner is almost always obliged to continue working as such to the end of his career.

(7) What is proposed is simply control by the State of the services of doctors. No one suggests that their work should be supervised in detail. General practitioners would be protected in great measure from the occasional frivolous or malicious complaints to which they are now exposed. Patients would have extra

because of limitations on freedom of treatment, and this would be aggravated under a fully integrated, State-controlled system.

(4) These bodies and such services as the mass X-ray units are adequate for the purposes of preventive medicine. Actual diseases remain to be diagnosed and treated, and the complete control of the doctor implied in a salaried service would destroy the valuable concept of the 'family doctor'.

(5) Before the National Health Service was established, a young doctor could settle anywhere he wished, with no further formality than that of putting up a plate. This freedom has already been curtailed, and the loss should not be aggravated by yet more government control. Complete freedom is as necessary to a doctor as to an artist, if he is to do his work in a creative way. When a doctor dies or retires, the patients usually prefer his son to a stranger.

(6) Promotion in any Civil Service sphere is low and hedged about with formalities. A junior would be compelled to wait, perhaps indefinitely, without any prospect of escape into other avenues. At present, a competent doctor is able to rise to consultant status by his own efforts.

(7) Even under the present modified system, too much power is wielded by the central authority. Diagnoses and treatment have not infrequently been disputed – and by persons remote from the scene and unfamiliar with the patient. Doctors are already protected by the British Medical Association and various legal defence bodies; patients with justifiable grievances are protected by the disciplinary powers of the Ministry's Executive Committee and by their own freedom to change doctors.

safeguards against careless or over-hasty treatment.

(8) With a wholly integrated system, provision could be made for research on a much larger scale than at present. The general practitioner could take his place in the system and provide clinical information arising out of his daily experience. Nowadays, this can usually be obtained only by special research projects or by erratically answered appeals to individual doctors. Medicine is often said to be an art, but contact with work in the more strictly scientific branches of the profession can do nothing but good to its practitioners.

(8) Research pursued under complete government control is generally stultified and frustrated. Only an ideal government department would allow the complete freedom necessary to research workers. But research, while obviously valuable, is not the only object of the profession. The emphasis on this aspect ignores the physician's role as guide and counsellor, which cannot be fulfilled in a regimented way.

(See also PRIVATE MEDICINE)

STATE-REGISTERED BROTHELS

Pro: (1) Prostitution is often called 'the oldest profession in the world' – which points to a fundamental truth. There have always been men, and probably always will be, who are led to seek the company of prostitutes because of inexperience, inadequacy, as a relief from domestic problems, to ease the tensions of over-sexuality, or whatever the cause may be. However much the Church condemns its immorality, however much we deplore it socially, it is a basic trait in human nature and nobody will change it. The State should recognise this fact of life and accept the urgent need to protect both the women and their customers from the disease, crime and other evils which surround prostitution in Britain today. The only effective way to do this is to sanction State-registered brothels, with legislation to ensure regular medical inspection and other necessary supervision.

Con: (1) The fact that vice and immorality exist is no justification whatever for the State to condone them. Even if we must recognise the weaknesses of human nature, the State has a prime duty to try to set and maintain standards of behaviour which all decent people would wish. By allowing officially-controlled brothels, it would not only give an appearance of participating in the trade but would actually be legalising permissiveness and encouraging promiscuity. State-registered brothels would also open the way to other forms of corruption (involving the police, etc.), which might well prove even less desirable than some of the present evils.

(2) Before this legislation was passed, the level of prostitution had become so serious that people could not walk down some thoroughfares in our main cities without being accosted

(2) Since the street offences legislation, prostitution in Britain has become a hole-in-the-corner business of tatty bars and clubs, 'call girls' surreptitiously advertising their phone numbers, and other such shoddy means of making contact. Nobody would want the streets to become infested with prostitutes again, as they were formerly, but an evil is always easier to control if it is in the open. A system of 'tolerated houses' (to use the French phrase) would provide this element of control and eradicate much of the present shady nature of the trade, while keeping our streets free of it.

(3) Venereal disease is rife – and getting worse. An essential condition for State-controlled brothels is that, as is the practice in Continental countries which permit them, the prostitutes registered for work there would all be subject to strict medical inspection not less than once a week, thus cutting down the dangers of disease.

(4) Among the chief hazards faced by prostitutes are the violent, evil men who bully and threaten them into carrying on the trade and who live off their earnings in exchange for supposedly 'protecting' them. If the women worked in officially sanctioned brothels, they would be safeguarded from these menaces.

(5) Before France abolished its 'tolerated houses' after the last world war – a move intended principally to protect Frenchmen from the rise in disease consequent on the successive presence of three foreign armies – it was not unusual for poor country girls to work in a brothel for a couple of years, to save up for the dowry which was then necessary before they could make a good marriage. Nobody despised them for it. Similarly, if there were State-registered brothels in every five or ten yards. Since then, the problem has not simply been swept under the carpet; all the evidence points to the fact that, overall, prostitution itself has decreased sharply. Immorality has a cumulative effect; so do measures to stop it. We may not be able to stop men seeking out vice, but we certainly shouldn't make it easier for them to find it. By tolerating brothels, the State would be abnegating its moral responsibilities – *and* encouraging a renewed increase in the total level of prostitution.

(3) The rise in vd is due to the increased permissiveness of our age and stems almost entirely from the 'amateurs', not the professionals. Most young women who become full-time prostitutes are already in the habit of getting themselves checked by a doctor regularly, for their own sake. In any case, experience in Continental countries has shown there is a danger that, because official medical inspections in brothels soon acquire the character of a weekly 'chore', they often become cursory and inadequate.

(4) Anyone who imagines that pimps would cease to batten on women, just because they worked in an official brothel – or, indeed, that no prostitute ever gives money to her 'boyfriend' of her own free will – simply does not know the harsh realities of life.

(5) Whatever the initial reasons may have been for the closures of France's brothels, the plain fact remains that they have not been re-sanctioned even now, more than forty years later – which shows that other moral and social considerations had greater weight. Nor can anything alter the fact that, however cosily you try to wrap it up, prostitution entails the degradation of women. And a British Government which permitted the

Britain, many prostitutes would feel that there was less stigma in working for such establishments; and this in turn would lead to a sharp reduction in the number of 'call girls' and other tawdry expedients for prostitution now current.

(6) The 'social approval' of brothels, in effect, would greatly reduce the incidence of sex crimes, such as rape. That has been the experience in all Continental countries which allow brothels. It has also been established beyond question that, in the Scandinavian countries which permit the open sale of pornography, the local people soon lose any interest they might once have had in the subject – to the point that, nowadays, the pornography shops rely almost solely for their trade on foreign tourists from countries where such wares are banned. Similarly, it is recognised that the State-tolerated brothels in West Germany are well-ordered, clinical, and frankly boring. In short, it is human nature that vice should be most attractive when it is illicit but rapidly loses its appeal once it is openly available.

opening of State-registered brothels would not merely be condoning but furthering such degradation. Moreover, the assertion that the existence of official brothels would cut the amount of other prostitution is sadly naïve. Human nature being what it is, there would much more probably be a considerable increase in the number of 'freelances'.

(6) The customs and experiences of Continental countries do not provide a valid yardstick; through differences of temperament, climate and many other factors, conditions and standards in Britain are quite different. Even the most permissive British 'liberals' have not raised protests against the crack-down on purveyors of hard-core pornography. Similarly, there was general public approval of the moves to stamp out the seedy 'bookshops' which so disfigured Soho and other city backstreets. By the same token, the great majority of the British public would strongly oppose any attempt to establish official brothels in this country.

STERILISATION OF THE UNFIT

Pro: (1) There is now conclusive evidence that certain types of mental deficiency and certain physical defects and diseases are transmitted to offspring according to known laws. The sterilisation of persons liable to transmit such defects would help substantially towards the eradication of these maladies, at a small cost and with the least possible interference with the present defectives' liberty and experience of life. (Modern sterilisation methods prevent them from

Con: (1) Sterilisation is an unwarranted interference with personal liberty and an infringement of the dignity which should be preserved even in the least fortunate of human beings. Geneticists have shown that most of such defects are transmitted to offspring only when both parents, who may themselves be normal, carry the weakness (a 'recessive gene'). Sterilisation of actual defectives would therefore merely touch the fringe of problem and, under random mating,

having children but do not otherwise affect their enjoyment of love-making.)

(2) Moral and religious duty impels us to take such a simple step towards ending a source of great suffering and degradation.

(3) Degeneracy is largely responsible for the worst social problems. A particularly high proportion of these unfortunates, for instance, is found among slum dwellers. It is cruel and absurd to try to palliate evil results, while failing to tackle the sources responsible for them.

(4) Owing to the greater security of life in modern times, this problem becomes worse, because defectives survive in a higher proportion than formerly, while people of intelligence above the average have smaller families than ever. This is a most serious matter for the future of civilisation in Britain and other countries.

(5) Great care must necessarily be exercised in carrying out the proposal, but doctors, who are traditionally and professionally jealous of the rights and well-being of their patients, and lawyers, who are notoriously cautious in their outlook, can be relied on to prevent abuses.

(6) The advance of civilisation comes from the superior stocks. The production of an occasional genius is not sufficient compensation for the harm done and suffered by an increasing number of defectives in the community.

would reduce the proportion of defectives only slightly in each succeeding generation.

(2) It is against all religious standards and scruples. The tradition of Christianity is hostile to such interference with the workings of nature.

(3) To a large extent, this confuses cause with effect. Much degeneracy is due to bad social conditions, inadequate attention and education during childhood, and poverty.

(4) The most promising attack on this problem is by way of scientific research into the effects of diet, sunlight, and the activities of various glands on the mental and physical growth of man. As our present social system favours the prosperity of those who can make money rather than of those who can contribute to the development of culture, the infertility of genius is not to be wondered at. (Plus the fact, of course, that people of intelligence deliberately have small families nowadays, in recognition of the environmental problem.)

(5) The administration of such a measure lends itself to great abuses. In Nazi Germany, where liberty of opinion and conduct was little valued, sterilisation was a punitive weapon against people who departed from the beaten track. It will always be used against the poor, never against the rich.

(6) Many of the geniuses to whom the world owes much of its culture belonged to families in which other members were defective. For the progress of mankind, sterilisation might well cause more losses than gains.

SUNDAY ENTERTAINMENT; SUNDAY SHOPPING

Pro: (1) There is a widespread demand for the lifting of all remaining restrictions on Sunday cinemas, the staging of many more professional football matches, and the opening of theatres and other forms of public recreation on Sundays. People quite naturally desire the most wholesome form of rest – that is, not inactivity but a salutary change from their normal occupations. The opposition to this demand comes from a minority of Sabbatarians, whose outlook is many years behind the times but who still wish to impose their views on the whole nation.

(2) In Roman Catholic countries on the Continent, full facilities for Sunday entertainment have been the practice for many years – and the Church makes no objection provided people go to Mass beforehand.

(3) The Act permitting the Sunday opening of cinemas makes the express provision that those employed on Sunday in places of entertainment shall have a complete day's rest on another day each week.

(4) In a complicated society like our own, it is impossible to prevent all labour on a particular day. Trains and buses must run. Electric power must be generated for lighting and transport. Postal and telephone services must be available. Monday morning's newspapers and Monday's bread are largely provided by Sunday labour. Few Sabbatarians would care to dispense with the protection afforded by the Sunday labours of the police, the fire brigades and the medical profession.

(5) Nearly all the same arguments

Con: (1) Where Sunday games and cinemas are the general rule, people are tending to discard all religious observances and Sunday has become a day of noise, frivolity and irreverence. If fewer people attend places of worship and fewer children go to Sunday School, there will be a general decline in morality. There has, in fact, been a continual lowering of moral standards contemporaneously with the decline in Sunday observance. Besides, the opening of places of amusement on a Sunday deprives the people who work in them of their day of rest.

(2) Notwithstanding the discipline imposed by Roman Catholicism and its attempt to ensure at least the essential minimum of religious observance among its adherents, the so-called 'Continental Sunday' is among the reasons why, in many ways, the trend away from religion has been even more marked in some of these countries than in Britain.

(3) A day off during the week is not equivalent to a free Sunday. It gives no opportunity for attending church or chapel, or for family reunion.

(Some) Sunday should be kept as a day apart. 'Remember the Sabbath day, to keep it holy.'

(4) It is not feasible to stop all labour on Sunday but at least there should be as few people employed as possible, and these only on essential services. No one can maintain that Sunday cinemas are a necessity. Many professional football managers still doubt whether the innovation of staging one or two League matches on Sundays has proved an unqualified success.

apply to Sunday shopping. That there is a clear public majority in favour of it is borne out by most opinion polls and also by the sizeable number of stores which have met this demand by opening on Sundays in defiance of the regulations (and irrespective of any subsequent fines they might incur for doing so).

(6) A Shops Bill, aimed at deregulating Sunday trading, had the full backing of the Conservative Government but was defeated in the House of Commons in April 1986, through a 'revolt' by about 100 Tory backbenchers. While not doubting the sincerity of many of them who said they wanted to preserve the 'traditional British Sunday', the fact remains that Conservative MPs came under intense pressure from a campaign launched by the churches, supported by many small businessmen – pressure which must have been particularly hard to resist for MPs representing marginal constituencies (or ones which might become so).

(7) Even opponents of the Shops Bill agree that the laws governing Sunday trading are a chaotic, irrational hotch-potch, in bad need of an overhaul. As things stand, people in England and Wales (Scotland already enjoys more freedom) can buy a bottle of gin on a Sunday but not a tin of child's milk powder, a plant but not a packet of seeds, a copy of *Playboy* magazine but not the Bible!

(8) Some of the 'rebel' MPs have since put forward proposals aimed at ending the many anomalies of the present regulations, while retaining the broad structure of the British Sunday. Among their ideas: the abolition of controls on Sunday trading for small shops (those with no more than three staff) and for certain listed premises, such as garden centres;

(5) With opinion polls, much depends on what questions are asked ... In one Harris Research Centre survey, only five per cent of more than 1,000 adults questioned said they were seriously inconvenienced by most shops being closed on Sundays, 70 per cent said that Sunday working in shops should be kept to a minimum, and 61 per cent said it was nice to have one day a week when the streets were quiet. The big department stores which flouted the regulations did so only during the few weeks prior to the final debate on the Shops Bill, in the belief that (with the Government behind the measure) it would soon become law. When this proved a misconception, the stores backed down immediately.

(6) Leaving aside the plain fact that the 'Keep Sunday Special' campaign was supported by all the leading churches, and that the Church of England Synod voted to oppose the Bill by a massive 367 to 1, it must be pointed out that the first really strong objections expressed publicly to the Sunday trading proposals came not from religious circles but from the business world. Small businessmen, in particular, were fearful that they simply could not afford the extra staff pay entailed and that their trade would be swamped by the big stores more severely than ever.

(7) When a whole range of regulations has been built up over many years, so that some have become self-contradictory, there must always be a case for preventing the law from being made to look an ass. Accordingly, as the Bill was passing through the House of Lords, a number of peers suggested various compromise proposals which would have combined reform with a continued measure of control. But the Government turned

permission for Sunday opening up to a maximum of four hours for larger shops involved in the recreation and leisure industry – including the big DIY stores (some of which already enjoy their most thriving trade on Sundays, in any case!). It is to be hoped that a compromise of this nature will be adopted before too long, if only as a first step.

(9) Nobody contests the Sabbatarians' right to observe the Lord's Day in their own way. The objection is the same applying to any aggressive orthodoxy: they should not try to interfere with other people's rights.

them all down – and thus, when the Bill came back to the Commons, duly paid the price.

(8) The ideas noted opposite were first voiced by a leading bishop and then espoused by the dissident MPs. This shows clearly that church objections to the total deregulation of Sunday trading were not dogmatic. They recognised that it is not just church people but a big majority of ordinary Britons who believe Sunday to be a special day.

(9) Sabbatarians are fully aware that their views are now unpopular and in a minority, but they believe sincerely that they have a duty to maintain the traditional Sunday, in the hope that (as happened before in history) many more people will eventually turn back to God.

SURROGATE MOTHERS

Pro: (1) The number of babies available for adoption is always far smaller than the demand, resulting in much sadness among childless couples who want to offer a loving home but are rejected by the official adoption agencies. For these agencies, the prime criterion is to try to do their best for the child; inevitably, therefore, they have to turn down many potential parents who would be perfectly competent to bring up a child but are less satisfactory than some other applicants on grounds of age, locality, or whatever it may be. In these circumstances, at least a small part of the gap could be closed by the use of surrogate mothers, i.e. women who, in effect, rent out their womb to produce a baby for the couple paying them. Ideally, such arrangements should always be subject to strict supervision – and the couple's feeling

Con: (1) Both surrogate agencies and the women they enrol to bear the babies have been described as 'living off immoral earnings'. If commercial surrogacy were ever to become a regular alternative to adoption, it could be so only for the wealthy. Poorer people, who might be just as deserving, or even more so, could never afford the fees demanded. (In one notorious British case in the mid-1980s, the fees paid totalled £13,000.) Moreover, there would be many instances when no amount of wealth could overcome the equivocal situation, in law, facing a child brought into the world by this route. Sad though it undoubtedly is to see an adoption refused to people who would make lovely parents, surrogacy can never be a satisfactory answer. For a start, such contracts are legally unenforceable; the courts would almost

that the eventual baby really does belong to them can be enhanced by the surrogate mother bearing the child after artificial insemination, having been implanted with sperm from the would-be father himself.

(2) It should be stressed that surrogate parenthood need not necessarily be commercial. The procedure can be arranged just as well through non-profit-making agencies, with the couple paying for no more than the actual expenses involved. Throughout history, there have been cases of childless couples resorting to expedients of this kind – for instance, through the sister of an infertile wife agreeing to be inseminated by the husband and to hand over the baby to them after birth. While this may be the ultimate in good will within a family, it is surely far less desirable morally than a properly conducted, virtually clinical arrangement through third parties who have no direct emotional involvement with the case (as in normal adoptions).

(3) Experience with surrogate agencies in the USA, particularly, indicates that most of them are fully respectable and well-motivated, exercising very close control over all medical and legal aspects of the contract.

certainly disregard any contract made in advance if the surrogate mother changed her mind and decided she wanted to keep the baby after all; yet, if she *was* still ready to part with it, for ultimate adoption by the couple who hired her, the legal situation would be analogous to that of making and accepting payment for the transfer of a child's custody with a view to adoption (which is a criminal offence).

(2) Even when couples enter surrogate agreements in good faith, even when commercial gain is not a factor, they must still be made to understand they have no claims that can override the interests of the child. To give just a few examples of the difficulties they would cause: children born through surrogacy are left in a legal limbo; the father who provided the sperm cannot claim parental rights, because the child is illegitimate; the only way he could claim such rights is through adopting the child – but, under British law, this would be illegal, because of the fees he had paid the agency and the surrogate mother. (Under the 1975 Children Act, any potential adoption where a fee has changed hands is rendered void.) On the other hand, if the baby were born to a married woman, the child is presumed to be the legitimate offspring of her and her husband, but is actually illegitimate. If a surrogate mother decided to renege on the deal, she could bring affiliation proceedings against the donor father only if she were single or separated. The donor's sole hope of remedy would then be in seeking an order for the custody of the child. And these, remember, are merely a few examples of the numerous objections that could be raised . . .

(3) On the contrary, some disputed deals in the USA have led to huge lawsuits, with the parties even airing their differences on TV. Horrific!

TAXATION, DIRECT, ABOLITION OF

Pro: (1) Although the level of direct taxation has come down somewhat in recent years, it is still so heavy (for peace-time conditions) that very little renewed extension of it would now be feasible. It is particularly unpopular with the lowest earning people caught in the income tax net, who believe firmly (whether rightly or wrongly is immaterial) that the burden of direct taxation weighs more heavily on them, relatively, than on higher earning groups. Many of them feel that a widely generalised system of indirect taxation, replacing direct taxes, would be more equitable.

(2) The advantage of the indirect over the direct system is, in effect, that people would pay taxes only on the goods or services they consumed. Thus, the poorest sections of the population, already having to take care over what they spend their money on, could be sure that they were not having to meet a higher proportionate share of the overall tax burden than was their strict due. At the same time, instead of flat-rate indirect taxation imposed on everyone irrespective of earnings levels (e.g. VAT at a blanket rate of 15 per cent), the rate could be varied on different goods and services to take account of the probable income levels of the people using them. As examples: the proportion of indirect tax chargeable on the purchase of a Rolls-Royce would be appreciably higher than that for a Ford Escort; likewise, the tax on food and drink consumed at a night club would be much stiffer than on the fare served at Joe's Transport Caff. Critics who claim that such differentiations

Con: (1) Indirect taxes violate the first principle of taxation, in that they cause more to be taken from the taxpayer than they bring to the State. Whether or not there is a case for reimposing much tougher rates of income tax on the highest earners who have benefited most from tax cuts in recent years, as some people argue, could be decided only as a political matter. But what nobody could dispute is that the essential flexibility of the direct taxation system has made it possible to remove the burden of income tax from increasing numbers of the lowest earners, during the same period.

(2) How do you estimate someone's 'consumption' of things like education or national defence – expenditures which necessarily have an eye on the long term but in which the individual taxpayer may well have no immediate involvement at the moment? This is just one example of the great many ways whereby trying to make things fairer by taxing solely in proportion to consumption would be so complex as to render any such system virtually impossible to administer – throwing profound doubt on whether it could ever achieve the benefits claimed opposite. On the other hand, many of such benefits *are* already feasible under the direct taxation system, through careful grading of the progressive tax bands. Varying VAT rates in accordance with the type of product or service may seem a good idea in theory and has, in fact, been tried in the past – when, for instance, quite ordinary electrical appliances like refrigerators were

(especially at less obvious extremes) would be too complex to work efficiently, and in any case would inject an undesirable 'class' element, need merely look at the variable VAT rates and sales taxes which work perfectly well in other countries.

(3) In some Continental countries, dodging income tax is almost a national hobby and their governments, therefore, already have to rely more on indirect than on direct taxation for the bulk of their revenues. The application of VAT in Britain has shown that, thanks to the efficiency and incorruptibility of the Customs & Excise officers responsible for its collection, evasion of such indirect taxes here is minimal.

(4) For some of the articles on which indirect taxation is already imposed, there is another, moral factor rendering it desirable to make them more expensive as a means of preventing excessive consumption. Two obvious cases in point are alcohol and tobacco.

(5) The revenue from direct taxation is uncertain and fluctuating.

(6) Proposals tabled by the Chancellor of the Exchequer in 1986 were designed to link pay to profits, giving workers a direct stake in the success of their own company. (*See: Profit-Sharing.*) Among the advantages, it was held, were that it would improve shopfloor motivation, lead to better performance, and create more jobs – since companies would be encouraged to hire more people (and sack fewer) if they knew that their wage costs would fall back automatically in times of recession, when profits were squeezed. As a further incentive, the proposals offered workers the possibility of tax relief of £12 a month (on the portion of their pay that was profit-related) – a concession which, it

classed as 'luxury goods'! But, in practice, it tends to be bad for the psychological health of the taxed community and also runs counter to any hope of eventually achieving greater rationalisation of taxation throughout the EEC.

(3) Those European governments which already relied more on indirect taxation, long before VAT became general under the EEC, still needed large amounts from direct taxation as well. Both systems remain essential, in tandem. We may pride ourselves that British taxpayers are more law-abiding than the Continentals (though this is not always borne out by experience in the courts!); but, in the absence of direct taxes, the vast expansion of indirect taxes necessary to fill the gap would increase both the temptation and the opportunities for evasion to such a degree that it is problematic whether even our incorruptible Customs men could cope with it all.

(4) Unduly high indirect taxes may restrict consumption, but a balance has to be struck between that and an equally undue drop in revenue.

(5) The yield from *all* forms of taxation is uncertain and fluctuating.

(6) The first reaction to the proposals from some trade union leaders was that this kind of pay flexibility was just another formula for pay reductions. It has also been pointed out that, if a company goes through a difficult period and has to cut costs in order to remain competitive, it will always be the wage element that is cut and not the still-to-be-earned profit element; so would this be any different from what already happens (except, perhaps, that the worker would be even worse off than now)? There's not much point in offering a slice of the cake as an incen-

was estimated, would cost the Exchequer £150 million a year. In effect, therefore, this scheme already represented a step along the path towards at least partial abolition of direct taxation.

tive, in the form of tax relief size of the cake itself is reduced people are having to tighter belts, the kind of items mostly subject to indirect taxation are the first to suffer a drop in demand.

(See also the next article)

TAXATION OF SINGLE PEOPLE

Pro: (1) Under the British taxation system, single people normally pay a higher proportion of their earnings in income tax than do married people with the same level of income. There is nothing inequitable about this, since single people generally have only themselves to support and can afford to pay more than those with family responsibilities. Taxation should always be based on the resources of the individual citizen.

(2) A family bringing up healthy children is automatically contributing to the welfare of the State, and it is only right that the parents should accordingly benefit from taxation relief. There is an equally good case, therefore, for the proposition that childless single adults, above a given age, should actually be taxed at a higher rate than they are at present, i.e. a new, additional tax on single people. Among its desirable effects would be the encouragement of marriage and a sharp reduction in the number of irregular unions, now all too prevalent.

(3) Official statistics show a marked increase in the number of illegitimate children. There are now more than 100,000 children a year born out of wedlock – twice as many as the rate ten years ago. Altogether,

Con: (1) It is implicit in this debating issue not simply that single people should be taxed but that they should be taxed more highly – and the argument opposite recognises that they already are, indirectly, through the granting of extra allowances to those who are married and have children. While such allowances are fully justifiable, it is nevertheless inequitable to impose a relatively heavier burden on single taxpayers, because this is, in effect, double taxation (which is contrary to the first principles of taxation). Moreover, it lacks sense from the national economic standpoint, since high taxes impair their ability to save money, at the very period of their lives when they are usually most free to do so.

(2) The theory that citizens exist for the benefit of the State finds favour only in totalitarian countries. No democracy should base its taxation on such exploded ideas, which represent gross interference with the liberty of the subject. Far from framing taxes to encourage marriage, present-day environmental problems – in particular, the need to combat over-population – make a strong case for giving people incentives to stay single longer. If the nation faced up to its environmental responsibilities prop-

it is estimated, close on four million people in Britain are illegitimate in the eyes of the law. Higher taxation of single people would not only curb immorality but would improve the lot of many children who now suffer from the lack of a true family life.

(4) Marriage is natural to mankind and the unmarried state is, in itself, undesirable. Most men are better for the responsibilities and influences of married life; all but a small proportion of women desire to get married and have children.

erly, the taxes imposed on single people should be proportionately *lighter* than on anyone else.

(3) To suggest that higher taxation would prevent immorality is unrealistic, to say the least. Even if it did lead more 'illicit' couples to decide to get married, which is extremely doubtful, marriage contracted under such economic threats would rarely make for a happy family life.

(4) The unmarried state is undesirable only for people who want to get married but are unable to do so. A growing number of people nowadays, women as well as men, prefer to stay single, as a matter of deliberate choice. Why should they be penalised?

(See also the previous article)

TERMINATION OF PREGNANCIES, LEGALISED

Pro: (1) Legislation to permit the termination of pregnancies, i.e. abortions, is necessary to avoid the incidence of 'back-street' operations by ignorant or ill-equipped persons and the consequent hazards for women who have sought their help: infection, injury or even death. No responsible woman deciding to seek an abortion would ever make such a decision lightly. But one point on which she can reassure herself is that a child has no legal existence before birth and, in any case, is not even recognisable as a human being until relatively late in a pregnancy.

(2) Abortions are particularly necessary for the relief of pregnancies resulting from rape or incest or in girls below the legal age of consent. Figures for England and Wales in 1983 show

Con: (1) Life begins at conception, when the passive egg is fertilised by the active sperm, and there can be no justification for ending that life. As the Roman Catholic Archbishop of Westminster wrote to MPs on the issue in 1985: 'The needs of some cannot be allowed to eclipse the rights of others.' Many women undergo abortions only through fears of disapproval, or perhaps even threats, from their family and friends or from the child's father. The operation is accepted reluctantly at a time when a woman's mind and body, even during the most normal pregnancy, both undergo significant additional stress.

(2) Violent end to an innocent life, one which is biologically half the own-child of its mother, is no answer to pregnancy caused by rape, incest or

that the number of live births to girls aged under 16 that year totalled 1,249 and the number of induced abortions for the same age group was 4,077. Over the preceding decade, the annual total of such abortions had risen by 40 per cent and the actual number of births had fallen by 250 – a conclusive indication, surely, of the extent of the misery which must have existed before legal abortions were obtainable.

(3) Abortion should never be looked at simply as a form of birth control, as many critics claim it to be. The Abortion Act 1967 specifies that the termination of a pregnancy is permitted in order to safeguard the physical or psychological health of the woman involved. That many women thus spared can go on later to exercise normal procreation, without having suffered any lasting mental or physical harm from the prior abortion, is shown by one statistic published in the mid-1980s, some 18 years after abortion was legalised in this country: by that time, it was calculated, about one woman in five bearing her first-born child, in Britain, had experienced a previous termination.

(4) Selective abortion can minimise the number of handicapped people in the community who will never be able to enjoy the full quality of life.

under-age sexual relations. Abortion is merely the easy way out. Statistically, moreover, it has been established that pregnancy follows rape relatively seldom.

(3) The great majority of abortions in the UK are carried out on psychological grounds. Psychology, however, is still a 'science' far less exact even than medicine; few doctors are trained in psychology, which points to a serious flaw in the legislation – because such training is not specifically required, by law, in those able to authorise an abortion. Little or no regard is paid to the woman's psyche after she has had an abortion. While there can be no grounds for suggesting that the lack of effective research into post-abortion psychology might be at least partly due to doctors' fears of jeopardising their future career prospects, the fact remains that the comparative absence of studies on the subject is quite remarkable.

(4) Abortion cannot be used to weed out the imperfect human beings, not only for all the obvious moral reasons but also simply because of the other side of the equation: how do you define the perfect, and just who would be qualified to do so?

(See also BIRTH CONTROL, VOLUNTARY OR COMPULSORY; CONTRACEPTION FOR GIRLS UNDER 16)

TERRORISM

Pro: (1) The essential point to bear in mind is that one man's terrorist is another man's patriot. People who resort to violent protests, such as time-bombs and the hijacking of aircraft, are not sadists or otherwise morally

Con: (1) One could more readily understand a terrorist's motives – however much one disagreed with them – if his acts were directed against the military or against armed police. While no revolt or violent defiance of

depraved; right or wrong, they believe that they have genuine political or social grievances, which governments have refused to recognise or remedy, and that a campaign of terrorism is the only way to overcome the apathy of the general public and of the authorities concerned. They decide on this course of action as a last expedient, when all conventional political or legal means have failed or are barred to them.

(2) In the words of a Russian terrorist, Zlelyabov, in 1879: 'History is terribly slow; it must be pushed forward.' History does, indeed, provide many examples of sustained terrorism achieving objectives which governments had previously been unwilling to grant (e.g. the Jewish militancy which helped to expedite Britain's decision to leave Palestine, thus leading to the creation of the State of Israel in 1948; and similarly, the four-year Arab terrorist campaign which brought about independence for the Republic of South Yemen in 1967).

(3) By threatening the lives of selected victims (e.g. aircraft passengers or diplomats in an embassy they have occupied), terrorists have frequently been able to win specific concessions – such as the release of jailed colleagues. More broadly, by creating a climate of fear and disrupting everyday life, they keep their viewpoint continually before the public eye. Eventually, this *can* succeed for them – either because public opinion gradually becomes convinced of the justice of their demands and swings behind them, or because more and more people grow so sick of the violence that, to have done with it, they force recalcitrant governments to give way.

(4) There was a considerable body

law and order can be condoned, this would at least have some character of openly declared warfare. As it is, though, most present-day terrorism involves the jeopardising or actual deaths of innocent civilians. Nothing can justify that. But terrorists become so obsessed by their supposedly righteous cause, so eaten up by their sense of grievance, that all moral judgments are excluded from their thinking, which is the worst form of perverted arrogance. They do not resort to terrorism out of desperation, as their apologists claim, but because its methods appeal to their own warped characters. They are not selfless heroes but criminals.

(2) On the contrary, the weight of historical evidence shows that terrorism rarely succeeds in its ultimate objectives. In Aden and pre-1948 Palestine, a virtual state of war existed and the terrorists' targets were, first and foremost, the British soldiers stationed there. When ordinary people are the main victims – as in South America and Northern Ireland – the terrorists end by alienating many sections of the population who might otherwise have had some sympathy for their aims. Most of those Middle Eastern countries which formerly supported the hijacking exploits of Arab guerrillas, if only tacitly, have now turned against them, recognising that the adverse reaction provoked by such acts, in other countries, does the Arab cause far more harm than good.

(3) Governments have a duty to protect human life, which always adds to the controversy over their decisions on how to deal with terrorism. If they resist, they endanger the victims held captive by the terrorists; if they yield, they lay themselves open to further terrorist attacks subsequently. It is a harsh dilemma – though, on balance,

of support among young people in West Germany and Britain for the aims of the so-called Baader-Meinhof gang and the 'Angry Brigade'. Their disgust with present-day society, and their desire to change it fundamentally, was shared by many – even if they did not go along with the extreme violence espoused by the groups concerned. The police themselves recognised that members of these groups were not criminals in the ordinary sense.

(5) When a cause is just, the end justifies the means.

those governments which have refused to surrender to terrorist demands, even at the risk of the victims' lives, have usually proved their case. Such governments were able to take this course because majority public opinion in their own countries was behind them. And that is the crux of the matter. If terrorism's bluff is called, whatever the immediate price, the fundamental lack of justification for its methods will lead to its collapse.

(4) The terrorism adopted by these would-be social revolutionaries was self-defeating, because it lost them whatever public sympathy their idealistic objectives might once have had. History is a natural evolutionary process, and any attempt to force extreme reform by violent means will succeed, at the most, in producing short-term changes which are swiftly followed by other upheavals. Changes, in short, which are without durability or permanence. Whether socially or politically motivated, this is the basic flaw in all terrorist philosophy.

(5) It doesn't, and never will.

THEATRES:
Are They In Need of Reform?

Pro: (1) The theatres of London have fallen into the hands of businessmen who openly admit they are concerned with nothing but profits. Many of them know little of dramatic art; they work on the principle that the largest profits are to be obtained from plays and entertainments which pander to the lowest tastes of the public. In the provinces, matters are worse than in

Con: (1) Theatres are *not* worse than they were. They give the public what amusement it wants, which is their proper function. Good plays are provided in sufficient numbers by the commercial theatre to satisfy those who wish to see them, and the present very high standard of drama in Britain is esteemed throughout the world – as shown by the many new British plays

London. In the mid-1980s, one leading provincial theatre, at Leicester, transferred more productions to London than at any time in its recent history; but only one made it any real profit and the theatre ended with a £200,000 deficit for the year. There could hardly be more eloquent testimony to the need to overhaul the British Theatre's economics.

(2) Landlords have put up rents to such an extent that serious producers can embark on new ventures only if they have a virtual certainty of packed houses or are backed by enormous capital. Even when these rare conditions are fulfilled, they may not be able to obtain a theatre for more than a very restricted period, if they get one at all. Plays or spectacles which achieve success are kept on for absurdly long runs, and many new plays never reach London at all. Many actors who wish to do good work are forced to remain performing drivel, unless they are content with the limited audience of a suburban 'little' theatre.

(3) The prices of seats in West End theatres are prohibitive for the majority of people, and this factor has obviously contributed to the large number of theatres which have gone out of business.

(4) The commercialised theatre is infested with unscrupulous men who would not be tolerated in any other business. As the profession is over-crowded, young actors and actresses are grossly exploited by managers and agents, especially in the provinces.

(5) The stage has a much deeper and more long-lasting influence than that of the screen, but many of the people running it have failed to measure up to their responsibilities, and the inadequacies of their present

which are produced soon afterwards in the USA and other countries. As for 'popular' shows, the not infrequent failure of very vulgar but expensive productions shows that the public has a remedy in its own hands. The nature of the theatrical business inevitably makes it subject to wide ups and downs. The provincial theatre cited opposite expected to clear its accumulated deficit within three years.

(2) If theatres are reformed as some people wish, many of them will fall into the hands of cranks who seem to believe that the only proper subjects for drama are gloomy and unsavoury treatments of moral problems. One of the reasons for the commercial conservatism of managers is the already excessive taxation to which they are subjected. Rents are admittedly high, but the remedy for this does not lie in further harrying of theatrical managements.

(3) Grants from the Arts Council and other bodies ensure a constant supply of works of high cultural standard, in both London and the provinces. The majority of people like theatres near their homes, and many of these small theatres in the suburbs or in towns near London are among the most thriving and progressive.

(4) The exploitation of young actors is much less common nowadays, and any abuses are dealt with by British Equity and the leading managers. The growth of trade union organisation among actors has brought them into the same social atmosphere as other workers.

(5) Television and the cinema are much more important than the theatre as an industry and a social influence, but the special impact of a 'live' performance must never be underestimated; theatres will always have this particular appeal and be sure of

policies have driven increasing numbers away to other forms of entertainment.

attracting a public, albeit possibly smaller than in former years.

TIED (PUBLIC) HOUSES, ABOLITION OF

Pro: (1) The tied house system deprives the licence-holder of full control of his public house, which remains under the aegis of a third party (the brewery company), although the licensee himself still has to take all responsibility in name. At the last count (1986), some 47,000 of Britain's 80,000 pubs were owned by brewers.

(2) Those who own tied houses impose strict terms on the managers and, by making their tenure terminable at short notice, keep them completely under their own control.

(3) The brewers are able to sell whatever beer they choose to their tenants, who in some cases are bound by agreement not to return any. Moreover, for the beer thus sold to them, many tenants have to pay a higher price than the owners of free houses pay.

(4) The tendency of some owners of tied houses is to extend the system to wines and spirits, as well as beer.

(5) The uncertainty of tenure and the onerous terms oblige the tied house licence-holders to increase their sales to the utmost, so that they may make money while the business remains in their hands. Thus the system is a direct incitement to excessive drinking.

(6) The system is actually illegal, since a licence, which is granted to one man, is granted to him alone, without power to assign it, so any such transfer

Con: (1) It is as much in the brewer's interest as in the tenant's that the public house should be conducted in a proper manner, so that the licence may not be endangered. Tenants of tied houses usually take a great pride in seeing that they are well run. According to the Brewers Society, a long EEC inquiry into the system concluded that it was fair.

(2) No publican need take a tied house, nor would he if the terms were too onerous; the eager competition for the tenancies of tied houses disproves all assertions as to the tyranny of brewers. Tenancy agreements nowadays normally provide for at least one year's notice on either side.

(3) No brewer would willingly or knowingly sell bad beer in a house under his own name. Most brewers allow their tenants to return beer if not good; and if the tenant has to pay a higher price for his beer, he receives an excellent *quid pro quo* in that he has to pay nothing for the goodwill of the business and gets possession for a lower rent than would be possible under any other system.

(4) Even where the tie extends to wines and spirits, these must be good or the public would not buy them. There is no tie on tobacco or food, which the licensee is free to buy wherever he can get the most advantageous terms for his own profit.

(5) Few customers want to get drunk; the vast majority drink only as

235

would be null and void. Accordingly, a brewery owning a tied house would, following such a transfer, be guilty of a breach of law if it sought to turn out the original licence-holder.

(7) Brewers very often fix the rent at a lower figure in order to reduce the rating assessment, and thus are able to evade their fair share of taxation.

(8) The drink trade, being a licensed one, cannot be compared with any other, and the publican should be regarded more as a public servant than as a tradesman.

(9) Brewers cannot complain if their 'rights' are ignored since, knowing the law, they yet choose to risk their money and trust that the strict letter of the law will not be applied. The publican himself has never been recognised as having a 'right' to renewal of his licence.

(10) The system has often ended in throwing the trade of a whole district into the hands of one brewery, or in the amalgamation of breweries, thus destroying all competition.

(11) The evils of the system are felt by all connected with the trade, and the system is almost universally condemned.

much as they wish, and no more. They are not likely to increase the amount at the bidding of the publican.

(6) If the tied house system is illegal, why is it necessary to introduce an Act of Parliament to say so? Magistrates have, as a rule, declined to interfere with the system. Brewster Sessions are held twice a year at which licences are renewed to existing tenants and transfers are approved.

(7) It is a matter for the authorities to see that the assessment is put at a fair figure, and it cannot be charged as a fault against the tied house system if they fail in their work.

(8) The tied house system also prevails in other businesses throughout the country where large firms have branches, and there is no reason why a distinction should be drawn between the drink trade and these others.

(9) Much money has been spent by brewers in improving their properties; no one could expect them to hand this over to the publican without a measure of compensation or safeguard. By the nature of the trade, it is only right that a publican should reapply for his licence every year.

(10) No district is so completely monopolised by any one brewery that competition is altogether destroyed. Brewery companies now make 'swap' agreements with each other in various towns (particularly those where one firm has a high percentage of the pubs), to ensure that customers get a choice of more than one brewer's beers.

(11) If the system were universally condemned (which it is not), it would be quite possible for the big breweries to combine to put an end to it.

TRADE UNIONS:
Do Their Powers Need Further Restriction?

Pro: (1) By their power to stage strikes as and when the leaders called for them, the more powerful unions had held industry up to ransom and injured the country in numerous ways. It was these excesses which eventually inspired proposals to make it obligatory for a union to hold a secret ballot of its members, both before any strike may go ahead and also for the periodic elections of union executives. Even the Labour Party's National Executive Committee has approved a new industrial relations policy giving union members the 'right' to such ballots, a reform intended ultimately for inclusion in union rule-books.

(2) The Social Democratic Party goes further, not only calling for it to be compulsory for such ballots to be, specifically, *postal* ballots (i.e. rather than work-place polls), but also proposing that arbitration prior to a strike should be compulsory as well (particularly for workers in the essential public services). Quite apart from SDP supporters, many others would agree that changes along these broad lines are needed in the light of plain evidence of the use of undue pressure, even intimidation, to try to force members to toe the line desired by the union leadership. There has been cause for distinct unease about the proper conduct of some unions' internal polls, above all as regards their secrecy.

(3) Unions should be prohibited from authorising or financing strikes on such relatively trivial issues as job demarcation or, in areas of industry where two or more unions overlap, on trying to make it compulsory to join

Con: (1) Strikes are never called unless union leaders have overwhelming evidence that their members desire such action. Most unions have elaborate machinery (including secret ballots, in many cases) for determining what their members want, and the influence of trade union leaders is more often exercised nowadays in moderating rather than provoking the impetus for strikes. To impose excessive restrictions on workers' freedom to withdraw their labour would be an infringement of their legally recognised rights. Whatever the ill will towards the trade unions of the Conservative administration which introduced the latest labour legislation, the plain fact is that many union members now see secret ballots as part of a restoration of their democratic freedoms which they value and are determined to retain. At the same time, there is a strong possibility that any intended governmental interference in union rule-books (even under a Labour regime) would infringe the right of freedom of association and would break International Labour Organisation conventions.

(2) Among several good arguments in favour of retaining the present arrangements are that (a) postal ballots do not necessarily rule out rigging, and (b) there is often a lower return – i.e. fewer members bothering to vote – than in properly conducted workshop ballots. Hence the case made by several of the top union leaders, during the framing of the Conservative Government's new legislation, when they pleaded successfully for the retention of flexibility and a

one union rather than another. Putting pressure on workers to make them become union members should be prohibited; unionists guilty of taking coercive steps against non-unionists should be subject to heavy penalties.

(4) Trade unionists have often claimed that employers perpetrate much more irresponsible acts than their own. But, even in any occasional instances where this might be true, it can never be a justification: the malpractice of one is no excuse for the misdeeds of another.

(5) Abuse of picketing – and especially the big increase in secondary picketing – made it necessary to introduce legislation imposing firmer control over union members' exercise of the right. So-called flying pickets (moved from one area to another) and the frightening violence of mass demonstrations at strike locations had made nonsense of the supposed use of reasoned persuasion implicit in 'peaceful' picketing. Despite the new legal restrictions, though, continued excesses by some strikers – e.g. in the Wapping printers' dispute – provided clear proof that, regrettably, the controls still did not go far enough. Equally manifest was that the legislation making trade unions liable for unlawful acts by their members has still not been implemented as effectively as it should have been.

(6) Under the system of unions raising political levies, members who disagree with their own union's political affiliations have the right of 'contracting out' (i.e. not having to pay the levy). But in many cases, although this is supposed to remain confidential, people are often afraid to exercise the right because of the likely repercussions from their workmates. While much could be said in favour

range of options, arguing that workshop ballots *could* be conducted efficiently and honestly.

(3) Union leaders have long recognised the need to tackle this issue by initiating discussions on demarcation problems in general. It is only natural for there to be some resentment against people who willingly accept all the benefits that fellow-workers secure for them but do nothing themselves to assist such efforts. Here again, though, trade union opponents tend to exaggerate the extent of the few abuses which do occur. Even the SDP proposals accept the 'closed shop' principle, calling for it to be accepted whenever a ballot of two-thirds of a workforce votes in favour of one.

(4) The whole idea of 'hamstringing' the unions, on the pretext of making them stick to their legitimate functions, is promoted first and foremost by the kind of people whose own activities militate against the interests of the community (for instance, by forming rings to engineer the restriction of output, the raising of prices, or the suppression of inventions which might offer a much longer living alternative to some mass-produced but relatively evanescent product.)

(5) Much of the violence in industrial confrontations has been provoked by the authorities' blatant use of the police to support their own political ends – a practice resented by many policemen themselves and also arousing some suspicion of incipient moves towards establishing a national police force, under direct control of the central government. The history of what trade unions have had to fight for, over the past 150 years, provides ample justification for their privileges. Any attack on their legal status will eventually boomerang on those who attempt it.

of changing the system to 'contracting in', whereby unionists would have to state specifically that they *wished* to pay the levy, this has so far been adjudged impossible politically. However, one necessary reform about which there can be no doubt is for unions to have to come clean about the purpose of the political levy. Hitherto, it has been represented all too often as a fund for securing a union voice in Parliament, rather than what it really is in practice: simply a direct payment to the Labour Party.

(7) Unofficial strikes, originating on the shop floor and often called on spurious or trivial pretexts, have destroyed the confidence which should be at the base of sound industrial relations. Dominating personalities gain power as shop stewards, and many of them turn out to have mainly political rather than industrial aims. Union leaders are almost powerless to prevent such incidents and are often reluctant to deal with them when they occur, especially when the leaders themselves may have gained power for political ends. Some have not scrupled to use this power illegally in tampering with union rules and voting procedures.

(8) Trade unions should be obliged by law to invest a given proportion of their money (pension funds, etc.) in their own particular industries, which would lead to readier co-operation between unions and managements *and* be a further aid in discouraging unnecessary strikes.

(6) Trade unions have just as much right to further the interests of their members in the political sphere as do the directors of large companies whose 'political contributions' – made, overwhelmingly, to Conservative Party interests – are decided without the slightest attempt to seek shareholders' approval. Much to the chagrin of right-wingers who hoped to 'nobble' Labour Party finances, moves to reform the political levy back-fired. Under the new Trade Union Act, unions with a political fund had to ballot their members for approval to continue raising money for the purpose. Every one of the 47 unions involved voted overwhelmingly in favour – and several other, smaller unions talked of establishing such a fund for the first time.

(7) Unofficial strikes are inevitable while union leaders remain inaccessible to the rank and file, but this is a matter of internal organisation which the unions should tackle themselves. Apparently frivolous pretexts are often merely the latest incidents in a long history of bad relations with the management. The remedy for infiltration of unions by unscrupulous people lies with the membership and, in cases of illegal conduct, with the courts.

(8) Many trade unions already do just that. But no amount of investment could exceed the biggest stake that all hold in their own industry – the mere fact that their members' livelihoods depend on it.

(See also CLOSED SHOP: SHOULD IT BE BANNED?)

UNEMPLOYMENT, STATE REMEDY FOR

Pro: (1) Unemployment is one of the worst misfortunes that can befall a person or family and has many harmful influences on industry and society at large. As in many cases it is a direct result of government decisions at home or political changes abroad, and tends to afflict whole regions whose workers were dependent on a particular superseded industry, the State should step in to help. It is unjust that workers should suffer for conditions which they cannot in any way control. America's unemployment problem during the Depression of the 1930s is a classic example. It was dealt with by President Roosevelt as a matter of national urgency – which indeed it was – with a considerable measure of success. In Britain, it must surely be crazy that the number of people claiming poverty-line benefits had risen by two million between 1979 and 1986 – and that unemployment, in June 1986, represented 13.5 per cent of the workforce (against 7 per cent in the USA and only 2.6 per cent in Japan).

(2) Only the State can provide facilities, on the scale now needed, to train the increasing number of redundant workers for new jobs in other industries. Only the State's ability to pay National Assistance (or 'dole', as introduced in 1918) has prevented large-scale unemployment from swelling into civil strife – at the same time, saving wages and conditions of work from deterioration and preventing adolescent workers from being forced into industry on a pittance.

(3) Unemployment cannot be made

Con: (1) The evils of unemployment are admittedly great, but they are due to conditions and circumstances which cannot be ended or mended quickly by any State action. Only by patience and the slow rebuilding of international trade can we look for relief. On the other hand, matters would be much improved by the withdrawal of trade union restrictions on rates of output and on the sort of job a tradesman can do, by the freeing of industry from the multitude of restrictions which hamper it, and, in the opinion of some experts, by the reintroduction of import quotas to protect our own manufacturers. The jobless figures in Britain failed to fall despite there being a record number of people on Government-sponsored training schemes. This is further confirmation that a State programme could never be the sole answer. The unemployment situation, especially in the export trades, has been distorted, in fact, by international political considerations and the present worldwide economic recession. Were it not for these, the problem would right itself without the need of further State intervention.

(2) It might be a help if more men agreed to such re-training and were willing to shift to new jobs in other parts of the country. As it is, too many try to stay within their own shrinking industries and, despite above-average unemployment levels in their own regions, refuse to move elsewhere. The remedies offered by the State, therefore, have not been a success. The 'dole' has proved the greatest single impediment to the adjustment of our

a direct charge on industry, because all sections of industry are not affected by it in the same way. Nor could this apply in the case of a whole industry which has become obsolete or contracted. There are also many workmen, chiefly unskilled, who shift about from one industry to another. Above all, the fact must be faced that, because of international economic conditions generally, the unemployment problem has reached a pitch where full-scale governmental action offers the only hope at present, if not of solving it, at least of palliating it.

(4) Thrift is not a virtue when the family income is inadequate to satisfy present needs. If unemployment were dealt with properly, trade unions would be willing to relax their regulations about permitted levels of output and so on, for these are mainly designed to secure that their members are not thrown out of work owing to redundancy or temporary gluts on the markets. It is well known that a period of unemployment decreases the skill and general efficiency of a worker by lowering his standard of living, so that the reduction of unemployment would raise the average efficiency.

(5) Many Conservative thinkers privately endorse the idea that large-scale unemployment is to be welcomed as the quickest way to remedy the country's economic ills. The argument is debatable; its immorality is uncontestable.

industrial system to changed conditions.

(3) The State is not the proper organ for relieving the misfortunes occasioned by unemployment. Since capitalist industry depends on a reserve of labour, each industry should be made to support its own unemployed. This is a charge which ought not to be spread over the general population. If each trade has to meet its own problems, it would quickly turn to reorganisation of its production and marketing, with most beneficial results.

(4) State maintenance of the unemployed tends to discourage thrift among the working classes and actually fosters idleness and inefficiency. Even on present standards, the unemployed sometimes draw allowances of as much or nearly as much as their fellows get for a whole week's work.

(5) Unpalatable though it may be, increased unemployment is both essential and inevitable in grappling with the problem of inflation, a far graver threat to any country's future. History shows that, once the rate of inflation is brought within reasonable bounds, restoring industrialists' confidence sufficiently for them to resume capital investment, the pool of unemployed is rapidly reduced.

(See also FULL EMPLOYMENT)

UNITED NATIONS ORGANISATION

Pro: (1) In spite of the failure of the

Con: (1) History is strewn with the

League of Nations in some fields, and fortified by the experience of another world war, the nations of the world deemed it necessary to form a successor organisation. A modern world without any international authority is unthinkable.

(2) The difficulties which the UN encounters in the field of high politics should not blind us to the useful work it does. It has proved invaluable in facilitating international co-operation in such matters as health, education, suppression of the white slave traffic and (through the associated International Labour Office) conditions of labour in industry, agriculture and shipping. Above all, despite its obvious political failures, it continues to provide a regular meeting-place for behind-the-scenes talks and negotiations between countries which are publicly at loggerheads. It has been well said that 'the mere habit of representatives of various nations meeting together and discussing matters for the general good will create a valuable habit of mind and temper which should have a wide and beneficent influence'.

(3) The UN's constitution – notably, the establishment of the Security Council and the right of veto among its Big Five members (the USSR, USA, Britain, France and China) – is far more realistic than that of the ill-fated League of Nations. While political rivalries may limit the scope of its effective decision-making, the system does ensure that whatever decisions are taken will correspond with the ability and willingness to carry them out of those Great Powers on whom such duties mostly descend.

(4) If there were no disagreements of principles between different countries, there would be no need for any such all-embracing body as the UN.

wreckage of attempts at international organisation, of which the UN is only the latest. They have all split on the same rock of sovereignty, and the UN, in the long run, will be no exception. Such an organisation cannot succeed because the necessary prerequisite – willingness on the part of member countries to recognise its overriding rights – is lacking. The scant respect with which its decisions on such questions as Palestine and South-West Africa (Namibia) have been treated by the States concerned; the tendency to bypass it in settling really important questions, such as the crises of Berlin, Cuba and Vietnam; the organisation's huge indebtedness, through the failure of many members to pay all the dues they owe; all these are signs of the process of decay.

(2) That international regulation of various social matters is a good thing cannot be denied, but this work can equally well be carried on by *ad hoc* bodies, as has been done in the past. In fact, it is endangered by being linked artificially to the controversial discussions on political and diplomatic issues on which there is continual disagreement. Wrecking of the UN on political issues would leave its social committees high and dry.

(3) The small nations are resentful of the right of veto enjoyed by the Big Five and would certainly try to end it, if they could. In the meantime, some of them have attached themselves to one or other of the two big power blocs, as the best way to promote their own interests, while the so-called non-aligned countries now form a third bloc of such size that their unrealistic conduct has largely discredited the General Assembly's proceedings. At the same time, the very narrowness of the conditions under which agreement must be reached in the Security

The function of the organisation lies precisely in making it possible for nations to act together on the basis of whatever agreement they can eventually achieve. Widely publicised international discussions put a brake on secret diplomacy and secret alignments. The symbolic presence of a UN 'buffer' force was a crucial factor in the successful efforts to avoid a new war between Israel and Egypt. UN forces also succeeded in keeping the inter-communal temperature down in Cyprus (prior to the Turkish invasion, at least). By remaining in the former Belgian Congo (now Zaire), they could have helped in bringing about a peaceful transition to stable government and prevented the tragedies subsequently caused by tribal violence and foreign intervention.

(5) The truly international spirit of the organisation is underlined by the fact that its officials are drawn from virtually every one of its member-nations and that they work together harmoniously, irrespective of any political or ideological differences between each other's countries.

(6) Economically, the world is moving towards the breakdown of national barriers. The formation of the Common Market and the general agreement on the desirability of lowering tariff barriers are illustrations of this tendency. Conditions are likely to grow more favourable to the success of the UN, not less so.

(7) Liquidation of the UN would leave sectional bodies, such as Communists and Roman Catholics, as the only ones internationally organised. The United Nations Organisation, essentially, defends the interests of the ordinary citizen throughout the world, without sectarian or sectional partiality.

Council gives rise to an inflexibility which, eventually, might well cause the breakage of the machinery itself.

(4) In hard fact, the nations are divided into three main camps, those of the Communist and capitalist countries, and the non-aligned bloc. At all UN meetings, decisions are taken, and arguments presented, in accord with one or other of these tendencies. But where formal international agreement is difficult, the UN is bypassed. The attacks on Unifil, its force in Lebanon, show how little the UN is respected, in this context. The Congo intervention was not conspicuously successful and, in overstepping the bounds of impartiality, the UN forces may actually have delayed the end of the war there.

(5) The UN Secretariat has become a top-heavy bureaucracy. Most posts are allotted on the principle of 'Buggins' turn', i.e. they go to someone from this-or-that country simply to ensure that the country in question is represented in the Secretariat – and quite irrespective of the ability, or otherwise, of the official concerned.

(6) Agreements to abolish tariffs and abide by international decisions on economic matters are apt to be flouted when conditions are unfavourable. The conclusions and decisions of the UN, as past experience shows, remain particularly vulnerable to the same tendency.

(7) Religious and political bodies are able to achieve a fairly stable organisation because they have a common purpose. With the aims of its members differing so widely, the UN has no such basis, to any effective extent. Nor does it operate with consistent even-handedness, any more than its individual members do.

UNITED STATES OF EUROPE

Pro: (1) The national idea was necessary in the Middle Ages to raise the world out of barbarism and help the development of modern civilisation, but it has served its purpose, and events since 1914 have finally shown that complete national sovereignty is unworkable. Ever since the Congress of Vienna (1814–15), the nations of Europe have been attempting to reach some form of unity. The League of Nations was wrecked on the rock of national sovereignty; if Europe is to have equal weight with other power groupings in world counsels, its constituent countries must consent to some form of federation among themselves.

(2) For various reasons, but mainly because of their sufferings as important theatres of war, the European countries lost much of the economic power from which their former dominant political influence was derived; yet European civilisation has a great tradition and a unique contribution to make to international life – and the formation (and expansion) of the Common Market has not only demonstrated their joint economic strength but has already provided ample proof as well that, when brought together politically, they can become a telling force and rank alongside the so-called Super-Powers, America and the Soviet Union (and eventually, no doubt, China).

(3) Modern economics demand a larger geographical unit than can be provided by any single country in Europe. The industrial and agricultural nations of Europe are complementary, natural resources are distributed over the whole continent, and their integration is essential for

Con: (1) The idea of European Federation is not practical. There is no true identity between the various States of Europe, and national sovereignty is necessary in order to preserve the distinctions to which they cling. The League of Nations failed because it was not content with limited achievements, based on the few common interests of its members, but strove after an unreal and unattainable unity. The same danger is still inherent in the UN, could yet afflict the EEC members (who are anything but united in their views about the nature of eventual European political unity), and would certainly become apparent in any United States of Europe.

(2) The British Commonwealth is still strong enough and united enough to constitute a cogent force in world policy, despite occasional disagreements. A United States of Europe might benefit some other countries but has no advantages for Britain and would complicate our relations with the rest of the English-speaking world. While recognising that the EEC's objectives are not merely economic but, in the longer term, political as well, Britain opposes anything more than a loose linking which would preserve national identities.

(3) It would be over-optimistic to expect any country to weaken the balance of its economic life for the benefit of a federation. So far from wishing to rise above nationalism, most countries are striving to advance the interests of their own populations. All the EEC's hard-fought economic agreements are still marked by forced concessions to individual self-interest among its member-nations.

(4) For the United States of Europe

their future economic survival – as the EEC has clearly shown.

(4) There is no reason for a United States of Europe to exclude any nation from its framework. All the nations have similar problems to face, and differences in ideology and the degree of State control are of decreasing importance these days. It is already foreseeable that Communist and capitalist countries could take part without any serious difficulties arising.

(5) The idea of federation is not new. It has worked very successfully in the USA, in spite of early growing pains, and the power of the federal organisation has developed in a natural manner. Moreover, the federal structure does not prevent the exercise of the individual 'state's rights', which are still jealously guarded. In the two centuries or more since establishment of the USA, political education in the world at large has so much advanced that federation could now be initiated much less painfully in Europe than might once have been the case. It has also worked well in the USSR, which is a federation of national republics, and notably in Switzerland.

to succeed, it would have to include all European countries. Serious divergences of economic interest exist between Western European nations, let alone between them and the countries of Eastern Europe. The Communist political and economic systems are too far removed from those of other countries to be easily absorbed into a federal system.

(Some) In practice, the USE idea is most popular among those who would exclude Russia and countries linked to her ideologically. A Western USE, which would in effect be based on NATO and thus tend to exclude neutral countries, would be more likely to result in renewed polarisation between East and West. During the 1975 European Security Conference in Helsinki, several Communist representatives stated bluntly that the conference agreements did *not* mean a United States of Europe was possible.

(5) The US federal organisation was effectively established by groups of people whose outlook and racial origins were similar at the time. In the USSR, state autonomy is slender and the federal authority overriding. Switzerland is composed of cantons with strong economic identity, whose local differences are more apparent than real. Europe, on the other hand, consists of old-established countries with long traditions and pronounced national differences. For Britain, entry into a USE would entail the abandonment of some of our most cherished institutions.

(See also COMMON CURRENCY; INTERNATIONALISM; and the preceding article)

UNIVERSITY REFORM

Pro: (1) Universities should be national, in that they ought to provide for the highest cultural requirements of the whole nation and that no individual university should cater, in the main, for just one or two classes of society. The scholarship system at Oxford and Cambridge, the independent procedures of the various colleges, and, until recent years, their relatively limited contact with State schools, discourage many would-be students.

(2) Some provincial universities are still largely without the indisputable benefits that come from residence in college. This can not only lessen the student's contact with many of the main currents of university life except in the lecture room (and, perhaps, the students' union!), but also with much of the regular contact with his teachers which is such a fruitful feature of life at Oxford and Cambridge.

(3) Internally, university legislation and administration should be in the hands of the teaching staff and others who are running the academic side of the university and who know its needs and difficulties. Overall, though, all universities should be controlled more closely by the Department of Education, because they form part of the national educational system. At present, there are too few universities to meet local needs in some regions and a surplus of choice in others. Most universities have insufficient staff for their needs (particularly since the swingeing economies imposed by the post-1979 Conservative Governments). Because of the big growth in the numbers attending universities, tutorial groups were averaging twelve students or more, whereas they should

Con: (1) Those who can benefit from university education now have ample opportunities to obtain it. By the mid-1980s, some 55 per cent of all students graduating from universities in England and Wales were from comprehensive schools (against 23 per cent from grammar schools and only 16 per cent from independent schools). As regards Oxford and Cambridge specifically, the fundamental soundness of their institutions is proved by the competition for admission. It would be more profitable to leave their unique character intact.

(2) Non-residence also has its advantages. Non-campus universities in large cities can offer the student a rich general experience which is denied to those who enter university as inexperienced schoolchildren and remain in its rarefied atmosphere. All good provincial universities have developed tutorial and counselling systems for their non-resident students.

(3) To limit the concept of a university to a body of resident dons marks a self-satisfied exclusiveness. A true university comprises all its members. The idea of direct control is repugnant to the traditions of academic independence which have been the special glory of our universities. At the same time, the University Grants Committee (allocating the funds) has enough control to guard against abuses or eccentricities. While the population explosion in students did lead to a dropping in the standards required for entry, this upsurge in numbers has now levelled out and begun to drop again – to the point that the problem is, if anything, the other way round. Over the next few

ideally comprise not more than six. There are too many students at university who should not really be there.

(4) Conditions of entry should be revised. The present specialised requirements involve intensive cramming in school and destroy every chance of achieving a general, *all-round* education. Many potential candidates from State schools are still at an unfair advantage compared with those from the better-staffed independent schools.

(5) University curricula remain extraordinarily narrow. American universities demand that all undergraduates, whatever their main subject, should take some science, some arts and some social science. In Britain, dual honours programmes are widely available on paper, but in practice the majority of students realise from their teachers' attitude that it is 'safer' to concentrate on one main subject, with perhaps just a token subsidiary. Educationally, and for the sake of the community's future needs, the curricula ought to be based much more than now on natural science. They should also be reorganised, especially in the scientific departments proper, so as to allow greater time for research. It is because universities do not give enough of the practical side that more and more money has been going to the polytechnics, which do recognise the importance of that aspect.

(6) There are already too many universities. However small and local in character, they still try to cover almost the whole field of university education. As a result, there is widespread overlapping and inefficiency.

years, it has been estimated, Britain will need 3,000 more graduates annually than the universities can supply.

(4) Students who cannot satisfy university entrance requirements are better accommodated in polytechnics or technological institutions. Candidates are not always assessed solely on examinations and academic records, and any inadequacies they may have in other respects are likely to be the fault of the schools or the candidates themselves.

(5) Without any need to impose reforms from outside, university leaders have always been aware of the need to adapt to changing demand. As an example, it was the committee of university vice-chancellors which, in 1986, first held a review of education aimed at reforms of the examination system and university courses to bring higher education in line with the new GCSE examination. Foreseeing the eventual abolition of A levels, they were seeking a sixth-form exam which would bring in students of a wider range of ability, doing a wider range of subjects. They would surely have held that a university of scientists would be a national calamity. Science without moral philosophy and liberal culture is a danger to the world. Many scientists, not excluding some eminent ones, are remarkably ignorant and presumptuous about subjects off their own special track. Several of the newer universities have shown their awareness of this by instituting mixed courses. In many fields (e.g. law, medicine, psychology, social sciences), university curricula do in fact incorporate a large proportion of practical work.

(6) No university is granted a charter until the institutions out of which it grows have reached a suitable status and can establish their case for

the grant. Local universities, by their appeal to local pride, divert funds to education which would otherwise be used for different, perhaps less desirable purposes.

VACCINATION

Pro: (1) Vaccination has eradicated epidemics of smallpox, world-wide, and has proved an efficient protection against other diseases. In the few cases where smallpox has occurred after vaccination, it is always modified to such an extent as not to be recognisable in its early stages. In pre-vaccination days, the mortality from smallpox, and the blindness, disfigurement and other injuries caused by it, were universally dreaded. It was fatal in about 30 per cent of cases and hastened death in most of the others. Apart from smallpox, the efficacy of vaccinations is shown by the fact that some countries make it compulsory for visitors to have them for yellow fever and cholera as well. The very success of Jenner's discovery has blotted out these dangers from our national consciousness.

(2) Statistics show an enormous difference between the relative numbers of cases of smallpox among the vaccinated and unvaccinated, which also show far fewer fatal cases. This was borne out strikingly in the case of the troops invading tropical countries in the Second World War. In an outbreak of the disease at Bradford in 1962, during which seven people died, four of the victims had never been vaccinated, one only in infancy, and one showed no trace of the vaccination he claimed; but all the people who recovered had been vaccinated. It was generally agreed that the

Con: (1) The only definition that can be found for 'efficient' vaccination is that which is not followed by smallpox. Even if this occurs in the individual, vaccination will not destroy the infectivity of the disease, so that a person immunised by vaccination might act as a carrier for non-immune people. The fact may easily disguise the serious nature of an epidemic at its start. In the present high state of development of preventive medicine in Britain, there is no likelihood that an epidemic will get far before control measures stop it.

(2) The Bradford outbreak was started by a child in whom the symptoms had been masked by an attack of malaria. That the outbreak did not spread further was due to the prompt measures of isolation, disinfection and tracing of contacts, in which the local doctors and authorities, the Ministry of Health and its laboratories, all played their part.

(3) The willingness of people to be vaccinated in times of panic only testifies to the depth and strength of propaganda on the subject. After vaccination of infants ceased to be compulsory in 1946, the proportion of infants vaccinated dropped to some 18 and 10 per cent in England and Wales respectively (in 1948), and it is admitted that the areas where vaccination figures are lowest are not those to suffer the greatest incidence of the disease.

epidemic had demonstrated the urgent need for vaccination at intervals throughout life, especially among hospital staffs and people working at shipping terminals and airports. The great increase in air travel particularly has made it possible for a sufferer to enter the country before the symptoms of the disease have appeared.

(3) Inoculations of various kinds are accepted nowadays and have reduced mortality in many other illnesses. The public confidence in vaccination was shown by the fact that more than 100,000 people in Bradford came forward and asked for it, as well as thousands elsewhere. When Edward Jenner carried out his first successful vaccination in 1796, one-fifth of all deaths in Britain were due to smallpox. In 1967, when the World Health Organisation began a mass vaccination drive to eradicate smallpox, the disease was endemic in about thirty countries and there were more than 2,500,000 cases throughout the world; five years later, there were only 150,000 cases; today, only a very occasional accidental case appears – just one in the USA in 1986, for example – and the disease is regarded as totally conquered. Similarly, in Britain, with the 'triple jab' introduced after the last world war (against diphtheria, whooping cough and tetanus), the figures speak for themselves. Deaths from diphtheria in 1941, 2,641; by 1972, none. From whooping cough, between 1941 and 1949, annual average of deaths, 1,008; by the mid-1980s, down to not more than 5. And, in 1983, only a single death from tetanus.

(4) Before antisepsis was practised, there was no doubt a small but real risk of conveying some form of sepsis. There was also some risk of inoculation by accident with other diseases.

(4) Coroners' inquests have over and over again proved that vaccination has been the cause of death. Jonathan Hutchinson in his *Archives of Surgery* recorded no fewer than 679 deaths from cowpox from 1881 to 1893, or more than one child a week. There is also a definite risk of other diseases being introduced with the serum. Some tragic cases have been recorded of children dying of other diseases in the absence of any risk from smallpox itself, or even from smallpox contracted as a result of vaccination. In 1974, a pathologist giving evidence at a Walsall inquest disclosed that, as a result of the standard 'triple jab', there had been 425 cases of adverse reactions in England and Wales during a seven-year period – and of these, 17 were deaths. In the same year, it was officially estimated that, out of about 600,000 children given the 'triple jab' each year, between 60 and 80 might suffer brain damage in consequence. Professor George Dick, microbiologist at the Middlesex Hospital, put it somewhat higher, producing data which showed that permanent brain damage could follow immunisation in two out of 10,000 children. He also observed that whooping cough (for which vaccination presents the most risk in the 'triple jab') is now usually a mild disease – and that this could be due to the natural waning of the disease rather than vaccination. Apart from all these dangers, there is the added risk of sepsis from inoculations. Despite the wide variance in estimates of brain damage (one other report puts it as low as 1 in 100,000), the fact remains that, by the mid-1980s, as many as 200 possible legal claims were anticipated on the issue.

(5) In the first day or two after vaccination, there is actually an

But these risks are infinitesimal since the introduction of glycerinated calf lymph, which is produced and tested in most rigorous conditions. Since direct inoculation from sufferers was abandoned, it is impossible to contract smallpox as a result of vaccination.

(5) The risk of vaccinia is extremely small. In 1958, there were only 25 cases, or one in 500,000 vaccinations, and five cases of encephalitis. Most of the few cases occur among older children and adults being vaccinated for the first time, which points to the advisability of doing the first vaccination in infancy.

increased liability to the disease in the patient. There is also the risk of complications giving rise to vaccinia or to a severe form of encephalitis which may cause permanent invalidism and mental derangement, if not death. If most of these cases do occur among older children being vaccinated for the first time, as is claimed, it would clearly be better if the schoolchildren in question were not vaccinated at all.

VEGETARIANISM

Pro: (1) The slaughter of animals bred for the purpose is cruel and degrading. The conversion of pasture into arable land would greatly benefit the nation, as would the cessation of expensive meat imports. Artificial manures can be derived in ample quantities from coal and the atmosphere.

(2) (Some) Darwinian theories add special force to the argument against domesticating cattle for the purposes of slaughter; for artificial selection with a view to the table only is substituted for the healthy operation of natural selection, and the animal is thus deprived of its capacity to improve and rise in the scale of being. Moreover, animals in a domestic state are more liable to disease than when wild.

(3) The process of evolution teaches us that man will have less and less to do with animals which are a fertile breeding-ground for disease, e.g. cows were largely responsible for tuberculosis.

Con: (1) Unless animals are kept for food, they will die out. If they are not kept in large numbers, arable land will not be properly manured, as artificial products are not a complete substitute for organic manures. These and fertilisers would have to be imported instead of meat if there were any large extension of arable farming. A general conversion to vegetarianism would not prevent the killing of animals. If cows are to be kept for milk and cheese, then bulls would have to be destroyed as non-productive.

(2) The only alternative to domestication in man's service is extermination by man. Either process is a part of man's survival and selection. It is erroneous to suppose that wild animals are freer from disease and parasites than tame ones, or that natural selection is not as cruel in its operation as artificial.

(3) A world in which man has left no room for other animals is inconceivable. The tendency of history is to make man more and more dependent

(4) (Some) The universe is a whole; animals are just as much a part of it as man. Mankind must not violate the harmony and plan of the world by destroying his fellow creatures.

(5) The slaughter of animals is accompanied by much cruelty, as when calves and lambs are separated from their mothers. Animals also suffer much in transit and, while the cruelties at present associated with the slaughterhouse might be abated, they could never be quite abolished.

(6) The work of destruction is demoralising and the surroundings of the slaughterhouse are degrading. We ought to relieve our fellow-citizens of such employment. If everyone had to slaughter his own meat, most people would be vegetarians.

(7) Revelations from time to time, such as Upton Sinclair's *Jungle*, show the abuses and horrors that the meat trade abounds in. Our markets, large and small, reveal themselves to ordinary observation as disseminators of dirt and disease.

(8) Vegetarianism fosters humanity and gentleness, while a meat diet produces ferocity.

(9) The formation of man's teeth (he has no teeth wherewith to tear flesh food), the fact that he has not a rough tongue, and the nature of his intestines, which are long and sacculated compared with those of flesh-eaters, prove him to be frugivorous by nature. The apes, which are nearest to man, are wholly vegetarian in diet. Neither man's strength nor his speed is as it would have to be if he were flesh-eating by nature. If man depended on his strength and speed for his flesh food, he would have to be a carrion eater.

(10) A vegetarian diet will give as much nourishment as a meat diet; while the consumer of meat, which is

on a rational exploitation of the lower animals.

(4) A universal harmony is accepted or desired by only a few. Destruction of one animal by another seems to be a part of the world plan.

(5) Much pain has been eliminated by the invention of the humane killer, and measures to ensure that animals are not unduly frightened have been greatly improved. A certain amount of suffering is inevitable in nature; we can alleviate but not eliminate it.

(6) The fact that a trade is disgusting is no reason for its abolition. Many industrial processes and sanitary services are also disgusting, but we do not abolish them.

(7) Abuses such as those referred to are not confined to the meat trade, nor to markets. They result from the consideration of profit at the expense of all else and are a question for economic and social reform. Cleanliness in markets is a matter for municipal regulation.

(8) Diet has no such influence on character. For instance, many Turks and Japanese, both peoples known for their ferocity as warriors, are practically vegetarian. A meat diet may be said to improve the temper, as a meal including meat produces in most people a feeling of satisfaction.

(9) It is impossible to judge of man's necessities by analogy with the ape's, but it is worthy of note that the human intestine does not resemble that of the vegetarian rabbit. Man's organs are adapted to a mixed diet; like the pig, he is omnivorous. His wits replace strength and speed.

(10) It is an advantage to the human organism to receive protein in a more concentrated form than can be obtained from vegetables. First-class protein, which is only to be found in meat, is an essential constituent of a

mostly protein, takes in addition a large amount of starchy food, the vegetarian balances his diet by living on pulses and cereals which contain a large proportion of proteins mixed with starch. No scientific vegetarian lives on vegetables alone; nuts and cheese contain no starch.

(11) The craving for stimulants results in many cases from the qualities of meat, which induce a craving for stronger stimulants. The nations which consume above-average quantities of alcohol are the meat-eating nations. The only hope of curing alcoholism lies in a non-meat diet.

(12) Animal fats are more likely than vegetable fats to cause arteriosclerosis, leading to premature old age. Sir Clifford Allbutt noted that there are comparatively few people over forty who do not show some such signs, so that vegetarian diet cannot be held responsible. The peoples in all parts of the world that avoid meat are less liable to cancer than meat-eaters. Statistical studies have shown that people who have always been vegetarians tend to live longer than meat-eaters.

(13) Vegetarian diet is capable of as much variety as any that meat diet can offer. Vegetarians can take the credit for making some vegetables (e.g. haricot beans and lentils) much more popular with the general public. While costly dishes are possible, the object of rational vegetarians is to bring people to a rational simplicity. According to a Gallup Poll in 1985, nearly three million people in Britain are vegetarians or have cut out all red meat from their diet.

(14) Diet should be settled scientifically, on the basis of man's basic requirements. It is natural that there should be different schools of vegetarians, but the principles remain

scientifically balanced diet. Vegetables are so overloaded with starch and cellulose that they are less assimilable than flesh and larger percentages escape digestion.

(11) Special complaints naturally need a special regime. Nations which are vegetarian are given to drug-taking, e.g. opium, betel, bhang, coca. The real hope for curing alcoholism lies in the development of mental therapeutics. Vegetarians are often of a slightly abnormal temperament and vegetarian literature tends equally often to be hypochondriac.

(12) An exclusively vegetable diet is liable to produce debilitating intestinal disorders, especially if the food is uncooked. Apart from other considerations, it is doubtful whether the British climate is suitable for large-scale practice of vegetarianism. The differences in expectation of life are in any case so small as to make it hardly worth while to deprive oneself of the advantage and enjoyment of eating meat.

(13) While in theory vegetarianism offers a new and large variety of foods, in practice the reverse is the case; the food habitually consumed by vegetarians and served in vegetarian restaurants is often singularly deficient in variety and cooked in unappetising ways. The 'scientific vegetarians' who add eggs, milk and cheese to their diets are not true vegetarians, for they can only get those things if the rest of the world is meat-eating. A vegetarian diet adequate to the body and pleasing to the palate involves much expense of time and money.

(14) Vegetarians are not agreed among themselves; their varieties are numerous (e.g., VEM – vegetables, eggs, and milk – fruitarians, purin-free, unfired), and they are as opposed to one another as they are to meat-

the same. Vegetarians who relapse do so through special causes or through their own errors.

(15) A vegetarian diet ensures that adequate amounts of mineral salts and vitamins are consumed. Meat-eaters take vegetables; but they are often cooked in such a fashion as to destroy these vital substances. Appetite is also destroyed by the indifferent cooking of vegetables, when their lack of flavour can be concealed by the taste of meat.

(16) The latest evidence goes to show that the low rating put on cereal proteins is unsound. At least one cereal – soya bean – contains 'first-class' protein. As the majority of people suffer from too great an intake of protein, this criticism of vegetarian diet is not important.

eaters. Equally good cases could be made out for Fletcherism ('chew, chew, chew again'), the fasting cure, and the exclusively meat diet. Quite a number of vegetarians take to meat again after some years.

(15) The remedy for such deficiencies in meat-eaters' diets is to see that they eat salads and cook their non-flesh foods properly, not give up meat. Vegetarian cooking is frequently poor.

(16) The quality of the proteins in cereals and vegetables tends to be low and, since quality of food is as important as quantity, the consumer of animal foods, including cheese, scores heavily in this respect. The amount of protein in a diet cannot in any case be prescribed for everybody on one scale; it is quite possible that sedentary workers can do with comparatively little, but very few heavy workers would tolerate the idea of vegetarianism – and, in fact, most vegetarians are drawn from the middle classes (in Britain, at any rate).

VIVISECTION AND EXPERIMENTS ON ANIMALS

Pro: (1) Before examining the reasons for experiments on animals and the many important advances which have resulted from them, it should be noted that key changes are in prospect from the new Animals (Scientific Procedures) Act, which passed into law in 1986. This has replaced the long-inadequate Cruelty to Animals Act of 1876, making some 20 large-scale revisions of the regulations which formerly governed animal experiments. Among the biggest changes are: (a) people

Con: (1) That it took 110 years to reform the law – and far from adequately, even now – can only be classed as an utter disgrace. Here are just a few of the many loopholes in the new Act: (a) there is not a single area of experiments in which the use of animals has been banned; (b) there is not a single attempt actually to stop pain in such experiments; (c) while the regulations do set out to reduce the degree of pain caused, and one Home Office Minister has given an assurance that 'no pain is acceptable unless it

licensed to carry out experiments have to meet stricter requirements showing their competence to do so; (b) licences are also now required, for the first time, for individual projects – it has to be shown that the potential benefits of a specific experiment justify the number of animals to be used and the degree of pain likely to be inflicted on them (what has been described as 'pain with a purpose'); (c) all laboratories have to appoint a member of staff, aided by a veterinary surgeon (either on staff or on call), to take responsibility for the day-to-day care of the animals; (d) control is extended to large areas of experimentation left uncovered by the 1876 Act (because they were developed later); (e) stricter controls are introduced on the breeding and supply of laboratory animals (a move designed to counter the illicit trade in stolen and abandoned domestic pets); and (f), the most far-reaching of all, the previous advisory committee on animal experiments is replaced by an Animal Procedures Committee, with statutory powers to monitor the issuing of licences, investigate types of experiments and recommend further restrictions or outright bans. All these new measures are accompanied by tougher penalties for offenders, who are now liable to unlimited fines and up to two years' prison. While the full impact of the reforms was not expected to make itself felt until the early 1990s, nobody claims that the Act is an entirely satisfactory answer to the problem. But many leading bodies, even including the British Veterinary Association, have welcomed the legislation as a realistic basis for achieving greater protection for animals – and as a good springboard for further reforms in future. Compared with only 273 permitted animal experiments in

passes very stiff criteria', those self-same 'criteria' will be decided by scientists who have a vested interest in the continuation of animal experiments; (d) the Act does not give animal welfare an equal say with industry and academics; (e) it increases the secrecy of animal experimentation, with the threat of prison sentences for people who breach 'confidentiality'; (f) it allows experiments for a much wider range of purposes than under the previous law. The much-vaunted Animal Procedures Committee was not expected to make its first report until two years after the 1986 Act came into operation. In any case – as intimated under (c), above – the committee will be stacked with scientists and, under the terms of the legislation, will be able to appoint powerful sub-committees composed entirely of the experimenters themselves. The British Union Against Vivisection has pointed out that these are the people given the task of deciding what an acceptable level of pain is, 'even though two Government committees have said it is impossible to lay down objective criteria'. The possibility of failure to deal sufficiently firmly with abuses is already evident from one glaring omission in the Act – the absence of any clauses tackling, specifically and immediately, two of the most notorious experiments, the Draize eye irritancy test and the LD50 toxicity test. In the former, pesticides and shampoos are squirted into the eyes of rabbits; in the latter, animals are pumped with fluids until half of them have died from poisoning (LD stands for 'lethal dose'). Both these tests are widely regarded as not only unnecessarily cruel but also as of diminishing scientific value. Yet, according to Government statistics, 6,800 of the

1876, the annual total by the time the latest Act became law was 3.3 million. But this was 2 million fewer than a decade earlier; since 1976, the number has been falling at an average rate of six per cent a year. It is clear that the trend will receive further impetus from the new regulations, through the weeding out of any unnecessary experimentation still in being. However, what is no less clear is that, throughout the two White Papers and more than three years that the 1986 Act was in preparation, at no time did the Government come anywhere near envisaging the abolition of animal experiments. The one salient fact underlying the whole procedure, in short, is a recognition that the overall benefits from such experiments are just too valuable to be discarded.

(2) The healing art depends for its advancement on all the sciences, but especially on biology. The laws of biology can be discovered only by observation and experiment, just as the laws of other sciences have to be discovered. Observation may suggest a law, but experiment is essential to substantiate the theory. As men can relatively rarely be observed under the strictest scientific conditions and can be the subject of experiments only in exceptional circumstances, animals which are closely similar in physiological processes have to be used. Few of these laws could have been elucidated without experiments on animals.

(3) Psychopathology depends largely on animal experiments, particularly the study of instinctive behaviour and reflex action. Vivisection has taught us much about the purely physiological side of sensation and thought. It has saved an enormous amount of suffering both for men and for animals.

Draize experiments were carried out on the eyes of rabbits in 1985. These figures show that, of all the animal experiments in Britain that year, mice or rats were involved in 80 per cent, birds in five per cent, rabbits in five per cent, guinea pigs in four per cent and fish in four per cent. Although the total number has fallen – more probably, it is to be feared, as a result of adverse economic conditions rather than any moral scruples – much could be said about a society which subjects well over three million fellow-creatures to laboratory experiments each year (experiments often so painful that the animals die or have to be killed). And even more could assuredly be said about the fact that no fewer than 16,600 of the 1985 experiments were still merely to test cosmetics and toiletries. Why hasn't the Act outlawed animal experiments for such trivial purposes? Why has it legalised previously banned areas such as micro-surgery and the re-use of the same animal in more than one experiment? No less alarming, on another plane, is the lack of safeguard for the Act's present operation and future development. Because of its 'enabling' powers, any further changes can be made without fresh legislation – so everything will depend on the commitment of the individual Home Office Minister responsible. Instead of relying on one politician's determination (or otherwise), why weren't such crucial aspects covered by explicit legal provisions?

(2) Medicine and surgery are arts as well as sciences, and the animal economy is much more than a piece of machinery which can be taken to pieces and investigated in a vivisector's laboratory. Experiments done on sub-human creatures are, when applied to man, apt to be misleading

(4) Vivisection has given us many facts about the functions of the body, and has confirmed or modified those discovered by other means, e.g. the laws relating to blood pressure and the functions of arteries and nerves.

(5) The surgeon has been enabled to localise the functions of the brain and bring to perfection such operations as lobectomy. By experiment on animals during his training, he gets an idea of the effect of any measures he takes. Having the broad lines of possible results before him, he can proceed at once more boldly and more skilfully.

(6) Vivisection has not only shown us the true causes of infectious diseases but, to a considerable extent, has enabled us to prevent and cure them. The Pasteur treatment has reduced the mortality among those bitten by rabid animals from at least 15 per cent to fewer than 1 per cent. The antitoxin treatment of diphtheria has reduced mortality to nil when applied in the first two days.

(7) In war, the methods of prevention and cure by antitoxins and serum injections have eradicated the danger of typhoid and reduced the risks of tetanus and gangrene to minor proportions. All the methods employed are based on knowledge gained through vivisection. The very methods employed for disinfection are based on experimental results.

(8) Cancer now has a much greater recovery rate, thanks to animal experiments. Influenza is better understood and more nearly under control, and deaths from scarlet fever and measles have vanished thanks to treatment with antibiotics. Virus diseases are being conquered, poliomyelitis being an outstanding example. Sanitation has undoubtedly reduced many diseases greatly, as also has a lessening

and therefore dangerous. The late Sir Frederick Treves, himself a vivisector, admitted this as regards certain of his own experiments. The artificial diseases of the laboratory are not the same as diseases occurring naturally.

(3) Vivisection has distracted medical science away from psychopathology, with the result that progress in mental science has been much slower than in other fields.

(4) Such important discoveries as the circulation of the blood were made not by vivisection but by clinical and post-mortem observation and inference. As for the nerves, no experiments at all are needed to demonstrate the process of reflex action, which is claimed as a triumph of vivisection. 'Living pathology' suffices for the purpose.

(5) Prehistoric man well understood trepanning. As the human brain and body differ from the animal brain and body, little is to be learnt from vivisecting the latter.

(6) Although Pasteurism has taught us much about the causes of disease due to microbes, it has been far less productive in practical results.

(7) The improved health of armies during war has been due to superior sanitation and better facilities for normal medical attention.

(8) The diseases over which vivisectionists have spent most time show no signs of being eradicated through their researches. The menace of influenza continues, despite the efforts of the vivisectionists to develop a serum or antitoxin to combat it. The death-rate from diphtheria had already begun to decrease, through the natural waning of the disease, before the introduction of the antitoxin treatment. In other diseases such as measles and scarlet fever, similarly, the fall in the death-rate had begun long before there was

of poverty. But the general advance in the treatment of all manner of complaints is bound up with the study of morbid conditions under laboratory control and with the advance in biochemistry, both of which are dependent on experiments with animals. The supply of insulin, which offers the victim of diabetes a successful life, was the work of vivisectors.

(9) The action and effect of drugs are the same on all animals; when there is a difference in the action of a drug on two animals, it is a difference of *degree*, not of *kind*. Though anaesthetics were not actually discovered by vivisection, their development is largely due to it, e.g. Simpson's discovery that parturition could take place under an anaesthetic. All new anaesthetic compounds are tried on animals first. More thorough and more carefully controlled experiments would have prevented the thalidomide tragedy.

(10) Naturally, biology is full of controversies, like all other sciences. Anti-vivisectionists select from such discussions whatever statements or opinions suit their case. Dr Walker [see Con (10)] actually criticised the use made of vivisection, not the practice itself.

(11) The greatly increased knowledge of foodstuffs, of the role played by vitamins, of the value of proteins, etc., is dependent on systematic experimentation with animals – mostly, of course, by giving them special diets and noting results. The value of experiments on animals is firmly justified and established in this field. To those experiments we owe the great diminution in the number of children deformed by rickets, the reduction of the death-rate from puerperal sepsis by some 95 per cent, from cerebro-

any treatment due to vivisection, and it was even more marked than in the case of diphtheria.

(9) Since very few medicines have the same effect on the lower animals as they do on human beings, it cannot be said that we owe any exact knowledge of the action of drugs to experiments on animals. The use of thalidomide was the result of unjustified reliance on animal experiments. Anaesthetics were discovered not by experiments on animals but by Simpson's experiments on himself and by the experiments of Morton, the dentist, on his patients.

(10) There is a minority of able doctors who themselves deny or drastically criticise the claims of vivisectors. For instance, Dr G. F. Walker, an authoritative writer on medical subjects and holding several important hospital appointments, declared that 'vivisection, overwhelmingly on the whole, has been wasteful and futile'.

(11) The results of the biochemists' researches into food, etc., merely confirm what medical men without faith in vivisection, unorthodox practitioners, 'food reformers', and others, have said for many years, viz. we must not sophisticate our foodstuffs more than is necessary, we must buy food of good quality, we must take exercise and get plenty of fresh air. The same is true of the vogue for sunbathing. Those who could afford it have always known it to be desirable to get sea air, avoid the chemical-laden atmosphere of the industrial town, etc., and those who could not afford it have always wanted to follow their example. But the . conservatism of the medical profession as a whole, with its excessive faith in laboratories, is demonstrated continually. Although a doctor in the eighteenth century proved that scurvy could be prevented

spinal meningitis by almost 90 per cent, and from pneumonia to under 2 per cent of cases in patients aged under 50. Can anyone maintain that the sacrifice of a few thousand mice is too high a price to pay for the saving of so many human lives?

(12) The fact that, in Britain alone, some 30,000 people die from lung cancer every year (1985 figures) is surely a far greater cause for public concern?

(13) The anti-vivisectionist has no case on scientific grounds. His moral principles are dubious. Most 'experiments' are of a minor character that involve only slight discomfort to the animals concerned, and often not even that. Serious operations are conducted under anaesthetics, and, moreover, are only 5 per cent of the total number of experiments. The other 95 per cent are simple experiments such as inoculations and feeding tests. Other animals are beneficiaries, too, because nearly all veterinary medicine derives from such experimentation.

by consuming fresh vegetables and citrus fruits, and Captain Cook kept his crews healthy by following this advice, British medical 'experts' still recommended a diet for the Army during the First World War which resulted in many of our soldiers suffering from scurvy.

(12) How can anyone condone the experiments, disclosed in 1975, in which beagle dogs were in effect forced to smoke cigarettes? (The precise object was to compare the irritant power of smoke from tobacco substitutes with that from cigarettes.) It is small wonder that there was a major public outcry at the disclosure.

(13) Although it is not denied that vivisection may have produced some good results, the foundation of the opposition to vivisection is moral. Not even the surest advance in knowledge justifies the infliction of excessive suffering on dumb animals. Even the serum experiments involve acute pain, while sensation experiments must necessarily be done without anaesthetics. In tacitly inviting the public to tolerate vivisection, the scientists are encouraging callousness and cruelty and are stifling compassion in the human heart.

(See also ANIMALS, RIGHTS OF)

VOTING, COMPULSORY

Pro: (1) It is the duty of every citizen to take an interest in the affairs of his community, and to express his opinion on the questions at issue and choose between rival policies. Voting should therefore be made compulsory, under penalty for failure to vote. The ballot paper can be drafted so that

Con: (1) Compulsory voting obliges electors to choose one out of two or three persons or measures, even though they might not approve of any of them. It endeavours to force them to give a practical assent to a system which they may not like and may even want to change. The negative

no one has any grievance about being made to support a policy or candidate that he dislikes. Such a measure would heighten the sense of civic responsibilities and would be a precaution against power getting into the hands of incipient dictators (whether in the State or the local municipality).

(2) In countries which already have compulsory voting – such as Australia, which introduced it as long ago as 1925 – the idea works smoothly and well, and no reasonable elector feels that it is onerous or restrictive.

comment implied by abstentions from the poll can at times be most valuable.

(Some) If people are so indifferent to what happens that they do not trouble to exercise their rights, they should be left alone to bear the results of their negligence.

(2) It may work in a country with a relatively small and scattered population but would create vast problems in Britain and other densely populated industrial countries, with a much higher number of inhabitants. The volume of paperwork alone, in checking who had or hadn't voted and going through any necessary court proceedings afterwards, would be a bureaucratic nightmare.

WAR:
Is It Desirable?

Pro: (1) It might be held nowadays that no one in his right senses would deem war to be desirable. Professional soldiers are the first to say that their prime aim is to prevent war. Yet the fact remains that war does have beneficial aspects, notably as a moral influence. It develops virtues such as patriotism, self-sacrifice, efficiency, inventiveness, courage and discipline. The 'Dunkirk spirit' embodied all that was finest in our national character, but no stimulus sufficiently powerful to arouse it exists in peace-time, although the need for it is as great.

(2) Military training in time of peace brings similar benefits. It educates and disciplines, preserves from idleness and greatly increases physical fitness and mental alertness. (See *Military Training, Compulsory*.)

(3) War is necessary for the growth

Con: (1) Whatever may have been the attitudes of past generations (often conditioned by those of empire-building and colonialism), most people today – particularly the young – have come to regard war, of any kind, as utterly (and rightly) repugnant and immoral. War promotes cruelty, vice and stupidity, as well as untold physical and mental suffering. Most people are content to exercise their limited capacity for adventure in their working and home lives. Those who wish for wider opportunities can go in for exploration, pioneering, reclaiming of waste places or voluntary social service.

(2) Military service is generally disastrous to the individual. It uproots him from normal life and often substitutes demoralising idleness for useful occupation.

259

of powerful States. Only in these can individual capacities develop most fully.

(4) Art and literature, and religion, are stimulated by war.

(5) It selects the fittest, and thus secures the progress of evolution.

(6) War is a cure for over-population. If that sounds callous, reflect how often in history the threat of over-population has been abated (in the absence of war) by massive epidemics or other natural disasters. This pattern has always been evident in nature, when any species of wild life becomes too prolific for its healthiest survival.

(7) Trade follows the flag. The prestige of a nation in war and its armed strength are the foundations of its commercial credit. Victory secures access to resources of raw materials and foreign markets.

(8) War is often undertaken to save people from oppression or aggression, when intervention becomes necessary as a matter of moral duty and national self-respect. The liberation of occupied countries from their oppressors, and the punishment of the guilty, advances the moral standing of society in general. If it had not been for Britain's determination to fight on alone in 1940, against all the odds, three-quarters of Europe might still be under the aggressor's heel.

(3) Citizens of small, peaceful States generally achieve a higher average standard of living and more individual fulfilment within society than those of big countries. Inhabitants of the most militant States usually tend to lose much of their individual liberty.

(4) Flourishing periods for art and literature are not confined to warlike nations or times of war. Some religions (e.g. Buddhism) are completely opposed to war. People's fears in wartime make any religious upsurge all too understandable. How else to explain the paradox of ourselves and our enemy praying to the same God for victory?

(5) War selects the physically fittest only to eliminate them. In modern warfare, a soldier's chance of survival does not depend on his personal qualities. In the social ruin that follows war, it is the most cunning that survive.

(6) On the contrary, the birth rate often increases during and immediately after a war. But in any case, the remedy for over-population must lie in education and social change (see *Birth Control.*) To regard war as a cure for anything is quite unspeakable.

(7) Nations lose more in war than they gain in the trade that is supposed to follow it; war, under modern conditions, will ruin both victor and vanquished; the Second World War resulted in the widespread destruction and paralysis of peaceful industry. The days when trade could be imposed on conquered countries are past; indeed, nations are now forced to spend time and money on rebuilding the countries they have destroyed.

(8) Though wars are sometimes fought for such ends, the fruits of victory are usually wilted by compro-

mise and intrigue between the victorious nations.

(See also ARMAMENTS, LIMITATION OF CONVENTIONAL; NUCLEAR WEAPONS: SHOULD THEY BE BANNED COMPLETELY?; and the next article)

WAR:
Is It Inevitable?

Pro: (1) Mankind has always been prone to war and, to judge from the past, always will be. For every one year of peace, in recorded history, there have been thirteen years of war. Throughout the early civilisations of Egypt, Assyria, Greece, Rome, etc., war was a prominent feature of life. It was characteristic of their highest development and greatest vigour.

(2) Human nature is unchangeable – and the aggressive instinct is one of its characteristics. Virile men enjoy a fight. Desire for adventure and the struggle for existence accentuate the tendency.

(3) Nations have the same characteristics as individuals. They have a sense of national honour which prevents them from submitting to outrage and indignity.

(4) All nations are not at the same level of civilisation or strength. Weaker or more primitive nations will always be in danger of ill-treatment by more powerful nations, and rising nations will always have a temptation to go to war to establish their domination and overthrow the older powers.

(5) The commercial and economic rivalries between various nations cannot always be displaced or removed by arbitration, international organisations, or merely good aspir-

Con: (1) The progress of anthropological research shows that war is a recent phenomenon in human history, arising a few thousand years ago, through a definite set of conditions. The earliest civilisation of all, of which the records are chiefly traditional and archaeological rather than historical, was most certainly a peaceful one. But in any case it is false to assume that the future must resemble the past.

(2) Man has gradually risen in the scale of evolution and should by now be able to control or sublimate his fighting instincts.

(3) The analogy between nations and individuals may be rejected. Even if it is accepted, however, it leans in favour of the disappearance of war, since individuals now co-operate more than they used to.

(4) Wars to replace one empire by another may have been natural in the past, but today it is more difficult to succeed in a war of aggression since it inevitably raises the threat of becoming world-wide in its scope.

(5) Economic rivalry has caused war, but that is only an argument for reforming the social system that causes such rivalry. Even without changing the whole social structure, a stable arrangement of economic interests could be made. The widespread economic devastation which results

ations. These rivalries subsist and cause wars even when most of the world is striving for peace.

(6) A nation which does not defend its honour and prestige, or is known to be unprepared for war, will invite aggression from other more virile or belligerent countries.

(7) War may have become much more horrible, but men will not cease to engage in it. Mankind has an enormous capacity for suffering, but the individual always enters a fight in the expectation that his enemy will suffer more than he does.

(8) Man is doomed to unhappiness by his nature. War will always be welcomed every now and again, as a relief from the boredom of everyday existence, especially in times of economic stagnation or depression.

(9) For these reasons, no amount of arbitration, UN resolutions or disarmament treaties will ever prevent occasional wars. On the contrary, since they induce a false sense of security, they might sometimes even be a danger to a country's welfare.

from war today is more than any nation can afford, even those nations which are only indirectly affected.

(6) The honour of the individual once maintained the duel. Today, the duel has disappeared and, if necessary, aggrieved parties turn to the courts. National honour can be dealt with in the same way, by substituting recourse to international law for summary action.

(7) Small wars risk growing into big ones and the horrors of nuclear weapons have rendered any large-scale war impossible, unless the human race as a whole is prepared to commit suicide.

(8) A rational system of society and a national mode of life will abolish poverty, unhappiness and boredom. People will then value life far too much to throw it away.

(9) Men have striven for international agreement since nations existed and are not likely to give up the effort at this stage. Already the principle is accepted, though not much has been achieved yet in practice. The hope for peace is fundamental, and the solution will one day be found.

(See also the preceding article)

WOMEN, MARRIED, MORE JOBS FOR

Pro: (1) Married women have as much right to take part in the general activities of the community as other people. They are just as likely to do good work, and many of them do not feel fulfilled solely by household and family duties.

(2) In many cases, the family income would be insufficient if the

Con: (1) A married woman should find scope enough in looking after the home and her husband. Her first duty is to care for her family.

(2) The entry of more married women into the labour market would risk keeping wages low and harming many other women who do not have the resource of a husband's income.

husband alone were working. For some, marriage would not even be possible if the woman could not continue her employment or profession.

(3) While young babies may need their mothers, older children are sufficiently cared for during the day by school facilities. All responsible mothers who take a job make sure that they or their husbands will be home in time to look after their children, as necessary. In other societies, the child is often felt to belong to the whole community and shows no sign of deprivation. On Israeli *kibbutzim*, children spend allotted time with their parents after working hours but are otherwise cared for separately – again, with no ill effects.

(4) Many married women lose contact with the outside world when they have nothing to occupy them but their own family affairs, and thus may become poor companions for their husbands and growing children. In some homes, there is also a danger of polarisation, whereby the husband becomes regarded simply as the provider of income, while the wife holds herself to represent the family's source of culture and refinement. Wives who take part in their husbands' business, as with women (many of them married) who run their own businesses, are usually far more interesting and intelligent than those who vegetate at home.

(5) The only valid test for employing people, in any work, should be their efficiency. This, and not the maintenance of obsolete traditions, is also the prime interest for the community as a whole. Since the task of rearing babies may lessen a woman's efficiency (by restricting the hours when she would be free to do an outside job, for instance), it is

Generally speaking, given the taxation differences, it is nearly as easy to support a man and wife on the husband's income as it is for a bachelor to keep himself in lodgings, where he must provide for his own needs and also, perhaps, save money with a view to marriage or the support of dependants.

(3) The rise in juvenile delinquency is partly due to working mothers' absence from home, which contributes to unconscious resentment, bewilderment, a generally negative attitude, and the build-up of an anti-social attitude in later years.

(4) Some women are completely absorbed by running their homes, and prefer it that way. Mothers of growing children certainly don't need to take a job to avoid vegetating or losing contact with the outside world. Vast numbers of them remain intelligent and interested in life, often using free hours in the middle of the day to help with voluntary activities in their local community. Many married women in industry – particularly those who have to carry out all their domestic work, as well as doing their jobs, but do not get as much help from their husbands as they should – quickly show signs of strain and become worn and nervous, with the result that domestic unhappiness follows.

(5) Family life is an older and more important basis of communal prosperity than any form of industrial production. Some factories run kindergartens to look after their women employees' children in working hours. There is also now a statutory requirement for expectant mothers in full-time employment to be given 'maternity leave' – and some businesses have their own, even more generous schemes, allowing up to six months after the birth before the

reasonable that young wives should have 10–15 years off work, if they can, to bring up their babies. But once the children are in their teens, married women should be given every encouragement to take a job – if they wish to, that is. Women themselves (and their husbands, should their opinion be sought!) are the only proper judges of whether they should seek work outside the home. However, there is no doubt that most wives in their mid-30s – particularly those who had a job before they married – welcome the outside interest of at least a spare-time job. Nor is there any doubt that women with previous working experience, especially of office jobs, are much valued by enlightened employers. For mothers of younger children who want to work in industry, more provision should be made for adjacent crèches or kindergartens to care for the children while the women are working.

(6) The 'equal pay' legislation now in force should be made truly effective by job re-evaluation and regrading, which should give proper weight (for instance) to the fact that men's physical strength is no more nor less valuable, in context, than some of women's special attributes, such as manual dexterity. In addition, there should be more facilities to train married women, if they wish, for promotion to the highest levels of responsibility in factories, shops and offices, as well as in the professions.

mother is expected to resume her job. However, while these measures may seem commendable, they do not alter the basic objection that industrial jobs for young mothers put unnatural pressures (of time and strain) on both woman and child. Another drawback arises when women in industrial jobs become pregnant; for monotonous factory work and sedentary occupations often produce deep-seated fatigue – even though the women may not realise it, thinking that they are so accustomed to the work that it does not particularly tax them. Nor do such jobs give any opportunity for the kind of healthy activity which is beneficial to child-bearing.

(6) It is not suggested that no married women should work in industry – that would be nonsense. But there can be no doubt that measures to encourage a sizeable increase in their number would be unwise, because the right conditions for it do not exist. Women still of child-bearing age, for example, need the opportunity for flexible hours, job-sharing, part-time work and re-training without loss of seniority, pensions or similar benefits. In present circumstances, even the most enlightened employer would find it difficult, if not impossible, to accord all these on a large scale. In boom periods, when there are labour shortages, the employment of more married women may be of temporary benefit to an industry. But, as is all too evident from Britain's sorry labour scene in recent years, any advantages are offset in the long run by the problems caused – for the industry and the women alike – as soon as an economic recession occurs.

(See also the next article)

WOMEN'S RIGHTS MOVEMENTS:
Are They Too Aggressive?

(The first women's suffrage committee was set up in Britain as long ago as 1866, yet it was another 52 years before some British women won the right to vote and a further 10 years before all did. Efforts to gain equal rights for British women in other fields achieved their biggest step forward at the end of 1975, when the Sex Discrimination and Equal Pay Acts came into force. ver the preceding decade, a new element had been introduced into the fight by an American writer, Betty Friedan; her book, *The Feminine Mystique*, published in 1963, led three years later to her foundation in the USA of the National Organisation for Women, which campaigned – often using deliberately aggressive means – for women to free themselves from traditional male dominance. The organisation, which soon had counterparts in many other contries, became known familiarly as the Women's Liberation movement (or 'Women's Lib'). Britain, by the early 1970s, had between 40 and 50 Women's Lib groups in the London area alone. In more recent years, Women's Lib has given way to activists who, in terms of media shorthand, may be broadly described as Feminists. This covers a wide range of groups campaigning for women's rights. A few are so militant that they reject all involvement with men; others have come round to the view that they can achieve more by exploiting political and other fields on conventional lines, thereby seeking to reach and persuade a much larger number of people. It should be emphasised that the following arguments are intended to be much less about the merits of women's rights, in general, than about the pros and cons of the various movements fighting for them.)

Pro: (1) Popular newspapers have focused mostly on the more extremist manifestations of women's rights campaigners, ignoring the fact that many of them have thought deeply about women's role in society and have simply refused to accept situations which had too easily become regarded as immutable. Among the great strengths of the various Feminist movements is that they draw their support from a wide range of women, and that they also embrace numerous individual viewpoints, of greatly varying intensity. However, one point on which all of them are agreed is that there are still a great many injustices and illogicalities to be overcome before women achieve anything like truly equal rights.

Con: (1) In the eyes of the general public, the image of any movement, however valid its fundamental aims may be, will always tend to be coloured by the excesses of its lunatic fringe. The broader that fringe, the less credibility a movement can retain. Before the First World War, the violence of the suffragettes, and the ridiculous extent to which some of them became hostile to anything masculine, soon alienated public opinion from what was otherwise a just cause. Nor could suffragettes claim to have won women the right to vote. It was the efforts of ordinary women during the war, in showing themselves fully capable of taking on jobs previously done only by men, which finally overcame Parliamentary resistance. Simi-

(2) The women's movements of past generations had two big flaws. First, they were open to criticism as being run almost solely by middle-class, professional people. Secondly, in concentrating on their demand for political rights, the suffragists became so pragmatic that they 'sold out' as regards more fundamental changes in attitude. Neither criticism can be made of Women's Lib or the present-day Feminists. The former, by its dynamism and questioning of attitudes, provided the main stimulus for the change in public opinion which brought about the 1975 sex equality legislation. Without its vision, the work of older groups like the Fawcett Society would never have lifted off the ground. It prepared the ground for popular support for these reforms from an extremely broad spectrum – not just middle class, but active trade unionists, married as well as single women, and from all age groups. And this led, in turn, to the general direction now taken by the Feminist movement as a whole, aimed at the removal of socio-economic inequalities over the broadest possible range.

(3) It took until the mid-1980s before the authorities (and the public in general) at last began to recognise the truly horrific scale of the problem of rape. Not until then was a start made in changing the previous police attitude to rape complainants – a reaction of (to all appearances) almost automatic disbelief and of sharp questioning of the woman (at least, until her charge eventually proved justified). This climate of hostile suspicion was to blame for many women's reluctance to report such offences. Among other hostile influences that women still have to combat are moves by some politicians and biased individuals (with specific

larly, today, the stupid belligerence of some Feminists – those, for instance, who call themselves 'wimmin' or take evening classes in 'herstory', rather than allow even any partial taint from such syllables as 'men' or 'his' – has lost rather than gained support for women's rights and has threatened to jeopardise the advances being achieved by more moderate women's movements.

(2) Members of Women's Lib must have been living in a fairy-tale world if they believed that such symbolic gestures as burning their brassieres in public would do anything at all to change the climate of opinion in favour of legislative reform. The real spadework in creating the ground-swell of popular support for it was done by much less abrasive bodies – notably, the Fawcett Society (descended directly from the original London Society for Women's Suffrage of 1866) and the Six Point Group (founded in 1921 to work for the *emancipation*, not spurious 'liberation', of women). Such bodies have solid achievements to their credit, both through their campaigns which led specifically to the 1975 laws and through their clear exposition of inequalities which still need remedying. What's more, unlike Women's Lib and later militant movements, their membership is also open to men who support their views.

(3) The big rise in the number of alleged rapes reported to the police reflects the greatly improved procedures now introduced for handling complainants – with a leading role, be it noted, played by *women* police. While these improvements were admittedly long overdue, the militants always seem to forget that men, too, are entitled to protection. It is all too easy for a woman to cry

Church interests often evident behind them), threatening to weaken, or even scrap, the Abortion Act. Feminists have called for every woman to have the right to free contraception and to abortion on demand. Many of them have also urged the establishment of a network of child care centres, open 24 hours a day, so that more women can be free to lead useful lives and not be pinned down by domestic drudgery forced on them by men. Today, women make up 40 per cent of Britain's labour force. Only one in five households contains a married woman who does not go out to work. Among all the others in paid employment, those with young children are either forced to work part-time or have to make special arrangements for them to be cared for immediately after school hours – usually through neighbours or, perhaps, through male partners adjusting their own working conditions – because the number of local authority nurseries available is woefully short of the total needed.

(4) A prime example of renewed prejudice against women is evident, sadly, within the Church. In 1975, the Church of England's ruling General Synod accepted that there was 'no fundamental theological objection' to the ordination of women priests. Today, women have already been ordained in eight provinces of the Anglican Communion, including the USA, Canada, Australia and New Zealand. But in Britain, opposition has strengthened once more; and by July 1986, even on a motion merely to allow women already ordained abroad to celebrate Holy Communion at services in this country, the General Synod failed to muster the two-thirds majority necessary for the Church to recommend the measure to Parliament. Some opponents said that they

'rape' spuriously – out of jealousy, desire for revenge on someone who has rebuffed her, or many other such wretched motives – but often all too difficult, at first, for a man to prove that her accusation is baseless. While abortion is a big issue in its own right (*see Termination of Pregnancy*), that is quite distinct from sanctioning abortion on demand, free of any further formality. Without some measure of medical control, however limited, the potential assault on morality would be incalculable. As for nursery schools: there is certainly a good case for the authorities to provide more of them, but the 24-hour centres demanded opposite would threaten to undermine the whole point of motherhood. Even in communes where children are brought up separately, as in some of Israel's *kibbutzim*, the children spend at least part of each evening with their parents.

(4) At a time when more than 500 full-time deaconesses (barred from giving Holy Communion or performing marriages) were waiting to become priests, three of the main reasons advanced by opponents of the ordination of women were that the priesthood is, by its nature, a male function, that it would break the tradition of the Church and that, above all, it would make unity with the Roman Catholic and Orthodox churches much more difficult to achieve. (In an exchange of letters with the Archbishop of Canterbury in 1986, the Pope gave a warning that it would pose 'an increasingly serious obstacle'.) On purely material grounds, another objection was that, with estimates that about 1,000 clergy might leave the CoE over the issue, the Church could face having to pay them compensation totalling £100 million – a crippling sum. Even so, it is quite

feared approval for women priests would split the Church irretrievably, with its more traditional members either forming an entirely new church or becoming Roman Catholics. But the secretary of the Movement for the Ordination of Women has described this as 'blatant scare-mongering'. One point raised by the opposition is that Jesus Christ did not choose a woman as one of his apostles nor appoint one to represent him in a ministerial way. But the answer is best summed up by a CoE deaconess: 'Christ died for all of us – not just the male half of the population'.

(5) The more education a woman has, the deeper she is committed to creative work and not to the kitchen sink. Women have a right to equal opportunities in public life and worthwhile careers. They must be given improved training facilities in every field, equal access to the professions, to universities (including medical schools), and to courses enabling them to obtain higher qualifications – and their opportunities for winning promotion in their chosen careers must be genuine and meaningful. To cite just one example in the educational field: out of more than 3,000 professors in British universities today, fewer than 50 of them are women. Well over a decade after the sex equality legislation became effective, the reality of the situation is that women now have choice but, still, not many options – freedom, but little power.

(6) From its earliest stages, education remains riddled with sex discriminatory attitudes and must be radically reformed in this respect. We must rid children's books of their habitual depiction of the sexes in stereotyped roles, with boys always portrayed in adventurous or exciting

untrue to imply that the General Synod has now barred the door to women priests indefinitely. After the 1986 debate, it was agreed that there should be a 'cooling-off' period until 1990 – at which time, a new synod will be elected. At the time of that debate, a poll of the CoE clergy and laity showed that only four per cent of them believed the ordination of women would never happen; even opponents of the move felt, by a clear majority that it would eventually be inevitable. Given these facts, it is surely significant that the Movement for the Ordination of Women and its supporters, while entirely free of any accusation that they had failed to campaign adequately for their cause, have nevertheless accepted that the only effective way to win their case, in the long run, is by reasoned persuasion, *not* by disruption.

(5) Women's rights militants always tend to talk about exciting careers, apparently forgetting that not every man gets fulfilment from his work or has a creative or high-powered job. In real life, only a small minority do. Society does indeed owe women the right to equal opportunities and has at last recognised this in law. But from that point on, it's up to each woman to choose how she is going to use those opportunities. Women themselves must realise – and an ever-increasing proportion of them are doing so – that having a career and a family is not incompatible but, often, merely a question of good organisation (and of true partnership with their husbands). It isn't a case of either-or, between motherhood and a career; in claiming that it is, the militants give many ordinary women, quite unjustifiably, a feeling of inadequacy and guilt.

(6) The more experienced women's

activities and the girls always steered towards domesticity and motherhood; and this change in attitude must be maintained right up the line. From childhood up to school-leaving age, the present system fails to give girls the full, rounded education that would enable each girl to develop her own potential. Instead, the orientation of girls by their teachers – and, too often, by their mothers – is still almost solely towards biological functions.

(7) Any situation or activity in which men retain a dominant role, not through any intrinsic merit or superiority but merely to preserve their accustomed privilege, is totally rejected by all Feminists. Some American militants have even advocated all-female communes, the violent overthrow of male domination and, since the human race must continue, the creation of a sperm bank for use by women who want children but do not want men for partners. Others, less militant, believe that marriage is outmoded, that women are exploited by the marital situation and its aftermath in the case of divorce, and they should be free to choose when and from whom to have babies, if they wish, without being shackled by matrimonial bonds. However, as proof of the breadth of opinions among Feminists, there are also increasing numbers of them who warn that the campaign for women's rights must win the support of many more ordinary married women if it is to succeed in its aims and therefore should not antagonise them by appearing to strike at their security.

(8) It is not a question of claiming that women are as good as or better than men – simply that they are (or should be) fully equal as human beings. If they were treated as no more and no less than that, they would not

movements go a great deal of the way with the militants in supporting these particular demands. Publishers and teachers have long since accepted the need for sex-stereotyped roles and attitudes to be eradicated from textbooks. Even before this, though, bodies like the Fawcett Society were already concentrating as well on trying to secure changes in school curricula, so that girls should be definitely encouraged to continue with mathematics and to take scientific and technical subjects – and, consequently, to think longer-term about their careers and the wider job horizons now opened up for them. The Society is also campaigning for the improvement of careers counselling for girls, which, it says, should start before examination courses are chosen.

(7) To hear the Feminist activists talk, one would think the average woman is servile, inefficient, inconsistent, passive and ignorant. Women who, through conscious choice, have made a home and brought up children are made to feel that they have done something wrong. By turning men and women against each other, the militants threaten ultimately to destroy the family – which is still the essential basis of our civilisation, whatever the extremists may claim.

(8) Few would now contest that parental responsibility should be shared genuinely, that married life should be a partnership in the full sense of the word, and that men ought to shoulder an equal burden of the family and domestic tasks formerly left almost solely to women. Indeed, this is now the rule rather than the exception, as a way of life, among men who have married since the mid-1970s (that is, in the main, those still on the 'right' side of 40). But that does not mean leaning too far in the other

need to demand any special rights. In our present society, though, they remain the 'oppressed majority'. Women's rights campaigners have exposed the blatant inconsistencies of movements which demand freedom, self-determination, or whatever, in the name of human rights, and then exclude more than half of the human race. To cite another, parliamentary example: in Britain, up to the mid-1980s, less than four per cent of the MPs were women (roughly 25 out of 650). The utter inequity of this situation is underlined by experience in Norway, where, following a conscious decision to remedy the imbalance, women MPs already made up more than 40 per cent of the ruling Labour Party's strength at that time.

(9) More than a decade after the passing of the sex equality laws and the establishment of the Equal Opportunities Commission, the average female wage was still only two-thirds that of the male and women still formed a clear majority of the two million people earning less than £80 a week. A survey carried out by one (woman) MP showed that women made up only 15 per cent of the people selected by Ministers for appointment to various governmental and other official advisory bodies (e.g. the standing conference on crime prevention and the advisory committee on advertising). True equality will be achieved only when there has been a total reorganisation of the work place, so that it is no longer biased in favour of the male. This, indeed, will probably be the next key phase for feminist campaigners. Among the many ingredients: working conditions; more job-sharing; an entirely new look both at how to pay everyone a decent wage for less work (i.e. because of job-sharing) *and* at the often-outmoded

direction. The sex equality legislation, it should be remembered, is a two-way matter – also giving men opportunities not previously open to them. (For example, men can now become midwives!) The salient point consistently ignored by many Feminists is that men and women *are* different genetically, irrespective of physical factors and conditioning.

(9) In calling for a total re-shaping of the present working structure, feminist militants show a typical lack of logic. For one salient fact they ignore is that, contrary to the philosophy currently held by many of them, such a change could be achieved only with the help and active cooperation of mere males! (i.e. Not simply in sharing the running of the household or looking after the children, as more and more men already do, but even to the extent of subordinating their own career prospects to those of their wives.) In the autumn of 1986, the Fawcett Society and the 300 Group (founded originally to try to get 300 women elected as MPs) jointly launched a campaign called Women Into Public Life. Its ultimate aim is to get 40,000 female appointments to public bodies. This kind of steady working from within to change the system – using the rules of the present framework of society, rather than staging some meaningless, aggressive 'fight' against them – must assuredly be the only way the objective can finally be won.

(10) Insisting on neutral words like 'chairperson', instead of the usual 'chairman', does not get to the root of the problem. Nor has it made the least contribution, of any real substance, to women's fight for equal rights. Cynics might well say that the only concrete change for which Women's Lib could actually take the (dubious) credit was

basis on which 'worth' has been calculated. The full absorption of women into the market, and its necessary evolution, will be the largest social change since work was first rewarded with money. Few can doubt that the fight for it will have to be long and hard!

(10) In adult as well as school life, even the English language is sexist – masculine-dominated and discriminatory. One notable achievement by women's rights movements has been their successful opposition to the use of words and phrases which have an exclusively male form or connotation, even though they describe functions, activities or job titles which apply to women as well. The agitation on this score has won increasing public acceptance of the need to employ alternative, non-discriminatory terms. Similar discrimination still needs to be fought, too, in the advertising field: not just the silly, titillating advertisements portraying women solely as supposedly desirable sex objects, but – perhaps more dangerously – those which, almost subliminally, are patronising or condescending in their attitudes to women, or which implicitly perpetuate the stereotypes indicated in (9) above.

(11) None of the women's rights movements has a top-heavy, bureaucratic organisation, dominating or controlling its national affairs from the centre. Most are made up of a large number of very small groups throughout the country, the members of which share similar ideals but have complete freedom to discuss and propagate their individual viewpoints on all issues they regard as important. As a result, the movements throw up a continual ferment of new ideas.

(12) Women's Lib may have aggravated and irritated many people, but the now-general use of 'Ms', as a form of address for women who wish to assert their individuality by refusing to be classed as either 'Miss' or 'Mrs'. If the acceptance of that hideous two-letter abbreviation is regarded as an achievement, how is it that no one has yet established for sure how it should be pronounced? (The Feminists should take note, too, that there are still innumerable women, married and single, who find 'Ms' repulsive and are just as determined in their refusal to let anyone apply it to *them*!) As for advertising, few incidents could be more telling than an exhibition held in the mid-1980s at County Hall, London. The exhibits included a poster, sponsored by wild life conservationists, depicting a woman wearing a fur coat, with the caption: 'It takes up to 40 dumb animals to make a fur coat but only one to wear it.' The extraordinary reason for showing the poster was that, entirely ignoring the serious point behind its message, the exhibition organisers had selected it as a example of publicity material held to be offensively *sexist*! Is it any wonder that such half-baked attitudes are counter-productive, diverting attention from genuine causes for concern?

(11) This lack of national organisation is not simply a structural weakness but debilitates the campaigners' very arguments. While avoiding the pitfalls of the suffragette movement, which was eventually distorted by the over-strong control of those at its top, the Feminist groups have gone too far in the other direction. Without some recognised leadership, responsible for defining agreed policy, a movement will always tend to have the character of an undisciplined rabble. What some women's rights movements claim as a virtue is, in the final analy-

that is precisely what it set out to do. However extreme some of its actions and statements may have seemed to the more conservative-minded, it succeeded in getting many members of the public to start thinking and talking about issues which had not interested or even occurred to them previously. On the principle that 'any advertising is good advertising', it had a vanguard role in getting much more attention paid to women's affairs. Without the 'ginger' provided by the Women's Liberation movement, progress towards equality would not have advanced so far or so fast as it has. This is the legacy it bequeathed to the Feminists as a whole – and perhaps the most significant result, latterly, is that a growing number of Feminist publishers and other activists, who had previously kept themselves as isolated from the male world as possible, have begun coming round to the view that working within the 'main stream' is now the best way of putting over their case.

sis, proof of their fundamental irresponsibility.

(12) The progress already achieved came about through the work of moderates, men and women, who recognised that it is better to concentrate on securing reforms rather than waste energy in attacking the whole system. The militants may have helped to stir up public interest in the issues, but they did not make the running. Vociferous, aggressive minorities always get publicity out of all proportion to their actual influence – and, in this case, their jeering and shouting has frequently had a backlash effect. By the intemperate lengths to which they carry their hostility to men, by making ordinary women feel inadequate and guilty, by their unnecessary offensiveness, the women's rights extremists have if anything set back the real advance.

(See also the preceding article)

WRITTEN CONSTITUTION

Pro: (1) The British constitution is largely at the mercy of the party in power in the House of Commons. Since it is unwritten, there is effectively no legal limitation on what Parliament can enact by ordinary legislation. The Government virtually controls Parliament and there is excessive power in the hands of the Prime Minister; as a result, precedence is always given to the interests of the parliamentary majority – even though that majority may be very small (and, on occasion, has actually gained office

Con: (1) Britain's unwritten constitution is the result of precedent and tried and tested experience, built up over many centuries. Among its great virtues is that it is extremely flexible and empiric in nature, not based on well-meaning theories. Its replacement by a written constitution, were that possible, would result in a rigidity which, under British conditions, would inevitably hamper the efficient functioning of government. Moreover, who could be sufficiently impartial to draw up a satisfactory written consti-

with a lower total of votes than those received by the Opposition). A ruling party naturally claims that the measures it carries through are in the national rather than its own interest, but it is highly doubtful if this is always so. A written constitution would reduce the danger of laws being passed for sectional instead of national reasons; it ensures that the exercise of power is kept within due bounds.

(2) One of the main purposes of enacting a constitution is to entrench the principal traditions and conventions relating to the Executive. At present, these can be altered by any party which has a majority of one in Parliament. The Legislature should guarantee the rights of the individual; but under the present British system, as we have indicated, those rights are in the hands of the government of the day, which controls the Legislature. A written constitution would establish a Legislature which had control over the government and thus provide a better safeguard, in all circumstances, for the rights of the individual.

(3) The drafting of a written constitution would provide a unique opportunity for clearing up existing anomalies and for a thorough overhaul of outmoded laws and conventions. Its enactment would fit in with the present codification of other English Law. In the process, it might well simplify the solution of such issues as the powers of the Second Chamber and the national rights of Scotland and Wales. (See *Lords, Reform of the House of; Parliament, Reform of.*)

(4) A written constitution can keep pace with the times no less effectively, by the introduction of subsequent amendments as and when new conditions arise which make them desirable. The United States consti-

tution for this country? Ideally, the task would have to be undertaken by the main political parties and all other political groups of any size; yet there could be no hope of them ever reaching full agreement on the subject. And if one majority party tried to do it, there would always be a suspicion (at the least) that some of its provisions favoured that party's own sectional interests.

(2) Under a written constitution, the very rigidity of its statutes renders them more liable to abuse. The establishment of one particular set of laws, intended to cover all eventualities, would probably lead to confusion rather than to better organisation. Under our unwritten constitution, on the other hand, the adaptability of our conventions makes it far easier to give rulings suited to each individual case. In this form, our conventions reflect the evolutionary nature of law, whereby the best remedies have been retained out of the progressive experiences of the past.

(3) Among the most serious drawbacks of a written constitution is that a good number of its provisions are likely to become outdated very quickly. Britain avoids this because the natural evolution of law keeps pace with the times (more or less!). Public opinion may often be slightly ahead of it, but it does provide a reasonably speedy response to the changing attitudes and needs of society.

(4) Some of the amendments to the American constitution have been the principal sources of abuse. Two other leading nations which also have written constitutions are France and the Soviet Union. In the latter, it is laid down statutorily that women have complete equality with men; yet, apart from the former Minister of

tution has preserved flexibility in just this manner. Since 1787, more than two dozen amendments have been added to its original written constitution.

(5) Britain is a liberal democracy with, in theory, strict separation of powers (i.e. between the Executive, Legislature and Judiciary). In practice, however, because of the vagueness consequent on having an unwritten constitution, there is blurring at the edges and these three bodies do not in fact retain complete independence from each other. With a written constitution, the separation of powers would be truly effective.

Culture, Mrs Furtseva, how many women have been Government Ministers in Soviet history? And in France, how many entire new constitutions have been introduced in the past century?

(5) The separation of powers is secured just as effectively under an unwritten constitution, in practice as well as in theory. The independence of the British Judiciary, for instance, is sacrosanct — and recognised as such throughout the world.

(See also CABINET GOVERNMENT)

INDEX

While this Index expands on the direct cross-references between related subjects already given in the text, it also offers a further dimension. Many of the individual debating subjects crop up a number of times because, clearly, they are relevant to more than one of the principal themes listed. (As a cardinal example: our lives are touched by politics in so many different ways nowadays that the section for Politics, while already requiring more entries than any other, could logically have embraced almost every subject in the book!) Accordingly, under each main theme, the page numbers are given not only for the obviously related subjects but for others which have a relevance to it that, at first sight, is not always so obvious. Finally, subsidiary references are listed as well for subjects which touch on the principal theme only tangentially or in passing.

Agriculture
Land nationalisation, 113–5
Preservation of beauty spots, 152–6
Other refs: 20–22, 144–50, 166–7, 250–53

Animals
Animals, rights of, 7–10
Blood sports, 23–8
Vegetarianism, 250–53
Vivisection, 253–8

Civilisation
Advertising, 1–6
Animals, rights of; Vivisection, 7–10, 253–8
Architecture, modern, 11–14
Artistic awards, 15–17
Birth control; High birth rate, 17–20, 20–22
Blood sports, 23–8
Calendar reform, 35–6
Capital punishment, 37–8

Censorship, 39–40
Civil disobedience, 46–8
Degeneracy of modern civilisation, 67–70
Divorce; Easier divorce, 77–9, 79–81
Euthanasia, 82–4
Gambling; Lotteries; Speculation, 91–3, 119–21, 211–12
Homosexuals, 93–4
Immigration, 95–8
Industrial expansion, 99–102
Marriage as an institution, 121–3
Minorities, rights of, 125–6
Multi-national firms, 129–33
National registration, 186–7
Newspapers, 133–5
Pollution, 144–50
Preservation of beauty spots, 152–6
Prison reform, 157–60
Science (a menace?), 191–2
Social service conscription, 197–8
Soft drugs, 207–8
State-registered brothels, 219–21
Sterilisation of the unfit, 221–2

Sunday entertainment, Sunday
  shopping, 223–5
Terrorism, 231–3
Tied (public) houses, 235–6
Vegetarianism, 250–53
Women's rights movements, 265–72
Other refs: 61–2, 66–7, 71–2, 87–90,
  225–6, 230–31

Commonwealth and International
Auxiliary languages, 105–6
British Commonwealth, 28–31
Channel Tunnel, 40–44
Common currency, 57–8
Immigration, 95–8
Internationalism, 106–8
Ireland, 108–10
Minorities, rights of, 125–6
Multi-national firms, 129–33
Space exploration, 209–11
Terrorism, 231–3
United Nations, 241–3
United States of Europe, 244–5
Other refs: 87–90, 137–9

Conservation and Environment
Architecture, modern, 11–14
Channel Tunnel, 40–44
Degeneracy of modern civilisation,
  67–70
Industrial expansion, 99–102
Motor traffic, 126–9; *see also* 177–8
Pollution, 144–50
Preservation of beauty spots, 152–6
Other refs: 191–2, 259–61

Economics
Co-operation, 62–3, 63–4
Direct taxation, 227–9
High birth rate, 20–22
Industrial expansion, 99–102
Privatisation, 162–5
Unemployment, 240–41
Other refs: 17–20, 57–8, 90–91,
  129–33, 223–5

Education
Classics, 48–9
Co-education, 53–5
Comprehensive schools, 59–61
Compulsory school sport, 190–91
Corporal punishment, 66–7
Examinations (abolish them?), 84–6
Intelligence tests, 103–4
International auxiliary languages,
  105–6
Public schools, 175–7
Religious teaching, 187–8
School-leaving age, 188–90
Social service conscription, 197–8
Spelling reform, 212–3
University reform, 246–8
Other refs: 15–17, 20–22, 265–72

Europe
Channel Tunnel, 40–44
Common currency, 57–8
International auxiliary languages,
  105–6
Internationalism, 106–8
Referendum, 182–5
State-registered brothels, 219–21
United States of Europe, 244–5
Other refs: 51–3, 67–70, 193–4

Industry (see also under TRADE
  UNIONS)
Co-partnership, 64–5
Industrial expansion, 99–102
Industrial psychology, 102
Married women, more jobs for,
  262–4
Multi-national firms, 129–33
Payment by results, 144
Privatisation, 162–5
Scientific management, 192–3
Unemployment, 240–41
Other refs: 62–3, 63–4, 71–2, 72–3,
  191–2, 265–72

The Law
Capital punishment, 37–8
Censorship, 39–40
Civil disobedience, 46–8

Contraception for under-16s, 61–2
Corporal punishment, 66–7
Easier divorce, 79–81
Euthanasia, 82–4
Freedom of Information, 87–90
Immigration, 95–8
Indeterminate sentences, 98–9
Jury system, 110–12
Legalisation of soft drugs, 207–8
Liquor laws; Prohibition, 115–17,
  167–8
National registration, 186–7
Pollution (tougher laws needed?),
  144–50; see also 152–6
Prison reform, 157–60
Sunday entertainment; Sunday
  shopping, 223–5
Surrogate mothers, 225–6
Termination of pregnancies, 230–31

Mass Communications
Advertising, 1–6
Artistic awards, 15–17
Broadcasting, control of, 31–4
Censorship, 39–40
Commercial radio, 56–7
Freedom of information, 87–90
International auxiliary languages,
  105–6
Newspapers, 133–5
Public opinion polls, 173–4
Theatres, 233–5

Medicine
Euthanasia, 82–4
Premature burial, 150–52
Private medicine, 160–62
Psycho-analysis, 171–3
Soft drugs, 207–8
State medical service, 217–19
Sterilisation of the unfit, 221–2
Termination of pregnancies, 230–31
Vaccination, 248–50
Vivisection, 253–8
Other refs: 61–2, 157–60, 225–6

Military
Armaments, limitation of, 14–15
Military training, compulsory, 123–5
Nuclear weapons, 135–7
Pacifism, 139–41
Terrorism, 231–3
War: Desirable? Inevitable? 259–61,
  261–2
Other refs: 40–44, 103–4, 197–8,
  209–11

Politics
Anarchism, 6–7
Bishops, 22–3
British Commonwealth, 28–31
Broadcasting, 31–4
Cabinet government, 34–5
Capital punishment, 37–8
Churches in politics, 45–6
Civil disobedience, 46–8
Coalition government, 51–3
Compulsory voting, 258–9
Delegation v. Representation, 70–71
Direct action, 71–2
Disestablishment of the Church of
  England, 74–7
Eighteen-year-old MPs, 81–2
Fascism, 86–7
Freedom of information, 87–90
High birth rate, 20–22
Immigration, 95–8
Internationalism, 106–8
Ireland, 108–10
Land nationalisation, 113–15
Lords, House of, 117–19
Parliament, reform of (Devolution),
  141–2
Party government, 142–3
Pollution, 144–50
Preservation of beauty spots, etc.,
  152–6
Privatisation, 162–5
Proportional representation, 168–71
Public opinion polls, 173–4
Rating reform, 178–81
The Recall, 181–2
Referendum, 182–5
Second ballots, 193–4

Single-chamber government, 194–6
Socialism and Communism, 198–207
Sunday entertainment; Sunday shopping, 223–5
Terrorism, 231–3
Unemployment, State remedy for, 240–41
United Nations, 241–3
United States of Europe, 244–5
Written Constitution, 272–4
Other refs: 40–44, 59–61, 62–3, 63–4, 90–91, 91–3, 119–21, 217–19, 219–21

Religion
Birth control, 17–20
Bishops, 22–3
Christendom, Reunion of, 44–5
Churches in politics, 45–6
Degeneracy of modern civilisation, 67–70
Disestablishment, 74–7
Divorce, 77–9; *see also* 79–81
Euthanasia, 82–4
Marriage as an institution, 121–3
Pacifism, 139–41
Religious teaching in schools, 187–8
Spiritualism, 213–17
Sunday entertainment, Sunday shopping, 223–5

Sex-related matters
Birth control, 17–20
Contraception for under-16s, 61–2
Homosexuals, 93–4
Termination of pregnancies, 230–31
Other refs: 121–3, 225–6

Sport
Blood sports, 23–8
Compulsory school sport, 190–91

Olympic Games, 137–9
Sunday entertainment, 223–5
Other ref: 91–3

Taxation (and other monetary matters)
Advertising, 1–6
Common currency, 57–8
Direct taxation, abolition of, 227–9
Rating reform, 178–81
Taxation of single people, 229–30
Other refs: 113–15, 162–5

Trade Unions (see also under INDUSTRY)
Anarchism, 6–7
Closed shop, 49–51
Co-operation, 62–3, 63–4
Direct action, 71–2
Direction of labour, 72–3
Full employment, 90–91
Further restriction needed?, 237–9
Profit-sharing, 166–7; *see also* 64–5
Scientific management, 192–3
Unemployment, 240–41

Women
Birth control; High birth rate, 17–20, 20–22
Co-education, 53–5
Divorce; Easier divorce, 77–9, 79–81
Homosexuals, 93–4
Marriage as an institution, 121–3
More jobs for married women, 262–4
Social service conscription for both sexes, 197–8
Surrogate mothers, 225–6
Termination of pregnancies, 230–31
Women's rights movements, 265–72
Other refs: 61–2, 67–70, 229–30